THE
Russian
CHRONICLES

THE
RUSSIAN
CHRONICLES

A Thousand Years that Changed the World

FOREWORD: NORMAN STONE
PREFACE: DIMITRI OBOLENSKY

Bramley
Books

4509 The Russian Chronicles
This edition published in 1998 by
Bramley Books, an imprint of
Quadrillion Publishing Ltd of
Godalming Business Centre, Woolsack Way
Godalming, Surrey, GU7 1XW, England

ISBN 1-85833-397-0
Printed in Italy
Phototypesetting: Tradespools Ltd, Frome, Somerset
Origination: Columbia Offset, Singapore

First published in 1990

This edition revised and edited by Joseph F Ryan PhD
who would like to thank Phoebe Phillips
for her assistance

FRONT COVER (from left to right): John Massey Stewart:
Catherine the Great, portrait from N. N. Bozherdnov, *Trista
Let Tsarstovivaniya Doma Ronanovykh*, St Petersburg, 1912.
Novosti (London): *Lenin Returns to Russia, April 1917*.
SCR Library: icon depicting the Virgin and child.
AKG Photo London/Claudia Quaukies: Catherine Palace.
AKG Photo London: *Peter the Great at Deptford Dock*,
painting by Daniel Maclise (1806-1870).

FRONTISPIECE *The cupolas of the Cathedral of St Basil the
Blessed, Moscow. Built by Ivan IV the Terrible in 1554, it is
one of nine churches dedicated to his victory over the Tartars.*

Created and produced by Garamond Publishers Ltd

Editorial Director: Tessa Clark

Editorial

Project Editor: Cecilia Walters

Susan George
Fred Gill
Maureen Maddren
Jenny Overton
Timothy Probart
Peter Rea
Liliane Reichenbach
Jennifer Speake

Design

Harry Green
Phil Kay
Tony Spaul

Production

Roger Multon
Patrick Holloway

Picture Research: Elizabeth Loving

Maps: Jeff Edwards, Malcolm Day

Special Acknowledgement

Professor H. Lunt, Professor O. Pritsak, *Harvard Ukrainian Institute, Cambridge, United States of America*

Consultant Editors

Dr Orlando Figes, *Lecturer and Fellow in History, Trinity College, Cambridge, United Kingdom*

Dr Lindsey Hughes, *Senior Lecturer in Russian History, School of Slavonic and East European Studies, University of London, United Kingdom*

Robin Milner-Gulland, *Reader in Russian, School of European Studies, University of Sussex, United Kingdom*

Translators

Translation Editor: Dr Ralph Cleminson

Louise Barrick
Margaret Condon
Rose Cullen
James Cutshall
Horace Lunt
Diane Nicholls
Brian Pearce
Stephen Rowell
Sylvia Trott
Maria Unkovskaya

Special thanks to

John Massey Stewart

Contributors

Efim Barban, *Music Correspondent, BBC World Service, London, United Kingdom*

Dr Jeremy Black, *Senior Lecturer in History, University of Durham, United Kingdom*

Dr Viktor Borovsky, *Lecturer in Russian Languages and Literature, School of Slavonic and East European Studies, University of London, United Kingdom*

Dr Sue Bridger, *Lecturer in Russian, University of Bradford, United Kingdom*

Dr Anthony Briggs, *Professor of Russian Languages and Literature, University of Birmingham, United Kingdom*

Dr John Channon, *Lecturer in Economic and Social History, SSES, University of London, United Kingdom*

Dr Ralph Cleminson, *Senior Lecturer in Russian and Soviet Studies, School of Language and Area Studies, Portsmouth Polytechnic, United Kingdom*

Cooperative Poseidon Publishers, *Leningrad, USSR*

Dr Isabel de Madariaga, *Professor Emeritus of Russian Studies, SSES, University of London, United Kingdom*

Dr Paul Dukes, *Professor of History, King's College, Aberdeen, United Kingdom*

John Erickson, *Professor of Defence Studies, University of Edinburgh, United Kingdom*

Daniel Field, *Associate Professor of History, Syracuse University, and Senior Fellow of the Harman Institute for Advanced Study of the Soviet Union, United States of America*

Dr Patrick Gatrell, *Senior Lecturer in Economic History, University of Manchester, United Kingdom*

Dr Janet Hartley, *Lecturer in International History, London School of Economics and Political Science, United Kingdom*

Peter Hayden, *Garden Historian, former Chairman of the Garden History Society, United Kingdom*

Oxana Ivanchenko, *formerly of the Tretyakov Gallery, Moscow, USSR*

Gareth Jones, *Reader in Russian, University College of North Wales, United Kingdom*

Dr John L. H. Keep, *Professor Emeritus of Russian History, University of Toronto, Canada*

Dr Catriona Kelly, *Junior Research Fellow in Modern Languages, Christ Church College, Oxford, United Kingdom*

Tony Kemp-Welch, *Lecturer in Politics, University of Nottingham, United Kingdom*

Natalia Kostotchkina, *formerly of the Hermitage Museum, Leningrad, USSR*

Dr Hiroaki Kuromiya, *Research fellow, King's College, Cambridge, United Kingdom*

William J. Leatherbarrow, *Senior Lecturer in Russian, University of Sheffield, United Kingdom*

Dr Lucjan R. Lewitter, *Professor Emeritus of Slavonic Studies, Christ's College, Cambridge, United Kingdom*

Dr Patrick O'Meara, *Head of Russian Department, Trinity College, Dublin, Ireland*

Dr William F. Ryan, *Academic Librarian, The Warburg Institute, University of London, United Kingdom*

Alexander Schouvaloff, *London, United Kingdom*

Dr Denis J. Shaw, *Lecturer in Geography, University of Birmingham, United Kingdom*

Dr Victor Terras, *Professor Emeritus of Slavic Languages and Comparative Literature, Brown University, United States of America*

Dr Chris Ward, *Assistant Lecturer in Slavonic Studies, University of Cambridge, United Kingdom*

Dr John Westwood, *Honorary Research Fellow of the Centre for Russian and East European Studies, University of Birmingham, United Kingdom*

Foreword

Why is Russia so different from the rest of Europe? How has the state lasted so long, given that it includes so many different peoples who, in the ordinary course of events, would have become independent? These questions can only be answered in historical terms. The present book uses these, with original documents and excellent illustrations; it is a first-rate piece of work, which I have read with great profit. The editors of each of the sections have thought long and deep about their formidable job: how to present such unfamiliar terrain to an enquiring reader.

The medieval section deals with that all-important but hideously difficult question, the influence of religion upon society. There is, in my opinion, a 'mind-set' attaching to the great religions, whether Catholic, Protestant or Orthodox. Orthodoxy has enormous strengths. It is tolerant of minor sins – drunkenness in particular – and has a magnificent ritual, which still pulls in crowded congregations. On the other side, it has never been very good at Rights, and was inclined to cave in before a tsarist state that had little room for individual liberties.

So the Orthodox tradition made Russia more likely than any other country to accept Communism, which triumphed in the wake of Russia's defeat by the Germans in the First World War. Today, however, Russia may at last fulfil the promise of her fantastic history and civilization – to which this elegant book is a suitable tribute.

NORMAN STONE

OPPOSITE   *St Vladimir, baptizer of the Russians, with his martyred sons, St Boris and St Gleb.*

Contents

Foreword by Norman Stone 7

Editor's note 10

Preface by Dimitri Obolensky 11

The Rulers of Russia 12

Part 1 The Land of Rus 16

The Land of Rus 22

Trade and Tribute 26

Part 2 The Grand Princes of Kiev (882-1240) 28

Oleg. Igor. Olga. Svyatoslav 31

The neighbours of Rus 42

Vladimir I 47

The religion of Russia 49

The Orthodox Church in Russia 52

Birth of the Russian language 57

Boris and Gleb. Vladimir Monomakh 59

The Kievan state 73

Part 3 The Birth of Great Russia (1240-1505) 76

The Golden Horde 79

Moscow 87

Finance and currency 93

Ivan III the Great 95

Appanage Russia 97

Medieval icons 101

Part 4 Russia under the Tsars (1533-1676) 104

Ivan IV the Terrible 107

Ivan IV the Terrible 113

The Cossacks 117

Boris Godunov 119

Boris Godunov 121

Mikhail Romanov 127

Serfdom 129

Arts and crafts 130

Part 5 Imperial Russia (1676-1825) 136

Fyodor and Sophia 139

The Russian Renaissance 145

Peter I the Great 151

Peter the technician   156

St Petersburg: the making of an imperial
city   161

The battle for the Baltic   165

The greatness of Peter the Great   169

Peter I   174

Peter I's successors   179

Elizabeth, daughter of Peter the Great   184

Mikhail Vasilyevich Lomonosov   190

Catherine II the Great   199

Catherine the woman   204

Popular arts   211

The Pugachev rebellion   217

Catherine the reformer   224

Radishchev: the first attack on serfdom   228

Catherine the ruler   232

Catherine II's successors   239

Napoleon in Russia   244

The Holy Alliance   254

The Decembrist movement   260

Part 6 The Last Tsars (1825-1917)   264

Nicholas I   267

Westernizers and Slavophiles   271

Literature – a social force   274

Crimean War   278

Alexander II   287

The end of serfdom   292

Peasantry and serfdom   300

Alexander III   307

Nationality groups in Russia around 1900   310

Jews and anti-Semitism   312

Nicholas II   319

A new proletariat   323

The 1905 revolution   324

Rasputin: saint or sinner?   340

Revolution in Culture   345

Art and architecture   346

Theatre   348

Literature   349

Ballet   350

Music   352

Opera   353

Decorative arts   355

Part 7 The Russian Revolution (1917)   360

Lenin   363

The Russian peasantry   369

Lenin: the first successful revolutionary   373

Glossary   378

Bibliography   380

Sources   384

Index   389

Notes on illustrations   398

Acknowledgements   400

MAPS

The Land of Rus   21

The Tartar conquests   81

The rise of Muscovy   109

The Baltic conquests of Peter I the Great   164

The empire of Catherine II the Great   208

Europe in 1815   252

The Crimean War   281

Editor's Note

The Russians have from the early middle ages been acutely history-conscious, interpreting and acting upon their often fluid concept of 'Russianness' and its relation to a land, a faith, a culture, a socio-political destiny. Such concerns are as acute to Russians of the modern era. The purpose of this book is to trace the origins and ramifications of this national self-consciousness.

We have used eye-witness accounts, letters, diaries, newspaper articles, speeches, memoirs, poems – to compile our narrative. Specialist chapter consultants have selected and introduced the extracts from these documents, and linked them with explanatory texts (printed in a different typeface – see diagram below). Within the longer extracts, some passages (and occasionally sentences and phrases) have been deliberately omitted to avoid repetition, or to clarify the style of the original. Names, dates and titles were supplied where elucidation was required.

The documentary narrative is complemented throughout by brief passages written by a team of leading scholars from different parts of the world, commenting on key topics and individuals. They are printed in the same typeface as the link texts and introductory material, to distinguish them from the original documents – see diagram below.

Finally, a word is needed on problems of transliteration and transcription of proper names, to which there is no completely satisfactory solution. Russian place names are given in their conventional western form, e.g. Crimea, Moscow, Ukraine; other place names follow *Times Atlas* spellings. Proper names in Old Russian sources are given in their modern Russian form; names of rulers from Peter I have been translated into English equivalents (except Ivan); otherwise in their generally accepted anglicized version.

Dates are according to the Julian calendar up to the end of January 1918, and to the Gregorian calendar thereafter.

LINK
TEXT

CHRONICLE
OR
DOCUMENT

'GOSSIPY'
EXTRACT
FROM
DOCUMENTS

MODERN
ESSAY

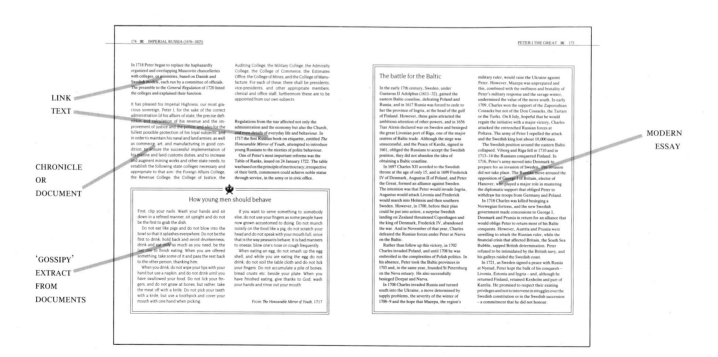

Preface

The term 'chronicle', usually applied to medieval historiography, is here given a wider significance. It designates a body of original texts composed between the 11th century to the October Revolution of 1917, and related to the history of the country generally known as Russia. These primary sources, arranged in chronological sequence and often written by eye-witnesses, may give the reader the impression of witnessing history 'as it really happened' unencumbered by modern interpretations, essential as these often are for a fuller understanding of the texts. There are many examples in this volume of this direct entry into the past. Autobiographies – those of Vladimir Monomakh in the 12th century and of the Archpriest Avvakum in the 17th – vividly portray, even in the brief extracts given here, their remarkable authors. Private letters, such as Tsar Ivan IV's ill-tempered epistle to Queen Elizabeth of England, uncover surprising moments of the past. And the encounter between widely differing societies is illustrated by the impressions of Russia recorded by visiting foreigners such as Richard Chancellor, Giles Fletcher, and the Marquis de Custine.

During the course of the book, the reader will notice a change of nomenclature. The country at first called *Rus* is later given its modern name, Russia. To avoid confusion a word of explanation is called for here, the more so since behind this change of name there lurks a still lively controversy. The term *Rus*, early in the Middle Ages, came to denote the home of the Eastern Slavs, centred on Kiev. These later divide into three ethnic groups which subsequently came to be known as Great Russians, Ukrainians, and Belorussians; and in the 13th century their paths began to diverge. The Ukrainians remained in the southern and western lands of Kievan Rus, and later became part of Poland. The Belorussians (together with some Ukrainians) formed the Slav component of the Grand Duchy of Lithuania. The Great Russians, who occupied the eastern and northern regions of Kievan Rus, gradually built round Moscow a centralized state, the later nucleus of the Russian Empire. The name 'Russia' can thus properly be applied only to the communities and state created by the Great Russian people. In the 17th and 18th centuries this state was to absorb or annex the greater part of the homeland of the Ukrainians and Belorussians.

Although the volume does not claim to be a detailed history of the country, nor a full-scale survey of her culture, the aim of *The Russian Chronicles* is to offer the reader an overview of the development, during the past thousand years, of the country known first as *Rus* and later as Russia.

D. Obolensky

DIMITRI OBOLENSKY

The Rulers of Russia

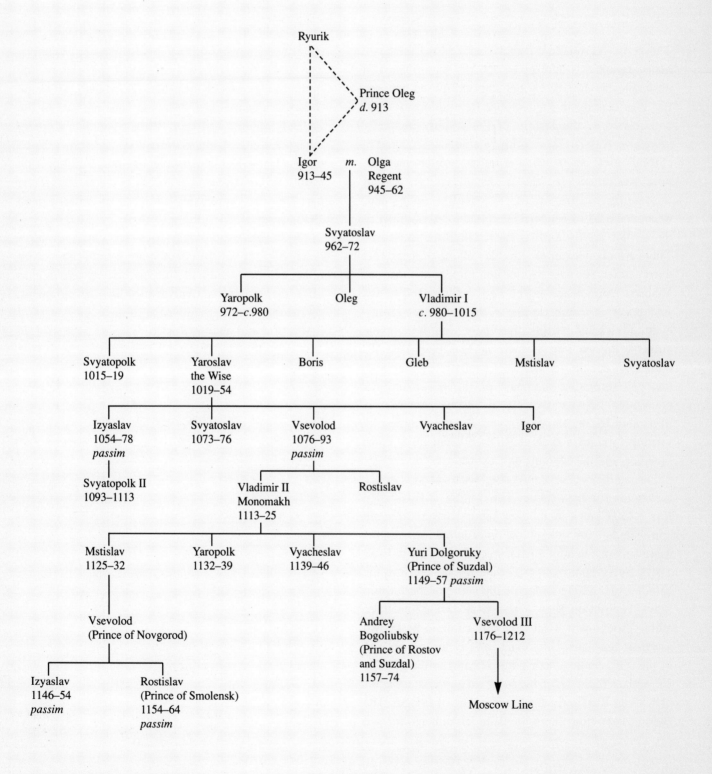

Ryurik

Prince Oleg
d. 913

Igor   *m.*   Olga
913–45   Regent
         945–62

Svyatoslav
962–72

Yaropolk   Oleg   Vladimir I
972–*c*.980   *c.* 980–1015

Svyatopolk   Yaroslav   Boris   Gleb   Mstislav   Svyatoslav
1015–19   the Wise
        1019–54

Izyaslav   Svyatoslav   Vsevolod   Vyacheslav   Igor
1054–78   1073–76   1076–93
passim   *passim*

Svyatopolk II   Vladimir II   Rostislav
1093–1113   Monomakh
            1113–25

Mstislav   Yaropolk   Vyacheslav   Yuri Dolgoruky
1125–32   1132–39   1139–46   (Prince of Suzdal)
                                   1149–57 *passim*

Vsevolod   Andrey   Vsevolod III
(Prince of Novgorod)   Bogoliubsky   1176–1212
                          (Prince of Rostov
                         and Suzdal)
                         1157–74

Izyaslav   Rostislav   Moscow Line
1146–54   (Prince of Smolensk)
passim   1154–64
          passim

Note: Dates refer to the years of reign

The Moscow line

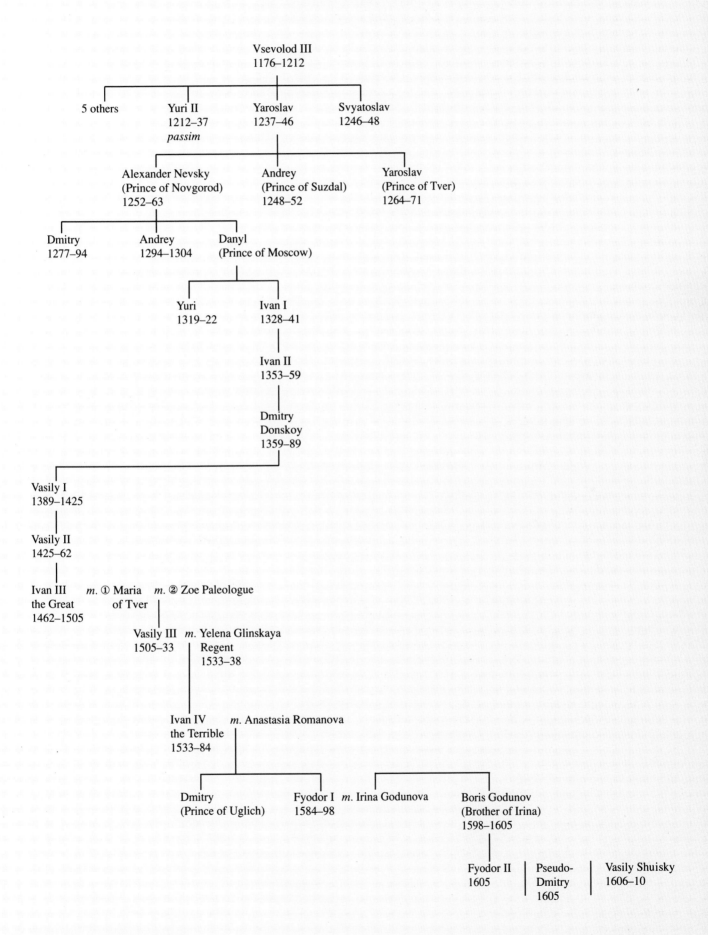

Vsevolod III
1176–1212

5 others

Yuri II
1212–37
passim

Yaroslav
1237–46

Svyatoslav
1246–48

Alexander Nevsky
(Prince of Novgorod)
1252–63

Andrey
(Prince of Suzdal)
1248–52

Yaroslav
(Prince of Tver)
1264–71

Dmitry
1277–94

Andrey
1294–1304

Danyl
(Prince of Moscow)

Yuri
1319–22

Ivan I
1328–41

Ivan II
1353–59

Dmitry
Donskoy
1359–89

Vasily I
1389–1425

Vasily II
1425–62

Ivan III   *m.* ① Maria   *m.* ② Zoe Paleologue
the Great   of Tver
1462–1505

Vasily III *m.* Yelena Glinskaya
1505–33   Regent
                  1533–38

Ivan IV   *m.* Anastasia Romanova
the Terrible
1533–84

Dmitry
(Prince of Uglich)

Fyodor I *m.* Irina Godunova
1584–98

Boris Godunov
(Brother of Irina)
1598–1605

Fyodor II
1605

Pseudo-
Dmitry
1605

Vasily Shuisky
1606–10

Note: Dates refer to the years of reign

The Romanov dynasty

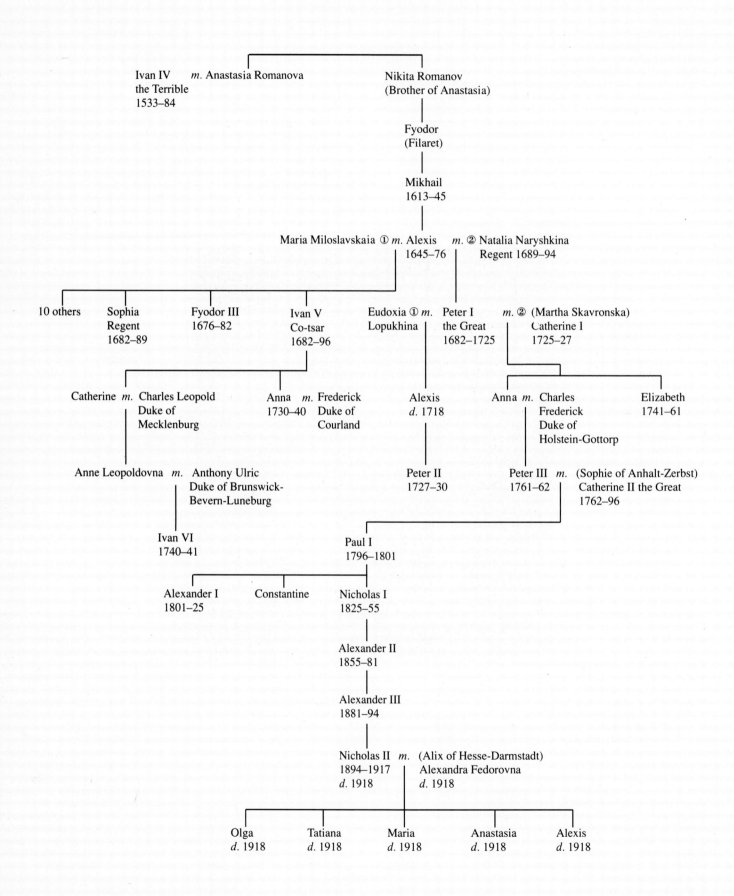

Ivan IV
the Terrible
1533–84

m. Anastasia Romanova

Nikita Romanov
(Brother of Anastasia)

Fyodor
(Filaret)

Mikhail
1613–45

Maria Miloslavskaia ① *m.* Alexis   *m.* ② Natalia Naryshkina
1645–76   Regent 1689–94

10 others   Sophia
Regent
1682–89

Fyodor III
1676–82

Ivan V
Co-tsar
1682–96

Eudoxia ① *m.* Peter I
Lopukhina   the Great
1682–1725

m. ② (Martha Skavronska)
Catherine I
1725–27

Catherine *m.* Charles Leopold
Duke of
Mecklenburg

Anna   *m.* Frederick
1730–40   Duke of
Courland

Alexis
d. 1718

Anna *m.* Charles
Frederick
Duke of
Holstein-Gottorp

Elizabeth
1741–61

Anne Leopoldovna   *m.*   Anthony Ulric
Duke of Brunswick-
Bevern-Luneburg

Peter II
1727–30

Peter III   *m.*   (Sophie of Anhalt-Zerbst)
1761–62   Catherine II the Great
1762–96

Ivan VI
1740–41

Paul I
1796–1801

Alexander I
1801–25

Constantine

Nicholas I
1825–55

Alexander II
1855–81

Alexander III
1881–94

Nicholas II *m.* (Alix of Hesse-Darmstadt)
1894–1917   Alexandra Fedorovna
d. 1918   *d.* 1918

Olga
d. 1918

Tatiana
d. 1918

Maria
d. 1918

Anastasia
d. 1918

Alexis
d. 1918

Note: Dates refer to the years of reign

PART 1 THE LAND

Rus (a term used anciently both of the land and its people) was a political entity that arose in the ninth century and quickly established itself over a large part of what are now Russia, the Ukraine and Belorussia, to become the largest early medieval European state. The bulk of its population belonged to the eastern branch of the Slavonic peoples (their languages then still inter-comprehensible) and consisted of a dozen or so main tribal units, which apparently had infiltrated and set-tled the main river-basins of zones of mixed forest and wooded steppe over preceding centuries. But the ruling dynasty of Rus and its retainers were Viking Scandinavians (soon to become Slavized). Among its population were some of non-Slav origin related to the modern Finns, Estonians and Baltic peoples. Rus, though Slav-dominated, was from the start multinational. Its name remained 'Russia' through many historical vicissitudes, until Peter the Great formally adopted the Latinate coinage *Rossiya*.

Before embarking on the history of Rus it is essential to understand the location in which that history has unrolled. The vast, undulating plain that is European Russia may seem from the map a confusing undifferen-tiated territorial mass, without natural landmarks to punctuate its monotony, or natural frontiers to set bounds on its inhabitants' slow aggrandisement.

Frontierlessness has indeed presented both a prob-lem and an opportunity throughout Russian history. Even 1000 years ago the Russian lands touched upon (though were not exactly bounded by) three great mountain-ranges – the Carpathians, the Urals and Cau-casus – and four seas – the Black, the White (Arctic), the Baltic and the Caspian, each of which beckoned its merchants by giving access to other peoples beyond. Yet on each of these the Russian state found inordinate difficulty in establishing a permanent foothold.

The geographical divisions of Russia are actually very striking, and though they have their analogues further west, they are far more marked and consistent than elsewhere in Europe. It is not too much to say that they have had an overwhelming impact on Russian his-tory, from the Slavs' first expansion eastwards in the early centuries of the Christian era to the present day. What is more, these divisions continue to the east – little interrupted by the Urals, the Caspian or the great Siberian river-systems – for thousands more miles, almost to the Pacific Ocean. They consist of a series of great zones of vegetation running latitudi-nally, and, despite all mankind's interference in the landscape, still giving way to one another quite ab-ruptly as one moves from north to south or vice-versa.

The two most characteristic, indeed famous, and sharply contrasted of the zones are the vast coniferous forest or *tayga* (the greatest such feature on our planet), occupying all the northerly parts of Russian and Siberia, save for the strip of tundra along the Arctic Ocean, and the treeless open grassland or steppe to the south, extending to the Black Sea and Caucasian foothills, but further east yielding to semi-desert and desert proper.

OF RUS

Both *tayga* and steppe offer considerable potential riches: furbearing animals, honey, wax and, of course, timber in the first, the humus-rich, fertile 'black earth' beneath the thick grass-roots in the second. Yet each, though looming large in the Russians' consciousness, proved curiously resistant to their permanent settlement. A thin scattering of Finnic hunter-gatherers could subsist in the *Tayga*, nomadic horsemen could easily dominate the steppe.

For settled agriculturalists (such as the Slavs were from prehistory onwards) both contrasting types of land were marginal, colonized only gradually, at first along the main river-valleys. These rivers, indeed, are the primary axes, or determinants, of the Russian civilizational landscape.

The northerly situation and general continental climate of Russia are the cause of difficulties. The *tayga* summer, though warm, is too short to ripen food-crops reliably; soils are poor and evaporation is slight, leading to frequent swampy conditions. The steppe, with low rainfall, is always at risk from drought: under the plough (as most of it now is) the 'black earth' can dry out disastrously and turn to dust-bowl.

Reliance on farming, the Russians' traditional primary source of wealth, would seem perverse, were it not for two vital further factors. The first is the climatic improvement that seems to have facilitated Russian settlement in the early middle ages, making marginal conditions tolerable, by the time of the early-modern 'Little Ice Age', the Muscovite state was already large and economically diversified. The second is the fact that between *tayga* to the north and steppe to the south, two much narrower, but crucial, intermediate zones are found.

The first (broadening out to the west to include the Baltic region and Belorussia) is that of the mixed, coniferous-deciduous forest. Easier to clear, with better soils and a slightly more temperate climate than the *tayga*, it gave Russians a forest foothold from which the latter could be exploited. The second, the so-called 'wooded steppe', is better watered than the steppe proper, more defensible and easier to cultivate, with extra resources provided by forest massifs.

Together, mixed forest and wooded steppe (in one or other of which zones historic capitals of Kiev, Vladimir, Moscow and St Petersburg all stand) gave Russians what seemed like limitless horizons for extensive farming, as well as a highway for eastward colonization.

Extracts from contemporary documents not only tell of the main historical events, but also show how people of the time made sense of them. The main criteria for the selection of chronicles was to illustrate the quest – which seems to have begun very early – for the elusive concept of 'Russianness', an ideological framework that would unite a sense of historical destiny with a geographical location, even if that location was a changing one.

It is not too much to claim that a knowledge of this quest is the key to an informed understanding of Russia to the present day.

Here is the tale of the seasons and the years, the tale of where the land of Rus came from, who first began to rule as prince, and how the land of Rus came into being.

Now we will begin this tale.

After the flood, the three sons of Noah, Shem, Ham, and Japheth, divided the land. The east was taken for Shem: Persia and Bactria all the way to India.

For Ham was taken the southern part: Egypt, Ethiopia, Thebes and Lybia.

For Japheth were taken the northern and western parts: Albania, Armenia Small and Great, the Slavs, the Pontic sea on the northern parts, the Caucasus mountains and from there all the way to the Dnepr and the Volga, which flows to the east into Shem's part.

Now Shem and Ham and Japheth divided up the earth by casting lots, so that no one would trespass on his brother's share and each lived in his own part. There was one tongue. And when people multiplied

LEFT *The Tower of Babel (Breughel); according to legend, Slav was one of the 72 languages that were scattered throughout the world when the tower was destroyed.*

took names for themselves, depending on the place in which they settled. Now, these also are Slavs: the White Croats and the Serbs and the Carinthians. The Slavs settled around Lake Ilmen, too, and they were called by their own name, Slovenins, and they built a town and called it Novgorod. And others settled along the Desna and along the Sem and the Sula, and they were called Severyanins. And in this way the Slavonic nation spread. Therefore the writing too was called Slavonic.

The crucial source for all Russian history up to the early 12th century is the *Primary Chronicle*. Compiled in the Kiev Monastery of the Caves in 1111–13, it is a remarkable attempt to tie in Russia with universal history. As the above extracts from its first section show, it places Russia among the world's nations, scattered at the fall of Babel. The people who were later to be called Russians descend from one of the three great branches of the eastern Slavs, who settled in separate tribal units along the great Dnepr river, united by a common Slav language.

Both Greeks and Arabs were interested in the peoples who lived north of their territories. The Pontic steppe beyond the Black Sea was controlled by a nomadic group of tribes who were largely Slav and probably the Russians' forebears. A Byzantine book on warfare, *Strategicon*, written in the reign of Emperor Maurice (582–602), describes them.

The Slavonic and Antian tribes are similar in their way of life, their customs, and their love of freedom. It is impossible by any means to force them into slavery or subordination in their own country. They are numerous and hardy, and they easily endure heat, cold, rain, nakedness, and lack of food. They are friendly to foreign visitors and protect them whenever necessary in their travels from place to place.

They have much livestock of all kinds and fruits of the land, piled in heaps, especially millet and wheat.

The modesty of their women exceeds all human nature, so that most of them consider their husband's death their own and voluntarily strangle themselves, not regarding widowhood as a fitting way of life.

on earth, they gathered in a place on the plain, to build a tower to the sky and the city of Babylon around it. The Lord God came down to see the city and the tower. And He confused the languages and divided them into seventy-two tongues and scattered them over all the earth. And God destroyed the tower of Babel with a great wind. One of these seventy-two tongues was the Slavic tongue, of the tribe of Japheth, who are Slavs.

Some of those Slavs scattered about the land and

These tribes settle in forests, along impassable rivers, swamps, and lakes, and build their homes with several exits, because of the many dangers that naturally occur in their lives. They bury the things they need in secret places, do not openly possess any superfluous belongings, and lead a nomadic life.

In the ninth and tenth centuries, Arab geographers came into contact with 'Russians' (Rus) who had begun to open up trade routes along the great south-flowing rivers towards Central Asia and Byzantium. Ibn Rusta, an Arab scholar writing at the opening of the tenth century, set a puzzle for future scholars by referring to Russia as an island in a lake. His account of 'Russians', however, seems to be based on observations of Varangians (Vikings) not Slavs.

Russia is an island around which is a lake, and the island on which the people dwell is a three days' journey through forests and swamps covered with trees.

They have a king who is called Khaqan, and they make raids against the Slavs, sailing in ships in order to go out to them, and they take them prisoner and carry them off to Khazar and Bulgar and trade with them there. They have no cultivated lands; they eat only what they carry off from the land of the Slavs.

When a child is born to any man among them, he takes a drawn sword to the new-born child and places it between his hands and says to him: 'I shall bequeath to thee no wealth and thou wilt have naught except what thou dost gain for thyself by this sword of thine.'

They have no landed property, nor villages, nor cultivated land; their only occupation is trading in sables and grey squirrel and other furs, and in these they trade and they take as the price gold and silver and secure it in their belts.

They are cleanly in regard to their clothing, and the men wear bracelets of gold. They are kind to their slaves and clothe them well, for they engage in trade.

These people are vigorous and courageous and when they descend on open ground, none can escape destruction; women are taken possession of, and men sent into slavery.

The Byzantine emperor, Constantine Porphyrogenitus (meaning Born-in-the-Purple), wrote an important work on historical geography, *De administrando imperio*, in the mid-tenth century. It includes this description of the Russian flotilla which annually sailed the trade route from Russia to Constantinople.

The single-straked ships, or dugouts, which the Rus sail down from Russia to Constantinople are from Novgorod. Others come from the city of Smolensk, from Lyubech and Chernigov, and from Vyshgorod. All these come down the River Dnepr, and are collected together at the city of Kiev.

The subject Slav tribes, who live in the mountains, cut the single-strakers there in time of winter and, when they have fastened them together, as spring approaches and the ice melts, they bring them on to the neighbouring lakes. And since these lakes debouch into the River Dnepr, they enter onto this river, and come down to Kiev, where the ships are fitted out, and then sold to the Rus.

The Rus buy these bottoms only, furnish them with oars and rowlocks and other tackle from their old single-strakers, which they have dismantled; and so they fit them out. In the month of June the Russians move off down the River Dnepr and come to Vitichev, which is a tributary city of the Rus. There they gather during two or three days, and when all the single-strakers are collected together, they set out and come down the Dnepr river.

They reach the island called St Gregory, on which island they perform their sacrifices because a gigantic oak tree stands there; and they sacrifice live cocks. From this island onwards the Rus do not fear the Pechenegs until they reach the River Selinas. After the Selinas they again fear nobody. Entering the territory of Bulgaria, they come to the mouth of the Danube.

The *Primary Chronicle* dates the entry of the Russians into history to the reign of the Byzantine emperor Michael III (AD 842), when they made spectacular

The Land of Rus

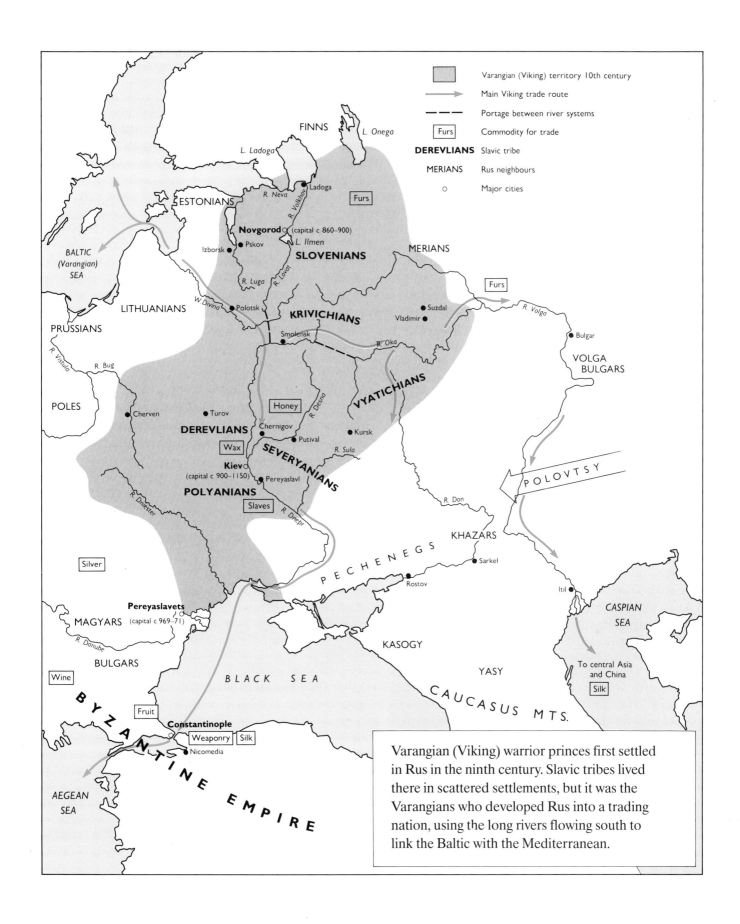

FINNS

L. Onega

L. Ladoga

BALTIC
(Varangian)
SEA

ESTONIANS

R. Neva

R. Volkhov

Ladoga

Furs

Novgorod (capital c 860–900)

Izborsk • Pskov

L. Ilmen

SLOVENIANS

MERIANS

LITHUANIANS

R. Luga

R. Lovat

W. Divina

Polotsk •

KRIVICHIANS

Suzdal

Vladimir •

Furs

R. Volga

Smolensk •

R. Oka

PRUSSIANS

POLES

R. Vistula

R. Bug

Cherven •

• Turov

Honey

R. Desna

DEREVLIANS

Chernigov •

Putival •

Wax

SEVERYANIANS

Kiev (capital c 900–1150)

Pereyaslavl •

POLYANIANS

Slaves

R. Sula

VYATICHIANS

Kursk •

Bulgar •

VOLGA
BULGARS

R. Dniester

R. Dnepr

POLOVTSY

R. Don

KHAZARS

Sarkel •

Silver

Pereyaslavets (capital c 969–71)

MAGYARS

R. Danube

BULGARS

Wine

PECHENEGS

Rostov •

BLACK SEA

KASOGY

YASY

Itil •

CASPIAN
SEA

CAUCASUS MTS.

To central Asia
and China

Silk

Fruit

Constantinople

Weaponry Silk

Nicomedia •

B Y Z A N T I N E   E M P I R E

AEGEAN
SEA

Varangian (Viking) territory 10th century

→ Main Viking trade route

- - - Portage between river systems

Furs Commodity for trade

DEREVLIANS Slavic tribe

MERIANS Rus neighbours

○ Major cities

Varangian (Viking) warrior princes first settled
in Rus in the ninth century. Slavic tribes lived
there in scattered settlements, but it was the
Varangians who developed Rus into a trading
nation, using the long rivers flowing south to
link the Baltic with the Mediterranean.

The Land of Rus

For its first 800 years of existence the land we call 'Russia' was known to its inhabitants as 'Rus' (a name probably applied in the first place to a people, and by extension to the country where they lived). The Latinate form *Rossiya* seems to have become widespread only in the 17th century. The Byzantine Greeks knew Russia as Rhôsia, and its people as Rhôs.

Much controversy has ensued since the problem of the origin of Rus was first raised in its modern form in the mid-18th century. What fundamentally is at stake is the question of whether Russia owes the origin of its statehood and culture to Viking or to native Slavonic sources.

Much chauvinist sentiment, pro or anti-Russian, has focused on the philological origin of the term 'Rus'. The Russian *Primary Chronicle* firmly identifies it as Viking: 'These Varangians were known as Rus, just as some are called Swedes, Norsemen, English, Gotlanders . . . on account of these Varangians the Russian land received its name'. However, the *Novgorod Chronicle* consistently applies the term 'Rus' to the lands around Kiev, not to the work where the Vikings (Varangians) first established themselves.

Writing in the middle of the ninth century, Constantine Porphyrogenitus, Byzantine emperor (913–59), listed placenames of evident Scandinavian origin as Russian; the Finnish for Swede is *Rotsi*; yet 'Rus' is not found in Viking sources (they termed the land *Gordariki*, 'land of enclosures', or forts). Much more conflicting evidence, usually from placenames, has been adduced: though a Viking origin seems more probable, it is by no means finally proved.

On the broader and more significant question of cultural origins, however, historians nowadays find much common ground. Nobody seriously holds that, beyond their political, mercantile and military skills, the Vikings brought the East Slavs any higher qualities of civilization. As a civilizational entity, ready to enter the medieval family of nations, Russia becomes a valid concept only with the fusion of a small number of Vikings with the settled population of East Slav agriculturalists and some Finno-Ugrian forest dwellers, perhaps also Balts – multinational state from its inception, from which, in turn, Great Russia, Ukraine and Belorussia would eventually be born.

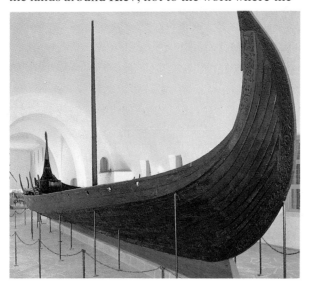

LEFT *Viking ship; boats like this carried the Varangian invaders from the Baltic to Byzantium.*

RIGHT *The domes of modern Kiev; the city, the capital of the first Russian state, was seized by Oleg in c. 879.*

Curious practices

St Andrew came to the Slavs, where Novgorod is now, and he saw the people there and what sort of customs they have, and how they wash themselves and whip themselves, and he was astonished. He went to the Varangians' territory and he arrived in Rome. There he told what he had taught and what he had seen, and said to them, 'I saw a wondrous thing in the land of the Slavs, when I was coming here. I saw wooden bath-houses. The Slavs heat them up greatly and take off their clothes and become naked. They douse themselves with tanning fluid; and they take young twigs and they beat themselves to the point that they can hardly walk out alive. And they douse themselves with cold water and thus revive. And they do this every day, not being tortured by anyone, but they torture themselves. They do it as washing, and not as torment!' All those who heard this were astonished.

From *Primary Chronicle*

contact with the Mediterranean world by raiding Constantinople. But first, the chronicler, coping with semi-legendary material, relates the foundation of Kiev – where he himself was writing years later – and the establishment of the Varangian Prince Ryurik as first ruler of Rus.

There were three brothers: the eldest one was named Kiy, and another Shchek and the third Khoriv, and their sister was Lybed. They built a town in the name of their eldest brother, and called it Kiev. Around the town was a forest and great pine woods, and they used to hunt wild animals. They were wise and intelligent men. They were called Polyanins, and from them there are Polyanins in Kiev to this day.

In the year 842, when Michael began to rule as emperor of Byzantium, the land began to be known as Rus. We have learned concerning this that in the time of this emperor the Rus came campaigning against Constantinople. Therefore we will begin from here.

In the year 862, the tribes drove the Varangians away overseas, and did not give them tribute. Then they began to rule themselves. But there was no justice among them, and family rose against family; there were quarrels among them, and they began to raid against one another. And they said to each other, 'Let us look for a prince for ourselves.' So they went over the sea to the Varangians, to the Rus. For it is so that these Varangians were called Rus, as now others are called Swedes, and others Normans, Angles, and still others Goths.

The Estonians, Slovenins and Krivichi and Vepsä said to the Rus, 'Our land is large and plentiful, but there is no order. Come to be prince and govern us.' And three brothers were chosen with their kin. They took with them all the Rus and came first to the Slovenins and built the town of Ladoga. The oldest, Ryurik, settled in Ladoga; the second, Sineus, in Beloozero and the third, Truvor, in Izborsk. From these Varangians the land of Rus was named.

After two years Sineus and his brother Truvor died. And Ryurik took the whole domain alone.

Ryurik had two men, Askold and Dir, not his blood-relatives, but boyars, and they obtained his permission to go to Constantinople with their kin. They started along the Dnepr, and, going past, they saw on a hill a little town. They asked, 'Whose little town is this?' And the people said, 'There were three brothers, Kiy, Shchek and Khoriv, who made this little town, and they perished. We live here in their town and pay tribute to the Khazars.'

And Askold and Dir remained in this town. They collected many Varangians, and began to rule the land of the Polyanins, while Ryurik was ruling as prince in Novgorod.

In the year 879, when Ryurik died, he gave his princely rule to Oleg, who was of his own kin, entrusting into his hands his son, Igor, who was very young.

RIGHT *Ryurik, the first ruler of Rus. A Scandinavian prince, he founded the dynasty that reigned from the ninth to the late 16th century.*

Trade and tribute

From the ninth to the 11th centuries, as the rule of the Varangian warrior princes developed into the more settled Kievan state, the distribution of goods moved from plunder to trade. At the time of Svyatoslav (964–72), it was still based on regulated plunder, or the tribute system; the princes exacted tribute from communities in their territories and exchanged much of it for products obtained outside their realms. Foreign trade developed and required the organization of domestic trade to feed it.

The rivers made this possible. Tributaries of different systems were in easy reach of each other and goods could be easily transferred from one major waterway to another. The Dnepr, on which Kiev was built, was a link in an important north–south river route that connected the Baltic with the Mediterranean. Moreover, because Kiev was also connected with the Bug, Oka, Vistula and Don rivers, products could be transported in all directions.

What the princes and their retainers wanted, for themselves and for trading, were the traditional products of the south: silk and other fine fabrics, and wine. Better-quality and certainly better-looking weapons were obtainable in Constantinople, and fruit was another worthwhile commodity.

Constantinople, reached by travelling down the Dnepr and along the Black Sea coast, was the main trading centre. The Russians brought their own products for exchange: furs, honey, wax and slaves.

During winter, the princes led, or sent, armed detachments to collect tribute from the settlements they claimed to rule. Sometimes such collections were peaceful and formalized, at others, violent and rapacious. Products were transported on horses or, when the amounts were considerable, on heavy sledges which, where possible, were hauled along frozen rivers. When the thaw came, goods for export rather than home consumption were loaded into boats made from hollowed-out giant trees. These craft could carry up to ten horses each and were large enough to survive coastal navigation. The princes usually accompanied these convoys, which set out in

Goods were distributed first by plunder, then through trade as the Kievan state became more settled, and included luxuries like jewellery as well as grain and other staple products.

ABOVE *Silver pendant.*

RIGHT *Earrings, also made from silver.*

spring from the main riverside towns, and, a peculiarity of Russian commerce at this time, often negotiated deals in person. Although a merchant class gradually developed, and properly carpentered boats were used, hostile tribes downriver strangled this flourishing trade towards the end of the Kievan period.

There was also internal trade as towns acquired specialized handicraft industries. At the same time, food was brought into them; Novgorod, for example, needed to import grain from the Kiev area. Although bartering was successful for main commodities the use of money became more widespread. The process began with the circulation of foreign money, but from the 11th century coins were minted in Kiev.

PART 2 THE GRAND

The period covered by this section is known as that of Kiev Rus (or Kievan Russia). Kiev was already important as a base in 860 when an advance guard of Vikings under Askold and Dir attacked Constantinople – the first historically attested entry of Rus into European history. It became the capital of a recognizable Russian state when, in or about 882, the Viking prince Oleg moved south from Novgorod and forcibly united northern and southern Russia, and one of the most glorious and prosperous European cities under Vladimir I (who accepted Christianity from Byzantium in 988–9) and his son Yaroslav. With the decline of the trade route from the Vikings to the Greeks its importance was reduced, and economic primacy passed to Galicia. The Tartar (Mongol) invasion of 1237–40 finally ruined Kiev for many generations to come, and marks the end of the first stage of Russian history.

From their different viewpoints, Byzantine, Arab and Scandinavian sources provide valuable information about Kiev Rus. But the importance of one documentary source overshadows all others, at least for the early (pre-1050) Kievan period. That is the so-called *Russian Primary Chronicle* (also known from its opening words as *Tale of Bygone Years*), traditionally ascribed to the monk Nestor, writing in the Monastery of the Caves at Kiev, under Vladimir II Monomakh in the early 12th century. From the mid-ninth century he can attach events to dates; but his account is no mere dry annalistic record. In fact it is a great civilizational compendium, containing the texts of varied documents (some very ancient, like the first treaties with Byzantium) and self-contained narratives. Its climax is the justly famous account of the conversion of Vladimir I. No other European medieval chronicle can match its richness.

Medieval Russian chronicles were not, as is sometimes assumed, kept and updated year-by-year as if they were diaries (though doubtless their compilers drew on notes made of events as they happened). In fact, the writing of a chronicle was a single largescale undertaking, perhaps to celebrate a public event such as the accession of a new ruler. The author of the *Primary Chronicle* shows an exceptional sense of historical awareness for a medieval writer. But vivid and generally reliable as the *Primary Chronicle* certainly is, we have to realize that fantasy may colour the famous accounts of such matters as the origin of the Ryurikid dynasty, the varied depravities of Vladimir and Olga before Christian conversion, the way in which Yaroslav (sole survivor of 13 brothers) gained the Kiev throne. In our volume we give many excerpts from the *Primary Chronicle*, in a new and hitherto unpublished translation.

PRINCES OF KIEV (882-1240)

From the later Kievan period there are several other sources that can supplement the *Primary Chronicle*, confirm it or correct its biases. Novgorod had its own literary tradition, and the *Novgorod Chronicles* not only give much north-Russian information but have a different tone from the *Tale of Bygone Years*: down-to-earth, full of items about the city's everyday life, the climate, odd portents, etc. Birch-bark scrolls – 'throwaway' documents about financial and domestic matters – have survived in large numbers in the exceptional anaerobic conditions of the Novgorod subsoil, and have been deciphered during the last 40 years. They are a unique and unexpected archaeological revelation, and examples date from the entire medieval period. The merchant-adventurer milieu of Novgorod also left the remarkable oral heroic epic of *Sadko* (Kievan epics also, of course, survived).

There are some fine Kievan religious works with political overtones: the *Sermon on Law and Grace* by Yaroslav's head of the church, the Metropolitan Hilarion; the *Lives* of the martyred princes, Boris and Gleb. Probably the greatest work to survive from Kiev (highly literary, though based on epic folk-poems) is secular in tone: the *Lay of Igor's Campaign*, presaging the downfall of Rus through political dissension, and by implication urging the quarrelling Russian princes to make common cause against the enemy.

Both Kiev and Novgorod left a longlasting impression on the Russian popular historical consciousness. The sudden obliteration of independent Rus at the hands of infidels invested it with the glamour of a lost (but perhaps recoverable) 'golden age', the object of nostalgic yearning almost from the start of the Tartar period. The Muscovite grand princes and tsars (and even the imperial rulers after them) would look at the old Kievan lands as their true patrimony, to be one day recovered. Kievan folk epic tales would continue to be sung by illiterate balladeers in the distant northern backwoods. Novgorod, with its traditions of citizenship, enterprise and liberatarianism – that survived indeed the Tartar onslaught, only to be eventually obliterated by Moscow – left a somewhat different but if anything more potent image for later Russians (particularly for the Decembrist revolutionaries of 1825 and subsequent 18th century Romantics): that of an alternative Russian cultural tradition to the oppressive centralization, arbitrary rule and tyranny that have all too often seemed the Russians lot.

Ψ

Oleg. Igor. Olga. Svyatoslav

The beginning of the Kievan period, following the beginning of Oleg's reign in Kiev, sees the emergence of Rus as a European power. It was not yet a state in the modern sense of the word. The native Slavonic population was still essentially tribal, without any national self-awareness, while their Varangian rulers, though gradually becoming assimilated to their subjects, still retained close links with Scandinavia. There was much travel to and fro between the two areas, attested by both Kievan chronicles and Norse sagas, and the outlook of the Rus of Gardariki was still basically that of Nordic freebooters, despoilers as much as governors of the land. constantly on the move between the enclosed towns that served as centres of their power in a country of uncertain temper. Their sporadic harrying of Byzantium typifies the relationship of barbarian rovers to the civilized world; and yet, in the person of Olga, widow of Oleg's successor Igor, a different attitude was already beginning to emerge, according to which the sophisticated Byzantine state was to be emulated rather than preyed upon. It was this attitude which, in the reign of Olga's grandson Vladimir I, was to prevail.

The documents in this chapter are all taken from the most important historical source for the period, the *Primary Chronicle*, the oldest manuscript of which, dated 1377, preserves a text which had probably taken shape in Kiev in the late 11th century. Drawing upon all the local historical tradition, it preserves both documentary sources like the treaties with the Greeks, and legendary and semi-legendary accounts like those of the death of Oleg (a wandering tale also found in other European literatures) and Olga's revenge on the Derevlyanins. With its unashamed bias in its decription of foreign affairs and its naïve delight in Olga's inventive deceit, its historical narrative also provides an insight into the early medieval Kievan mind.

OPPOSITE *Oleg, Kiev's first ruler (882–c. 912), with the young Igor who succeeded him as grand prince in 913.*

In the year 882 Oleg set out from Novgorod, taking many soldiers. He came to Smolensk and he took the town. From there he went on down and took Lyubech. Then they came to the hills of Kiev, and Oleg found out that Askold and Dir were ruling as princes. He concealed some of his soldiers in boats and left the others behind, while he himself came on, carrying the baby Igor.

Oleg sent to Askold and Dir saying, 'You are not princes, nor of princely lineage, but I am of a princely lineage, and this is the son of Ryurik.' And he killed Askold and Dir.

Afterwards, Oleg settled as prince in Kiev. And he said, 'Let this be the mother of the towns of Rus.' He had Varangians and Slavs and all the others with him.

And from that time on they were called Rus.

This same Oleg began to build towns and he decreed to levy tributes from the Slovenins, the Krivichi and the Merya. He established that the Varangians were to be given coin tribute from Novgorod at the rate of three hundred grivnas per year, for the sake of peace.

According to the *Primary Chronicle*, from which a brief passage is quoted above, Oleg, a Varangian, captured Kiev in 882 in the name of Ryurik's young son, Igor, and became its ruler.

This account in the *Primary Chronicle* describes the mission to the Slavs of Moravia undertaken by learned Byzantines, Cyril and Methodius, from 862 onwards. Among the fruits of the mission were the Slavonic translations of Holy Scripture and the service books, later adopted by the Eastern Slavs.

Now the Slavs were living in baptism, and their princes too. They sent to Emperor Michael, saying, 'Our land has been baptized, but we have no teacher who could admonish us and teach us and interpret the holy books. For we do not understand either the Greek language or the Latin. And some teach us this and others teach us that way. Therefore we do not understand the sense of the letters or their meaning. Send us teachers who can explain the words of the books and their sense.'

Hearing this, Emperor Michael called together all the philosophers and explained all that the Slavic princes had said. And the philosophers said, 'There is a man in Salonika named Leo. He has sons who understand the Slavic language, two clever sons of his are even philosophers.' The emperor sent for them and they were persuaded by him and went to the land of the Slavs to Rastislav and Svyatopolk and Kocel. When they arrived, they began to devise letters for a Slavonic alphabet; and they translated the Gospel. The Slavs were glad that they heard the greatness of God in their own language.

When Igor grew up, he followed Oleg and obeyed him. And they brought him a wife from Pskov, named Olga.

In the year 907, Oleg went against the Greeks, leaving Igor in Kiev. He took a multitude of Varangians and Slovenes and many others. With all these Oleg set out on horses and in boats; the boats were two thousand in number. He came to Constantinople and disembarked onto the shore. He murdered many Greeks; destroyed many palaces and burned churches. Of the prisoners they took, some they slaughtered, others they tortured, still others they killed, while others they threw into the sea. And the Rus did many other evil things to the Greeks, of the kind men at war do.

Oleg ordered his soldiers to fashion wheels and to put the boats on the wheels. When there was a favourable wind, they raised their sails and went from the field toward the city. Seeing this, the Greeks became afraid. They said, sending out to Oleg, 'Do not destroy the city! We agree to tribute as you wish.' So Oleg halted the soldiers, and the Greeks brought out food and wine to him, but he did not accept it. For it was prepared with poison.

The Greeks were afraid, and asked for peace. Oleg began to negotiate with the Greek emperors, Leo and Alexander. He sent envoys to them saying, 'Agree to pay tribute to me.' And the Greeks said, 'We will give what you wish.'

Emperor Leo, with Alexander, made a pact with

Oleg, agreeing to tribute and swearing oaths to each other. They themselves kissed the cross, while Oleg and his men took an oath according to the religion of Rus and swore by their weapons.

Oleg said, 'Sew brocade sails for the Rus, and silken ones for the Slavs.' And it was done. He hung his shield on the gate, showing victory, and set out from Constantinople. The Rus raised their brocade sails and the Slavs their silken ones, and the wind tore them. So the Slavs said, 'Let us stick with our canvas; silken sails are not meant for Slavs.'

Oleg returned to Kiev carrying gold and brocades and fruits and wines and all sorts of decorated things. And they called Oleg a seer, for the people were pagan and uneducated.

In the year 911, a big star appeared in the east, in the shape of a spear.

In the same year, 911, Oleg sent his men to lay down the terms of peace between the Rus and the Greeks. The Byzantine Emperor Leo honoured the envoys of Rus with gifts, gold and brocades and silks.

He assigned his men to them to show them the beauty of the churches and the golden halls and the riches in them, much gold, and brocades and precious stones, and the relics of the passion of the Lord – the crown of thorns and the nails and the purple robe – and the relics of the saints, thereby teaching them the Greek faith and showing them the true faith. So he sent them to their own land with great honour. When the envoys sent by Oleg returned, they told him everything the two emperors had said, how they had made peace, and established order between the land of the Greeks and of Rus, and that neither the Greeks nor the Rus were to betray their oaths. Afterwards Oleg lived in peace with all countries, reigning as prince in Kiev.

In the year 913 Oleg died, and the people all lamented for him with great sorrow. They took him and buried him on the hill which is called Shchekovitsa. His burial mound is there to this day. It is known as Oleg's mound. And all the years of his reign were thirty-three.

Ψ

A death foretold

When autumn came, Oleg remembered his horse, which he had put out to be fed but not ridden. For he had asked the magicians and wizards, 'From what am I to die?' And one wizard said to him, 'Prince, the horse you love and ride on – from him you will die.' Oleg, accepting this in his mind, said, 'I will never again mount my horse nor see him!'

Oleg ordered that his horse should be fed and should not to be brought to him; and he passed several years without seeing the horse, while he went against the Greeks.

When he had returned to Kiev and spent four years, he remembered, during the fifth year, the horse that the magicians had said would cause his death.

Oleg summoned the head groom and said,

'Where is my horse, which I had put out to be fed and cared for?' The groom said, 'He has died.' Then Oleg laughed and made fun of the wizard, saying, 'See, magicians speak falsely: all that is a lie. The horse has died, but I am alive.'

He ordered a horse to be saddled and said, 'Let me see the bones of my old horse.' He came to the place where the bones were lying bare, and the skull bare. Oleg dismounted from his horse and laughed, saying, 'Was it from this skull that I was to die?' And as he said this, he trod on the skull with his foot.

Then a snake, coming out of the skull, bit Oleg on the foot. From that snake-bite he became sick and died.

From Primary Chronicle

Oleg's successor was Igor, Ryurik's son. He ruled as prince of Kiev until 945. His freebooting raids on Byzantium, although ending in a defeat by the Byzantine navy, which used the much-feared 'Greek fire', nonetheless enabled him, in 944, to conclude a peace and trade treaty, rather less favourable to the Rus. Igor was killed soon after while collecting tribute from the Derevlyanins.

In the year 941 Igor went against the Greeks. And the Bulgars sent word to Emperor Romanus: 'The Rus are coming against Byzantium! Ten thousand boats! They have ravaged along the province of Pontus and having pillaged the whole area of Nicomedia they burned the whole Golden Horn. Some of their captives they chopped up, others they set up as targets and shot arrows at them and they took them and tied their hands behind them and pounded iron nails into their heads. They set many of the holy churches afire, they burned monasteries and villages, and they have taken a good deal of property from both regions.'

The Rus then came against the Greeks. There was fierce battle between them, and although the Greeks barely won, the Rus returned to their boats and fled. The Greeks met them in their boats and began to shoot fire through pipes onto the Russian boats. And a fearsome wonder was to be seen. The Rus, seeing the flame, threw themselves into the sea, wishing to

RIGHT *Constantinople, capital of the Byzantine empire. Igor concluded a favourable peace treaty with the Greeks in 945, shortly before his death.*

BELOW *Enamelled gold earring; Kievan, c. 1150. A product of the treasure captured in Byzantium.*

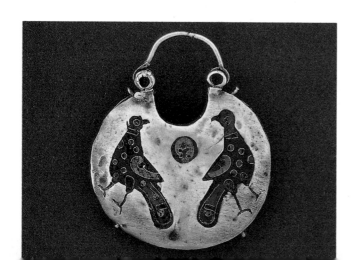

swim away; and thus the rest returned home. When they came to their own land each one told his own people about what happened. 'The Greeks,' they said, 'possess something like the lightning in the heavens, and they released it and burned us. For this reason we did not conquer them.'

In the year 944, having collected many soldiers, Igor again set out against the Greeks in boats and on horses, wishing to avenge himself.

Hearing this, Emperor Romanus sent his leading officials to Igor, pleading and saying, 'Do not attack, but take the tribute which Oleg used to take; I will also add more to that tribute.' To the Pechenegs too he sent brocades and much gold. Igor, having reached the Danube, summoned his army, and began to confer; he told them the emperor's words. And Igor's men said, 'If that's what the emperor says, what more do we want than to take gold and silver and brocades without fighting? Who knows who will win, we or they? Or who is in counsel with the sea? For we are not travelling on land, but on the depths of the sea: death is common to all!' Igor heeded them.

In the year 944, Emperor Romanus sent envoys to Igor to make the first peace treaty. Igor, having spoken with them about the treaty, sent his own envoys to Romanus. And Romanus summoned his officials and dignitaries. The envoys of Rus were brought in and ordered to speak, and the words of both sides were to be written on parchment.

The envoys sent by Igor returned to him with the Greek envoys, and they told him everything that Emperor Romanus had said. Igor then summoned the Greek envoys, who said, 'See, the emperor sent us. He wants to have peace with the prince of Rus and amity. Your envoys have taken an oath from our emperors, and they have sent us to obtain your oath and that of your men.'

Igor promised to do this. And having affirmed peace with the Greeks, he dismissed the envoys, after having given them presents of furs and slaves and wax.

Then Igor began to rule as prince in peace with all countries. But when autumn came he began to think of going against the Derevlyanins [an East Slavic tribe], wishing to increase their tribute.

In the year 945 Igor's retainers said to him, 'The Derevlyanins have adorned themselves with weapons and clothing, while we are naked. Go with us, prince, to obtain tribute, so you will profit and we too.' Igor heeded them; he went and did violence to the Derevlyanins. Then he returned home to his town of Kiev.

When the Derevlyanins heard that he was coming again, they conferred with their prince, Mal, and said, 'If a wolf gets the habit of coming among the sheep, he will carry off the whole flock unless he is killed. So with this man: if we don't kill him, he will destroy all of us.' So the Derevlyanins, coming out of the town of Iskorosten to meet Igor, killed him and his company; for there were few of them.

Igor was buried, and his burial-mound is near the town of Iskorosten to this day.

The curious and gruesome account of Igor's widow Olga's revenge is luridly depicted by the *Primary* chronicler perhaps to contrast the better with her later Christian personality.

Olga, Igor's widow, was in Kiev with her son, the child Svyatoslav. The Derevlyanins said, 'Now we have killed the prince of Rus. Let us take his wife Olga to marry our prince Mal; and let's take Svyatoslav and do what we want with him.'

The Derevlyanins sent their best men, twenty in number, in a boat to Olga.

Olga was told that the Derevlyanins had come. She summoned them to her and said: 'Welcome, strangers. Tell me why you have come here.'

The Derevlyanins said, 'The land of Dereva sent us to say this: "We have killed your husband. For your husband was like a wolf, stealing and plundering, while our princes are good and have taken good care of the land of Dereva. Marry our prince Mal!"'

OPPOSITE *'Greek fire', a favourite Byzantine weapon. Its use defeated the Rus forces that Igor led against Byzantium in 941. Many of his men were so terrified that they threw themselves into the sea.*

RIGHT   *Igor, grand prince
of Kiev (913–45). Not
satisfied with the great
wealth acquired from the
Greeks, he raided the
Derevlyanins to raise their
tribute. But his greed cost
him his life.*

For his name was Mal, the prince of Dereva. And Olga said to them, 'Your words please me. I cannot resurrect my husband. But I want to honour you tomorrow before my people. Go to your boat, and wait there with pride. Tomorrow I will send for you. You will say, "We will not ride on horses, nor go on foot; carry us in the boat!" And they will carry you up in the boat.' Then she dismissed them.

Olga ordered a big and deep pit to be dug at the tower yard outside the keep. In the morning, sitting in the tower, she sent for the guests. The Derevlyanins replied, 'We will not ride on horses or on carts nor will we go afoot; carry us in the boat!' So they began to carry them in the boat.

The Derevlyanins sat on the benches with their great buckles, proudly, and were carried into the yard to Olga. When they had arrived, the Kievans threw them into the pit, with the boat as well. Leaning down, Olga said to them, 'Is this honour good enough for you?' And they said, 'It is worse for us than Igor's death.' She ordered them to be buried alive, and they buried them.

Olga then sent to the Derevlyanins and said to them, 'If you are really asking for me, send distinguished men, so that I may come in duly great honour to marry your prince; otherwise the people of Kiev will not let me go.' When the Derevlyanins heard that, they chose the best men, who were in charge of the land of Dereva, and sent for her. When the Derevlyanins came, Olga ordered a bath to be prepared, saying, 'Wash yourselves and come to me.' The hut was heated up and the Derevlyanins went in. They began to wash. Olga's men barred the hut around them, and she ordered that it be set on fire, starting from the door. They all burned inside.

Olga hastened with her son to the town of Iskorosten, for they were the ones who had killed her husband. And she took up positions around the town with her son. She stayed through the summer but couldn't take the town. So she thought up this plan.

She sent to the town, saying, 'Why do you want to sit out the siege; all your towns have surrendered and agree to pay tribute? They are working their fields and land, but you will die from hunger, because you do not agree to pay tribute.'

The Derevlyanins said, "What do you want from us? We will gladly give honey and furs.' She said, 'Now you have neither honey nor furs, but I ask little of you. Give me three doves and three sparrows from each house. I do not want to levy heavy tribute like my husband, for you have become weak in the siege. Just give me this little bit.' And the Derevlyanins were glad. They collected three doves and three sparrows from each household, and sent them to Olga. Olga said to them, 'Now you have submitted to me and my child. Go into the town and tomorrow I will move out and go to my own town.'

The Derevlyanins were glad. They went into the town and told the people, and the people rejoiced. Olga distributed doves to some soldiers and sparrows to others, and ordered them to tie tinder to each dove and sparrow, wrapping it up in little pieces of cloth and tying it with thread to each of them. She ordered that as soon as it began to get dark her soldiers were to release the doves and sparrows. The doves and sparrows flew to their nests, the doves to the dove-cotes, and the sparrows under the eaves. In this way the dove-cotes caught fire, here outbuildings, there towers, elsewhere barns. There was no household where there was no fire, and it was impossible to put it out, for all the households had caught fire. The people fled from the town, and Olga ordered her soldiers to capture them. As soon as she took the town, she burned it. The elders of the town she captured, and as for the rest of the people, some she killed and others she gave to her men as slaves, the rest she left to pay tribute.

She levied a heavy tribute on them. Two parts of the tribute went to Kiev and the third to Vyshegorod to Olga; for Vyshegorod was Olga's town. After that, Olga went about the Derevlyan land with her son, Svyatoslav, and her retinue setting up regulations and taxes.

Her encampments and hunting grounds still exist. She came to her town of Kiev with her son, and remained there one year.

RIGHT *The interior of Hagia Sophia, Constantinople. A Christian church when the city was the centre of the Greek Orthodox religion.*

Olga's visit to Constantinople when she was over 60 years of age, and where she was baptized, is described by the chronicler. She was later canonized; but at the time, the ruling circle, including her own son Svyatoslav, clung largely to paganism.

In the year 955 Olga went to the Greeks and arrived in Constantinople, at the time Constantine, son of Leo, was emperor. And Olga came to him, and seeing that she was very good looking and intelligent, the emperor was amazed at her understanding. He conversed with her, saying to her, 'You are fit to reign in this city with us.' When she understood she said to the emperor, 'I am a pagan, but if you want to baptize me, baptize me yourself. If not, I will not be baptized.' So the emperor baptized her, with the patriarch. When she was enlightened, she rejoiced in soul and body. And the patriarch instructed her in the faith. He said to her, 'Blessed are you among the women of Rus, for you have come to love the light and abandoned the darkness. The sons of Rus will bless you even to the last generation of your grandchildren.' He gave her the commands about the rules of the Church, about prayer and about fasting, about alms and about maintaining the body pure. Bowing her head, she stood, taking in the teaching, like a sponge being given water.

After Olga's baptism, the emperor invited her and said to her, 'I want to make you my wife.' But she said, 'How is it you want to marry me, when you yourself baptized me and called me your daughter? Among Christians that is against the law, as you yourself know.' Emperor Constantine said, 'You have tricked me, Olga.' But he gave her many gifts, gold and silver, brocades and various vessels, and dismissed her, calling her his daughter. When she was about to go home, Olga went to the patriarch, asking his blessing to take home with her. And the patriarch blessed her.

Olga returned to Kiev, where she lived with her son Svyatoslav. She kept instructing him to be baptized, but he would not even hear of it. However, he said, if anyone wanted to be baptized, it was not forbidden; but he would be ridiculed.

Olga often used to say, 'I have come to know God, my son, and I rejoice. If you come to know him you too will begin to rejoice.' But he did not listen, saying, 'How can I alone accept another faith? My retinue will laugh at it.' And she said to him, 'If you are baptized, everyone will have to do it too.' But he did not heed his mother, and kept pagan customs, not knowing that he who does not heed his mother will fall into misfortune. However, Olga loved her son Svyatoslav, saying, 'May God's will be done. If God wants to have mercy on my family and the land of Rus, let him put it into their hearts to turn to God, as God granted me that gift.' After she had said this, she prayed for her son and for the people all the time, night and day, while she nourished her son to manhood.

Having reached maturity – and his mother Olga the ripe old age of 80 – Svyatoslav ruled as prince of Kiev from 962. The *Primary Chronicle* shows him to have been Spartan in his habits, fierce but chivalrous in warfare, politically naïve and uninterested in government. He nevertheless held down an empire that reached from the borders of the Byzantine empire to those of Central Asia. But his rash destruction of the Khazars opened the steppe corridor to nomad invasions, among whom were the fierce Pechenegs.

In the year 964, when Svyatoslav had grown up and become a man, he began to collect numerous and brave soldiers. For he himself was brave. And moving lightly, like a leopard, he waged many wars. When travelling, he did not take any carts with him, nor a kettle, nor did he cook meat. But cutting off a thin slice of the meat of a horse or a wild beast or an ox, he would cook it on the coals and eat it. Nor did he have a tent, but would spread out his saddle-blanket and put his saddle as a pillow. The rest of his soldiers were all like that.

In the year 965, Svyatoslav went against the Khazars. When the Khazars heard, they came out to meet him with their prince the Kagan, and they came together to fight. When the battle took place, Svyatoslav defeated the Khazars and took their town, Bela Vezha. And he defeated the Ossetians and Circas-

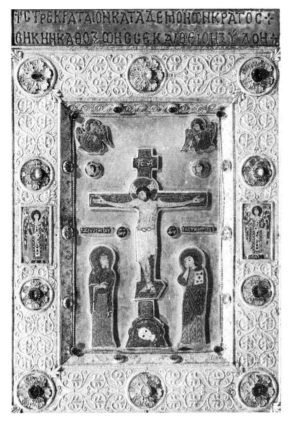

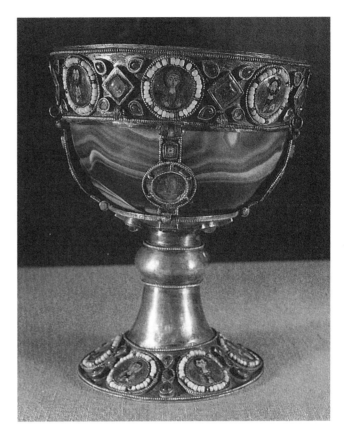

ABOVE LEFT *Byzantine votive panel studded with jewels.*

ABOVE *Byzantine chalice: sardonyx mounted in silver-gilt, decorated with pearls and enamel.*

LEFT *The baptism of Olga in Constantinople.*

sians. The following year, Svyatoslav defeated the Vyatichi and levied a tribute on them.

In the year 967, Svyatoslav went to the Danube to fight against the Bulgars, and conquered them. He took eighty towns along the Danube, and he settled as prince there, at Pereyaslavets, taking tribute from the Greeks.

In the year 968, the Pechenegs came against the land of Rus for the first time, while Svyatoslav was at Pereyaslavets. Olga shut herself up in the town of Kiev with her grandsons Yaropolk and Oleg and Vladimir. The Pechenegs surrounded the town in great force, and it was impossible to go out of the town or to send news. The people became weak from hunger and lack of water.

The people of the other side of the Dnepr assembled in boats. They remained on that side, for it was not possible for any one of them to enter Kiev, nor for anyone in the town to get out to them. The people in the town complained and one boy said, 'I will go.' He

The neighbours of Rus

The emergence, from the mid-ninth century, of Rus as a state took place within a triangle of forces: three of the major powers of the period, very different from one another though interdependent.

To the south of Rus lay the Byzantine (East Roman) empire. Centred on Constantinople and at the height of its early medieval glory, Byzantium, Christian capital of the world, gave Rus its religion, intellectual life and general world-view.

To the north-west were the still-pagan Vikings of Scandinavia, embarking on their phenomenal expansion of trade, plunder and exploration; to them the new state owed its political structures and spirit of expansionism.

To the south-east was Khazaria, a large state that crystallized when semi-nomadic Turkic tribes settled along the lower reaches of the great rivers – Volga, Don and Terek – that intersected the arid country north of the Caucasus and west of the Caspian. The Khazars chose Judaism as their state religion. Their territory controlled ancient trade-routes to the Islamic world and the east, and was also a buffer-zone absorbing nomad and Arab incursions. Their influence extended north and west: some Russian tribes became their tributaries.

In the 960s the Russo-Viking prince Svyatoslav destroyed their power.

The Vikings moved first south-eastwards, then south from the Gulf of Finland, seeking trade through Khazaria and with Byzantium. From its inception the new entity, Rus, was multinational: Slav, Scandinavian, perhaps Baltic and Finnic. Relations between Rus and Scandinavia were close until the 12th century, and in Novgorod whose traders had a depot on Gotland, remained so up to the late 15th.

Russo-Viking expeditions periodically tried to plunder Byzantium from 860 on. The Byzantines characteristically responded with diplomatic initiatives, which led to early 10th-century treaties and in 988–9 to the official conversion of Rus to Christianity.

Rus had other neighbours, in particular Slav peoples only slightly differentiated in language: Poles, Czechs, Slovaks, 'White Croats', Moravians (the first Slav nation to accept Christianity), and Bulgarians.

The Bulgarians, who occupied a strategically important location between Rus and the Byzantine empire, were the western branch of a Turkic people fused with a large Slav population and Christianized.

Their cousins, the 'Volga Bulgars', had moved north and founded a state in the region of modern Kazan. They adopted Islam as the Khagars did, but were the only Muslims in direct contact with Rus.

Further afield were the Germans of the Holy Roman Empire, then expanding east along the Baltic; the Magyars who had passed through the steppe on their way to Hungary; Vlachs (ancestors of the Romanians); Lithuanians and Latvians; Georgians beyond the Caucasus.

The Rus dynasty intermarried with most of the royal houses of Europe, including the English and French.

New neighbours in the steppe, however, fatally weakened the new state: first the Pecheneg in the 10th century, and from the 11th, the Polovtsian nomads, whose constant attacks eventually rendered its southern flank and trade-routes untenable.

RIGHT *An evocative portrayal of Mount Elbrus, Georgia's highest mountain. The region, beyond the Caucasus, was one of the more distant neighbours of the emergent state of Rus.*

went out of the town with a bridle and ran through the Pechenegs, saying, 'Has no one seen my horse?' For he knew the Pecheneg language, and they thought he was one of their own. When he got close to the river, he threw off his clothes and began to swim. When the Pechenegs saw this, they rushed at him, shooting at him, but they could not do anything to him.

When they saw him from the other side the people came in boats to meet him. They lifted him into a boat and took him to the prince's retainers. The boy said to them, 'If you do not come up to the town tomorrow, the people will surrender to the Pechenegs.' Their commander, Pretich by name, said, 'We will come up to the town tomorrow in boats.' When morning came, having got into the boats by dawn, they blew hard on their trumpets and the people in the town gave a shout. The Pechenegs fled in various directions away from the town. Olga came out with her grandsons and with the people to the boats.

When the Pecheneg prince saw this, he returned alone to the commander, Pretich, and asked, 'Who is it that has come?' The commander replied, 'The people from the other side.' The Pecheneg prince said, 'Are you the prince?' And Pretich said, 'I am his man, and I have come as a vanguard; his troops are coming behind me with the prince, a countless multitude.' The Pecheneg prince said to Pretich, 'Be my friend.' And Pretich said, 'I will.' They shook hands, and the Pechenegs retreated from the town.

The Kievans sent to Svyatoslav, saying, 'Prince, you are seeking other people's lands and taking care of them, but abandoning your own. The Pechenegs almost captured us and your mother and your children. If you do not come and protect us, they will capture us again. Are you not sorry for your patrimony, or your mother, who is old, and your children?' When Svyatoslav heard that, he quickly mounted his horse and, with his retinue, came to Kiev, kissed his mother and his children, and expressed regret at what had happened because of the Pechenegs. Then he assembled his soldiers and chased the Pechenegs into the steppe, and there was peace.

In the following year, Svyatoslav said to his mother and his boyars, 'I do not like being in Kiev; I want to live in Pereyaslavets on the Danube, for that is the centre of my land. There all the good things come together, from the Greeks – gold, brocades, wine and various fruits; from the Czechs and the Hungarians – silver and fine horses, and from the Rus – fur and wax, honey and slaves.' Olga said to him, 'You see that I am sick, how can you leave me?' For she had already fallen sick. 'After you have buried me, go wherever you want.'

After three days Olga died, and her son sorrowed for her and her grandsons and all the people with a great lamentation. And they carried her and buried her. And Olga had ordered that no funeral feast was to be held over her. For she had a priest, and he buried the blessed Olga.

In 969, Svyatoslav felt threatened by the Byzantines who wanted him to leave the Balkans. In characteristic style he immediately invaded the Byzantine empire; but he was defeated. After a Greco-Russian treaty which obliged him to return to Kiev, Svyatoslav was killed in 972 in a Pecheneg ambush at the Dnepr rapids.

In the year 971, Svyatoslav moved against the Greeks and they came out to meet the Rus. When the Rus saw them, they became frightened of the multitude of soldiers. And Svyatoslav said, 'There is no place for us to go now, we have no choice but to stand against them. Let us not shame the land of Rus, but lay down our bones, for the dead have no shame.' The armies clashed, and the battle was great. Svyatoslav was victorious and the Greeks fled. Svyatoslav moved on toward Constantinople, harrying and smashing towns which still stand empty to this day.

The emperor called his officials to his palace and said to them, 'What shall we do, since we cannot stand against him?' And the officials said to him, 'Send him gifts. Let us tempt him to see whether he is desirous of gold or brocades.' So they sent gold to him and brocades, and a clever envoy, saying, 'Observe his appearance and his face and his mind.' The envoy took the gifts and went to Svyatoslav. When Svyatoslav was told that the Greeks had come with obeisance, he said, 'Bring them here.' They came and bowed to him and put gold and brocades before him. Svyatoslav, looking aside, said to his servants, 'Put them away,' and they did so.

The emperor's envoys returned to the emperor and he summoned his advisers. The envoys said, 'We came to him and gave him the gifts; he did not look at them and ordered that they be put away.' One of the advisers said, 'Tempt him again, send weapons.' The Greeks heeded him and sent him a sword and other weapons. Svyatoslav, taking them, began to praise and admire them, and sent greetings to the emperor.

The envoys came back once more to the emperor and told him all that had happened. The officials said, 'This man must be fierce, since he does not care for possessions but takes weapons. Agree to pay him tribute.' So the emperor sent to Svyatoslav saying, 'Do not come to the city. Take whatever tribute you wish.' For Svyatoslav had come up almost to Constantinople. He took some gifts for those who had been killed as well, saying, 'Their families will take it.' He returned to Pereyaslavets with great praise.

Afterwards he sent envoys to the emperor saying, 'I want to have a firm peace treaty and amity with you.' Hearing this the emperor was glad, and sent him gifts greater than the previous ones.

Having made peace with the Greeks, Svyatoslav set out in boats toward the rapids. The people of Pereyaslavets sent to the Pechenegs, saying, 'Now Svyatoslav is coming your way, returning to Rus with only a small company, having taken many possessions and uncountable booty.' When the Pechenegs heard this they occupied the rapids. Svyatoslav came to the rapids, and since it was not possible to pass through the rapids, he stopped to winter there. They had no more food, and there was great hunger.

When spring came, in the year 972, Svyatoslav went to the rapids. Kurya, the Pecheneg prince, attacked him, and killed Svyatoslav. The Pechenegs took his head and they made a cup of his skull, putting metal around the forehead, and they drank from it. And all the years of the reign of Svyatoslav were twenty-eight.

RIGHT *Funerary statue of a Pecheneg leader. Svyatoslav, Kiev's last non-Christian ruler, was killed by the Pechenegs, who made a cup from his skull.*

Ψ

Vladimir I

For over a thousand years, with only a brief respite in the 19th century, the Land of Rus and its successor states were troubled by the problem of the transfer of power from one ruler to the next. The death of Svyatoslav in 972 precipitated one of these crises as his three sons, Yaropolk, Oleg and Vladimir, contended for the absolute overlordship that their father had enjoyed. The eldest, Yaropolk, already established in Kiev after Svyatoslav's removal of his seat to Pereyaslavets, soon disposed of Oleg and initially prevailed against Vladimir, who was forced to flee from his city of Novgorod to Scandinavia. Returning with an army of Varangians, Vladimir renewed the war on Yaropolk, whom he defeated and killed, thereby becoming the sole ruler of Rus.

At the beginning of his long reign (980–1015), Vladimir continued his ancestors' practice of raiding the Byzantine empire (specifically the Greek town of Cherson in the Crimea), but he soon concluded that it was better to enter the Byzantines' culture orbit than to oppose them. His adoption of Christianity on behalf of his people in *c.* 988 was one of the most decisive events in his country's history, and its results can be felt in Russia's cultural orientation to this day, while at the time an organized religion both answered the needs and facilitated the development of an increasing national and social cohesion in Rus.

The stability afforded by the presence of a powerful individual on the throne for 35 years also greatly aided the development of the emergent nation, and later generations were to look back on the reigns of Vladimir, and his son Yaroslav, as the golden age of Kiev. Only the nomads of the southern steppes, the Pechenegs, threatened the prosperity of the realm. But even they were contained by Vladimir's military prowess.

OPPOSITE   *The cathedral, in Kiev, of St Vladimir, the first Russian ruler to accept Christianity.*

In the year 980, Vladimir, son of Svyatoslav, came to Novgorod with Varangians. He said to his brother Yaropolk's governors, 'Go to my brother and say to him, "Vladimir is coming against you; get ready to fight against him."' And he took up residence in Novgorod.

He sent to Rogvolod in Polotsk, saying, 'I want to take your daughter to be my wife.' Rogvolod had come from over the sea and had his domain in Polotsk. Rogvolod said to his daughter, 'Do you want to marry Vladimir?' and she answered, 'I will not take the shoes off the son of a slave-woman; I want Yaropolk instead.' Vladimir's servants came and told him what Rogned, daughter of Rogvolod, had said.

Vladimir collected many soldiers, Varangians and Slovenins, Estonians and Krivichians, and went against Rogvolod at the very time they were to marry Rogned to Yaropolk. And Vladimir came against Polotsk; he killed Rogvolod and his two sons, and he took his daughter Rogned for his wife.

After that he set out against his brother Yaropolk. He arrived in Kiev with many soldiers, and so Yaropolk was killed.

Now Vladimir lay with his brother's wife, a Greek woman, who was already pregnant. And from her Svyatopolk was born. From a sinful root comes evil fruit. Because his mother had been a nun, and secondly, because Vladimir lay with her out of wedlock, even his father did not love him, for he was of two fathers, Yaropolk and Vladimir.

The above account from the *Primary Chronicle* gives an idea of the confusion and the ruthlessness which marked the war of succession that ensued, after the death of Svyatoslav, between his three sons. The youngest, Vladimir, eventually emerged victorious.

The remarkable story of Vladimir I's religious quest begins with his setting up of a synthetic pantheon of Slav gods from various parts of Rus.

Vladimir began to reign alone in Kiev. He set up idols on the hill outside. One was Perun, a wooden thunder god with a silver head and golden moustaches; they sacrificed to them, calling them gods. They would bring their sons and daughters and sacrifice to the demons, and they defiled the land with their sacrifices. The land of Rus was defiled with blood.

The elaborate account of Vladimir's conversion is the climax of the *Primary Chronicle*. Vladimir sent emissaries to visit the lands of other faiths. He based his choice on their reports; but he delayed until he had captured the important Byzantine Crimean outpost of Cherson, and obtained the sister of the Byzantine emperors, Basil and Constantine, in marriage. Vladimir's conversion led to a mass baptism of the Kiev population in the River Dnepr.

In the year 987, Vladimir summoned together his boyars and the city elders and said to them, 'The Bulgars came before me urging me to accept their

Eight hundred concubines

Vladimir was overcome by lust for women, and these were married to him: Rogned, daughter of Rogvolod, whom he seated at Lybed. From her he begat four sons, Izyaslav, Mstislav, Yaroslav, Vsevolod, and two daughters. From the Greek woman, Svyatopolk. From a Czech woman, Vysheslav, and from another, Svyatoslav and Mstislav. And from the Bulgarian woman, Boris and Gleb. He had three hundred concubines at Vyshegorod and three hundred at Belgorod, and two hundred at Berestovo. He was insatiable in fornication, having married women brought to him, and deflowering virgins. He was a lover of women like Solomon. Solomon, it is said, had seven hundred wives and three hundred concubines. He was wise, but in the end he perished. Vladimir was an uneducated man, but in the end he found salvation.

From *Primary Chronicle*

The religion of Russia

St Vladimir, grand prince of Kiev from 980 to 1015, is revered by his people today as 'Equal of the Apostles', a title he shares with Emperor Constantine, who, like Vladimir, made Christianity the official religion of his people. The grand prince possessed in abundance the qualities needed to be a successful ruler: a forceful personality, he was ruthless in establishing his personal power, an energetic and able warrior, and, before his conversion, violent and sensual.

The story of the 'testing of faiths', despite its 'literary' nature, also reflects a measure of reality. The Slavs, like their Finnic neighbours, practised a form of shamanism, but had little in the way of organized religion. Even the heathen pantheon erected in Kiev by Vladimir before his conversion was an artificial device, a final unsuccessful attempt to accommodate the old practices to the more highly developed social and cultural structures of the late tenth century. The leaders of Rus were seeking a faith more structured and evolved than their native religion.

It was inevitable that Byzantine Christianity should have become the established religion. Byzantium, the major power in the region, and by far the most advanced culture, had important commercial links with Rus. A Slavonic version of the Byzantine rite existed, and was in use, for example, in Bulgaria; this same rite was probably used by Christian communities already in Rus, whose most distinguished convert had been Vladimir's grandmother Olga.

The year 988, the date of the conversion, therefore marks not the beginning of Christianity in Rus, but the country's acceptance into the commonwealth of Christian nations, and the establishment of the Christian culture of Constantinople as the model for that of Rus.

The old religion was unstructured, and there was little or no organized resistance to Christianity. However, native beliefs were not a distinct institution and could not be simply abolished. Customs of pagan origin survived for centuries despite the clergy's frequent denunciations of the people's 'double faith'. Although they accommodated themselves to the Christian calendar, the Church was never reconciled to them, and the resulting duality in popular culture, a coexistence of the divine and the diabolical, played a large part in forming the Russian outlook on life.

ABOVE *Vladimir I of Kiev, later St Vladimir.*

religion. Then came the Germans and praised their own faith; and after them came the Jews. Finally the Greeks appeared, criticizing all other faiths but commending their own. What is your opinion on this subject, and what do you answer?' The boyars and elders replied, 'You have your men at your disposal. Send them to enquire about the ritual of each and how they worship God.'

Their counsel pleased the prince and all the people, so that they chose good and wise men to the number of ten. Then they went their way.

When they returned, Vladimir called together his boyars and elders and commanded the envoys to speak out, and so they did, saying: 'Among the Bulgars, we beheld how they worship in their temple, called a mosque, while they stand ungirt. The Bulgar bows, sits down, looks hither and thither like one possessed, and there is no joy among them, but only sorrow. Their religion is not good. Then we went among the Germans, and saw them performing many ceremonies in their temples; but we beheld no beauty there.

Then we went to Byzantium, and the Greeks led us to the places where they worship their God, and we knew not whether we were in heaven or on earth. For on earth there is no such splendour or such beauty, and we are at a loss how to describe it. We only know that God dwells there among men, and their service is fairer than the ceremonies of other nations. For we cannot forget that beauty. Every man, after tasting something sweet, is afterward unwilling to accept that which is bitter, and therefore we cannot dwell any longer here.' Then the boyars spoke and said, 'If the Greek faith were bad, it would not have been adopted by your grandmother Olga, who was wiser than all other men.' Vladimir then enquired 'from which religion they should all accept baptism', and they replied whichever he wished.

After a year had passed, in 988, Vladimir proceeded against Cherson, a Greek city [on the Black Sea] and the people of Cherson surrendered.

Vladimir and his retinue entered the city, and he sent messages to the emperors Basil and Constantine, saying, 'Behold, I have captured your glorious city. I have also heard that you have an unwedded sister. Unless you give her to me to wife, I shall deal with your own city as I have with Cherson.'

When the emperors heard this message they were troubled, and replied, 'It is not meet for Christians to give someone in marriage to pagans. If you are baptized, you shall have her to wife, inherit the kingdom of God, and be our companion in the faith. Unless you do so, we cannot give you our sister in marriage.' When Vladimir learned their response, he directed the envoys of the emperors to report to their masters

RIGHT *Icon depicting the Virgin and Child. Vladimir forcibly converted Kiev and Novgorod to Christianity after his own acceptance of the faith.*

A miraculous cure

By divine agency, Vladimir was suffering at that moment from a disease of the eyes, and could see nothing, being in great distress. The princess said to him, 'If you desire to be relieved of this disease, you should be baptized with all speed, otherwise it will not be cured.' When Vladimir heard this, he said, 'If this proves true, then indeed is the God of the Christians great,' and gave order that he should be baptized. The bishop of Cherson, together with the princess's priests, admitting him as a catechumen, baptized Vladimir, and as the bishop laid his hand upon him, he straight away received his sight. Upon experiencing such a sudden cure, Vladimir glorified God, saying, 'I have now perceived the one true God.' When his followers beheld this miracle, many of them were also baptized.

From *Primary Chronicle*

that he was willing to accept baptism, having already given some study to their religion, and that the Greek faith and ritual, as described by the emissaries sent to examine it, had pleased him well.

When the emperors heard this report, they rejoiced, and persuaded their sister Anna to consent to the match.

Anna, however, departed with reluctance. 'It is as if I were setting out in captivity,' she lamented; 'better were it for me to die at home.' They overcame her hesitation only with difficulty. The princess embarked upon a ship, and after embracing her kinfolk, she set forth across the sea and arrived at Cherson. The Chersonites came forth to greet her, and conducted her into the city, where they settled her in the palace.

Vladimir was baptized in the church of St Basil, which stands at Cherson in a square in the centre of the city, where the Chersonians trade. After his baptism, Vladimir took the princess in marriage. As a wedding present for the princess, he gave Cherson over to the Greeks again, and then departed for Kiev. When he arrived at his capital, he directed that the idols should be overthrown, and that some should be cut to pieces and others burned with fire.

Thereafter Vladimir sent heralds throughout the whole city to proclaim that if inhabitants, rich or poor, did not go to the river, they would risk his displeasure. When the people heard these words, they wept for joy, and exclaimed in their enthusiasm, 'If this were not good, the prince and his boyars would not have accepted it.' The next day, Vladimir went to the Dnepr with the priests of the princess and those from Cherson, and a countless multitude. They all went into the water: some stood up to their necks, others to their breasts, the younger near the bank, some of them holding children in their arms, while the adults waded farther out. The priests stood by and offered prayers. There was joy in heaven and upon earth to behold so many souls saved.

When the people were baptised, they each returned home. Vladimir, rejoicing that he and his subjects now knew God, looked up to heaven and said, 'O

OVERLEAF *St Sophia Cathedral, Kiev. It was in Kiev that the conversion of Russia first took place.*

The Orthodox Church in Russia

When Rus accepted Christianity in 988–9, Christendom was still one. But a series of rivalries, disagreements and differences of ritual culminated in the mid-11th century schism between its western ('Roman Catholic') and eastern ('Orthodox') branches. This turned into deep hostility with the sack of Constantinople by the crusaders in 1204. COnversion to Christianity on the Byzantine model implied not just a confessional choice, but the 'transplanting' of an entire civilization, including its art, music, building, writing, law and international relations.

The 'white' or secular clergy, priests and deacons who served the parish churches were invariably married, and in time were drawn almost exclusively from the sons of the clergy, rather than from other classes. Their way of life and outlook therefore resembled that of ordinary parishioners much more closely than did that of their celibate counterparts in the West. Children of clergy played a significant part in the growth of the 19th century intelligentsia.

A member of the secular clergy might be raised to the rank of archpriest or archdeacon (a senior deacon), but the upper hierarchy was drawn exclusively from the 'black' or monastic clergy, whose calling was open to all, from prince to peasant. The vast majority were simple monks who devoted themselves to prayer, fasting and manual labour, without aspirations to preferment, learning, or spiritual authority. Their communities varied from large monasteries with extensive lands to small groups of hermits in the depths of the forests. Both were subject to an abbot who, if he was in priest's orders, might have the title of archimandrite. All orders followed one rule; within this, individuals might elect to take the 'great habit', which entailed an even stricter asceticism.

The most senior clergy bore the title of bishop,

archbishop, or metropolitan, depending on the importance of their sees. The head of the Russian Church was the metropolitan of Kiev, (often a Greek). The metropolitanate moved to Vladimir in 1300 and to Moscow c. 1328, enhancing the prestige of the latters' rulers in their struggle for supremacy. Problems of accommodation with secular power were to trouble the Russian Church on many occasions.

The metropolitan was appointed by the patriarch of Constantinople until 1438, when an abortive union with Rome was negotiated at the Council of Florence-Ferrara. The then metropolitan, Isidore, was party to the agreement, which was not accepted by the Muscovites, who deposed Isidore and consecrated Metropolitan Jonas in his place without reference to Constantinople, establishing their *de facto* independence. The establishment of the patriarchate of Moscow, to which the first patriarch, Job (canonized in 1989) was consecrated in 1589, was the final step in the emancipation of the Russian Church.

God, who hast created heaven and earth, look down on thy new people, and grant them, O Lord, to know thee as the true God.' And he began to found churches and to assign priests throughout the cities, and to invite the people to accept baptism in all the cities and towns.

After these events, Vladimir lived in the Christian faith. Intending to build a church dedicated to the Holy Virgin, he sent for and imported artists from Byzantium. After he had begun to build, and the structure was completed, he adorned it with images, and entrusted it to Anastasius of Cherson. He appointed Chersonian priests to serve in it, and bestowed upon this church all the images, vessels and crosses which he had taken in that city.

Ten years after his conversion to Christianity, Vladimir inflicted a serious defeat on the Pechenegs at Belgorod. But there was constant and desperate conflict with them, and in 1015, as they attacked once more, Vladimir died, leaving several sons to claim his throne. The *Primary Chronicle* relates how the Pechenegs were tricked with the help of porridge and honey.

In the year 997, Vladimir went to Novgorod to find troops with which to fight the Pechenegs (for there was great and constant war with them), and the Pechenegs on perceiving that for the moment there was no prince at hand, came and besieged Belgorod. They allowed no sally from the city, and great famine prevailed. Vladimir could not bring succour, for he had no troops with him, and the number of the Pechenegs was great. The siege was thus prolonged, and the famine grew increasingly severe.

In the year 1015, the Pechenegs came against the Rus; so Vladimir sent his son Boris to meet them, while he himself was gravely ill with the very disease which ended his life on 15 July. He died at Berestovo, but it was not made public. During the night Vladimir's men removed the floor between two rooms and, having wrapped him in a carpet, they lowered him with ropes to the ground. Then putting him on a sleigh, they took him to the church of the Holy Mother of God, which he himself had built. When the people learned of this, they assembled in countless numbers and lamented for him: the boyars lamented him as the protector of their land, and the poor as their protector and provider. They placed him in a marble coffin and buried the blessed prince with lamentations.

Ψ

Silver spoons

With the thought that the weak and the sick could not easily reach his palace, Vladimir arranged that carts should be brought in, and after having them loaded with bread, meat, fish, various fruits, mead in casks, and kvass, he ordered them driven out through the city. The drivers were under instructions to call out, 'Where is there a sick man or a beggar who cannot walk?' To such they distributed according to their necessities. Moreover, he caused a feast to be prepared each Sunday in his palace for his subjects, and invited the boyars, the court officers, the centurions, the decurions, and the distinguished citizens, either in the pre-

sence of the prince or in his absence. There was much meat, beef, and game, and an abundance of all victuals.

When they became tipsy, they would grumble against the prince, complaining that they had to eat with wooden spoons, instead of silver ones.

When Vladimir heard of this complaint, he ordered that silver spoons should be moulded for his retinue to eat with, remarking that with silver and gold he could not secure a retinue, but that with a retinue he was in a position to win these treasures.

From Primary Chronicle

Birth of the Russian language

Old Russian (which later evolved into modern Russian, Ukranian and Belorussian) was the language of the eastern branch of the Slav peoples. The Slavonic language belong to the Indo European group; their speakers spread westwards, southwards and eastwards in the first centuries of the Christian era. In the early middle ages they were still intercomprehensible. To this day the Slav nations, for all their discords, retain an awareness of belonging to a family. Though there is fragmentary evidence that writing systems may have been in use earlier, full-scale literacy came to the Slav nations, including Russian, with Christianization. Their linguistic closeness had important historical consequences, since a written language devised on a South Slavonic basis proved suitable for West and East Slavs too. The circumstances are famous.

Two early Slav alphabets are known. The Cyrillic (named after St Cyril) is of course still used, with modifications, among Orthodox Slavs today; it is largely based on Greek letters. The other, Glagolitic, perhaps even more ancient, has strange and elaborate letters, with the character of a "secret scrip": it was in church use till recent-time in Croatia. The literary language the brothers devised (a considerable feat) is usually called "Old Church Slavonic", and is still the Orthodox ecclesiastical language. In the middle ages it was the language of "high culture" generally, and because it was not felt to be remote from Russian, it has influenced the latter enormously, both stylistically and in vocabulary, contributing much to its present day richness.

The newly-literate society of post-conversion Rus required schools and books: Vladimir I and, particularly, Yaroslav are recorded as encouraging both. Standard medieval literary forms (saints' lives, homilies etc) followed

ABOVE *Cyrillic script; its alphabet was invented by the followers of St Methodius.*

Byzantine patterns, but a distinctively Russian literary tone imbues the *Primary Chronicle* and certain other works characterized by poetic "word-weaving", echoes of oral epics, or both (notably the *Lay of Igor's Campaign*). On a humbler level, the thousands of birchbark documents recently unearthed from the peaty subsoil of Novgorod testify to surprisingly widespread urban literacy.

Ψ

Boris and Gleb. Vladimir Monomakh

After the death of Vladimir I in 1015, the sorry business of strife between his heirs over the succession began again. The Kievan chronicles record that the eldest, Svyatopolk, murdered his brothers Boris, Gleb and Syvatoslav before himself being driven out by Yaroslav, who was prince of Novgorod. Of the surviving sons of Vladimir, Izyaslav in Polotsk was outside the established limits of Kievan dominion, the powerless Sudislav was imprisoned, and only the valiant Mstislav in his southern fastness of Tmutorokan prevented Yaroslav, until his death in 1036, from enjoying the same absolute authority as his father.

The murdered princes Boris and Gleb, whose meek acceptance of suffering at the hands of evildoers was venerated as the ideal of Christian humility, became the first saints of their newly converted land.

Like Vladimir I, Yaroslav reigned for 35 years, and this long period of political stability brought prosperity to the land. The arts and literature flourished, and the cathedral of St Sophia in Kiev (the dedication deliberately recalling that of the Great Church in Constantinople) was built and adorned by Byzantine craftsmen. It says something of the progress of civilization that Yaroslav's death was not followed by the traditional blood-bath: instead, the realm became the common inheritance of the family. In practice a lot of feuding took place, which at times, weakened resistance to the attacks of the Turkic nomads of the steppe, the Polovtsy (or Cumans).

Novgorod, the second city of Rus, remained outside this system. Though it owed ultimate allegiance to the grand prince, its actual government was in the hands of an oligarchy of leading citizens enriched by the city's extensive trade, and able to expel the prince himself, whose functions at Novgorod were largely confined to the military sphere. Its local affairs are recounted in one of the oldest historical documents from Rus, the *First Novgorod Chronicle*.

OPPOSITE   *Boris and Gleb, ill-fated brothers*
of Yaroslav the Wise (1019–54).

After his father Vladimir had died, Svyatopolk took his seat in Kiev; and he summoned the Kievans and began to give them property. They took it but their hearts were not with him, for their brothers were with Boris. When Boris returned with the soldiers, not having found the Pechenegs, the news was given to him, 'Your father has died.' He lamented for his father a great deal, for he was beloved of him most of all. His father's retinue said to him, 'Go, sit in Kiev on the throne of your father.' But Boris said, 'It is not for me to raise my hand against my brother. Since my father has died, let him take the place of a father to me.' But Svyatopolk, filled with lawlessness, adopted Cain's design and sent to Boris, saying, 'I wish to be in amity with you, and I will give you more than father gave.' He was deceiving him, planning to kill him.

Svyatopolk came at night to Vyshgorod. He secretly summoned Putsha and the boyars and said to them, 'Without telling anybody, go kill my brother Boris.' They at once promised to do it for him. The envoys came to Boris's camp at night, and they attacked him like wild beasts around his tent. They thrust a lance and pierced Boris through. Along with him they pierced through his servant who had fallen on him to protect him. This servant, a Hungarian called George, was beloved of Boris, who had put on him a large golden necklace which he wore when he attended his master. The boyars not being able to take the necklace quickly from George's neck, cut off his head. They took the necklace, but the head they threw away. For this reason his body was not found among the corpses afterwards.

When they had pierced Boris, the cursed ones wrapped him in a tent, put him on a cart and drove him away, even while he was still breathing. When the accursed Svyatopolk saw that Boris was still breathing, he sent two Varangians to finish him off. When they came and saw that he was still alive, one of them pulled out his sword and plunged it into his heart. And so the blessed Boris died, receiving from Christ our God a crown among the just. His men laid his body in the church of St Basil, having brought it secretly to Vyshgorod.

Then Svyatopolk, the accursed, thought to himself, 'Now I have killed Boris, how can I kill my brother Gleb?' And adopting Cain's design, he sent with deceit to Gleb, saying, 'Come quickly. Your father is calling you, for he is very ill.' Gleb quickly mounted his horse and set out with a small company, for he was obedient to his father.

At this same time, news came to Gleb's brother Yaroslav about his father's death. Yaroslav sent to Gleb, saying, 'Do not go; your father is dead and your brother has been murdered by Svyatopolk.' Hearing this, Gleb cried out greatly, lamenting for his father, and particularly for his brother. He began to pray with tears, saying, 'Woe is me, Lord! It would be better for me to have died with my brother than to live in this world.'

While he was praying, those sent by Svyatopolk for the destruction of Gleb suddenly came upon him. The envoys seized Gleb's boat and bared their weapons. The servants of Gleb despaired. And the accursed envoy Goryaser ordered the servants to slaughter Gleb quickly; and Gleb's cook, named Torchin, unsheathed his knife and slaughtered Gleb. Like a spotless lamb he was offered as a sacrifice to God. When Gleb had been murdered, he was thrown on the bank between two logs. Later he was taken and laid beside his brother Boris, in the church of St Basil in Vyshgorod.

The above version, from the *Primary Chronicle*, of the memorable story of Boris and Gleb, the prince-martyrs, is the most concise and vivid of many. Vladimir's death had led to another civil war. The eldest of several sons, Svyatopolk committed many crimes in the hope of succeeding his father, including the murder of his brothers Boris and Gleb. But another brother, Yaroslav, was the ultimate victor.

How Yaroslav I came to the throne is only sketchily recounted in the *Primary Chronicle*. For the first ten years he was forced to share power with his brother, Mstislav.

In the year 1026, Yaroslav recruited many soldiers and came to Kiev, where he made peace with his brother Mstislav, near Gorodets. They divided Rus according to the course of the Dnepr. Yaroslav took the Kiev side, and Mstislav the other. They thus began to live in peace and fraternal amity. Strife and tumult ceased, and there was a great calm in the land.

In the year 1027, a third son was born to Yaroslav, and he named him Svyatoslav.

In the year 1028, a serpent-shaped portent visible to the whole country appeared in the heavens.

In the year 1030, Yaroslav attacked the Estonians and conquered them, and founded the city of Yuryev. At this same time, there was a revolt in the Polish land. The people arose and killed the bishops, the priests and the boyars.

The following year, Yaroslav and Mstislav gathered a large force and marched against the Poles. They recaptured the cities of Cherven, and ravaged the Polish countryside. They also captured many Poles and distributed them as colonists in various districts. Yaroslav located his captives along the Ross, where they live to this day.

When his brother Mstislav died in 1036, Yaroslav, the tough survivor, proved as memorable a ruler as his father Vladimir. Dubbed 'the Wise', he encouraged learning and the arts, probably commissioned the oldest known Russian law-code, strengthened international links and, by defeating the Pechenegs, secured the vulnerable steppe frontier.

In the year 1036, while on a hunting expedition, Mstislav fell sick and died. He was laid in the church of the Redeemer, which he himself had founded. Thereafter Yaroslav assumed the entire sovereignty and was the sole ruler in the land of Rus. He went to Novgorod, where he set up his son Vladimir as prince and appointed Zhidyata bishop.

At this time, a son was born to Yaroslav, and he named him Vyacheslav. While Yaroslav was still at Novgorod, news came to him that the Pechenegs were besieging Kiev. He then collected a large army of Varangians and Slavs, returned to Kiev, and entered his city. The Pechenegs were innumerable. Yaroslav made a sally from the city and marshalled his forces, placing the Varangians in the centre and the men of

For the love of God

Yaroslav loved the ritual of the Church and was devoted to priests, especially to monks. He applied himself to books, and read them continually day and night. He assembled many scribes, and translated from Greek into Slavonic. And they wrote and collected many books through which true believers are instructed and enjoy religious education.

Yaroslav founded other churches in the cities and districts, appointing priests and paying them out of his personal fortune. He instructed them to teach the people, since that is the duty which God has prescribed them, and to go often into the churches. Priests and Christian laymen thus increased in number. Yaroslav rejoiced to see the multitude of his churches and of his Christian subjects.

From *Primary Chronicle*

Kiev on the right flank; and the men of Novgorod were on the left.

When they had taken position before the city, the Pechenegs advanced and they met on the spot where the metropolitan church of St Sophia of Kiev now stands. The combat was fierce, but toward evening Yaroslav, with difficulty, won the upper hand. The Pechenegs fled in various directions, but as they did not know in which quarter they should flee, they were drowned, some in the Setoml, and some in other rivers, while the remnant of them disappeared and were not seen again.

In the year 1037, Yaroslav built the great citadel at Kiev, near which the Golden Gate stands. He founded also the metropolitan church of St Sophia, the church of the Annunciation over the Golden Gate, and also the monastery of St George and the convent of St Irene. During his reign, the Christian faith was fruitful and multiplied, while the number of monks increased and new monasteries came into being.

RIGHT *The cathedral of St Sophia, Kiev, built by Yaroslav the Wise in 1037. Two years later he founded a patriarchate in the city.*

ABOVE *The monastery of St George, Novgorod. The number of religious establishments increased during Yaroslav's rule as grand prince of Kiev.*

In the year 1045, Vladimir founded the church of St Sophia at Novgorod.

In the year 1050, on 10 February, the princess, wife of Yaroslav, died.

In the year 1051, Yaroslav, after assembling the bishops, appointed the Russian, Hilarion, metropolitan in St Sophia of Kiev.

Much is known about the Monastery of the Caves from the tales of its early monks, some incorporated in the *Primary Chronicle*, which include the story, given here, of its foundation.

Let us now relate why the Monastery of the Caves bears this name. Prince Yaroslav was fond of Berestovo and the church of the Holy Apostles situated there. He gathered a large company of priests, among whom was a priest named Hilarion, a virtuous man, learned and ascetic. Hilarion used often to walk from Berestovo toward the Dnepr to a certain hill, where the old Monastery of the Caves now is, and made his orisons there, for there was a great forest on the spot. He dug a little catacomb two fathoms deep, and often went there to chant the hours and offer his prayer to God in secret. Then God inspired Prince Yaroslav to appoint him metropolitan in St Sophia; and the cave remained as it was.

A monk called Antony came to the hill where Hilarion had dug the cave, and liked this site and rejoiced. He took up his abode there, praying to God, eating dry bread every other day and drinking water moderately. He gave himself rest neither day nor night, but persevered in daily labour, in vigil and in prayer. Afterward, good men noticed his conduct, came to him and supplied him according to his needs. So he became known as the great Antony, and those who drew near to him sought his blessing. Brethren joined him and he welcomed and tonsured them. Twelve brethren gathered about him.

They constructed many cells, completed the church and adorned it with icons. Such was the origin of the Monastery of the Caves, which was so named because the brethren first lived in the cave.

The main monastery church was founded in 1073 and consecrated in 1089. It must have been then that Greek (i.e. Byzantine) painters were hired to adorn it with mosaics, frescos and icons. The narrative is taken from tales collected at the beginning of the 13th century into the Kiev *Patericon* (Book of the Fathers).

Once upon a time, several Greek painters came to complain to Abbot Nikon, the abbot of the Monastery of the Caves at Kiev. They said, 'We want to see the men who hired us. We want justice. They hired us to decorate a small church, and we made the contract in the presence of witnesses. But this church is very large. We received gold as payment; take it back, and we will return to Constantinople.' Abbot Nikon did not understand their accusations and therefore asked them, 'Who were the people who made this agreement with you?' And the Greeks described these people, and named them as Antony and Feodosy. To this the abbot replied, 'My children, we cannot bring them before you, for they died ten years ago.'

The Greeks were awestruck at these words. Nevertheless they confronted the abbot with numerous merchants who had travelled with them from Constantinople to Kiev. The painters declared, 'In the presence of these merchants we made the agreement with the men who hired us, and accepted gold in payment. But since you, abbot, are either unwilling or unable to bring before us the men who commissioned us, show us their portraits so that our witnesses can see them.'

When the abbot brought them the icons of St Antony and St Feodosy the merchants looked hard and then bowed deeply. They said, 'Indeed, these are true likenesses. We now believe that even after death these men still live and can protect, help and save those who turn to them for aid.' Whereupon they decided to donate, for the embellishment of the altar, the mosaic which they had brought with them from Constantinople to sell.

After this the painters began to confess their sins. 'When we arrived by boat at the city of Kanev, on the River Dnepr, we had a vision. We saw a mountain, on which stood a large church. We asked other travellers, "What church is this?" They replied, "It is the church of the Monastery of the Caves, and you are its painters." We became angry, because the work would be so much greater than we had bargained for. We decided to go back, and started to go downstream. But that same night there was a severe storm; and when we awoke the next morning we found that we were at the village of Tripole, further up the river, and that an unseen power was continually pulling us upstream. We stopped our boat, only with great difficulty. We remained at Tripole the whole day, turning over in our minds the meaning of these events, for in one night, and without any rowing, we had travelled up the river for a distance that usually requires three days' journey.

'The next night the vision was repeated. When we woke up the next morning we again attempted to escape and made a great effort to row downstream. But the boat moved continually upstream. Of its own accord it soon came to land at the shore beneath the monastery.'

After the Greeks had finished their tale, both they and the monks gave praise to God, to the miraculous and holy icon of His most pure Mother, and to the holy fathers Antony and Feodosy.

The painters and the builders became monks and lived and died in the Monastery of the Caves. They were buried near the altar; their robes still hang there, and their books are preserved in this monastery in commemoration of this miracle.

Before his death in 1054, Yaroslav distributed principalities to his five sons, admonishing them to co-operate and hold Kievan Russia together. But as the *Primary Chronicle* recalls, signs pointed to the civil wars which ensued, thereby starting the decline of Kiev.

In the year 1054, Yaroslav, great prince of Rus, passed away. While he was yet alive, he admonished his sons with these words: 'My sons, I am about to quit this world. Love one another, since you are brothers by one father and mother. The throne of Kiev I bequeath to my eldest son, your brother Izyaslav. To Svyatoslav I give Chernigov, to Vsevolod, Pereyaslavl, to Igor the city of Vladimir, and to Vyacheslav, Smolensk.' Thus he divided the cities among them, commanding them not to violate or despoil one another's boundaries.

At the time, there was a portent in the west in the form of an exceedingly large star with bloody rays, which rose out of the west after sunset. It was visible for a week and appeared with no good presage. Much internal strife occurred thereafter, as well as many pagan incursions into the land of Rus, for this star appeared as if it were made of blood, and therefore portended bloodshed.

At this time a child was cast into the Setoml. Some fishermen pulled it up in their net. They gazed upon it until evening, when they cast it back into the water because it was malformed; indeed, it had its privates upon its face, and for reasons of modesty no further account need be given regarding it.

Somewhat before this moment, the sun also suffered alteration, and instead of being bright, became rather like the moon.

Such signs portend no good.

Miracle of the ghosts

In the year 1092, there was a most wondrous miracle at Polotsk. In men's imagination, when night fell, there would be a thumping along the street as though demons were galloping in the shape of men. If anyone came out of a house, wishing to see, a wound would at once be invisibly inflicted on him by the demons, and from this he would die. People did not dare go out of their houses. After this the demons began to appear on horses during the day, and they themselves could not be seen, but the hooves of the horses could be seen. And thus they inflicted wounds on the people of Polotsk and its region.

And when men saw this miracle, and its effect upon the people, they said, 'Ghosts are striking down the people of Polotsk.'

From Primary Chronicle

Any concord between the princes of Rus in the decades following the death of Yaroslav the Wise could be achieved only by voluntary agreement, which became ever harder to reach as the royal family subdivided with each generation. The *Primary Chronicle* records how Yaroslav's grandson, Vladimir, coped with this situation.

In the year 1093, the Grand Prince Vsevolod, son of Yaroslav, grandson of Vladimir, passed away on 13 April. And he was buried on the 14th, it being Holy Week, on Thursday, when he was placed in a tomb in the great church of St Sophia.

When Vsevolod had become very sick, he sent for his son Vladimir in Chernigov. When Vladimir came and saw that his father was very sick, he began to weep.

While Vladimir and Rostislav, a younger son, were sitting by him, the time came and Vsevolod passed away quietly and meekly and joined his fathers, having ruled for fifteen years in Kiev, a year in Pereyaslavl and a year in Chernigov.

Vladimir began to plan, saying, 'If I assume my father's throne, I will have to undertake a war with my cousin, Svyatopolk, for the throne formerly belonged to his father [Izyaslav].' After thinking it over, he sent to Svyatopolk in Turov. On the Sunday after Easter, 24 April, Svyatopolk arrived in Kiev. The Kievans came out to meet him with obeisance, and received him with joy, and he assumed the throne of his father and his uncle.

Vladimir II Monomakh (son of a Byzantine princess of the Monomachos family) succeeded to the Kievan throne in 1113. *The Legend of the Princes of Vladimir*, possibly based in part on an earlier oral tradition, was written in the 16th century, in order to provide support for imperial prestige and authority with its fictional account of how Vladimir Monomakh had received imperial regalia from the Byzantine emperor, Constantine Monomachus, who in reality was probably his grandfather and had died when Vladimir was only two years old.

In the year 1114, Grand Prince Vladimir Vsevolodovich Monomakh, the great-grandson of Vladimir, was grand prince of Kiev. He was called Monomakh for the following reason. When he began to reign in Kiev he held a council of his princes and boyars and lords, and said, 'We by the grace of God are the heirs and successors of our ancestors.

Now I seek counsel of you, princes of my chamber and boyars and commanders and all my Christ-loving army, that the name of the Holy and Life-Giving Trinity may be exalted through the might of your courage, by the Grace of God and at our command. What counsel do you give me?'

The princes and boyars and commanders answered Vladimir and said, 'The heart of the king is in the hands of God, as it is written, and we are all your servants and at your command.'

So Vladimir assembled skilled and wise and judicious commanders and appointed officers and heads of companies of fifty and a hundred, and gathered together many thousands of soldiers and sent them to Thrace, a province of Constantinople. And they took many prisoners and returned home safely with great riches.

At that time the pious emperor of Constantinople, Constantine Monomachos, was fighting wars with the Latins and the Turks. He summoned his imperial council and sent his ambassadors to Vladimir: Metropolitan Neophytos of Ephesus in Asia, and the bishops of Mitylene and Miletus and others of his noblemen.

He took from his neck the life-giving cross, made from the very wood of the cross on which Christ our Lord was crucified; he took the imperial crown from his head, and placed it on a golden plate; and he commanded that his envoys should bring him the box of sardonyx which had delighted the Roman emperor Augustus.

He sent also the necklace to Vladimir, that is to say the holy regalia which he wore on his shoulders, the chain of beaten Arabian gold, and many other royal

OPPOSITE *Vladimir Monomakh's crown, 13th–14th centuries. It was the oldest crown used for the coronation of all the tsars until Peter I.*

gifts, with the following entreaty: 'Receive from us, loving and faithful prince, these honourable gifts, which are from the beginning of the endless years of your royal house and lineage, for honour and glory and for the crowning of your free and autocratic tsardom. Our ambassadors shall entreat you, that we seek peace and love of your highness, that the churches of God shall be untroubled, and all Orthodox people shall abide in peace under our empire and your free autocracy of Russia, and that you shall be called the Emperor Crowned by God, being crowned with this imperial crown by the hands of Metropolitan Neophytos and the bishops.'

And thenceforth Vladimir was called Monomakh, tsar of Great Russia. Afterwards Vladimir remained in peace and amity with the Emperor Constantine. And from that time to this the grand princes of Vladimir have been crowned with the imperial crown which the Byzantine emperor, Constantine Monomachos, sent, when they are crowned as grand princes of Russia.

Vladimir Monomakh, grand prince of Kiev, died in 1125. He reigned in Kiev for thirteen years, and lived seventy-three years in all. He was buried in St Sophia in Kiev on 19 May.

One manuscript of the *Primary Chronicle* includes an unusual text: the *Testament* (or *Instruction*) of Vladimir II Monomakh, addressed to his sons. It includes characteristic early medieval good advice. Vladimir and his son Mstislav were the last Kievan rulers successfully to unite the realm and hold the steppe nomads at bay.

As I sat upon my sledge, I meditated in my heart and praised God, Who has led me, a sinner, even to this day. Let not my sons or anyone else who happens to read this brief discourse laugh at its contents. But rather let my sons or anyone else [who reads it] take my words to heart and not be disposed to laziness, but labour zealously. First, for the sake of God and your own souls, retain the fear of God in your hearts and give alms generously, for this is the beginning of all good. When you are on horseback with nothing to do, and if you know no other prayers, say 'Lord have mercy' in your mind, for this is the best prayer of all. Give to the orphan, protect the widow and permit the mighty to destroy no man. Take not the life of the just or the unjust, nor permit him to be killed. Destroy no Christian soul even though he be guilty of murder.

When you speak either good or evil, swear not by the name of God, nor cross yourselves, for that is unnecessary.

Receive with love the blessing of bishops, priests and abbots and shun them not, but rather, according to your means, love and help them, that you may receive from them their intercession in the presence of God.

Be not lax in the discipline of your homes, but rather attend to all matters yourselves. Rely not upon your steward or your servant, lest they who visit you mock your house or your table. When you set out to war, be not lazy, depend not upon your captains, nor indulge in drinking, eating or sleeping. Guard against lying, drunkenness and fornication, for therein perish soul and body.

Visit the sick and accompany the dead, for we are all mortal. Pass no man without a greeting; give him a kindly word. Love your wives, but grant them no power over you. This is the end of all things: to hold the fear of God above all else. If you forget all my admonition, read this counsel frequently. Then I shall be without shame and you shall profit thereby.

Let not my sons or whoever else reads this discourse criticize me. I do not commend my own boldness, but I praise God and glorify His mercy because He guarded me, a sinful and a wretched man, for so many years from the hour of death and did not make me inactive or useless in all the necessary works of man. As you read this, prepare yourselves for all good works and glorifying God and his saints. Without fear of death, or war, or of wild beasts, do a man's work, my sons, as God sets it before you. If I suffered no ill from war, from wild beasts, from flood, or from falling from my horse, then surely no one can harm you and destroy you, unless that too be destined of God. But if death comes from God, then neither father, nor mother, nor brethren can save you from it, although it

is prudent to be on one's guard, the protection of God is better than the protection of man.

Among the *byliny*, or oral epics of the Russian folk tradition, are a number relating to early Novgorod. One of the best known, *Sadko*, reflects the city's preoccupation with wealth and trade. It has also provided the subject for Rimsky-Korsakov's opera of the same name.

Sadko the merchant began to trade and great were the profits he won. In his white stone palace in Novgorod Sadko re-created the heavens. In the sky hangs the sun and in his palace a sun hung; in the sky gleams the moon and in Sadko's palace a moon gleamed; the stars shone in the heavens and in the palace of Sadko too.

Then Sadko the rich merchant invited the men of Novgorod to a glorious feast. He invited the chief burghers Foma Nazaryev and Luka Zinovyev. All ate their fill at the banquet, all drained their cups dry and made their boasts at the feast. One man boasted of his countless treasure of gold, another vaunted his dashing might.

Some sang the praises of a doughty steed or their glorious fatherland – the glories of the land of their fathers and the mettle of their youth. The wise man praised his aged parents while the foolish man boasted of his youthful wife.

At length the elders of Novgorod spoke out: 'We have all eaten our fill at the feast, at this glorious table we have all sated our thirst and sung our swaggering songs of praise. Why does Sadko not praise anything with us? Why does Sadko not boast of his possessions?'

Sadko the rich merchant replied, 'Of what should I boast; whose praises ought Sadko to sing? My treasury of gold will not waste away; my coat of many

RIGHT *Novgorod; the city was the chief centre of foreign trade during the Middle Ages.*

colours will not wear thin and my valiant band of followers will not betray me. Perhaps I should boast of my countless treasure of gold. Yes, I shall buy up all the merchandise of Novgorod, good and bad, with my countless treasure of gold.'

No sooner had he uttered these words than the chief burghers of Novgorod struck a great wager concerning Sadko's countless treasure of gold. Sadko wagered thirty thousand silver pieces that he could buy up all the merchandise in Novgorod, good and bad, leaving no goods on sale in the whole city.

The next day Sadko rose at first light and roused his gallant followers. He gave his men countless sums of gold from his treasury and sent them out into all the trading rows of the city. He went straight to the Merchants' Row and bought up all the merchandise of Novgorod, valuable and shoddy together, with his countless treasure of gold.

The second day Sadko rose at first light and roused his gallant followers. He gave his men countless sums of gold from his treasury and sent them out again into all the trading rows of the city. He marched directly to the Merchants' Row. Twice the amount of merchandise had been brought out, and twice as much merchandise filled the stalls to the great glory of Novgorod.

Again Sadko bought up all the merchandise of Novgorod, valuable and shoddy together, with his countless treasures of gold.

On the third day Sadko rose at first light and roused his gallant followers. He gave his men countless sums of gold from his treasury and sent them out once more into all the trading rows of the city. He marched directly to the Merchants' Row. Three times the amount of merchandise had been brought out and three times as much merchandise filled the stalls, for wares had been sent from Moscow to Novgorod to the great glory of Novgorod.

Now Sadko set to thinking: 'I cannot buy up the wares of the whole wide world. If I buy up merchandise from Moscow then goods will only sail in from across the seas. Certainly I am not the richest merchant for glorious Novgorod is richer than me.'

So Sadko surrendered to the chief burghers of Novgorod his wager of thirty thousand silver pieces.

From his countless treasure of gold Sadko built thirty ships, thirty scarlet prows and into these thirty scarlet ships he piled the merchandise of Novgorod. He sailed along the Volkhov to Lake Ladoga and from Ladoga to the River Neva. From the Neva he reached the blue ocean. As he sailed the ocean blue, he turned towards the Golden Horde and there he sold his Novgorodian wares for a great profit. He piled his forty-gallon barrels high with burnished gold and pure silver and returned home to Novgorod.

The *First Novgorod Chronicle* provides an independent record chiefly of events concerning Novgorod from the early 11th century. Here, the

chronicle gives evidence of a self-confident city-state, able to impose conditions on its princes, with an oligarchic aristocracy.

In the year 1136, the men of Novgorod summoned the men of Pskov and of Ladoga and consulted with them on how to expel their prince, Vsevolod. On 28 May they imprisoned him in the bishop's court with his wife and children and mother-in-law, and put an armed guard of thirty men over him day and night. He spent two months in prison, and on 15 June they allowed him to leave the town and made his son Vladimir prince in his stead.

In the year 1137, Prince Vsevolod Mstislavich, who had been expelled the previous year, came to Pskov, intending to take the throne of Novgorod again. He had been called in secret by certain men of Novgorod and Pskov, his friends saying, 'Come, prince, they want you back.'

When it became known that Vsevolod was at Pskov there was great turmoil in Novgorod. The people did not want Vsevolod; but Mayor Kostyantin, Nezhatin and many others fled to Vsevolod at Pskov. The people plundered their houses, and sought out those among the boyars who supported Vsevolod, despoiling them of about fifteen hundred coins which they gave to the merchants to finance a war to prevent Vsevolod's return; Some innocent people were also affected. Then Prince Vsevolod died at Pskov, and the people followed his brother Svyatopolk. And there was no peace with them. And all year a large ration of bread cost seven rezanas.

In the year 1138, on 9 March, there was great thunder, so that we heard it clearly, sitting in our homes.

In the year 1139, on 25 December, Svyatoslav Olgovich came from Kiev and entered Novgorod and sat upon the throne.

In the year 1140, on 20 March, there was a sign in the sun, and only as much of it was left as a four-day-old moon, but it returned to its full size before sunset.

In the year 1141, on 1 April, there was a very wonderful sign in the sky – six rings, three about the sun, and three other large ones away from the sun, and it remained for almost the whole day. In that year, Novgorod was without a prince for nine months. Then they sent to Prince Gyurgy at Suzdal; he did not come, but sent his son Rostislav, who had been before. On 26 November of the same year Rostislav entered Novgorod and took the throne.

In the year 1143 the autumn was rainy, and from 8 September to the solstice there was warm weather and rain. There was a great flood by the River Volkhov which carried off the hay and the wood. The lake froze in the night, and the wind broke up the ice, which was carried down the Volkhov and destroyed the bridge, and carried away four piers without trace.

In the year 1144, a completely new bridge across the Volkhov was made where the old one had been. In the same year Kholm, a quarter of Novgorod, and the church of St Elias were burned and completely destroyed by fire.

Also in that year Archbishop Nifont decorated all the chapels in the church of St Sophia at Novgorod. In the same year the stone church of the Mother of God at Torgovishche in Novgorod was completed.

In the year 1145, there were two whole weeks of great heat, before the harvest; then came rain, so that we saw not a clear day till winter; and they were unable to harvest a great quantity of corn and hay, which went to waste.

That autumn the water was higher than three years before; and in the winter there was not much snow, and no clear day, not till March.

The same year, two priests were drowned and the bishop did not allow singing over them. The same year was founded the stone church of Boris and Gleb, at Smyadino by Smolensk.

In the year 1156, the whole town of Novgorod gathered together and decided to appoint, as bishop for themselves, Arkady, a man chosen of God. The people went and took him out of the monastery of the Holy Mother of God. The whole choir of St Sophia, all the town priests and the monks led him in, having entrusted him with the bishopric in the Court of St Sophia, until the metropolitan should come to Rus.

In Kiev, the struggle for succession to the Kievan throne was renewed after the reign of Vladimir II Monomakh. One of the contenders was Prince Andrey Bogolyubsky, of Rostov and Suzdal. A contemporary account from the Hypatian text of the *Primary Chronicle*, written in Kiev, relates how, in 1169, he successfully attacked and sacked Kiev.

In the winter of 1169, Prince Andrey Bogolyubsky sent his son Mstislav with his troops against the prince of Kiev, Mstislav Izyaslavich. With him went the men of Rostov, Vladimir and Suzdal and eleven other princes.

Mstislav Izyaslavich, the prince of Kiev, shut himself in Kiev and fought from there. The battle was fierce on all sides. The town was besieged for three days, then the armed followers of all the princes gathered at Serkhovitsa and swept down behind Mstislav, shooting arrows. Mstislav's men said to him, 'Why do you remain, prince? Leave the town. We cannot overcome them.'

God helped Mstislav Andreyevich and his brothers. Kiev was taken on 10 March, on the Wednesday of the second week of Lent, and the whole town was plundered for three days – the lower and upper parts of the town, the monasteries, St Sophia and the Tithe Church of Our Lady. No mercy was shown to anyone: churches were burned down, Christians were slain, some were shackled, women were taken into captivity, forcibly separated from their husbands, and children wept to see their mothers taken away. Much property was seized and the churches were stripped of icons, books, vestments and bells. The Monastery of the Caves was set on fire by the heathens, but God preserved it by the prayers of the Holy Mother of God. There was much moaning and grief and inconsolable sorrow in Kiev and tears were ceaseless. All this took place owing to our sins.

The Lay of Igor's Campaign is the most celebrated work of Kievan literature. These extracts describe the foolhardy – and unsuccessful – expedition in the 1180s against the Polovtsian steppe nomads of a minor prince, Igor of Novgorod-Seversk, his capture

The Kievan state

Kiev Rus, which reached a peak of prosperity in the first half of the 11th century as the largest state of early-medieval Europe, was a loose federation of principalities bound together by language and cultural traditions, and by a common interest in exploiting the trading possibilities of the great waterway systems of eastern Europe.

The full exploitation of their potential could come only with political stability, and this was achieved by Viking adventurers known to Greeks and Russians as 'Varangians', who were to supply Russia's first dynasty of rulers from the ninth century.

The principalities of Rus were largely successors to the dozen or so tribal groups that colonized various parts of it in the first centuries of our era, and are discussed in the *Primary Chronicle*. The princes of Kiev 'ruled' only in the sense that they could impose their will by force and install their relatives in the main towns. Their opportunism culminated with Svyatoslav, a wanderer-warrior prince who showed little commitment to Kiev, somewhat casually conquered a vast steppe empire, and finally (969) transferred his capital to Pereyaslavets on the Danube. A more responsible attitude to government seems to have been shown by Vladimir I (and maybe by his grandmother Olga). Meanwhile the Vikings' Slav subjects must have been capable of organizing customary law, religion, small-scale trade and agriculture – the real foundation of Kievan prosperity – for themselves.

The cohesiveness of the federation depended on personalities rather than institutions, and there was frequent squabbling – sometimes bloody feuding and warfare – between members of the ruling dynasty. Their exploitative attitude to the realm was to be mitigated, but never wholly eliminated, by subtler Christian concepts of stewardship. At first, princes frequently changed their residences, particularly when the Kievan succession passed from brother to brother: later, branches of the dynasty tended to put down local roots (thereafter subdividing), a situation recognized in the Lyubech accord (1097) engineered by Vladimir Monomakh. There was a hierarchy of principalities: Chernigov and Pereyaslavl followed Kiev in importance. Polotsk early established its own dynasty (on the territory later to become Belorussia). Novgorod, the ancient trading city that had its own vast motherly 'empire' to exploit, had special status from an early stage. By the 12th century its townsfolk could hire and fire their princes (its 'offshoots', Pskov and Vyarka, later developed similarly). The 'Land beyond the Forest' (*Zalesskaya zemalya*, often called the 'Vladimir-Suzdal Principality') actually usurped Kiev as seat of the Grand Prince in the mid-12th century, and was to be the progenitor of Muscovite Russia. A strange principality was isolated Tucutorakan, on the Black Sea near the Crimea; in the 12th century the Kievans could no longer defend it.

Free peasant farmers, able to change their masters and residence, seem to have constituted the bulk of the population of Kiev Rus: serfdom was a later development (though there were also slaves – in whom the Vikings traded through Constantinople. At the opposite end of the social spectrum were boyars – an aristocracy originating in the *druzhina* or retinue (both bodyguard and advisory committee) of a prince. A variety of urban classes – their distinctions not now fully understood – played a significant social role. All free adult men belonged to the town *veche*, an informal but important assembly, summoned by a bell. This highly democratic institution died out with the Tartar invasions, save in Novgorod, where it flourished till the 15th century Muscovite conquest.

and escape. Although it relates only a minor incident in a long record of skirmishes, it is a plea for the princely dynasty to stop the internecine quarrels that were weakening Russia in the face of outside threats. Partly through Borodin's opera, it has implanted itself firmly in the Russian literary consciousness.

Let us then, brothers, begin this tale of Igor who, filled with a warlike spirit, led his brave hosts against the land of the Polovtsy, for the land of Rus.

Igor looked at the bright sun and saw that all his warriors were covered by the darkness it cast [eclipse of the sun, 1 May 1185]. And he said to his men, 'Brothers and retainers! Better it would be to be slain than to be taken prisoner; so let us, brothers, mount our swift horses, that we may look upon the blue Don.' The prince's mind was ablaze with eagerness and his longing to taste the great Don veiled the omen from him. 'I want,' he said, 'to break a lance at the limit of the Polovtsian steppe; with you, O Sons of Rus, I want to lay down my life, or else to drink of the Don from my helmet.'

Igor awaited his dear brother Vsevolod from Trubchevsk. And Vsevolod the fierce aurochs said to him: 'You are my one brother, my one bright light, Igor; saddle your swift horses, brother; mine indeed are prepared.'

Then Prince Igor stepped into his golden stirrup and rode out into the open plain. The Polovtsy hastened by untrodden roads to the great Don; their carts screeched at midnight like swans let loose and Igor led his warriors towards the Don.

The night was slow in falling; the glow of sunset faded. Mist covered the plain. The nightingales' songs were stilled, the jackdaws' chatter was aroused. The Rus barred the great plain with their scarlet shields, seeking honour for themselves and glory for their prince.

From dawn on Friday they trampled the infidel Polovtsian hosts and, scattering like arrows over the plain, they carried off the fair Polovtsian maidens, and with them gold and brocades and precious cloths of samite. With coverlets, mantles, cloaks lined with fur, and with all manner of Polovtsian finery they began to lay pathways over swamps and marshy places. Scarlet is the standard, white is the banner, scarlet the horse tail, silver the shaft for the valiant son of Svyatoslav.

On the next day, very early, a blood-red glow heralds the dawn; black clouds come in from the sea, and streaks of blue lightning quiver within them. There will be a mighty thunder! Rain will come, a rain of arrows, from the great Don!

Behold, the winds, grandsons of the god Stribog, blow arrows from the sea upon the valiant hosts of Igor. The earth rumbles, the rivers flow with turbid stream, dust covers the plain, the banners announce: the Polovtsy are coming from the Don and from the sea; on all sides they have surrounded the Russian hosts. The devil's children have barred the plain with their war-cry, and the valiant Russians have barred it with their scarlet shields.

A like battle was never heard of – from dawn till evening, from evening till dawn tempered arrows fly, sabres thunder against helmets, lances of Frankish steel crash in the unknown steppe amid the Polovtsian land. The black earth beneath the hooves is sown with bones and watered with blood.

What is this noise, what is this ringing that I hear far away, early before dawn? Igor is wheeling his troops: for he has pity on his dear brother Vsevolod. They fought for a day, they fought for a second day; on the third day, towards noon, Igor's standards fell. Here the two brothers parted on the bank of the swift Kayala and were laid low for the land of Rus. The grass bows low with pity, and the tree in sorrow bends to the ground.

And Kiev, brothers, groaned with sorrow, and Chernigov with affliction. Anguish flowed over the land of Rus, sorrow in abundance spread across the land of Rus, while the infidels, victoriously invading the land of Rus, took tribute of a squirrel-skin from every homestead.

For Igor and Vsevolod now roused the dissensions which their father, the redoubtable Svyatoslav, the great prince of Kiev, had curbed by the fear he inspired in his enemies. Now Germans and Venetians, Greeks and Moravians who sing the glory of Svyatoslav, now rebuke Prince Igor, who has sunk his wealth at the bottom of the Kayala, the Polovtsian river, and scattered

Russian gold. Prince Igor has exchanged his golden saddle for the saddle of a slave. The ramparts of the cities are downcast, and joy bowed down.

On the Danube the voice of Yaroslavna [Igor's wife] is heard from Putivl; like a desolate cuckoo she cries early in the morning. 'I will fly,' she says, 'like a cuckoo along the Danube, I will dip my sleeve in the river, I will wipe my prince's bleeding wounds.'

Yaroslavna, early in the morning, laments on the rampart of the city of Putivl saying: 'O Dnepr! You have battered your way through the rocky mountains across the land of the Polovtsy. You have rocked Svyatoslav's boats upon your waters. Carry, O Lord, my beloved back to me, that I may weep no more.'

The sea breaks into foam at midnight; waterspouts advance like mists. God shows Prince Igor the way out of the land of the Polovtsy to the land of Rus, to his father's golden throne. Igor measures the steppe in his mind, from the great Don to the little Donets. Ovlur, having brought a horse, whistles from across the river: he bids the prince understand: Prince Igor shall not be a captive any longer!

The grass rustled, the tents of the Polovtsy stirred. And Prince Igor sped like an ermine into the rushes and like a white duck on to the water. He sprang upon his swift horse, and sped towards the meadows of the Donets, and flew like a falcon beneath the mists, slaying geese and swans for his meals.

The sun shines in the heavens: Prince Igor is back in the land of Rus. Maidens sing on the Danube, their voices twine across the waters to Kiev. Igor rides up to the church of Our Lady of the Tower. The countryside is happy, the cities are joyful.

BELOW *Prince Igor in battle; a romantic portrayal of Russia's legendary hero.*

PART 3 THE BIRTH

Between the downfall of Kiev and the re-emergence of an independent and unified Russian state under Moscow at the turn of the 15th to 16th centuries, stretches a lengthy period, at least a quarter of a millennium. Some historians pass over it quickly, treating it as little better than a 'dark age'. Yet dark ages do not last that long: it was a period not just of military and economic eclipse, but equally of artistic and spiritual achievement; not just of political fragmentation, but of the forging of new social structures, and a concomitant ideology that, for better or worse, set Russia on its subsequent historical path to greatness.

The Tartars, in a series of sudden blows, plundered and destroyed the cities of the central, eastern and southern principalities, forcing the population back on a subsistence economy.

The immediately post-conquest literature is filled with a desperate yearning for lost freedom and glory and a desire to salvage something from the wreckage. Hence, in part, the building-up of the image of Alexander Nevsky, prince of Novgorod, who defeated the encroaching Swedes and German knights, but agreed to pay tribute to the Tartars, whose armies did not get as far as Novgorod or Pskov.

Despite the sheer psychological difficulty for the Russians of admitting that their Christian realm was under the permanent overlordship of heathens (leading to a curious absence of reference to what later was called the Tartar 'yoke' in the literature of the time), the Russian princes – who were allowed to retain their lands as long as they were obedient to the new masters – soon had to make the best of things and carry on with business as usual. From late-Kievan times, the princely families who regarded the realm as property, to be divided among their legatees, tended to split their territories into ever-smaller units or appanages, which suited the Tartars' divide and rule policies well. Princes were glorified tax-gatherers and policemen: severe retribution would fall upon them for any popular uprising or insubordination.

In the mid-14th century there was a long period of relative tranquillity during which Russia began to rebuild itself, both economically, with a revival of trade, and culturally. First Novgorod, then increasingly Tver and Moscow, grew in prosperity. Princes of Moscow managed generally to ingratiate themselves with the Tartars of the Golden Horde, and they reversed the previous trend by absorbing smaller appanages wherever possible. The metropolitan of the Church – still an all-Russian institution which had profited by being exempted from Tartar taxes – made Moscow his seat from c.1328, adding to its prestige. By about 1400 Moscow, though still not rivalling Novgorod, was becoming an important centre of architectural, artistic and literary patronage; this was the age of the greatest painter associated with Moscow, Andrey Rublyov, and his school. Quite minor places, however, sponsored art and chronicle-writing, and cultural links with the Balkan countries, including Byzantium, revived.

The remarkable spiritual movement associated with St Sergius of Radonezh started in mid-century – appar-

OF GREAT RUSSIA

(1240-1505)

ently independently of official church and state, though both soon interested themselves. Sergius's Trinity monastery became a most important all-Russian cultural centre; from it a large number of hermitages and monasteries fanned out through the whole northern forest zone, assisting colonization. The best late-medieval Russian writer, Yepifany the Wise, wrote classic lengthy *Lives* both of Sergius and of his friend, Stephen of Perm, who converted the pagan Komi people to Orthodoxy, devising for them an alphabet and a literature.

The Russian revival under Moscow was signalled by Prince Dimitri Donskoy's victory over a large punitive Tartar force at Kulikovo on the Don in 1380: an epic account of this, known as the *Zadonshchina*, cleverly reverses motifs from the Kievan *Lay of Igor's Campaign* (the story of a defeat). Though there were damaging Tartar raids thereafter, time was running out for the Golden Horde, which began to disintegrate in the 15th century. Ivan III ceased to pay tribute to it, and Rus was again independent. Ivan (who became Grand Prince in 1462 after a lengthy civil war among claimants to the Muscovite throne) had a long agenda in his 43-year reign, the chief item of which was to restore what he understood to be his ancestral patrimony. Ideological writings of the period took pains to construct an impressive lineage for the Russian grand princes and the Russian Church: not only Moscow, but Tver and Novgorod participated in this process. But Ivan III and his successor Vasily III curtailed pluralism in the Russian lands – both by gradually introducing conditional land-tenure (turning his aristocrats into servitors) and by bringing the remaining independent principalities (Novgorod, Tver, Vyatka, Ryazan and Pskov) under Muscovite control. Most of the populous West Russian lands, however, had passed into Lithuanian possession, and Ivan could do no more than push back the frontier somewhat: some historic Kievan territories were not reabsorbed into Russia until the partitions of Poland in the 1790s. The crushing of Novgorod – whose leaders, desperate to preserve their freedoms, had rashly parleyed with Lithuania – was accompanied by mass deportations and confiscation of lands. Novgorod, richer and more populous than Moscow, fell to the latter because it could neither adequately feed itself nor defend itself militarily.

Since the fall of Constantinople (1453) Russia had become the major free Orthodox nation, very conscious of its role (supported by the fantastical ideology that Moscow had become the 'third Rome'). A sharp debate on the position of the Church and its relation to the state (earlier adumbrated by Sergius's activity) characterized the years around 1500: those who supported a spiritualized church free of worldly encumbrances (the 'Non-Possessors') eventually lost, and the Muscovite Church, with rich landholdings, generally cooperated closely with the state.

Ψ

The Golden Horde

The expansion of the Mongol empire in the 13th century radically altered the course of the history of the Eastern Slavs. The Mongol armies that invaded the Land of Rus were predominantly Turkic, and are known to the chronicles as Tartars.

The Tartars' first contact with the Slavs was in 1224, when they inflicted a crushing defeat on the princes of Rus at the battle of the Kalka. Withdrawing immediately, for internal political reasons, the Tartars reappeared in 1237, devastating the principalities of Rus and imposing their rule upon them.

Only Novgorod, protected by its geographical situation, escaped the general ruin. Its prince, Alexander Nevsky, by submitting voluntarily to Tartar overlordship, avoided a Tartar invasion of his territory. Thanks to his victories over the Swedes and Germans (neither in reality of any great strategic importance), Alexander has become a symbol of Russian nationalism, and specifically in the context of rivalry with Western Europe. This image of Alexander has been deliberately fostered from the composition of his *Life* in the 1280s to his canonization in the 16th century, to the dedication of the great monastery bearing his name in the newly founded St Petersburg in the 18th, and to Eisenstein's film in our own.

The Tartar invasion also completed the process of the shift of power from Kiev to the northern principality of Suzdal, which had begun a century earlier. This was due in part to a shift in patterns of trade, and in part to the fact that Suzdal and its associated cities had enjoyed the political stability that Kiev had so conspicuously lacked. Already in 1169 Andrey Bogolyubsky, having sent his son Mstislav to sack Kiev, had assumed the title of grand prince, but continued to reign in Vladimir. After the Tartar devastation, a power vacuum developed in Kiev and the rest of the southern and western Rus; this was later filled by the rising power of Lithuania.

OPPOSITE *A Tartar khan.*

In the year 1224, for our sins, there came unknown people out of the East; no one knows for sure who they are or whence they came, or what is their language, or of what tribe they are, or what is their faith.

They are called Tartars, or some say, Taurmens, or others, Pechenegs. Wise men who understand books know them well; but we do not know who they are. We have written of them here for the sake of the memory of the princes of Rus and the misfortune that they brought upon them. For they made many countries captive, and slaughtered a multitude of the godless Polovtsy, and drove others out.

In 1224 the Rus (together with the Polovtsy, their erstwhile enemies) encountered a new menace in the steppe country: a detachment of armed horsemen who appeared from the south-east and demanded submission. Above, the *First Novgorod Chronicle* records that in fact this was a Tartar (i.e. Mongol) advance guard. On the River Kalka near the Sea of Azov the Rus gave battle, and were defeated; the enemy gave no mercy. The victors then rode off, no one knew whither, and the Russian princes resumed their quarrelsome ways.

This disaster was followed by another: an early frost killed the crops and a severe famine spread across the land. It was regarded at the time as God's punishment for not having overcome the pagan Tartars.

In the year 1230, on 14 September, the frost killed the grain in our lands, which caused much distress. We began to buy bread at eight kunas, and a measure of rye at twenty grivnas, and at fifteen in the homesteads, and wheat at forty grivnas, and millet at twenty, and oats at thirteen. People left the town and region of Novgorod, so that other towns and lands were full of our brothers and sisters. Those who remained began to starve. Who would not shed tears, seeing dead bodies lying in the streets, and infants eaten by dogs? So God put it into the heart of Archbishop Spiridon to do a good work; he had a burial pit dug out, close by the Church of the Apostles on Prosskaya Street, and appointed a good and humble man,

Stanilo by name, to bring the dead on a horse as he went round the town. Stanilo brought them constantly every day, and the pit was filled to the top; three thousand and thirty persons were buried in it.

The Tartars returned to devastate and subjugate Russia in 1237–40. They picked off principalities and cities one by one, demanding from each submission and tribute. The first important princely capital to succumb was Ryazan, and later a colourful tale of its destruction at the hands of Batu, the Tartar commander in Russia, was widely circulated. Extracts are given here.

Ψ Cannibalism in Novgorod

What shall I say of the punishment of God that came upon us in the winter of 1230? For some among the common people murdered living people and ate them, and others ate carrion and dead bodies, and others ate the flesh of horses, dogs and cats. But those who were caught doing such things were burnt with fire, or cut to pieces, or hanged. And others ate moss, or thistles, or pine, or lime bark and leaves, or elm, whatever they could think of; and other evil men began to burn the homes of good people where they found there was rye, and so they plundered their goods instead of repenting. And we did worse things than this, even though we saw the wrath of God before our eyes: dead men that could not be buried eaten by dogs in the streets and in the market and on the great bridge. Fathers and mothers sold their children to the merchants for bread. And this calamity was not in our land only, but in every region of Rus except Kiev alone. And so God requited us according to our works.

From First Novgorod Chronicle

The Tartar conquests

At the death of Yaroslav the Wise (1054), the Kievan state became divided into independent principalities. The Tartar invasion began in 1237, culminating in the sack of Kiev in 1240. For over 200 years, the Russian princes paid tribute to the Khanate of the Golden Horde.

Arctic Circle

NOVGOROD EMPIRE

Pinega

VYATKA

SWEDEN

L. Onega

L. Ladoga

(1240) ×
R. Neva

ESTONIANS

× (1242)

Luga
L. Peipus
Pskov

Riga

TEUTONIC KNIGHTS

LITHUANIANS

R. Neman

W. Dvina

Polotsk

POLOTSK

Minsk

POLES

TUROV-PINSK

Drogochin

Pinsk   Turov

VOLHYNIA

Vladimir

KIEV

Galich

GALICH

Kamenets

R. Dniester

Novgorod

VLADIMIR-

Galich

(1238) ×
R. Sit'

Yaroslavl

Rostov

Tver   **SUZDAL**

Suzdal

Moscow   ○ **Vladimir**

SMOLENSK

Smolensk

CHERNIGOV

NOVGOROD-SEVERSK

Novgorod Seversky

Chernigov

Kiev   **PEREYASLAVL**

Pereyaslavl

R. Dnepr

R. Oka

Ryazan
× 1237

RYAZAN

R. Voronezh

R. Volga   Kazan

Bulgar   **VOLGA BULGARS**

U R A L   M O U N T A I N S

KHANATE OF THE GOLDEN HORDE

GERMANIC TRIBES

MAGYARS

Pereslavets

POLOVTSY

R. Kalka   × (1223)

R. Don

Sarai

Sarkel

Itil

AZOV SEA

BLACK SEA

CASPIAN SEA

Legend

- Novgorod Empire
- Russian principalities under Mongol control from 1240
- → Mongol invasion route 1237–40
- Khanate of the Golden Horde
- ○ Major cities
- × Battle and date

0 ———— 400km

In the year 1237, the godless Batu Khan invaded the land of Rus with his Tartar host and set up camp on the banks of the River Voronezh, on the borders of Ryazan. He despatched his useless envoys to Grand Prince Yury of Ryazan to demand tithes from everyone, prince and commoner alike. Grand Prince Yury Ingvarevich of Ryazan immediately sent word to the pious Grand Prince Yury Vsevolodovich of Vladimir, requesting him to send aid to combat godless Batu Khan or to come with his men to Ryazan. Yury of Vladimir did not come in person, however, nor did he send aid for he wished to fight against Batu Khan on his own.

Seeing this, Grand Prince Yury of Ryazan sent his own son, Fyodor, to the godless khan with gifts and an ardent entreaty not to make war on Ryazan. Prince Fyodor rode to the River Voronezh where Batu Khan was encamped. He brought Grand Prince Yury's gifts and implored the khan not to make war on Ryazan.

Godless Batu Khan, who was false and merciless, accepted the gifts and swore falsely that he would not attack Ryazan. However, the braggart boasted that he would make war on Rus. He demanded the daughters and sisters of the princes of Ryazan as concubines. Driven by jealousy, one of the Ryazan noblemen reported to Batu Khan that Prince Fyodor of Ryazan had taken to wife an imperial Byzantine princess, Evpraksia, who was exceedingly beautiful. Batu Khan, who was sly and deceitful, was aroused by carnal passion and said to Prince Fyodor, 'O prince, reveal the beauty of your wife to me.' At this, the pious Prince Fyodor laughed and replied, 'It is not meet that we Christians hand our wives over as concubines to you, infidel tsar. Only if you conquer us will you possess our wives.'

This reply infuriated Batu Khan; he took offence and gave orders for the immediate murder of Prince Fyodor. He commanded that the prince's body be tossed to the wild beasts and the birds of the air to devour. He also killed other princes and warriors.

Only one of Prince Fyodor's teachers, Aponitsa by name, managed to hide, and he wept bitterly as he beheld the blessed body of his noble master. Aponitsa saw that there was no one to tend the corpse, so he carried away the body of his beloved master and

committed it to secret burial. Then he hastened to tell blessed Princess Evpraksia how the infidel Batu Khan had slain her husband, the pious Prince Fyodor.

Evpraksia was standing in the upper apartments of the palace cradling her beloved child, Prince Ivan, when she heard this message of death. She was overcome with grief, and flung herself and her infant son Prince Ivan from the palace heights onto the earth below, where they were smashed to pieces.

Grand Prince Yury heard how his beloved son Fyodor, and the other princes and many of their servants, had been slain at the hands of the godless Khan and he began to mourn them with his wife, the other princesses and his courtiers.

For a long time the whole city wept. But scarcely had they recovered from their great tears and wailing

than they mustered an army to march against the infidel Batu Khan. They encountered his forces near the borders of Ryazan. There was a fierce and bitter battle; many of Batu's mighty forces fell.

Batu Khan was afraid to see so many of his Tartar host slain. So he began to wage war on the land of Ryazan, and eventually came to Ryazan itself. He laid siege to the city and attacked relentlessly for five days. Many citizens were slaughtered or wounded by the heathens, and some were exhausted by the great hardship they suffered. On the morning of the sixth day the pagans advanced on the city. Some carried torches, some battering rams and others a myriad scaling ladders. On 21 December 1237, the heathens captured the city of Ryazan.

The pagans entered the cathedral church of the

Most Holy Mother of God, and there they put Yury's mother, Grand Princess Agrippina, and her daughters-in-law and the other princesses, to the sword. They consigned the bishop and the clergy to the flames and burned them in the holy church. They drowned some people in the river and they killed every last monk. They burned the whole city and seized all the renowned beauty and riches of Ryazan. They destroyed the churches of God and spilt much blood on the sacred altars. Not one man was left alive in the city. All lay dead together. And all this came to pass because of our sins.

Defeated and disunited, the princes of Rus were unable to prevent the further devastation of their land. The *Typography Chronicle*, a late 15th-century compilation, shows that perhaps the heaviest moral blow was the sack of Kiev, the old capital and 'mother of the towns of Rus', in 1240.

In the year 1240, the godless Batu came against Kiev with a strong army and besieged it. Kiev was surrounded by the Tartar forces, so that people inside the city could not hear each other speak for the creaking of Batu's carts and the noise made by his camels and horses, and the whole land of Rus was filled with warriors.

Batu placed siege engines against the wall near the Lyadsky Gate, and the Tartars beat against the wall day and night until they breached it. The citizens came out upon the wall where it was breached; there was a breaking of spears, a clashing of shields, and arrows darkened the sky. The townsfolk fled and the Tartars took the wall. But that day and that night the townsfolk built another wall by the church of the Mother of God. The next day the Tartars attacked it, and there was another fierce battle.

Meanwhile people had fled with their goods to the church roofs, and the walls of the churches collapsed with the weight. The town fell to the infidels on 6 December, St Nicholas' day. Then, having taken Kiev, and hearing that Daniil, prince of Volynia, was in Hungary, Batu went on to Vladimir.

conquer his land.' He gathered a great army, embarked it upon his ships and departed with this great force, blazing with the spirit of war.

Intoxicated with madness, he reached the River Neva and, puffed up with pride, he sent his ambassadors to Prince Alexander in Novgorod with this message: 'How can you fight against me? I am here already and will conquer your land!'

Prince Alexander, hearing these words, became enraged. He went to the church of St Sophia, knelt in front of the altar and prayed to God. Having finished his prayer, he bowed to Archbishop Spiridon, who blessed and dismissed him. Alexander walked out of the church, wiping away his tears, and started to gather his army. Then he went against the enemy, not waiting for all who were going to join him, trusting in the protection of the Holy Trinity.

On the Sabbath, at the sixth hour of the day, Alexander joined battle with a sudden attack. The destruction of the Catholic Swedes was terrible. Hosts of them were killed; Alexander himself branded the face of their king with his lance. The rest of the enemy had fled to their ships, which they loaded with their dead. The number of corpses was so great that the ships sank.

Prince Alexander returned home victorious, praising God and glorifying his Creator, the Father, the Son and the Holy Ghost, now and ever unto the ages of ages.

In the 1240s the young prince of Novgorod, Alexander, had to face attacks from Swedes and German (Teutonic) knights intent on colonizing the Baltic shoreline. Passages from *The Life of Prince Alexander Nevsky*, produced a few decades after his death by a member of the prince's retinue, record how Alexander defeated the Swedes by the River Neva (hence his surname Nevsky).

In the year 1240, the Catholic king [actually Earl Birger] of Sweden heard about the great bravery of Prince Alexander of Novgorod and said, 'I will go and

Having defeated the Swedes, Alexander Nevsky turned against the other invaders, the Teutonic Knights. The *First Novgorod Chronicle* relates the crucial battle which took place on the frozen Lake Peipus, on 5 April 1242. It became known as the Battle of the Ice, and was celebrated in Eisenstein's film *Alexander Nevsky*.

In the year 1242, Prince Alexander and the men of Novgorod, together with his brother Andrey and the men of Nizhny Novgorod, marched against the Germans in Estonia, and cut off all the roads to Pskov, on Lake Peipus. The prince drove them out of Pskov,

The battle took place on Saturday, 5 April 1242. In the same year, the Germans sent a message: 'Those lands of the Udmurts, Luga, Pskov and Latgallia, that we took with the sword while you were without a prince, we relinquish in their entirety, and those of your men whom we have taken prisoner we will exchange: we will let yours go, and you will let ours go.' And they released the hostages and made peace.

Meanwhile the Tartars were spreading their domination across the land. The *Novgorod* chronicler describes how they exacted tribute from the Christians.

In the year 1245, on 18 September, Batu Khan killed Prince Mikhail of Chernigov and his boyar Fyodor at the Golden Horde. This is how they were killed.

Now Batu followed the Tartar custom: if anyone came to do homage to him, he ordered his priests to lead them through the fire and the one doing homage had to worship a bush and fire.

Mikhail said, 'It is not right for Christians to pass through the fire or to worship the idols.' The priests went to tell Batu Khan, 'The Grand Prince Mikhail is not obeying your commands or going through the fire or worshipping your gods.' And Batu Khan was enraged, and sent to Mikhail one of his lords, his steward Yeldega, who said, 'If you will not pass through the fire and worship the bush and the idols, then you will die a cruel death.' Mikhail replied, 'I do not want to be a Christian in name only, and do the works of the heathen, but rather I believe in Christ, the only God.'

Then the executioners arrived, jumped down from their horses, and took hold of Mikhail. They stretched him out, holding him by the arms, and began to beat him over the heart with their hands; then they threw him prostrate on the earth, and began to beat him with their feet. After this had continued for a long time, a certain heathen renegade, called Doman, cut off the head of the holy Grand Prince Mikhail and cast it aside. Then they began to torture Fyodor as they had tortured Mikhail, and cut off his head too.

ABOVE *Alexander, prince of Novgorod, and after the death of his father Yaroslav II, grand prince of Kiev.*

captured both Germans and Estonians, and sent them in irons to Novgorod, while he marched upon Estonia. When they were there, Alexander sent out all his army to forage. The Germans and Estonians met the foraging party by a bridge, and many were killed.

The prince retreated to Lake Peipus, pursued by the Germans and Estonians. Seeing this, Prince Alexander and the men of Novgorod drew up their army on Lake Peipus, at Uzmen, at Voroney Kamen. The Germans and Estonians attacked and drove a wedge through the army; but many were slaughtered. Then God and St Sophia and the holy martyrs Boris and Gleb helped Prince Alexander: the Germans fell and the Estonians fled, and Alexander and his men pursued and killed them for nearly three miles over the ice, as far as the Subolich bank. Innumerable Estonians fell, and four hundred Germans, and fifty were taken prisoner and brought to Novgorod.

Ψ

Moscow

The battle of Kulikovo Pole (1380) occupies a place in the Russian historical consciousness similar to that which the English reserve for Agincourt. After over a century of foreign domination, the princes of Rus demonstrated their ability to defeat their seemingly invincible enemy, with permanent results for their national self-perception.

This was a period of religious and cultural as well as political revival. Prominent in the renewal of the Church were St Alexis, metropolitan of Moscow, and St Sergius of Radonezh, whose influence over the princes helped to calm their internecine squabbles and promote concerted action to the national good. In the 15th century the Russian Orthodox Church finally became independent from Constantinople when the latter, desperate for western aid against the Turks, accepted papal authority in an abortive union which Moscow rejected. Spirituality and culture were combined in the person of the icon painter Andrey Rublyov (c. 1370–1430), canonized in 1988, whose work is still unsurpassed in Russian art.

Throughout the 14th and 15th centuries Moscow progressively grew in importance. This was initially due to the good relations which the princes of Moscow enjoyed with the Tartars, who supported them against their less loyal rivals; but later, as the Tartar hold upon Rus became more tenuous, the khans built up the power of Moscow to counteract the growing influence of Lithuania, to which the princes of Tver were becoming dangerously close. This eventually led to the point where Moscow, with the lands that it had absorbed, became sufficiently strong to act on its own account.

OPPOSITE   *Spires of the Kremlin in Moscow,*
heart of Christian Russia.

Grand Prince of Moscow Dimitri Ivanovich and his cousin Prince Vladimir Andreyevich, filled with a martial spirit, appointed valorous commanders from all over the land of Rus.

O lark, delight of fair days, fly up beneath the blue sky, look on the powerful city of Moscow, and sing the glory of Grand Prince Dimitri and his cousin Vladimir.

The standards were raised on the banks of the great River Don, the fringed banners waved, and the gilded mail glistened.

All the princes of Rus gathered to Grand Prince Dimitri, saying, 'Grand prince, the heathen Tartars are already entering our fields and taking our patrimony from us. They stand between the Dnepr and the Don, and are about to ford the Mecha and sacrifice their lives to our glory.'

Then Grand Prince Dimitri said to his cousin Prince Vladimir, 'Come, cousin, across the swift River Don, let us win for ourselves something that will be a wonder to the nations, let us try our brave men, and make the River Don run with blood for the land of Rus and the Christian faith!'

The Tartar carts creaked between the Don and the Dnepr, the Tartars came upon the land of Rus. Grey wolves ran from the mouths of the Don and the Dnepr; but they were not grey wolves, they were the heathen Tartars, intent upon making war upon all the land of Rus, the heathen Mamay, chief of the Tartar army, bringing his forces upon Rus.

Now the princes of Rus fell upon the great armies of the Tartars, striking their steel lances upon Tartar armour. The steel swords rang on the helmets of the Tartars, at Kulikovo Field, at the River Nepryadva.

At Kulikovo Field strong clouds came together, and out of them flashed much lightning, and great thunder. That was the sons of Rus joining battle with the heathen Tartars for the great wrong they had suffered, and their gilded armour flashing and their steel swords clashing upon the Tartar helmets.

At that time, in the land of Ryazan, neither the ploughmen called, nor the trumpets sounded, only the ravens croaked and cuckoos called in expectation of the bodies of men. It was dreadful and sorrowful to behold, for the grass was covered in blood, and the trees bent down to the ground with distress.

That day, on Saturday, 8 September, the Christians slew the heathen armies at Kulikovo Field, at the River Nepryadva.

The black earth beneath the horses' hooves was sown with Tartar bones and watered with their blood. The strong armies joined battle and trampled down the hills and meadows. The rivers and streams and lakes were muddied.

Glory extended to the sea and to the Iron Gates on the Danube, to Rome and Constantinople, announcing that Rus had overcome the heathen.

The sons of Rus plundered the treasure of the Tartars, taking back to their own land the horses and camels, silks and satins, silver and gold, strong armour and pearl beads.

The women of Russia adorned themselves with Tartar gold. Joy and merriment spread through the land of Rus, and the glory of Rus exulted over the heathen. The whole earth was in awe of the grand prince.

Grand Prince Dimitri and his cousin, Prince Vladimir, and the other commanders stood upon the bones at Kulikovo Field, at the River Nepryadva; dreadful and sorrowful, brethren, was it then to behold.

Christian corpses lay by the banks of the great Don like ricks of hay, and the Don ran red with blood for three days.

Then Grand Prince Dimitri said, 'Brethren, princes and boyars and descendants of boyars, you have laid down your lives for the holy churches, for the land of Rus, for the Christian faith. Forgive me, brethren, in this life and the next. Come, cousin, Prince Vladimir, to our own land, to the glorious city of Moscow, and resume the rule of our principalities; for we have attained honour and a glorious name.' To God be the glory.

The Tartars exercised efficient indirect control over Russia through its princes, who had to be confirmed in office at the Tartar court and acted as tax-collectors. The princes of Moscow, a previously insignificant place, most often found Tartar favour and gained the title of 'Grand Prince' during the 14th century. In 1380, the Muscovite ruler Dimitri defeated a large

Tartar army, sent to punish him for insubordination, at Kulikovo on the Don.

The above extracts from the work called *Zadonshchina*, written by Sofony of Ryazan, show that the battle was crucial to Russia's national awareness and pride.

The 14th century saw a remarkable religious movement, with large social consequences, in northern Russia: the founding of dozens of hermitages and monasteries throughout the forest zone. Settlers followed, and Moscow did its best to profit by the process. It was instigated by Sergius of Radonezh, later considered Russia's patron saint. Some passages from a *Life of Sergius*, composed by Yepifany (Epiphanius) the Wise, a Russian writer who had known him, are quoted here.

Kirill of Rostov had two sons, the first called Stefan, and the second Sergius, whom he brought up in great piety and purity. Stefan learnt to read and write quite successfully, but his brother slowly.

One day Sergius went out for a walk, as was his habit, for he greatly loved silence, and passing a certain oak wood, he found there an elder in priest's orders standing under a tree and praying.

The child approached and when the elder finished praying he called him and said, 'Do you want anything, child?' And the child replied, 'Father, my soul is very sorrowful, because I have been sent by my parents to learn the Holy Scriptures, and I cannot understand what they say. Therefore, reverend father, pray to God for me.' The elder beheld him with his inner sight: his words were sweet to him, because he understood that grace would be upon the boy; he prayed, and called the child, and blessed him. Then he said, 'From this moment, child, God has given you the ability to read and write, whereby you may also be of help to others.'

After the death of his wife, Stefan left the world and became a monk. His brother Sergius came to him, entreating him to go with him to seek out some deserted place. Finally, by God's guidance, they came to a deserted place, provided with woods and oak thickets and water. It pleased them greatly, so they prayed and set to work at once.

First they built themselves a little hut in which they could rest a little from their labours; likewise they built a little church, for they had not the strength for a large building. When it was time for the church to be consecrated, they petitioned the metropolitan, and he sent priests who came and brought all that was necessary for the consecration of a church. So they consecrated it in the name of the Holy and Life-Giving Trinity.

Now it came to pass that Prince Mamay of the Golden Horde had raised a great army of godless Tartars, and was coming upon the land of Rus. All the people were oppressed with great fear. But the great and praiseworthy and victorious Grand Prince Dimitri of Moscow and Vladimir, who then held the sceptre of the land of Rus, came to Sergius to enquire of him whether he should go out against the godless.

The saint said, 'It is right for you to take care of the Christian flock that has been entrusted to you by God. Go forth against the godless, and by God's help you will conquer and return safely to your home.' The grand prince said, 'If God helps me, father, I shall found a monastery in honour of the most pure Mother of God.'

God helped the victorious Dimitri, and the heathen Tartars were defeated, and utterly routed.

After his glorious victory, Grand Prince Dimitri returned to his fatherland with great joy, and came without delay to his elder, St Sergius, thanking him for his good counsel. The prince wanted to turn his promise into deed swiftly, and to found a monastery. The elder went and searched and found a suitable place on a river called the Dubenka, and through the

goodwill of the grand prince, St Sergius built a church there, dedicated to the Dormition of Our Lady, the most pure Mother of God.

In a short time, thanks to the sovereign's assistance, there was a wonderful monastery there.

Only two years after the great Russian victory at Kulikovo the Tartars came back and sacked Moscow while Grand Prince Dimitri was away. Dimitri had to accept Tartar overlordship but until his death, in 1389, successfully rebuilt Moscow's strength.

In the year 1382, the Tartar Khan Toktamysh attacked the land of Rus with a great army and laid waste to much of it: he took Moscow and burnt it, and likewise Pereyaslavl.

The Grand Prince Dimitri, seeing how many godless Tartars there were, did not oppose them, but went to Kostroma with his princess and children, and Prince Vladimir went to Volok, and his mother and wife to Torzhok, and the metropolitan to Tver, and Bishop Gerasim of Kolomna to Novgorod.

The growing authority of the Russian Church in the 14th century is reflected in the second great *Life* by Yepifany, written in *c.* 1397. This is of Stephen, apostle to the Permians (Komi), a pagan people occupying an extensive territory west of the middle Urals.

The following extracts relate how, for his successful mission, Stephen devised a written Permian language.

Our holy father Stephen was a Rus by birth, of the Slavonic race, from the Dvina country in the north.

While he was but a youth, he became a monk at the monastery of St Gregory Nazianzen at Rostov, called

RIGHT *Dimitri, grand prince of Moscow, reviews his troops before attacking and defeating a Tartar army at Kulikovo in 1380.*

солебⷧетсѧ а шоломы наглаваⷯ ихъ а҃нꙇоутренаа
а свѣтаꙗщисѧвоⷡⷬꙗемѧбера елобⷰцышоломоⷨꙇапламеⷡ
гненыиипоⷬебⷩесѧ

the Enclosure, near the bishop's cathedral, for there, in the time of Bishop Parfeny, were many books which he needed for reading.

He taught himself the Permian language and devised new writing for it, inventing new letters to express it adequately; and he translated and transcribed Russian books into Permian. He also learnt Greek and how to read Greek books. So he was able to speak three languages, and also read and write them, namely Russian, Greek and Permian.

Taking with him relics of the saints, and altar cloths, and the other things that are necessary for the consecration of a church, and the holy chrism and the holy oil and such like, he boldly set out towards the land of Perm. He was on fire with divine zeal, and went in amongst them as a lamb among wolves, there to teach them about God and the Christian faith.

When they heard the Christian faith preached, some of the Permians believed and wanted to be baptized, but others did not, and prevented those who would. Those few of them who first believed and were baptized by him often came to him. They sat by him and talked, and remained constantly by him and loved him greatly. But those who did not believe, thought to kill him.

The servant of God, Stephen, prayed to God, and after his prayer set about founding a church, which he built at a place called Ust-Vym, where the River Vym flows into the Vychegda. When he consecrated the church, he dedicated it to the Annunciation of Our most Holy, most Pure, most Blessed Lady the Mother of God and Ever-Virgin Mary. Then the unbaptized Permians wanted to be baptized, and many people, men, women and children, came to him.

Stephen journeyed to Moscow, and was there consecrated by the metropolitan bishop of the Permian land. One day he summoned his clergy and his clerks and all those whom he had brought from the land of Perm, and after short conversations on spiritual matters, he lay down upon his bed, and the brethren sang the canon and worshipped.

While the words of thanksgiving were yet upon his lips, like one who falls asleep or begins to rest with sweet slumbers, the holy father Stephen quietly and peacefully gave up the ghost.

In March 1423, Grand Prince Vasily made a will. Extracts given here represent the first evidence of dependants registered on country estates of the reigning family.

I give to my princess half of all my customary dues from Nizhny Novgorod, in as full a manner as my mother held them. Likewise I bequeath to her the villages that belonged to my mother, together with their customary dues and whatever services were liable to be rendered.

When my children come into their inheritance and begin to draw the income from their estates, my princess and my sons, Ivan and Yury, and my other children, shall send out their clerks who are responsible for making surveys. These clerks shall record on oath the portions of each, and they shall impose taxes by ploughland-unit and people in accordance with that register.

By the same register, and in proportion to their estates and their income, my princess and my children shall begin to give my son, Ivan, general tax for the payment of the tribute to the Golden Horde. But if God changes the Horde, my princess and my children shall take the tribute to themselves, and my son Ivan shall not interfere.

I bequeath to my princess Sophia half of all my customary dues from Novgorod.

My son Vasily and my princess shall set up a commission of enquiry, and impose tribute on the people, according to their ability to pay.

She shall give tribute to the Golden Horde from those regions and villages according to the reckoning and the dues for the upkeep of the post-horse stations, whenever it shall be required.

If God changes the Horde and ends their domination, then my princess shall take that tribute for her own use; and my son, Prince Vasily, is not to interfere.

Sophia is to have the administration of justice within her lands: my son, Prince Vasily, is not to send into her regions or her villages for any reason at all. And these regions and villages are to be my princess's for her lifetime. On her death, they are to descend to my son, Prince Vasily.

Finance and currency

The Mongol invasion in the 13th century disrupted Russian economic life. Settlements were destroyed, fields laid waste and trades depressed. But it was not long before the Russians rebuilt their dwellings and began to work in their old ways. And the Mongol occupation, by encouraging the emergence of a common market with free-trade understandings between the principalities, stimulated economic development.

There were new opportunities for Russian traders to meet merchants from China, the Mediterranean and other parts. Foreign craftsmen, often Germans, settled in towns and helped raise the technical standard of manufacture, which had fallen drastically during the decline of Kievan Russia.

Novgorod, which had been largely unaffected by the Mongols, became a centre for Russia's foreign trade with western Europe in particular, which was conducted through the Baltic ports. Exports remained forest products, with the addition of flax and fish oil. Imports from the west were beginning to include articles for general consumption, as well as luxury items.

The princes were vassals of the Mongols and paid them tribute, but continued to finance themselves by fees, fines, and levies on trade. There was a revival of money, and at first Mongol silver and copper coins served this purpose in many territories. But Russian-minted coins began to reappear; in the 14th century Dmitry Donskoy was probably the first Muscovite ruler to mint his own coins, which, apart from a Russian inscription on one side, closely resembled those of the Mongols.

The new Russian coinage had at least three functions: to provide a medium of trade, to assert Muscovite independence and to undermine the Mongol economy. It was probably for the last

ABOVE *Tax officials raise money required by Ivan I to pay the tribute demanded by the Tartars.*

purpose that the coins looked like Mongol ones but contained less silver, a feature that also provided a source of income for Dmitry (who issued the coins at face value). Bad money drives out good, and the 'good' Mongol coins soon went out of circulation because nobody wished to spend them. In an attempt to revive their currency, the khans were forced to reduce the content of their coins.

In the 15th century, coinage remained a medium of propaganda as the Russian princes struggled for independence and hegemony: the operation of a mint was a symbol of independence. When the princes of Tver and Moscow were struggling for supremacy they minted coins that were intentionally very different, each of which was intended to drive out the other. The climax of this propaganda war was during the reign of Ivan III, grand prince of Moscow (1462–1505), who minted coins on which he was described as 'Lord of All Russia', emphasizing that Moscow would dominate the new, emergent Russia.

Ψ

Ivan III the Great

The reigns of Ivan III and Vasily III are the culmination of the process of the 'gathering of the Russian lands' about Moscow. By Vasily's time a state had emerged that was recognizably the Russia we know today. In 1480 Ivan III had completed the process begun exactly a century earlier by his great-grandfather Dimitri Donskoy, by formally renouncing his allegiance to the khan. The Russian and Tartar armies faced each other for several days across the River Ugra, but the Tartars withdrew without giving battle, thus signalling the end of their dominion over Russia.

Ivan was equally successful in his internal policies. At his accession Moscow was already the most powerful of the Russian principalities, and he proceeded to enlarge it by annexing the others. Sometimes this was a peaceful process, but his two greatest acquisitions – of the republic of Novgorod and of Moscow's great rival, Tver – were achieved by force of arms. Vasily, his son, found that he had little to do besides the annexation of Pskov to complete the process.

Under Ivan, the people of north eastern Rus found themselves united under a single ruler for the first time since the days of Yaroslav the Wise, and once again began to think of themselves as a nation. The fall of Constantinople in 1453 had radically altered not only the political map but also the ideological frame of reference of Orthodox Christendom, and notions of Russia as Byzantium's spiritual heir became increasingly prevalent in Moscow. Inseparable from this was the concept of the imperial dignity. In 1472 Ivan III married Sophia Paleologina, niece of the last emperor of Byzantium, and adopted the Byzantine double-headed eagle as his own emblem. Spiritual and political ideas fused in the concept of 'Moscow the Third Rome', which was first expressed in the monk Filofey's epistle to Vasily III.

OPPOSITE *Ivan III the Great (1462–1505).*

Grand Prince Vasily Vasilyevich, feeling that he was ill of a wasting disease, ordered that he should be burnt, as is the custom with those who are ill in this manner; he ordered the fire to be applied in many places of his body, even to those where he had no illness, and at the time he did not even feel it.

When the wounds festered, and he became seriously ill, he wished to become a monk, but they would not let him and he died of that illness in the third hour of the night on Saturday, 27 March 1462.

He was buried the following day in St Michael the Archangel's Cathedral in Moscow, where all the grand princes are buried.

With his blessing his eldest son, Ivan, succeeded him as grand prince. To his second son, Prince Yury, Vasily Vasilyevich gave Dmitrov, Mozhaysk, Serpukhov and so on, with their lands, villages and revenues, which he had inherited from his grandmother Grand Princess Sophia. To Prince Andrey the Elder he gave Uglich, Bezhitsky Verkh, Zvenigorod and many other lands and villages; to Prince Boris he gave Volok Lamsky, Rzhev, Ruza and all the lands and villages of his great-grandmother Maria Goltyayev, as she had ordained; to Prince Andrey the Younger he gave Vologda with its lands, and the Zaozerye and many other lands and villages.

To Grand Princess Maria, his widow, he gave all the revenues, and Romanov Gorodok, and the lands and villages throughout the realm that had belonged to the former grand princess, to which he added much he had purchased or confiscated from traitors.

In the year 1464, Grand Prince Ivan and his mother, Grand Princess Maria, let Prince Vasily Ivanovich depart to be grand prince of his patrimony Ryazan. The following winter, on 9 January, Prince Vasily came to Moscow and married Anna, the grand prince's sister, and went back to Ryazan with the princess.

It was under Ivan III, called the Great, that the main 'gathering of the lands' – the unification of various territories under the rule of Moscow – took place. Ivan used various means to achieve this end, including dynastic marriages, purchase and simple aggression. The first thing he did on acceding to the throne, however, was to follow the old practice of distributing appanages to his close relations.

The above account of the death of his father, Vasily II, and Ivan III's accession, is taken from the so-called *Nikon Chronicle*, compiled in Moscow in the first half of the 16th century.

The consolidation of power in Moscow caused problems for Novgorod, which had maintained its independence in part by its ability to choose its own prince. When this came to an end, in the latter part of the 15th century, some elements in the city began to look towards Lithuania, which had never belonged to the commonwealth of East Slavonic principalities, and was, moreover, a Roman Catholic state. The resultant dissensions within Novgorod provided Ivan III with his opportunity to act. This account, taken from a late 15th-century chronicle known as the Moscow compilation, takes Ivan's side in the conflict.

Hearing that there were great disturbances in his patrimony of Great Novgorod, Grand Prince Ivan Vasilyevich sent messengers to the town, saying, 'Men of Novgorod, you are my patrimony, and have been from the beginning the patrimony of my grandfathers and great-grandfathers, since Grand Prince Vladimir, who converted the land of Rus, the great-grandson of Ryurik, who was the first grand prince in your land. From his time to mine we have ruled you and bestowed favour upon you and defended you on all sides, and we are at liberty also to punish you if you start to regard us contrary to tradition. You have never been the subjects of any king, nor of the grand prince of Lithuania, since your land has existed. But now you are renouncing Christianity for Latinism, while I, the grand prince, am doing you no violence, nor laying any heavier dues on you than did any of the grand princes of our line.'

But after great deliberation, the grand prince announced to his spiritual father, Metropolitan Filipp, to his mother, Grand Princess Maria, and to his boyars, his intention to use military force against Novgorod. Hearing this, they advised him to put his

Appanage Russia

Primogeniture never took root in Russia, even among its rulers. When a prince died, his property was normally divided, according to the appanage system, among his sons, with provision for his daughters and widow (who might inherit fully if there were no sons). The early Russo-Viking princes regarded their realm as the common property of their dynasty.

In Kiev Rus, however, brother often succeeded brother. Provided the ruler of Kiev could exercise central control, and while princes still frequently moved their residence, the Kievan federation held together. In the 12th century, when central power weakened and branches of the ruling family began putting down local roots, the inheritance system became utterly important. A principality was subdivided in nearly every generation, until even the smallest towns became 'capitals', with their own chroniclers, monasteries and painters.

Because free peasants and landowners could enter the service of any prince they wished, appanage princes were able to exercise only the weakest political control over their lands. Effectively they were little more than estate-owners, dependent on their household servants or *kholopy*, who in fact fulfilled the tasks and role of slaves.

The princes had to rely for military support on the forces fielded by almost equally powerful landowners or boyars.

The appanage system held sway from the mid-12th to the late-15th century.

The Tartars (Mongols), who were Russia's overlords for most of the period, took full advantage of its inherent weakness, confirming princes in office and using them as tax-gatherers. However, ambitious principalities, notably Moscow after c. 1300, absorbed lesser territories through war, cajolery, purchase, marriage, or inheritance.

By the 16th century the Moscow grand princes regarded all the Russian lands as their patrimony.

RIGHT *View of the country south of the Black Sea. Under the appanage system, whole regions were divided up into small estates, thereby losing all political control.*

trust in God and carry out his intention to move against Novgorod to punish it for its treachery.

So the grand prince set out, leaving his son Ivan and his brother Prince Andrey the Younger in Moscow. On 29 June 1471 he came to Torzhok.

Meanwhile the grand prince's brothers each took his own road towards Novgorod, burning and taking prisoners as they went, as did the grand prince himself and his commanders. Two of them, Prince Danilo Dmitrievich and Fyodor Davydovich, approached nearer to Novgorod. When they reached the banks of Lake Ilmen, they were suddenly ambushed by a force that had come from Novgorod by boat and, disembarking, crept up on their camp. But the grand prince's commanders' sentries saw them and informed their commanders, who immediately attacked them and killed many and took others prisoner. They compelled those whom they had taken prisoner to slit each other's lips and noses, and sent them back to Novgorod, and threw the armour that they had taken from them into the water, or else burnt it, for they had no need of it.

Then the Archbishop-elect Feofil and the prominent citizens from all the districts of Novgorod came across Lake Ilmen in boats, to petition the grand prince's boyars so that they would intercede with the grand prince. So the boyars went and petitioned the grand prince.

The grand prince was gracious to them and immediately ordered that all plundering, burning and taking of captives should cease, and that those who had been taken should be released. Novgorod paid reparations of sixteen thousand Novgorod silver roubles to the grand prince, besides what they paid to his brothers and the other princes and boyars and commanders.

Then the grand prince sent the Archbishop-elect Feofil and the others who had come with him back to Novgorod with honour, and after them he sent his boyar Fyodor Davydovich to administer the oath of allegiance to all Novgorod, both small and great, and to receive the money.

So Fyodor Davydovich went to Novgorod and did as he was commanded, while Grand Prince Ivan Vasilyevich of Vladimir and Novgorod, Autocrat of All Russia, returned to Moscow in great triumph on 13 August.

Ivan III died in 1505 and was succeeded by his son Vasily III, who continued his father's policy of extending Muscovite dominion over the remaining Russian lands. In 1510 he turned his attention to one of the most important areas that were still self-governing, the city-state of Pskov, the western neighbour and former dependency of Novgorod. The *Sophia Chronicle* is an unofficial record associated with Novgorod. It was compiled in the 15th century with 16th-century additions, from which this account is taken.

The people of Pskov lived according to their own will and had no sovereign prince over them, but chose their prince, receiving him from the great powers, be it Moscow or Lithuania, and his position was more like that of a hireling than of a prince. It was their custom that if he should offend them in any way, they would send him back to where he had come from. Now they had a prince, Ivan Obolensky, called Repnya, whom they had received from Grand Prince Vasily Ivanovich of Moscow, and he lived among them in a violent and overbearing manner, according to the custom of Moscow, and not according to the custom and law of Pskov.

The men of Pskov, unable to tolerate this sort of evil for long, chose envoys from all Pskov and sent them to Grand Prince Vasily Ivanovich in Moscow, complaining of the prince and asking him to send them another one who would behave better and judge more justly. The grand prince sent them back to Pskov, saying, 'I am going to Novgorod, and when I come I shall have your prince brought before me in irons with great shame and dishonour as a criminal, and I shall judge between him and you, and condemn him to death as a robber, and hand him over to you, and you shall do as you like with him.'

On 26 October 1510, Grand Prince Vasily Ivanovich came to Novgorod with his brother Prince Andrey and his boyars. And all the posadniki and chiliarchs and the entire ruling class of Pskov went to see the grand prince and complain of their own prince, and only the

RIGHT *St Sophia, Novgorod. Ivan III conquered the city and brought it under Moscow's control in 1478.*

abbots and priests and the lower classes and the women and girls were left in the town.

The grand prince's idea, which had brought him to Novgorod from Moscow, was to impose his own rule on Pskov. So the grand prince sent his secretary Tretyak Dolmatov, who told them his first new conditions at the town assembly. 'If you, posadniki and people of my patrimony Pskov, desire to live according to your ancient ways, you must accept two things that I want: you must have no town assembly, and take down the assembly bell. But if you will not do these two things that the sovereign desires, there will be bloodshed amongst those who resist his will. And our sovereign lord the grand prince desires to worship at Holy Trinity in Pskov.'

The men of Pskov bowed down to the ground and could not answer him, but their eyes filled with tears like babes in arms, and only those who were too young to understand what was happening did not weep. Only they answered the emissary, 'With God's help we shall think about it and give you an answer tomorrow.' And the men of Pskov wept.

As the next day, which was a Sunday, dawned, they rang the bell for the assembly, and Tretyak came to the assembly, and the posadniki and people of Pskov addressed him, 'It is written in our chronicles that in his father's and grandfather's and great-grandfather's time we swore to the grand prince that we, the people of Pskov, were the subjects of whatever prince should reign in Moscow. Now, God's will be done, and the sovereign is free to dispose of the town of Pskov, and us, and our bell. And if the grand prince wishes to visit his patrimony of Pskov and worship at Holy Trinity, we shall be glad with all our hearts to receive him.'

On 13 January they took down the assembly bell at Holy Trinity, and the people of Pskov watched this being done, and they wept for their freedom and their ancient customs.

The same month, a week after the grand prince's arrival, Prince Pyotr Veliky, Ivan Vasilyevich Khabar and Ivan Andreyevich Chelyadin administered the oath of allegiance to the people of Pskov. And on Thursday, 24 January, our sovereign lord Grand Prince Vasily Ivanovich of All Russia entered Pskov.

Though the people of Pskov may have mourned their loss of independence, there were those among them who were ready to support the idea of a centralized state. One of these was the monk Filofey of the Elazarov Monastery, who in his epistle to Vasily III, written about 1520, first propounded the ideology of 'Moscow the Third Rome'. According to this, Rome lost its primacy within Christendom because of its apostasy from the true faith, and its successor Constantinople likewise lost its position when it fell to the Turks in 1453; their dignity was then inherited by Moscow, the only remaining Orthodox Christian state, and its ruler.

By the exalted and omnipotent and all-sustaining right hand of God, through whom monarchs reign and the great and mighty are magnified, righteousness is ascribed to you, most serene and most august Grand Prince Vasily Ivanovich of Moscow, Orthodox Christian tsar and lord of all and protector of the altars of God and of the holy ecumenical Catholic and Apostolic church of the holy and glorious Dormition of our Most Holy Lady the Mother of God, which has now shone forth instead of the churches of Rome and Constantinople. For the church of Old Rome fell through the Apollinarian heresy, and the Ishmaelites have broken down the doors of the church of the New Rome, Constantinople, with pikes and axes.

This, then, is now the holy Catholic and Apostolic Church of the Third Rome, your sovereign realm, which shines brighter than the sun in its Orthodox Christian faith to the very ends of the universe.

Let it be known to Your Majesty, O pious tsar, that all the realms of Orthodox Christendom have been reduced to your realm alone, and you alone on the earth bear the name of a Christian emperor.

And you shall be called a citizen of the Heavenly Jerusalem for the justice of your rule; for to them that order earthly things well, heavenly things will be given.

Observe then, and take heed, O pious tsar, for all Christian realms are reduced to your realm alone, and two Romes have fallen, the third stands, and a fourth there will not be.

Medieval icons

'Icon' is the Greek word for an image. In the Orthodox world it came to have the narrower sense of the representation of a holy personage or event, most often painted in tempera on a portable wooden panel, though it should be noted that the frescos with which Orthodox churches are normally adorned are no less 'iconic' than panel-paintings.

When in the ninth and tenth centuries the Slav nations, including Russia, were converted to Christianity, Eastern Christendom had just experienced (AD 726–843) the protracted religious, political and social crisis associated with 'iconoclasm' ('image-breaking'). From this there emerged a whole theology of the holy images, which thereafter were regarded as a central part of Orthodox worship – not, however, to be idolized superstitiously, but to be venerated. Orthodox Christian culture had a strong visual orientation: the image, accessible to the illiterate and literate alike, was a powerful cohesive force in society as well as the bearer of theological, social or historical messages. Nowadays we can also appreciate the aesthetic appeal and art-historical importance of icons from which European easel-painting ultimately derives. They transmitted many aspects of the Greco-Roman classical heritage (facial types, postures, drapery, etc.) while transforming it for spiritual purposes through stylization and symbolization.

Russia is fortunate in the number, age and artistic quality of the medieval icons that have survived there. They had a pervasive role in old Russian life, standing not only in churches but in private houses and wayside shrines. Some icons – notably of the Virgin and Child – were associated with particular localities; some were considered 'wonder-working'; some reflected, or were at the centre of large historical movements or events.

ABOVE *An icon of the Novgorod school depicting the Annunciation.*

Early Russian icons are often characterized by expressive directness; only in the late 17th century do we find finicky over-refinement.

Icon-painting, often regarded as a static art, in fact evolved stylistically: in particular the late middle ages – in Byzantium and Serbia as in Russia – witness a remarkable aesthetic quest to portray emotion and dynamism. The classic moment of the Russian icon is the early 15th century, the age of a painter whose individuality we can assess, Andrey Rublyov (d. 1430). The development of the multi-tiered icon-screen (*iconostasis*) in churches gave painters unprecedented opportunities, while the relative autonomy of Russia's principalities led to a creative diversity of local manners.

Three examples of the work of Andrey Rublyov, who led the Moscow school and influenced the development of icon painting throughout Russia.

ABOVE LEFT   *The Trinity; Christ is in the centre with God the Father on the left and, on the right, the Holy Ghost.*

ABOVE   *The Dormition of the Virgin; Christ stands above her holding her soul.*

LEFT   *The archangel Michael; detail from the Deisis of Zvenigorod.*

RIGHT   *St Nikolai Lipensky; an example of the Novgorod school with its massive composition and warm colours.*

PART 4 RUSSIA

When the 17-year-old Ivan IV (the 'Terrible' or 'Awesome') had himself crowned tsar with great ceremony, he was not only upgrading the Muscovite ruler's title from grand prince, but signalling the authority of Moscow over All Russia (*vseya Rusi*, often wrongly translated 'all the Russias'). The title of tsar, presumably a very early import into the Slav languages, and derived from 'Caesar', had always been used by the Byzantine emperor and latterly of the Mongol khan: the tsars were effectively laying claim to both rather different heritages. The concept of a ruler took on a grander, more spiritual aura than the proprietorial attitude the Viking-descended dynasty had hitherto claimed, and tsars were seen as divinely ordained: hence there arose the new phenomenon of numerous pretenders, often supposedly bearing physical marks to witness to their God-given status. There was much ideological literature of the time testifying to these concepts, but of particular interest are the writings of Ivan IV himself, often in the form of personal, yet still public, letters, in an inimitably powerful if incoherent rhetorical style. His longest and most remarkable correspondence was with Prince Kurbsky, an important adviser who escaped into Lithuanian service; this move shocked Ivan and he considered it treasonable.

Ivan IV's long reign (1533–84) is the quintessentially Muscovite period. A carefully structured service society, resistant to intellectual change (though not to all contact with the West), extremely hierarchical, it seemed entirely watertight. Ivan's early military successes (notably against the Kazan Tartars), the downgrading of the boyars and the stout defence of Orthodoxy, made him a folk hero. Yet in the second half of his reign everything turned sour: his firm rule turned to cruelty on a massive and unpredictable scale, wars were lost and Muscovy faced internal crisis.

The crisis arrived with the extinction of the Ryurikid dynasty on the death of Ivan's successor Fyodor I. His prime minister, Boris Godunov, was elected tsar, to the anger of the old boyar families. A pretender claiming to be Ivan's dead son Dimitri launched a successful civil war; thereafter followed a period of chaos with further pretenders, a boyar tsar Vasily IV Shuysky and nearly a Polish takeover of the realm; the Swedes also intervened. Finally the Church, with popular provincial support, launched an appeal for Russian unity that succeeded in calling an 'assembly of the land' and electing 16-year-old Mikhail Romanov, a kinsman of Ivan IV's popular first wife, the new tsar.

This 'Time of Troubles' was a traumatizing event, threatening disintegration of the country. It led both to a series of literary works which tried to make sense of

UNDER THE TSARS
(1533-1676)

the events, and also to the long-lasting concept of 'Holy Russia', whose special destiny was not necessarily linked with the person of a given ruler.

The Muscovite institutions and service state were reimposed intact after 1613, already, from a European perspective; a curiously backward-looking move, Muscovite backwardness begins to permeate the accounts of western travellers.

In fact, in the 17th century, Moscow became excessively dependent on western technological and military help (long before Peter I's reforms), and this in turn gave rise to considerable xenophobia. This is the background to several of the crises of this and the following century. The greatest of these erupted in the reign of Mikhail's son, Alexis Mikhailovich, and is known as the Great Schism of the Russian Church. The Old Believers (in their own eyes, the true believers) resisted certain reforms of ritual that had wider implications, and the upshot was close to civil war. Historians seem undecided as to whether the Old Belief (soon subdividing into often eccentric sects) was totally retrograde, a form of eastern Protestantism, or a phenomenon embodying the essence of true Russianness. In any case it gave rise to a copious and sometimes very moving literature: the autobiography of the Archpriest Avvakum is not only the last great medieval Russian devotional work, but one that is arrestingly modern in the vigour of its language and immediacy of its perceptual world. Women – reduced to low status in Muscovite theory – played an active part in the schism and provided several of the saints of the Old Belief.

Muscovy in the 17th century laid the foundations of a power and prosperity that were to become evident in the 18th, by expanding across the entire Eurasian land mass to the Pacific, and attempting to push the powerful Ottoman Turks back to the Black Sea. In the west it was still unable to reclaim all the historic Kievan lands: but there was a resurgence of Orthodox feedling that led to the reincorporation of Kiev and the eastern Ukraine. The concerns and problems of late Muscovy were not remote from those of Peter the Great (who revered the memory of his father Alexis): the dislocation between the old, fundamentally medieval culture of Muscovy and Russia's new age is not as great as was thought at the time, or as subsequent historians have assumed.

Ψ

Ivan IV
the Terrible

The 16th century in Russia is dominated by the figure of Ivan the Terrible, who indeed reigned for over half of it, from 1533 to 1584. This is partly due to his having come to the throne as a child of three, but he was only 16 when he began to rule in earnest. His coronation in 1547 was the first at which a Muscovite ruler formally assumed the title tsar, which had previously been applied to biblical rulers like King Solomon, and above all to the emperor in Constantinople. However, it was not to the Byzantine imperial heritage alone that Ivan was laying claim. His coronation ritual makes clear reference to the *Legend of the Princes of Vladimir*, an apocryphal history that tried to establish imperial status for Ivan's ancestor Vladimir Monomakh, the implication being that the imperial dignity belongs to Moscow as of right, and not as a substitute for Byzantium. It is remarkable how little is made of Ivan's genuine descent, through his grandmother Sophia Paleologina, from the Byzantine imperial line.

Ivan was in many ways a brilliant man – a composer of liturgical music and a writer of vigorous if undisciplined prose, as well as an energetic ruler. More than anyone else, he determined the image of the Russian tsar, and his shadow lay, to a greater or lesser degree, upon all his successors.

Ivan's reign saw an extensive and rapid expansion eastwards – by the end of it he had added the titles of tsar of Kazan, tsar of Astrakhan and tsar of Siberia to his already impressive list – but his wars in the west were fruitless. However, this was a time of increasing contact with Western Europe, in which English merchants of the Muscovy Company were prominent. There is a corresponding increase in the number of foreign sources for the country's history, as the native chronicles are supplemented by the witness of English and other visitors.

OPPOSITE *Ivan IV the Terrible (1533–84).*

On Sunday, 16 January 1547, Grand Prince Ivan Vasilyevich of All Russia was crowned tsar by Metropolitan Makary of All Russia, and the archbishops, bishops, archimandrites and all the clergy of the metropolitanate of Russia, with the life-giving Cross and the tsar's crown and diadem.

The coronation of Grand Prince Ivan Vasilyevich followed the ancient tradition of his fathers. The large space in the middle of the cathedral in Moscow of the Holy and Glorious Dormition of Our Lady, the Most Pure Mother of God and Queen of Heaven, was prepared, and two thrones placed there, one for the tsar, and one for the metropolitan. When the time came, and Metropolitan Makary and the archbishops and bishops and archimandrites and other clergy had put on their vestments, the metropolitan had a faldstool placed in the middle of the cathedral, and on it he placed the cross and crown and coronation garments of Emperor Constantine Monomachus, with which Grand Prince Vladimir Monomakh had been crowned tsar of Russia.

When Grand Prince Ivan Vasilyevich entered the cathedral, the metropolitan and clergy began the service. Then the metropolitan took the cross from the golden plate and placed it upon Grand Prince Ivan Vasilyevich.

After the prayer the metropolitan, making the sign of the cross over the grand prince, placed the crown upon his head. Then a litany was said, and a prayer to the Mother of God, and then the tsar sat upon his throne, and the metropolitan on his, and in a loud voice the archdeacon intoned a polychronion to Tsar Ivan Vasilyevich of Russia, which was sung by all the clergy.

Then the metropolitan bowed to the tsar, and after this the autocrat was acclaimed by the clergy and the boyars and all the people. Next the tsar left the cathedral, and they spread velvet cloths in his path as he went.

Though the title 'tsar' had been applied occasionally to his predecessors since the 11th century, Ivan IV was the first to adopt it officially at his coronation in 1547. Previously, the title tsar (which is derived from Caesar), had been applied pre-eminently to the

Byzantine emperor, and Ivan, in adopting it, was laying claim to a similar status.

As can be seen from the above account in the *Nikon Chronicle*, the coronation ritual emphasized this imperial heritage.

One of several attempts to codify the developing body of medieval Russian law was the Law Code issued by Ivan the Terrible in 1550.

The passages from it quoted here reflect the progressive restrictions of the peasants' rights and freedoms, which was eventually to develop into total serfdom.

Peasants are to migrate from region to region or from village to village only during the week before, and the week after, 26 November, St George's day.

For their lands and tenements, the peasants are to pay the dwelling payment, and for a holding in the fields.

A priest is not liable to the dwelling payment, and may leave at any time.

If any peasant sells himself into bondage as a villein, away from the arable land, he may leave at any time and he is not liable to the dwelling payment. But there is this condition: if any of his grain remains growing in the ground, he shall pay from that grain the dues of the tsar and the grand prince; if he does not want to pay the due, his crop is confiscated.

One of Ivan IV's key commanders at the siege of Kazan and a trusted friend, Prince Andrey Kurbsky, was alarmed by Ivan's increasing use of terror towards his boyars. In 1564 he left Muscovy and went into the service of its arch-rival, Lithuania.

There ensued a remarkable correspondence stretching over 15 years, in which Kurbsky's reproachfulness is more than matched by Ivan's sarcasm and thundering rhetoric. Implied in the short extracts given below are questions of the tsar's rights and duties.

The rise of Muscovy

WHITE
SEA

● Kholmogory

PRINCIPALITY OF NOVGOROD

R. N. Dvina

L. Onega

● Ustyug

R. Sukhona

● Olonets

L. Ladoga

GRAND
PRINCIPALITY
OF
MOSCOW

Vologda ●

GULF OF FINLAND

Narva ●

Reval ●

L. Peipus

Novgorod

L. Ilmen

R. Volkhov

Kostroma ●
Yaroslavl ●

Nizhny
Novgorod

● Kazan

R. Volga

● Suzdal
● Vladimir

● Murom

● Pskov

Riga ●

● Tver

Zvenigorod
Moscow

R. Oka

● Ryazan

S
W
E
D
E
N

BALTIC SEA

Memel ●

Vyazma ●

Kaluga ●

X Kulikovo (1380)

KHANATE
OF
KAZAN

● Saratov

● Königsberg

Danzig ●

PRUSSIA

L I T H U A N I A

Vitebsk ●

● Minsk

Smolensk ●

R. Neman

R. Vistula

● Warsaw

● Pinsk

HOLY
ROMAN
EMPIRE

P O L A N D

● Chernigov

● Krakow

Kiev ●

● Kharkov

R. Dnepr

R. Don

● Galich

H U N G A R Y

R. Dniester

● Rostov

Belgorod ●

	Principality of Moscow in 1300 (Under Mongol rule)
	Grand Principality of Moscow 1462
	Union of Lithuania-Poland by 1462
	Lands gained by Ivan III (1462–1505)
	Lands gained by Vasily III (1505–33)

× **Battle and date**

○ Major cities

0 ————————— 400 km

Ivan III the Great began the process of Russian unification, under the rule of Moscow, by marrying into neighbouring dynasties and making gifts of land to relations. To preserve its independence, Novgorod allied with Lithuania and Poland against Muscovy.

To the tsar, glorified by God, who appeared most illustrious in Orthodoxy, but is now found not to be so because of our sins.

What evil and persecutions have I not suffered from you! What tissues of cruel lies have you not woven about me! Are there any sins and treacheries of which you have not accused me? You have paid me with evil for the good I have done you, and with boundless hatred you have repaid me for my love. My blood, which I have spilt for you as if it were water, is crying out to God against you.

God is my witness as to how many times I have been wounded in various battles by the barbarians. Because of these wounds, my whole body is covered with scars. All this, O tsar, you regarded as nothing, and you have repaid all of us only with a hatred so bitter that it resembles a burning furnace.

I am drawing to a close now. This letter, soaked in my tears, I will order to be laid in my coffin when the time comes for you and me to appear in judgement before my God, Jesus Christ.

A. KURBSKY

To A. Kurbsky

Here is our Christian and humble reply to him who once was a truly Christian boyar, adviser and general of our autocratic state, and now has become an apostate from the holy life-giving Cross and a destroyer of Christians.

Your epistle has been received and clearly understood. Although, having concealed your venom under your language, you may think that your letter is full of honey, yet its taste is more bitter than that of wormwood.

Is this the way which you, a Christian, learned to serve a Christian monarch? Is this how you render homage to an anointed ruler, by vomiting poison like a devil? You wrote the beginning of your letter without thinking about repentance.

Torments, persecutions and deaths in many forms, these we have not conceived against anyone; as for traitors and witches, such dogs are executed everywhere.

In your madness, you say that the blood you have spilt for us, fighting foreigners, cries out to God

Beat your children

If you have a daughter, make her afraid of you, and you will preserve her from bodily impurity. Let her walk in obedience, lest you be put to shame, and lest she, being allowed her own way, foolishly lose her virginity: when it becomes known, people will laugh at you. If you give your daughter in marriage unsullied, you will have accomplished a great work, and will be praised in the assembly, and at the end you will not complain of her.

If you love your son, beat him frequently, and you will rejoice over him afterwards. Chastise your son when he is a child, and you will be glad of him when he is a man: you will be praised even among the wicked, and your enemies will envy you.

Bring up your son with threats, and you will

have quietness and blessing from him. Do not laugh or play with him, for if you relax in small things, you will certainly end by suffering in great things, and you will find that your soul will be heartily sick of it.

Do not give your son authority in his youth, but bruise his ribs while he is growing, or else he will become wayward and disobedient to you, and you will have difficulties, and sorrow in your soul, and commotion in your house, and loss in your property, and reproach from your neighbours; and you will be a laughing-stock to your enemies, and the authorities will give you much trouble and make you pay for it.

From *Domostroy*

RIGHT *The crown of Ivan the Terrible. Known as his 'Kazan hat', it was made to commemorate the tsar's capture of Kazan, a Tartar khanate close to Moscow, in 1552. Studded with turquoises, rubies and pearls, edged with sable and topped by a single topaz, the crown is the work of Russian artisans.*

against us. This is laughable, for it was not we who spilt it; blood cries to God against the person who has spilt it. You were fulfilling your duty to your fatherland, not to us.

My blood cries louder to God against you, blood spilt not in wounds, not in bloody streams, but in sweat and abundantly heavy toil because of you! Because of your hatred, insults and persecution, many tears, sighs and groans have been shed by us.

IVAN

Ivan IV seems to have been a man of copious intellectual energy and learning. As well as those to Kurbsky, many other letters are ascribed to him: they are marked by a powerful, rhetorical style.

Towards other rulers he is often captious, complaining of slights to emissaries or questioning their credentials as true autocrats on equal terms with the tsar.

An example of this is given below, in a letter which was written to Queen Elizabeth of England in 1570.

Ⲯ

Ivan IV the sadist

I shall draw a veil over what he did before he came of age at about twelve years old, but of this I shall now speak. At an early age he began to spill the blood of dumb animals by hurling them down from great heights (in their language 'from the porches and towers'). He did many other improper things which revealed his taste for arbitrary mercilessness. His tutors permitted him to commit such acts, and even praised him for his cruelty.

He was just entering his fifteenth year or so when he took to harming people. He gathered around him gangs of youths and the relatives of the aforesaid counsellors, and began to ride with them around the streets and squares and bazaars to beat and rob people of all classes, men and women alike.

Indeed, as a boy Ivan acted like a true brigand, and committed other brutalities which are shameful to relate.

When Ivan had begun to surpass even himself in all manner of countless evil deeds, the Lord, to tame the tsar's cruelty, visited an especially harsh fire on the city of Moscow and by this sign clearly manifested His wrath.

From A. Kurbsky, *History of the Muscovite Grand Prince*

You have now sent our ambassador back to us, without sending your own. You have dealt with our business in a manner different from that which was agreed upon between us and your ambassador. Your letter to us is as casual as if it were a travelling pass, whereas such great affairs cannot be decided without the exchanging of pledges and ambassadors.

You have taken no interest in this affair, leaving your ministers to negotiate with our ambassador, and then only about trade. But the real power in these negotiations was with your merchants, Sir William Hart and Sir William Chester.

We had thought that you were the monarch in your own kingdom, ruling yourself, that you cared about your queenly honour and the welfare of your state. That is why we wanted to treat with you. Now we see that it is really your people who have the power, and not just the people, but mere trading yokels who care nothing for our royal persons, our honour and the welfare of our lands, but are concerned only with their own profits.

In your virginal state, you are just a simple old maid. This being so, we will leave this affair to one side. As to your trading yokels who have neglected our royal persons, let them see how they will fare when they try to continue their trade. So far the state of Muscovy has managed to prosper without English goods. We would like you to return the trade charter which we have granted to you. Even if you should fail to return the charter, we shall order that its provisions are to be ignored. Furthermore, all the charters concerning trade heretofore granted by us we regard as invalid from this day forth.

This letter was written in our kingdom's city, Moscow, on the 24th of October, 1570.

Richard Chancellor, an English merchant seeking a northern passage to the East, was by a remarkable series of chances washed up in the White Sea in 1553 and brought to Moscow. He impressed Ivan IV sufficiently for permanent trade connections with England to be established. This is an extract from Chancellor's own vivid account of his presentation to Ivan IV, written in a letter to his uncle.

This is the story of my meeting with His Majesty. After

Ivan IV the Terrible

Ivan IV, 'the Dread' or (a mistranslation) 'the Terrible', began his reign auspiciously, but egocentricism gave way to paranoia, expressed in irresponsible, cruel and tyrannical behaviour.

Ivan was only three when his father, Grand Prince Vasily III, died in 1533. On coming of age in 1547 he had himself crowned as tsar (emperor), symbolizing his determination to rule as an autocrat whose power was subject only to God. He summoned two councils to regulate the affairs of church and state. A new law code in 1550 strengthened control over the notoriously arbitrary provincial governors. Other reforms systematized the duties and rewards of the middle service class (gentry) and established an élite force of musket-bearing infantry (*streltsy*).

These measures were designed to promote imperial expansion in the east. In 1552–6 Ivan conquered the Tartar khanates of Kazan and Astrakhan, which controlled the strategic Volga artery, enabling Russian merchants and Cossacks to penetrate western Siberia, where another Tartar khanate, that of Sibir on the River Ob, was overthrown in 1582. Russia also gained a foothold in the northern Caucasus.

Ivan chose not to tackle the more formidable Nogai and Crimean Tartars to the south-east and south, who were backed by Ottoman Turkey, but instead turned west. In 1558 he found a pretext to invade the territories of the Livonian knights on the Baltic seaboard. This alarmed neighbouring European states such as Denmark, Sweden and especially Poland-Lithuania (then much stronger than Muscovite Russia), and Ivan waged war with them intermittently until 1582/3, securing only temporary territorial and commercial gains.

The Livonian war strained the country's modest resources and aggravated the internal security problem, especially in the tsar's fevered imagination. He suspected that his wife Anastasia Romanov, who died in 1560, had been poisoned, and disgraced two close advisers who had been associated with his earlier reforms. Other unjustified repressive acts followed: aristocrats had their properties confiscated and some were put to death. The defection to Poland-Lithuania in 1564 of a trusted general, Prince Andrey Kurbsky, seems to have unhinged Ivan's mind. He set up the *oprichnina*, a separate court and administration which took control of certain profitable areas of the realm. Its most trusted members, the *oprichniki*, formed a 'police force' several thousand strong, charged with rooting out alleged subversive elements in the rest of the realm, or *zemshchina*. Nearly two hundred nobles were exiled to Kazan; others were seized, tortured, and executed, sometimes by extraordinarily sadistic means such as impaling, along with their kinsmen and retainers. In 1570 the tsar launched a military campaign against Novgorod; over 2000 people perished. The total number of his victims is thought to have been more than twice this number.

A devastating Crimean Tartar raid on Moscow in 1571 forced Ivan to reunite his tsardom, but in 1575 he apparently contemplated a new purge; he temporarily delegated his powers to a converted Tartar princeling. In 1581, in a fit of rage, he struck dead his son and heir, whose wife thereupon had a miscarriage. Such a deed caused the tsar deep anguish, and made civil war inevitable.

Ivan died in 1584. During his reign thousands of peasants fled to the comparative freedom of the southern borderlands, undermining the state's economic and military power, and alarming landowners. In the 1580s the government responded by limiting peasants' legal right to move, the first major step in the legal imposition of serfdom, which culminated in 1649.

Ψ
All that shines is gold

Long tables were set around the room, on a dais raised two steps higher than the body of the floor. These tables were fully occupied by those who dined with the tsar: each man was dressed in white.

In the middle of the chamber there stood a table or cupboard for the display of plate. It was full of cups of gold. The treasure displayed there included four great pots, or *crudences* as they call them, of breath-taking magnificence. They were of gold and silver and, as I think, a good yard-and-a-half high.

Two gentlemen waited by the cupboard. Each had a napkin on his shoulder, and held a cup of gold which was set with pearls and precious stones. These were the tsar's own drinking cups. When he was so minded, he drunk them dry at a single draught.

Two hundred persons dined that day: and each was served with gold vessels. All the gentlemen that waited at table were dressed in cloth of gold. When serving the tsar, they wore their caps on their heads. Before dinner, the tsar changed his crown; during the meal he changed it twice more.

From a letter by Richard Chancellor

I had been there twelve days, the secretary, who has the audience of foreigners, sent for me, telling me that the tsar's pleasure was that I should come before His Majesty, bringing him the letters of my master King Edward VI. I was glad to receive the summons, and obeyed.

When the tsar was in his appointed place, the interpreter came for me in the outer chamber, where more than one hundred gentlemen sat, each one dressed very sumptuously in cloth of gold. From there I progressed to the council chamber, where I found the tsar himself, surrounded by his nobles. They presented a magnificent spectacle. They sat around the chamber on a dais: yet the arrangement was such that he himself was raised well above his nobles, enthroned on a gilded chair. On this he half leaned, resting one hand on the chair. In his right hand he held a staff of crystal and gold. The tsar wore a long gown of beaten gold and had an imperial crown on his head. The chancellor and the secretary stood before him.

After I had paid my respects, and delivered my letter, he welcomed me, and enquired concerning the health of King Edward my master. I replied that he was in good health at the time of my departure from his court, and trusted that this was still the case. The tsar dismissed me with an invitation to dinner.

Giles Fletcher, English ambassador to Moscow in 1588 and 1589, published his book *Of the Russe Commonwealth* in 1591.

In the passage below he describes Ivan IV's institution of the *oprichnina* (literally, that part of a prince's possessions administered as his private property, and not as part of the state), which he used as an instrument of terror.

Besides the sovereign of Russia himself, there are various degrees of persons or estates, of which the first is the nobility.

These held jurisdiction and absolute authority within their precincts.

Tsar Ivan Vasilyevich began, by degrees, to clip off their greatness until, in the end, he made them his very bondslaves – for so they term themselves.

So that now they hold their authority, lands, lives and all at the tsar's pleasure.

RIGHT *Russian dress of late 14th century; golden robes were often worn at court, favoured as a status symbol.*

BELOW *Another example of Russian costume. Here, boyars and merchants in their respective ceremonial dress.*

To achieve this, Ivan IV divided his subjects into two parts. One he called the *oprichniki*, or special men. Selected from the nobility and gentry, they were placed under his own control and taken as his faithful subjects. The other part he called *zemskie*, or commons. The *zemskie* included those noblemen and gentlemen whom Ivan suspected of disliking him or his government.

The *oprichniki* far exceeded the other part in numbers, money and arms; the *zemskie*, moreover, were deprived of his protection, so that if any of them were harmed or killed by the *oprichniki*, there were no amends to be sought from public justice or by complaint to the tsar.

This freedom of action of the one part to spoil and kill the other enriched that side, and the tsar's treasury, and removed such of the nobility as Ivan disliked. Within one week, three hundred were slain in the city of Moscow alone.

A turning-point of history came when the Stroganovs, a rich family of industrialists, sent the freebooter Yermak, with a tiny force of about 1000, across the Urals in 1581. Yermak's force managed to defeat the Muslim khan of Western Siberia, Kuchum. Yermak and most of his followers were Cossacks: free descendants of often runaway peasants, settled along the southern rivers. Extracts from a folk-song celebrate Yermak's exploits.

On the far-famed steppes of Saratov, a little above the town of Kamyshin, a little below the town of Saratov, there gathered the free Cossack bands.

The Cossacks converged, brothers, in one ring from the Don and Grebni and the Yaik. Their leader was Yermak Timofeyevich, and Astashka Lavrentyevich was their captain.

On the broad and level square in the glorious city of Astrakhan, the Cossacks gathered in one ring and turned their minds to one thought: 'Since chill winter has passed and summer, the warm days of summer will soon be upon us, it is time for us to go on campaign, brothers.' Yermak Timofeyevich addressed his men. 'Let us row up the Volga river, brothers, and cross the towering peaks to reach the Muslim realm. Let us wage war on the realm of Siberia, brothers, and subdue it for the White Tsar. We shall take Khan Kuchum captive, and on this account will our tsar have mercy upon us. Then brothers, I shall go to our White Tsar and plead our case before him, saying, "Hail, our life's hope, O Orthodox Tsar! I am Yermak. I bring you my rebellious head, and along with my head I bring you Siberia's unbounded realm." Then the formidable Tsar Ivan himself will say, "Hail, Yermak! I pardon you and your warriors. On account of the faithful service which you have rendered me, I pardon you, and behold, I grant you the silent expanse of the far-famed Don."'

Ivan the Terrible accepted the newly conquered territory into his realm, which marked the beginning of Russian control over Siberia. Two years later he died; and since, in 1581, he had killed his son and heir, Ivan, in a fit of rage, it was Fyodor, the oldest surviving son, who acceded to the throne, as the *Nikon Chronicle* briefly records.

That winter, in 1584, there appeared a sign in the heavens over Moscow – a cross and a comet. Tsar Ivan's courtiers told him about it, and he came out onto the Red Porch and looked at it, and said to them, 'This is a portent of my death.'

He gave his son the Tsarevich Fyodor Ivanovich his blessing to be tsar in Moscow, and he gave his younger son the Tsarevich Dimitri Ivanovich the town of Uglich with all its revenues for his appanage.

And this done, Tsar Ivan gave up his soul to God on 18 March.

In the same year, after Tsar Ivan's death, people came to Moscow from all the towns of the Muscovite state and implored the Tsarevich Fyodor with tears, that he should, without delay, take up the rule of the Muscovite state and be crowned with the tsar's crown.

Fyodor was crowned soon after the death of his father Tsar Ivan, on Ascension Day.

The Cossacks

The Cossacks were Russian and Ukrainian peasants who sought a distinctive life, free from serfdom and taxation, in a distinctive environment: the valleys of the great steppe-country rivers (Dnepr, Don, Kuban, Terek, Yaik/Ural). They banded together for self-protection in democratic, semi-military, strongly disciplined, self-reliant hosts under an elected leader (*hetman* or *ataman*), and from the mid-16th century, these tough soldiers and adventurers began to play a significant part in Russian history.

The best-known and westernmost host, the Zaporozhians, established themselves on the Dnepr below the rapids, their capital an island called Sech or Sich, from where, for well over a century, they played off Poles, Russians and Ottomans. The Stroganov merchant family, granted the right to exploit the Ural area on behalf of Ivan IV and Fyodor I, hired a force of over 1000 volunteers, mostly Cossacks under the legendary Yermak, who before being killed in 1585 initiated the great Russian eastward expansion. The Cossacks were vitally necessary to Muscovy as crack soldiers, frontiersmen and trouble-shooters, and because of their unpredictability, turbulence and independence, a thorn in its flesh.

The great peasant rebellions of 1670–1 and 1773–4 were both led by Don Cossacks: Stenka Razin (a daring pirate on the Caspian and Volga), and Yemelyan Pugachov, who claimed to be Peter III, and whose manifestos promised a return to ancient peasant and Cossack rights and to the Old Belief. In the 18th century, many Cossacks became settled landowners and their privileges were eroded. However, they remained a powerful cavalry force with a strict, archaic code of honour.

BELOW *Yermak's Cossacks defeat Tartar forces of the khan of Sibir, or Siberia, in 1581.*

Ψ

Boris Godunov

The period of ruin and disorder, known as the Time of Troubles, which followed the extinction of the dynasty of Ryurik, cannot have seemed inevitable at the time. The last tsar of the old line, Fyodor Ivanovich, was succeeded without conflict by his brother-in-law Boris Godunov, who had for all practical purposes ruled the country during Fyodor's reign. Despite some aristocratic disaffection, Boris continued to be an effective ruler during his seven years as tsar, but his sudden death in 1605, leaving a 16-year-old boy as his heir, opened the way for the False Dimitri, a pretender who had challenged Boris by claiming to be the son of Ivan IV, to seize the throne. Soon disposed of despite Polish support, he was replaced by Vasily Shuysky, the head of one of the most prominent noble families. It says something for Vasily's abilities that he was able to survive for four years in the face of the chaos into which the country now descended.

It was to Wladyslaw, son of King Sigismund III of Poland, that the boyars offered the crown when they deposed Vasily in 1610, but this initiative came to nothing as a result of the increasingly demanding conditions imposed by Sigismund. As the country plunged deeper into anarchy, with the Poles occupying Moscow, the Swedes in Novgorod, and the boyar council hardly in control of the rest of the country, salvation appeared from Nizhny Novgorod in the form of a national army headed by the able administrator, Kuzma Minin, and the experienced general Prince Dimitri Mikhaylovich Pozharsky. Free of factional loyalties and with the sole aim of restoring independence and order to the Russian state, this disciplined force succeeded in expelling the Poles from Moscow and pacifying the land sufficiently to allow the convocation of an assembly of the land to elect a tsar, thus establishing the new dynasty of the Romanovs.

OPPOSITE *Boris Godunov (1598–1605).*

Eight years after the death of Tsar Ivan IV, God, on account of our sins, allowed envy and pride and injustice to multiply amongst the tsar's subjects, so that many of them not only hated each other, but even conceived the idea of murdering Tsar Fyodor.

One of these subjects was the boyar Boris Fyodorovich Godunov. The Devil put it into Boris's mind to do away with his righteous lord, Tsarevich Dimitri, and he thought, 'If I get rid of the tsar's line, I shall be master of Russia.'

Boris Godunov sent to Uglich to poison the tsarevich. But whenever they gave the righteous Tsarevich Dimitri the poisonous herbs in his food or drink, God preserved him. When Boris heard that nothing did Dimitri any harm, he was very downcast. He called his friend Mikhail Bityagovsky and gave him presents, and promised him great honour, and sent him to Uglich with his son Danilko Bityagovsky and Mikitka Kachalov.

When they arrived they soon took control of everything. They plotted with Dimitri's nurse Marya Volokhova and her son Danilko, and decided to murder him on 15 May 1591. This accursed nurse, Volokhova, took the tsarevich out into the courtyard. His mother, who had suckled him at her breast, did not want to let him go, so that the wicked woman very nearly dragged him to his death by force, and his mother followed them down onto the lower porch.

Then the wicked Danilko Volokhov took him by the hand and said, 'Is this a new necklace you have, my lord?' 'It is an old necklace,' Dimitri replied in a quiet voice, lifting up his neck towards him. Then Volokhov stabbed him in the neck with a knife, but failed to cut his throat. The tsaritsa, seeing that her son was being murdered, threw herself over him and began to shout. The accursed Danilko threw away his knife and fled, but his accomplices Danilko Bityagovsky and Mikitka Kachalov began to beat the tsaritsa, and leaving her barely alive, took the tsarevich from her and killed him, like a lamb unblemished. He was eight years old.

The above account of the death of Tsarevich Dimitri Ivanovich, taken from the Continuation of the

Nikon Chronicle, represents a version of events which was generally accepted as late as the 19th century, and forms the basis of Pushkin's drama and Mussorgsky's opera, *Boris Godunov*. Most modern historians, however, consider Dimitri's death to have been accidental.

After the extinction of the dynasty of Ryurik, the obvious candidate for the throne was Tsar Fyodor's brother-in-law, Boris Fyodorovich Godunov, who had been in effective control of the administration during the tsar's reign. Boris's show of reluctance, related here by the Nikon continuator, was a political device designed to leave no doubt that he was responding to the will of the nation.

In the year 1598, Tsar Fyodor Ivanovich fell ill, and seeing that he was soon to depart from this vain world into eternal rest, he called for the pious Tsaritsa Irina Fyodorovna, and kissed her and said farewell to her, and told her not to remain on the throne, but to enter a convent. Then he called for Patriarch Job.

The tsar asked to be anointed with the holy oil, and to receive Holy Communion, and he rendered up his honourable and righteous soul to God on 7 January.

There was such great weeping and wailing in Moscow on the day of his burial, that people could not hear the singing, or what they were saying to one another. His reign had lasted fifteen years and ten months, and he had lived thirty-three years.

The boyars and the army and all the people of the realm of Muscovy and people from the capital city of Moscow and from all the towns and villages met Patriarch Job, and implored him to choose a tsar for the country. The patriarch and all those in authority, and the whole country, held a council, and decided to make Tsar Fyodor's brother-in-law, Boris Godunov, tsar, for they had seen his just and firm administration of the country under Tsar Fyodor. But he refused with his lips, though in his heart and mind he had long desired it.

They implored him with tears for many hours not to reject their entreaty. He agreed, and was proclaimed tsar that very day.

Boris Godunov

In the English-speaking world, Mussorgsky's opera *Boris Godunov* has come to be pronounced *Boris Good-enough*, an imprecision that conveys an accidental insight, because Godunov, tsar from 1598 to 1605, has been portrayed as an exceptionally good ruler with a bad and fatal streak. He was handsome and gracious, considerate of the poor, and an advocate of education. But many regarded him as a murderer, intriguer and cruel despot.

Ivan IV's son, Tsar Fyodor, was mentally unfit to rule and Godunov, the new tsar's brother-in-law, soon became regent despite the opposition of several aristocratic families. A favourite of Ivan IV, he had enriched himself, and his wealth was an additional source of power and influence. Most important, perhaps, he had inherited from Ivan a primitive but powerful secret police organization.

Under Godunov, Ivan IV's harsh and unpredictable regime was replaced by a more moderate atmosphere. Territorial expansion was resumed. The patriarch of Constantinople agreed that the Russian Orthodox metropolitan should be re-titled as patriarch, giving Moscow additional prestige. Russians were sent to study abroad. Laws were passed to prevent big landowners kidnapping peasants from small landowners.

In 1598, however, Tsar Fyodor died. Godunov was proposed as his successor but insisted on election by a popular assembly, the *Zemskii sobor*. His detractors asserted that this was window-dressing, to give him extra legitimacy; there were other claimants to the throne. Although Godunov was elected, he was fearful of rivals and, as a result, revived the secret-police tactics perfected by Ivan; unlike his predecessor, he preferred to exile rather than execute his enemies. Of his two most prominent rivals, one went to prison after torture and the other, a Romanov, became an unwilling monk in a distant monastery.

But Godunov could not prevent sporadic disorders in the countryside. His repressions became increasingly paranoid, and his political weakness was aggravated first by a disastrous famine in 1601–3, and then the appearance of a pretender, the so-called 'False Dimitri'.

The original Dimitri, another son of Ivan IV, had died in 1591. His death was implausibly attributed to an accidentally cut throat during an epilepsy attack. As Godunov became increasingly unpopular, rumours spread that he had engineered Dimitri's death, in order to clear the way for his own elevation to the throne; according to his enemies, his repressions were the result of a bad conscience. His supporters claimed that they were reactions to the machinations of his rivals. However, most Russians believed in the justice of God's hand, and drew their own conclusion when Godunov unexpectedly died while rallying support against the forces of the False Dimitri.

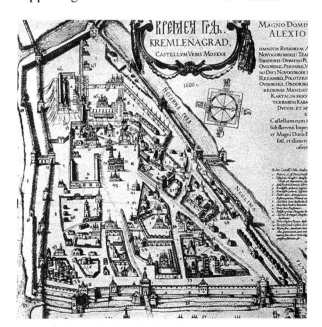

ABOVE *Boris Godunov's plan of the Moscow Kremlin. His building projects included a water conduit to the Kremlin.*

On 1 September 1598, Tsar Boris was crowned in the Cathedral of the Most Pure Mother of God by Patriarch Job and all the rulers of Moscow. Tsar Boris feasted for three days and honoured many of the chief people and appeared good to everyone.

Boris, though an able and energetic ruler, had difficulty in establishing his authority over the members of the aristocratic milieu from which he had himself emerged. Prominent among these were the Romanovs, who like the tsar were connected by marriage to the old dynasty. The 17th-century author of the Continuation of the *Nikon Chronicle*, writing under a Romanov tsar, naturally takes the Romanovs' side against Boris.

Tsar Boris considered that he had cut off the imperial line when he had the Tsarevich Dimitri killed, and wanted to do away with the rest of the old imperial family, that is, Tsar Fyodor Ivanovich's cousins Fyodor Nikitich and his brothers. Tsar Boris hated them, because he wanted to extirpate the imperial family. He incited many people to inform against them, and acting on that information he arrested many of their people.

Their servants, male and female, were tortured to make them give evidence against their masters, but they had no such evil intent, and many of them died under torture rather than slander their masters. Tsar Boris, seeing their innocent blood, had Tsar Fyodor's cousins detained in Moscow for a long time, and eventually had them imprisoned in various towns and monasteries.

The last years of Boris's reign were troubled by the appearance of a pretender, the runaway monk Grigory Otrepyev, who claimed to be the Tsarevich Dimitri Ivanovich and who, with Polish help, raised an army with which he contended for the Russian throne. The outcome of the conflict was determined by Boris's sudden death in 1605.

In Holy Week, on the day before the feast of the women bearing myrrh, as Tsar Boris got up from the table after a meal, he was suddenly taken violently ill, so that there was scarcely time to tonsure him, and he died of that illness within the space of two hours.

He was buried in St Michael's Cathedral in Moscow in the chapel of St John Climacus, where Tsar Ivan Vasilyevich and his children are buried. Tsar Boris died in April 1605, having reigned seven years.

Russian sauna

The Russians heat their *pechi*, which are made like the German bathstoves, that warm their houses to extreme temperatures, especially in winter, which contrast with the severe cold outside.

Because the Russians are used to these extremes of both heat and cold, they bear them patiently. You can see them at times come out of their bathhouses steaming and sweating, and fuming as hot almost as a pig on a spit, and yet, immediately, to season their bodies, leap into a river stark naked, or douse themselves with cold water, and in the depth of the winter at that.

From Giles Fletcher, *Of the Russe Commonwealth*

A highly partisan Russian account of False Dimitri, from which extracts are given below, was written by Avraamy Palitsyn, a monk at the great Trinity Monastery which withstood a long Polish siege – hence a participant in the historical events.

There was a certain monk named Grigory who, whilst still a callow youth, became proficient in necromancy and other evil arts. During the reign of Tsar Boris, he fled Russia and settled within the borders of the kingdom of Poland.

There the false monk lived, penning false letters which he sent everywhere, to announce that he was the living son of Tsar Ivan IV, the Tsarevich Dimitri. In two years he seduced a quarter of the entire world and the whole of Europe with his letters.

In the same year as Boris died, this monk ascended the throne of Boris, adopting the name Dimitri. We know from many witnesses that Grigory was a mere monk who wished to exalt himself as tsar of Russia. This unfrocked monk was always accompanied by a large armed escort. Before him and behind him marched armed soldiers bristling with pikes and halberds and many other weapons. This mass of glinting weaponry made a terrifying spectacle.

The whole court, including the common servants, obeyed his command to revel like bridegrooms. They caroused through the street and decked themselves out in foreign cloth of gold and silver and purple.

Before he was joined in wedlock, the accursed pretender forcibly defiled many virgin souls, male and female, and he even raped pious nuns.

That unfrocked monk connived with the Polish heretics to mow down all ranks of Muscovite society, from the magnates to the humblest functionaries. However, within two days, this cruel plot was uncovered, and ten days after his unrighteous wedding, on 26 May 1606, the accursed pretender himself died a violent death. He had reigned but twelve months.

ABOVE *Tiled stove, or* pechi, *17th century. It was used to heat Krestovaya Palace, Suzdal.*

The following passages from the Continuation of the *Nikon Chronicle* show how Vasily Shuysky, head of one of the most prominent noble families, claiming descent from Ryurik, emerged as leader in the crisis following the removal of the False Dimitri

After the usurper Dimitri had been killed, the boyars followed the advice of Prince Vasily Ivanovich Shuysky: not only failing to consult with the whole country, but without even the knowledge of many

people in Moscow, on 30 May 1606, they came and took Prince Vasily to the Place of Proclamations and proclaimed him tsar.

Then they went with him to the Cathedral of the Mother of God in Moscow, and he began to speak in the cathedral (which had never been done in the whole history of Muscovy), saying that he swore an oath to the whole country, that he would do no ill to anyone without the consent of the council; and that whatever misdeeds had been committed under Tsar Boris, no one was to take vengeance for them.

This period, the Time of Troubles, was one of devastation in Russia. With the old dynasty extinct, how could a true tsar, divinely ordained, be recognized? Such questions were at the root of dozens of popular uprisings. An anonymous English witness, 'J.F.', testifies to this and to the sufferings of Moscow, occupied by the Poles.

On 20 May, Prince Vasily Shuysky was elected tsar.

The nobility and clergy, however, proceeded to elect Wladyslaw, eldest son of the king of Poland, as their tsar. Upon this, Wladyslaw sent a certain Stanislaw Zolkiewski to the imperial city of Moscow, with a force of ten thousand horses, to take possession of the throne and to hold the country for him, an act which caused several riots. The lords of the council, in consequence, caused all the citizens to be disarmed, allowing only one hatchet to every three houses, to be shared by them in order to be able to split their wood for fuel. This act infuriated the citizens, and turned them against the lords and the Poles.

Zolkiewski realized his predicament and pondered on the power of the citizens, weighing it against the weakness of his army in keeping possession of so vast a city. He decided to administer an oath of loyalty to his soldiers, commanding them that on the sixth day of May, at one o'clock in the morning, each one should set fire to his lodgings, and that he should not spare man, woman, or child. These things were done according to his instructions, and more than one hundred and thirty thousand people were massacred, in addition to those who were burned to death.

Thus within a single day all the buildings of that famous city, which was said to cover an area of more than twenty-six miles, were burned to ashes. Only the three stone walls which circled each other, with great distances between them, and the tsar's palace, some monasteries, and some other stone buildings, survived.

But the just hand of Heaven gave retribution for this bloody tragedy. The country forthwith raised two mighty armies under the command of the lords Trubetskoy and Pozharsky. They set a close siege on the city, and blockaded it, and the Poles within. The siege lasted two years, until extreme famine forced the Poles to surrender that famous capital city and, with it, the prince of Poland's claim to the throne and empire of Russia. Out of thirty-five thousand brave men not twenty persons returned to Poland. In this siege a loaf of bread was sometimes sold for a thousand roubles, which is five hundred pounds sterling.

The siege of Moscow

During the time of this cruel siege, in which I was involved for twenty-two months, being lodged in the imperial palace, I observed several causes and instances of misery and wretchedness on the part of the besieged. These included the eating of the flesh of horses, dogs, and cats, and of all sorts of leather, boiled in ditch water, which served instead of tripe. But what left the deepest impression, and most aroused my compassion, was to see many Russian ladies of noble birth, and fair young gentlewomen, who not long before would have scorned the idea that the earth should touch their feet, but who were now constrained to go bare-foot, and to prostitute their bodies to every mean person in order to obtain food. Truly, when they were discarded by some, I have seen them proffer their services to others. I recalled the old proverbs, 'Pride must have a fall', and 'Hunger will break stone walls'.

From an anonymous English witness, J.F.

For four years Tsar Vasily had to contend with political chaos, Polish invasion, and the appearance of yet another False Dimitri, who succeeded in establishing himself at Tushino outside Moscow and is hence known as the Brigand of Tushino. Tsar Vasily's troubles were compounded by the unreliability of the leading boyars, who succeeded in forcing his

deposition, as described in the Continuation of the *Nikon Chronicle*.

In July 1610, Tsar Vasily became very unpopular in Moscow, and the people began to establish communications with the army of the Brigand of Tushino, saying that they would choose a tsar together with them. At the same time, the boyar Prokofy Lyapunov and all his advisers went to the Place of Proclamations and began to cry out that the people should renounce their allegiance to Tsar Vasily.

Many villains and the whole of Moscow joined their side, and they entered the Kremlin and laid violent hands upon the boyars and Patriarch Germogen, and took them across the river to the Serpukhov Gates, crying out that they should reject Tsar Vasily. Only a

ABOVE The All Saints Bridge, Moscow, in the 17th century. The city flourished after its victory over the Poles (1612).

few of the boyars stood by the tsar, and even they quickly deserted him.

During his reign, Tsar Vasily had suffered much misfortune and shame and criticism, but he suffered the final dishonour from his own family, for his brother-in-law, the boyar Prince Ivan Mikhaylovich Vorotynsky, led the crowd into the Kremlin and deposed Tsar Vasily and his tsaritsa from their throne, and took them back to their old residence. He had been tsar for four years and three months.

Tsar Vasily was made a monk and taken to the Monastery of the Miracle (Chudov). The tsaritsa likewise was made a nun against her will and taken to the Convent of the Ascension.

Ψ

Mikhail Romanov

The fate of his immediate predecessors would have been enough in itself to explain Mikhail Fyodorovich Romanov's reluctance to accept the Russian throne, but even without this he seems to have had no enthusiasm for public life or taste for the responsibilities of government. Fortunately he was relieved of the necessity to bear them for the greater part of his reign by the presence of his father Patriarch Filaret, a strong and experienced politician, who governed the country as much in his own name as his son's, even receiving embassies from foreign monarchs.

Mikhail's reign was largely a period of recovery from the Time of Troubles, but his son, Alexis, though he still had serious economic and social problems to contend with, was able to do more to develop his realm. Alexis's reign had its dark side: among the provisions of the law code of 1649 was the final step in the enserfment of the peasants, and any civil disorder was put down with ruthless severity, but it must be remembered that to contemporaries both of these may have seemed welcome steps in the direction of social stability.

Alexis encouraged a movement for reform within the Russian Church which aimed to purge both its ceremonies and its liturgical texts of corruptions that had entered them during the centuries of isolation. The progress of reform was disrupted by the consecration of the peremptory and intemperate Nikon as patriach in 1652. Both the nature of Nikon's reforms, which were perceived by many as innovations rather than as the restoration of the ancient tradition, and his dictatorial manner of introducing them, provoked furious opposition, culminating in the secession from the church of a large body, known as the Old Believers, who continued to worship according to the unreformed tradition. Their most prominent leader was the Archpriest Avvakum.

Alexis Nikhaylovich was the last of the great medieval rulers of his country. By the time of his early death in 1676, the old order was coming to an end.

OPPOSITE *Mikhail Fyodorovich Romanov*
(1613–45).

The metropolitans and the archbishops and all conditions of men came to Moscow from all the towns and monasteries and they set about choosing a sovereign.

Not only the great lords and the state servants, but the ordinary people and even the children as well, they all cried out with a loud voice that they desired Mikhail Fyodorovich to reign over Muscovy.

There was great joy in Moscow that day. All the people went to the cathedral of the Mother of God, and sang prayers and rang the bells and wept, as if they had come out of darkness into the light.

Tsar and Grand Prince Mikhail Fyodorovich of All Russia approached Moscow, and the people came out to meet him with bread, and the lords and boyars met him outside the city with crosses.

The tsar Mikhail Fyodorovich came to his throne in Moscow on the second Sunday after Easter, 1613, and there was again great joy in Moscow, and they sang services.

To complete the restoration of order within the Russian state, it was necessary to elect a new tsar. An Assembly of the Land was convened for this purpose in 1613, and, as described above in the Continuation of the *Nikon Chronicle*, chose the 16-year-old Mikhail Romanov. He belonged to the popular boyar family the Romanovs, and was related to Ivan IV's first wife, Anastasia.

One of Mikhail Fyodorovich's first actions as tsar was to ensure the return from captivity in Poland of his father, Fyodor Nikitich, who had been forcibly tonsured under Boris Godunov, and under the name of Filaret had risen in the Church to be metropolitan of Rostov.

Tsar Mikhail Fyodorovich sent a number of boyars as ambassadors to Vyazma, in west Russia, with Pan Strus, the Polish representative.

When they arrived in Vyazma, the tsar's representatives had to wait a long time for the arrival of the Lithuanian ambassadors to negotiate the exchange of prisoners.

Eventually the ambassadors from Lithuania arrived, bringing with them Metropolitan Filaret Nikitich, Mikhail's father, and all the gentlemen who had been taken prisoner.

There was then another long delay, because the ambassadors wanted them to cede land. But Metropolitan Filaret Nikitich sent to the Muscovite ambassadors, saying that they should not cede an inch

LEFT *Ambassadors of the Moscow* zemstvo *and the people entreat Mikhail Fyodorovich to accept the tsar's crown.*

Serfdom

Serfdom developed with the rise of the Muscovite 'service state' in the 15th and 16th centuries. Kievan Russia's population included a class of slaves, but no serfs; peasant farmers were freemen who could migrate at will, and labourers normally hired themselves out by the year.

In Moscow, under Ivan III (1462–1505) and his grandson Ivan IV (1533–84), the old land-owning boyar aristocracy was gradually ousted by 'service nobility', who held their estates conditionally upon their performance of service, normally military. Because the lands that were their basic remuneration were worthless unless worked, the labour-force had to be legally 'fixed' to them: the peasants, therefore, were in their turn doing state service of a kind, and were under the state's protection. In remote areas such as the north and Siberia, where there were few if any estate-holders, peasants remained freemen.

Serfdom was legitimized by Alexis I in 1649. Peter the Great (1682–1725) strengthened the service state. In the 18th century serfdom was more efficiently enforced, and the serf's position worsened as he was increasingly regarded as his master's possession, with ever-less protection.

Serfs discharged their obligations by working a certain number of days, often three per week (*barshchina*), for their landlord, or by paying a quit-rent (*obrok*). This, more usual where the land was poor, allowed a peasant to take up other employment, with the permission of his master, often in towns: some prospered. A landlord was responsible for his serfs' poll tax; a village commune, *mir* or *obshchina*, distributed land and tasks, and negotiated with the authorities.

Serfdom, though arbitrary, was not slavery. Serfs envied the 'state peasants', who lived on state land and who, although bound to their place of residence, were free to arrange their lives. However, the Crown could hand the land on which they lived to a landlord, enserfing them overnight. The gentry were 'liberated' from service in 1762, but it was 99 years before Alexander II emancipated the serfs.

---

of land to Lithuania. The Lithuanian ambassadors, seeing the strong stand taken by Metropolitan Filaret Nikitich, then agreed to exchange prisoners.

Serfdom spread gradually in late-medieval Russia. Peasants could usually flee to new employers or empty lands in the south or east; but losses of labour caused havoc to landowners, and the state's efforts to reclaim fugitives were steadily extended, as this decree shows, promulgated by Tsar Mikhail in 1634–5.

The Sovereign Tsar and Grand Prince of All Russia, Mikhail Fyodorovich, made a decree, to which the boyars assented.

These are the terms of the decree.

The Tsar and Grand Prince Mikhail Fyodorovich of All Russia is to give back the runaway peasants who have fled in the past ten years, to his, the sovereign's, crown villages and lands.

Further, the patriarch, the metropolitans, the arch-bishops, the bishops, and the monasteries; and the boyars, chamberlains and councillors; and the Moscow gentlemen, the household servants and every rank of Moscow people; and the gentlemen of the towns, and the junior boyars; and the foreigners, and the widows and the minors, whoever they are: all these landlords are to give back the runaway peasants and labourers who ran away to them ten years ago, or less.

Simultaneously, the claimants are to proceed with their suit against the peasants, as chattel property, and against their goods and holdings.

Ψ

Paid to creditors: five children

I, Nikula Leontyev, gardener, of Novgorod, acknowledge that I, Nikula, owe the Novgorod merchants Semyon and Ivan Ivanovich Stoyanov, fifty roubles.

I, Nikula, have no money or goods with which to honour that debt. And in order to pay that debt I, Nikula, have delivered to the merchants' house, my son Senka, my other little son, who is in his second year, and my three daughters, Natalka, Oksyushka, and Ovdotitsa.

My children are to serve them and all those in their house until their masters' death, and are to do any work required of them. My children are to be obedient and submissive to their masters. Semyon Ivanovich and Ivan Ivanovich are free to discipline my children by any means if they are at fault.

I, Nikula, am not to interfere in any matter that affects my children. And since I have nothing to give with which to feed or clothe or provide shoes for my children, they are to receive nothing but their keep. I, Nikula, am guarantor for my children if they steal or run away.

Under these conditions I, Nikula, have made this deed of gift of my children. The public notary Vaska Okhanatkov wrote this deed of gift on the 5th day of May, in the year 1647.

At the request of Nikula, the gardener, and in his stead, Grishka Timofeyev Deksha, a man of the artisan quarter, signed this deed of gift.

Deed of gift by Nikula Leontyev, 5 May 1647

Arts and crafts

Novgorod silversmiths were renowned in the 16th century for innovative and individual work.

Pectoral crosses, almost round with the points of the cross taking the form of a trefoil, and sometimes with enamel decoration, are typical of the period; closely related to ancient stone wayside crosses, within a circle, they indicate the survival of a folk tradition that is also reflected in the silversmiths' translation of the ancient wooden *kovsh* (ladle) into silver. These new precious utensils, richly decorated with foliar ornamentation and enamel, and often made with spoons to form a set, were very popular in 16th- and 17th-century Russia. Most *kovshi* stand on a raised base, or on legs in the form of griffins or lions, an idea taken from western European art, but assimilated to Russian traditions. Inscriptions around the rim wish good health to the drinker, or provide specimens of popular wisdom.

In 1645, at the age of 48, Tsar Mikhail Romanov died, leaving his one remaining son, Alexis Mikhailovich, to succeed him at the age of 16.

The execution of King Charles I of England in 1649 outraged the tsar, who revoked the considerable

Novgorod craftsmen also made silver bookbindings and covers for icons, using complicated and intricate techniques; silver filigree was often combined with enamel, precious stones and pearls.

The best examples of embroidery, one of Russia's oldest forms of artistic creativity, were made in the 15th and 16th centuries. Images, ecclesiastical vestments, shrouds, altar frontals and banners were essential to church ceremonies, while embroidered objects could be carried by travellers and used on military campaigns. Ornamental embroidery was widely used in domestic utensils, fine clothing and headgear. Skilled women embroiderers worked with icon painters and were responsible for selecting the background material: satin, velvet, brocade, or silk of a single colour. Then the pattern would be drawn on it by painters, each of whom specialized in a particular aspect of the work: the icon painter was responsible for the composition and for the faces of the saints, while the ornamental foliage or 'herbs' (*travy*) was by a foliage painter, the inscriptions by a calligrapher and so on. Only when they had completed their tasks was the actual work of embroidery begun.

The embroidered representation of saints is known as 'painting with a needle'. At the same time, ancient folk traditions are evident in images derived from pagan symbolism. Embroideries were kept with care, handed down from generation to generation, and often given to monasteries, whose inventories and donation records provide far more information about embroidered works of art than icons.

Special embroidery workshops in the households of princes, boyars and rich merchants were run by the lady of the house and produced pieces in silver and gold thread, coloured silk, pearls and precious stones. The most prominent of these were at the courts of the grand princes (subsequently tsars) of Moscow.

RIGHT *Bag for salt made of wool, 19th century. The tradition of embroidering utensils has not changed.*

FAR RIGHT *Woman's costume, Armenia. Made of velvet, silk and cotton. Silver amulets are to ward off evil spirits.*

LEFT *Weathervane. Metal craft from the Ukraine.*

trading privileges the English had hitherto enjoyed in Russia. After the Restoration, English merchants again appeared in Moscow, where they were observed by Deacon Paul of Aleppo, a Syrian Christian who visited Russia in the 1660s in the train of Patriarch Macarius of Antioch. In his *Travels of Macarius*, Paul left a voluminous account, in Arabic, of the journey.

All the English ships come to Archangel, which is a port of the empire on the shore of the White Sea. They bring to Moscow all kinds of merchandise; loads of Cretan wine; and wines from Spain and France, and from their own country, of various sorts; and with the wine, oil, also olives, nuts, sugar, biscuit, glass, senna, house furniture, clothing, and other European goods. From the Russians they take sables with the tails, ermine, which they stamp with gold in their country and afterwards export to them and to us, together with fish-teeth. At the feast of the Dormition of Our Lady, on 15 August, is held a great fair for buying and selling when the Muscovite merchants repair to the English with their merchandise, which they sell to them, and purchase theirs.

The principal commodity which the English carry away in their ships is wheat and rye; for the food of the Frank countries is all supplied from the provisions of this. The emperor gives them the wheat and the rye, and receives from them steel coats of mail of wonderful beauty, called *jabakhanah*, arms of all kinds, etc: these are the articles which he wants from them.

We were informed that the distance of the great islands of England from Archangel, when the wind is favourable, is fifteen days' voyage. They are three magnificent islands, near each other, in the midst of the ocean, eight thousand miles in circumference. The first is called Ingliterra, the second Filondra, and the third Scotsia.

One of the greatest upheavals in Russian history began when the zealous and domineering Patriarch Nikon, with the tsar's approval, in 1654 began to revise the service-books and some practices of the Russian Church. The reforms provoked a schism that alienated perhaps half the Russian population from the authorities, who persecuted them, at times harshly. Nikon's doughtiest opponent was the Archpriest Avvakum. His opposition to the reforms earned him exile to Siberia, and eventually martyrdom in the far north. Shortly before this (1672–6), he wrote his own *Life*, the classic 'Old Believer' text. It was unpublished in Russia until the 1860s.

It is thirty years in all that I have been in orders, and I am now over fifty years old.

In the year 1652, the tsar called on Metropolitan Nikon to be patriarch. Once Nikon had become patriarch, he really began to spit venom! During Lent, he sent an instruction to Archpriest Ivan Neronov of the Kazan cathedral, who was my spiritual father. Nikon wrote in his instruction, 'According to the tradition of the Apostles and the Holy Fathers, it is not right to bow down while kneeling, but you should bow from the waist; also you should cross yourselves with three fingers.' The fathers and I met and considered this; we could see that winter was upon us – our hearts were cold and our legs trembled.

Archpriest Daniil of Kostroma and I copied out extracts from the holy books concerning the position of the fingers and bowing down, and we presented them to the tsar. There was a lot written down, and I do not know where he has hidden it, but I suspect he gave it to Nikon. Soon after that Nikon had Daniil seized. After much ill-treatment, Daniil was exiled to Astrakhan, where they put a crown of thorns on his head, and he died there of his treatment, in an underground prison.

After this I was arrested during the night service by a company of *streltsy*, and I was chained up at night at Patriarch Nikon's court. When Sunday dawned, they put me, with bound hands, in a cart, and took me from the patriarch's court to the Andronyev Monastery. I was chained up in a dark subterranean room, and was kept there for three days without food or drink; chained up in the darkness I did not know whether I was bowing to the east or to the west. Nobody visited me except mice and cockroaches, and the crickets chirped, and there were a fair number of fleas, too.

RIGHT The Patriarch Nikon and his clergy. Nikon's reforms caused a great schism in the Church.

I was imprisoned there for four weeks. Then I was exiled to Siberia with my wife and children. We endured too much hardship on the journey to recount it all, except to say that my wife had just given birth, and she was taken along on a cart, ill as she was. It is two thousand miles to Tobolsk, and it took us about thirteen weeks by cart and by water, and half the journey by sledge.

Then an order came that I should be removed from Tobolsk on the Lena for reproaching Nikon the heretic. I was to be sent to Dauria [on the Amur], in the custody of Afanasy Pashkov, who was sent there as commander, and for my sins he was a severe man.

When we were on the River Tunguska, my boat was swamped by a storm: it was filled full of water in the middle of the river and the sail in rags. Pashkov was angry, and at the next rapid started to drive me out of the boat, saying, 'You heretic! It's your fault that the boat is sailing so badly. Go across the mountains, and

Russian fauna

The mountains were high, the woods impenetrable, and there was a stone cliff like a wall so high you could scarce see the top of it. There are big snakes in those mountains, and ducks and geese with fine feathers, and the crows are black and the jackdaws are grey — they have different feathers from the Russian birds. There are also eagles, and falcons, and gerfalcons, and Indian fowl, and pelicans, and swans, and a whole multitude of other wild birds. The mountains are also inhabited by wild animals — goats, and deer, and bison, and elks, and boars, and wolves, and wild sheep: we could see them, but we could not catch them.

From Avvakum, *Life*

keep away from the Cossacks.' Later we travelled five weeks over bare ice on sledges. They gave me two horses for my children and luggage, and my wife and I stumbled along on foot, constantly slipping on the ice.

I returned to Moscow after eight years. The tsar allowed me to kiss his hand, and spoke graciously to me. He commanded that I should be housed in the monastery buildings in the Kremlin. My custodians often took me to the Monastery of the Miracle, where the authorities skirmished with me like dogs. Their final words were: 'Why are you so stubborn, Avvakum? All Palestine, and the Serbs, and the Albanians, and the Wallachians, and the Romans, and the Poles, all cross themselves with three fingers, and only you in your obstinacy insist on crossing yourself with five fingers. It is not right.'

I answered them. 'It is the wolf Nikon and the Devil who have decreed that we should cross ourselves with three fingers, but our first pastors both crossed themselves and blessed others with five fingers.'

Then the tsar sent some *streltsy* and they seized me and also Lazar, the priest, and the elder, Epifany. They took us to St Nicholas' in Moscow and then took depositions from us regarding our faith.

So, after cutting out the tongues of our brethren Lazar and the elder, but without inflicting any such punishment on myself, they exiled us to Pustozerye in the north.

The great Church schism cut across the barriers of class and sex that in Muscovy had been so rigid. The highborn Morozova suffered as painful a martyrdom for the Old Belief as her hero, low-born Avvakum. Her arrest is recounted in the *Life of Morozova*, written in the last quarter of the 17th century.

When this blessed Morozova found out about the innovations in the dogmas of the Church, and the corruption of the ancient traditions and of the church worship, she became very zealous for Orthodoxy and was filled with revulsion and disgust for all the new introductions.

Morozova began to think of greater things, and greatly desired monastic orders. Seeing her unshakable reason and faith, her spiritual mother agreed. Then the blessed Morozova, whose name in religion was now Feodora, saw herself in monastic orders, having received such a great gift of God, and entrusted all her legal business to her faithful servants.

When the time of the tsar's wedding approached (for the Tsaritsa Maria had died, and Alexis wanted to marry Natalia), the blessed lady did not want to go with the other noblewomen to the tsar's wedding.

The holy woman preferred to suffer rather than have to call him 'orthodox', and kiss his hand, and receive a blessing from his bishops.

The tsar was very angry with her all that summer, and began to look for a plausible pretext for persecuting her. Then Joachim, archimandrite of the Monastery of the Miracle, came to her. He asked, 'How do you cross yourself, and how do you say your prayers?' And she, holding her fingers according to the ancient tradition of the holy fathers, replied, 'Lord Jesus Christ, Son of God, have mercy upon us. This is how I cross myself, and this is how I pray.'

Members of the tsar's council came to her and brought chains and put them on her neck; and the blessed Feodora made the sign of the cross and kissed the chains, saying 'Glory to thee, O Lord, that the bonds of St Paul are placed upon me!' They took her in a sledge without respecting her rank, and drove her past the Monastery of the Miracle under the Tsar's Passage within the Kremlin.

And as she sat there, the blessed Feodora stretched out her right hand, showing clearly how she held her fingers, and lifting it up high, made the sign of the Cross frequently and made her chains rattle; for she thought that the tsar was watching her, and therefore she wanted to show him that not only was she not ashamed of their abuse, but she was greatly comforted in the love of Christ and rejoiced in her bonds.

Nikon's arrogance and intransigence eventually proved his downfall. After quarrelling with the tsar, he refused to carry out his functions in Moscow. The *Moscow Chronicle* briefly describes the meeting in 1666–7 of the Church Council, at which Nikon was deposed, defrocked and sent into exile.

In October 1667, the most holy ecumenical patriarchs, namely Paisius, by the grace of God pope and patriarch of Alexandria and ecumenical judge, and Macarius, by the grace of God patriarch of Antioch and all the East, arrived in the great and famous capital city of Moscow, invited by Meletius the Greek at the behest of the most pious Tsar and Grand Prince Alexis Mikhailovich, to deal with Nikon, patriarch of Moscow and All Russia, on account of his having abandoned the patriarchal see of Moscow.

The most holy ecumenical patriarchs decided that Nikon should no longer be patriarch, and divested him of his orders, and decreed that he should be a simple monk, and he was exiled to the Ferapontov Monastery at Beloozero.

Although the Church council condemned Nikon, it nonetheless upheld his reforms, and the last decade of Alexis's life witnessed cruel persecution of the Old Believers. But the greatest upheaval of the reign was political: in 1670, six years before Tsar Alexis died, a bloody and extensive popular rebellion erupted. A river-pirate of Cossack stock, Stenka Razin, sailed up the Volga, slaughtering officials and proclaiming freedom. Soldiers and peasants welcomed Razin, eager to overthrow the corrupt system. A foreign eyewitness, Ludwig Fabricius, left an account of it.

When Stenka Razin with his company reached Pan-shin, a small town situated on the River Don, he stealthily began to recruit the common people, giving them money and promising great riches if they would be loyal to him and help wipe out the treacherous boyars. This process lasted the whole winter, until, by spring, he had assembled four to five thousand men.

In the meantime, four regiments of *streltsy* were despatched from Moscow to subdue these brigands. They arrived with their big boats and, as they were not used to the river, were easily beaten. Stenka Razin gained a large arsenal of ammunition and artillery pieces, and everything else he required. Simultaneously about five thousand men were ordered up from Astrakhan, by water and by land, to capture him.

Stenka prepared for battle and deployed his forces along a wide front. To all those who had no rifles he gave a long pole, charred at one end, to which a rag or a small hook was attached. From afar, they presented a strange sight, and the common soldiers in our army imagined that, since there were so many flags and standards on the plain, there must be a host of people. These soldiers held a meeting and at once decided that this occasion was the chance for which they had been waiting for so long. With all their flags and drums they straightaway deserted to the enemy. They began kissing and embracing one another, and swore to stand together and fight with life and limb in order to exterminate the treacherous boyars, to throw off the yoke of slavery, and to become free men.

PART 5 IMPERIAL

By the time the 'most pious' Tsar Alexis died in January 1676 a number of cracks had already begun to appear in the façade of traditional Muscovite culture, as Russia drew closer to Europe through war, diplomacy and territorial expansion. The Russian Orthodox Church had been divided and weakened as a result of the reforms of the 1650s. A few bold individuals at court even began to adopt a semi-westernized life style. But by western standards Russia still seemed backward, at best a fringe nation of Europe, ruled by an autocratic monarch and hampered by a serf-based economy, without the benefit of a middle class, universities, academies or secular culture.

Foreigners contemptuously referred to Muscovy as a 'rude and barbarous kingdom'. But under Alexis's immediate successors Russia was to become more fully involved in European affairs, for example by joining the Holy League against Turkey during the regency of Alexis's daughter Sophia (1682–9), whose participation in public affairs heralded the emancipation of women from virtual seclusion. The bloody rebellion of the musketeers, or *streltsy*, however, which inaugurated the regency in May 1682, revealed a darker side of Russian life, exposing a web of internecine feuds, religious superstition and xenophobia.

One of the observers of this rebellion was the new tsar, Alexis's nine-year-old son Peter I (1682–1725), who is said to have been alienated once and for all from traditional Muscovy by the horrors that he witnessed.

Of Peter's three boyhood passions, one, a taste for warfare, might have marked him out as a traditional Orthodox sovereign, but his love of foreigners and the sea hinted at new orientations. These three themes dominated his reign, of which the warship is a potent symbol. Peter's reform of the army culminated in Russia's victory over Sweden at Poltava in 1709, one of the decisive battles in European history. He founded the navy, and as its base the new Baltic port of St Petersburg, soon to be the capital of a more westward-looking Russia. He vastly expanded his father's policy of hiring foreigners and outwardly transformed his nobles, depriving them of their beards, dressing them in western fashion by royal decree and forcing them to serve the state.

Whether he was a revolutionary, or an energetic reformer building on the foundations of his predecessors, Peter the Great wrought immense changes, seeking to impose order from above on both society and the environment.

There is much to admire in the Petrine legacy, but it also had its negative side. The new law of succession of 1722, designed to introduce meritocracy at the top, instead brought palace revolutions and court intrigues for the rest of the century. More seriously, Peter created a rift between the Europeanized upper classes and the peasant population, many of whom lived in bondage as serfs, their way of life little different from that of their remote Muscovite ancestors.

A major weakness of Peter's reforms was that so many of them were inspired solely by Peter himself. After his death in 1725, it looked as though a series of ineffectual or under-aged rulers might allow a return to the old ways: Peter's wife Catherine (1725–7), illiterate and self-indulgent, his twelve-year-old grandson Peter (1727–30), his niece Anna (1730–40), a woman with no interest in politics, and Ivan VI (1740–1), a mere infant when he came to the throne. Yet somehow Peter's system, rooted in autocracy and universal state service, survived.

At the beginning of Anna's reign a clique of aristocrats failed to impose a constitution which would have limited the power of the monarch. The reform was opposed by the Guards, a decisive factor in the accession of Peter's successors. It was they who raised

RUSSIA (1676-1825)

Peter's daughter Elizabeth to the throne in 1741, as a counterweight to the unpopular German party at Ivan VI's court. Elizabeth's reign, of which the splendid baroque palaces designed by the architect Rastrelli are the most vivid symbols, saw a consolidation of western education and culture, as German influence gave way to French. Russia basked in military glory as her soldiers won victories over Prussia in the Seven Years War, taking Berlin in 1760.

But just over a year later Elizabeth's successor, her nephew Peter III (1762), recalled his troops and returned Russia's gains to his hero Frederick the Great. After only six months on the throne, Peter was overthrown by a Guards' coup in favour of his German wife, Catherine, soon to be known as the Great (1762–96).

Schooled in the ideas of the Enlightenment (she corresponded with Voltaire and Diderot), Catherine regarded herself as the spiritual daughter of Peter I. She favoured religious toleration, justice tempered with mercy, education for women, civil rights determined within the bounds of class and estate, and the classical style in art and architecture. She also gained military glory for her adopted country, presiding over two successful wars against Turkey and three partitions of Poland, whereby Russia acquired vast territories and stored up political problems along her western borders.

Such territorial acquisitiveness was in keeping with the spirit of the age, but Enlightened theories and domestic realities were often at odds, as the bloody rebellion led by Cossack Pugachev in 1773–4 showed too well. Catherine disapproved of serfdom in theory but could find no painless way to abolish it in practice.

While her reign was dubbed the Golden Age of the nobility, epitomized by their 1785 Charter of Privileges, Catherine has been criticized for neglecting the lower orders. Frightened by the French Revolution, in 1790 she banned a denunciation of autocracy and serfdom written by one of her own nobles, accusing the author of being infected with the French madness.

The reign of Catherine's son Paul (1796–1801), who has gone down in history as the Tsar Madman, served to underline some of the advantages of the Catherinian age, to the nobles at least. A group of them assassinated him in 1801.

The accession of his son Alexander I (1801–25), a young man of liberal convictions, was greeted with enthusiasm. Napoleon's ignominious retreat from Moscow in 1812 and the entry of Alexander's troops into Paris in 1814 gladdened the hearts of patriots and raised hopes of political liberties. Ironically, the French-speaking Russian officer élite who had 'liberated' France enjoyed no institutionalized political power in their own country, outside the privy councils, civil service and army high command, the rank-and-file troops were still drawn from the serfs.

Alexander toyed with the idea of constitutional reform, but his reign ended in reaction. Disillusionment with tsarism, fuelled by a strong dose of European ideas, was the driving force behind the revolt which occurred in St Petersburg shortly after Alexander's death, in December 1825. Young educated army officers from Russia's leading families acted on the best patriotic and humanitarian impulses when they denounced autocracy and serfdom, but they were poorly organized and inadequately supported.

The five who were executed in 1826 were regarded as martyrs by a new generation of revolutionaries, who learned by their mistakes. How remote these young 'Decembrists', educated in the ways of the West, seem from their semi-literate 17th-century boyar ancestors, steeped in Muscovite patriarchal religious culture. Yet Russia's basic institutions changed little in the 150 years which separated them, not excluding the rulers themselves.

Fyodor and Sophia

At the end of the 17th century Russia was a country in transition. During the reign of Alexis she had drawn closer to Europe through war, diplomacy and the hiring of foreign specialists. But by western standards Russia was still culturally backward, a landlocked country ruled by an autocratic monarch, its economy based on serfdom. The short reign of Fyodor III (1676–82), Tsar Alexis's son by his first marriage to Maria Miloslavskaia, saw some internal reforms and an inconclusive war with Turkey. Fyodor, only 14 when he came to the throne, was weak and ailing. Sadly, he did not even have time to continue the dynasty. His first wife and her new-born son died in 1681, and a second wedding in 1682 was followed two months later by Fyodor's death. The senior claimant to the throne was 16-year-old Ivan, mentally and physically handicapped, also the son of Maria Miloslavskaia. Only one other male Romanov survived, nine-year-old Peter, fit and intelligent, but the offspring of Tsar Alexis's second marriage to Natalia Naryshkina.

Peter was proclaimed tsar, and a bloody struggle for power between the Miloslavsky and Naryshkin factions ensued. Moscow's armed guards, the *streltsy*, insisted upon Tsarevich Ivan's right to the throne. In May 1682 a compromise was reached, by which Ivan and Peter were declared joint tsars. A few days later their sister Sophia, then aged 25, was made regent. Her chief minister and reputedly her lover was Prince Vasily Golitsyn. Under his direction Russian diplomatic activity in Europe became more intensive than ever before, the regime's greatest triumph being the 1686 Treaty of Eternal Peace with Poland by which the tsars gained permanent possession of the city of Kiev at the cost of aiding Poland in her war against the Turks. The Russian campaigns were waged against the Tartars of the Crimea, but on two occasions, in 1687 and 1689, Prince Golitsyn returned empty-handed. Military failure precipitated the overthrow of Sophia's regime in September 1689.

OPPOSITE *Fyodor III (1676–82)*

In the present year 1678, on 24 March, on the festival of Palm Sunday, the Great Sovereign Tsar and Great Prince Fyodor Alekseyevich, Autocrat of All the Great and Little and White Russias, was pleased to attend divine liturgy in the church of the Image of Christ Not Made by Hands, in the great sovereign's palace. After the liturgy he was pleased to leave his royal chambers and come out to the cathedral and apostolic church of the Dormition of the Holy Mother of God in the fifth hour of the day.

The great sovereign was clad in a robe of gold cloth embroidered with pearls, and a cap of finest fur. He was followed by the boyars and lords-in-waiting, men of the council and privy councillors, table attendants, crown agents, Moscow servitors, state secretaries and chief merchants, all dressed in gold-spun robes and in caps of finest fur. Officiating in the cathedral at that time was the Great Lord His Holiness Joachim, patriarch of Moscow and All Russia, and their graces the metropolitans with all the clergy. As the sovereign proceeded into the cathedral the choristers, deacons and sub-deacons sang the Polychronion.

After the singing, the Great Lord His Holiness Joachim, patriarch of Moscow and All Russia, with the clergy chanted prayers, and left the cathedral with the precious crosses and the holy icons to go to St Basil's cathedral on Red Square. The great sovereign was pleased to go to that same church, following behind the precious crosses and the holy icons.

Along the route, on both sides of the road marched colonels and captains of the *streltsy* to clear the great sovereign's path.

In the enclosure to the left, going from the town towards the Place of Proclamations, stood the donkey on which His Holiness the patriarch was to ride into the city. Next to the donkey, in the same enclosure, were willow branches set out in a sledge, and the sledge was covered in red cloth. The willow had been decorated and brought from the palace and the armoury. Then the great sovereign arrived, with His Holiness the patriarch and the clergy, at the Place of Proclamations and took up his position at that spot.

Now there began the ceremony of Palm Sunday, during which His Holiness the patriarch presented the great sovereign with a palm leaf and a willow branch. Then His Holiness distributed palm and willow branches to the metropolitans and archbishops and boyars and lords-in-waiting and men of the council and privy councillors.

After the reading from the Holy Gospels, His Holiness Patriarch Joachim of Moscow and All Russia took the precious and life-giving cross of Our Lord in his right hand and the Holy Gospels in his left, and sent Archpriest Michael of the Dormition Cathedral and Iakov the sacrist to the place where the donkey had been tied, with orders to untether it and bring it to the steps of the Place of Proclamations. Then the Great Lord His Holiness Patriarch Joachim of Moscow and All Russia mounted the donkey and rode towards the cathedral in the Kremlin, and the Great Sovereign Tsar and Great Prince Fyodor Alekseyevich, Autocrat of All the Great and Little and White Russia, was pleased to take the end of the donkey's reins and lead it to the cathedral.

Much of Tsar Fyodor's time was spent performing ceremonial duties amidst the pomp of Russo-Byzantine ritual. The above description of a religious procession from the Moscow Kremlin to Red Square in 1678, taken from the official Court records, provides a characteristic example. Shortly after Fyodor's death on 27 April 1682, however, the Kremlin was to witness a less edifying spectacle. Two factions engaged in a murderous struggle for the succession: claimed by the Naryshkin heir Peter, and by Fyodor's young brother Ivan, son of Maria Miloslavskaia. Moscow's armed guards, the *streltsy*, seized the opportunity to air their complaints against cruel commanders and to express their objection to Ivan being passed over by a Naryshkin.

The following description by Andrey Matveyev, an adherent of the Naryshkin camp and later a fervent supporter of Peter I, is one of a number of conflicting accounts of the *streltsy* rebellion; contemporaries were at odds, especially on the degree of pre-planning and collusion with the *streltsy* on the part of Ivan's sister, Sophia Alekseyevna, who soon emerged as the real power in the palace. Matveyev describes the scene when, after two days spent massacring those deemed to be hostile to the Miloslavsky faction and to their own interests, the *streltsy* came to the Moscow Kremlin to demand Tsaritsa Natalia's younger brother Ivan who, it was rumoured, had abused Tsarevich Ivan and even desired the crown for himself.

On 17 May 1682, in that most bitter time, the wicked *streltsy* rebellion reached its height. After their intrusion into the Kremlin the savagery grew greater still, quite beyond human comprehension. For the Moscow *streltsy* shamelessly set off in a frenzy of hard-hearted rage and bestial fury; marching with their pole-axes and pikes to the ceaseless tolling of the great Kremlin bell and the beating of drums, insolently they went forth. Most of them were quite inhuman in their drunken and noisy state, more like wild beasts than men as they proceeded in a great throng. They approached the palace, coming right up to the entrance closest to the tsar's chambers with its golden barrier, and with a great shout, angrily and uncouthly, they demanded that those listed be handed over to them. Threatening violence to all the boyars, they demanded the immediate hand-over of Tsaritsa Natalia's brother, the boyar Ivan Naryshkin, without whom they refused to leave the Kremlin that day.

The boyars conveyed to Tsaritsa Natalia the *streltsy's* urgent demand for her brother. It was now that Tsarevna Sophia Alekseyevna could no longer keep her secret concealed, and for the first time brought public suspicion upon herself by telling Her Majesty the tsaritsa in a sharp voice that there was no way now they could avoid giving up her brother to the *streltsy* this very day without bringing general calamity upon themselves and everyone else.

Heinrich Butenant, a German resident in Moscow who had himself narrowly escaped being murdered the previous day, here gives his own version of how Ivan Naryshkin was handed over to the *streltsy*, and describes the gruesome fate that awaited him.

ABOVE *The Kremlin, target of the rebellious streltsy.*

The *streltsy* cried: 'We know that you have Ivan Naryshkin hidden. Give him up or we shall search for him ourselves until we find him, and then it could be worse for all of you. We give old Naryshkin and his three younger sons their lives, but Ivan Naryshkin shall and must die by our hands.'

The elder tsaritsa, Natalia, begged them to have a little patience. She went upstairs and persuaded the younger tsaritsa, Martha (widow of Fyodor III), and the Tsarevna Sophia to go out with her and beg for the life of her brother Ivan Naryshkin. She also persuaded a metropolitan to come down with an icon of the Virgin. Natalia brought out her brother, who hid behind her, with the icon of the Virgin which the metropolitan held on his chest. Both tsaritsy, together with Tsarevna Sophia Alekseyevna, fell down on their knees and prayed for Ivan Naryshkin's life, but it did

ABOVE *Sophia Alekseyevna, regent of Russia 1682–89.*

no good. A *strelets* (armed guard), casting aside all shame and restraint, grabbed Ivan Naryshkin by his long hair and dragged him to the torture chamber (which was not far off, between the palace walls).

Ivan Naryshkin was strung up, yet no matter how much they tortured him, he spoke not a word but kept his teeth firmly clenched; whereupon he was sent to the marketplace with some *streltsy* and in all haste was chopped into small pieces, and his head, hands and feet were set up on stakes.

With Ivan Naryshkin's execution, the rage of the *streltsy* abated. A compromise was reached and on 26 May 1682, Ivan and Peter were named joint tsars. Sophia, aged only 25, became regent. Under her rule, Russia saw more diplomatic activity than ever before. Russian embassies were dispatched all over Europe. Ambassador Vasily Postnikov brought the following credentials to London, where he arrived in September 1687 at the Court of King James II.

Through the mercy and grace of Almighty God, through whom we are established and led in the way of peace, We, the most serene and most powerful Sovereigns, Tsars, and Grand Princes of All Russia, etc., send you, our dearly beloved and most powerful brother, James II, by the grace of God king of Scotland, England, France and Ireland and other dominions, etc., our most friendly and most fraternal greetings.

We have always wished to advance the cause of unity in Christendom. Certain events have alerted us to the increasing numbers of the enemies of Christendom. They, finding us unallied with other realms, took advantage of our isolation by warring against us. Nevertheless, we have withstood and dispersed their armies without help or assistance from any other kingdom.

These enemies, finding that they were losing both the war and men, made a truce with us for a fixed period. This done, they turned their forces against our dearly beloved brothers, his Imperial Majesty, the Emperor, and his Royal Majesty of Poland. Whereupon we have been pleased to conclude a treaty with his Royal Majesty of Poland establishing perpetual and inviolable friendship and alliance against those above-mentioned enemies, so that by this concord the whole Christian world might flourish and the enemies of the Holy Cross be suppressed and routed.

To further strengthen the alliance with our beloved brother, the king of Poland, we, through our honourable envoy Vasily Postnikov, are pleased to acquaint you with all the details of this alliance; and to tell you of our own good health and prosperous government. He is likewise to enquire concerning your Majesty's health and prosperity, and to congratulate your Majesty on your accession. He is to inform you of our desire for friendship and closer co-operation, so that brotherly love and friendship may always increase between such powerful princes.

We, the most powerful Sovereign Tsars, are confident that your Royal Majesty will accept our envoy's account of affairs as a matter pleasing to God, and necessary for all Christendom, and that you will show to a greater degree than usual the proof of your goodwill and friendship. We shall not fail to do likewise. By

ABOVE *The centre of Moscow, described by Schleissing in the 17th century as a 'miserable little village'.*

these efforts our friendship will continue to increase, to our mutual comfort and aid. In the same spirit of peace and Christian aspiration we wish your Royal Majesty many years of good health, prosperous rule and increase of good government.

Given at our court in our city of Moscow, 16 February 1687, in the fifth year of our reign.

Many foreigners visited Moscow, some of them entering the tsar's service. Georg Adam Schleissing, a soldier from Saxony, records his impressions of the city from a visit in 1684–6.

The main seat of government, the town of Moscow, is big and quite extensive – viewed from afar the residence of the tsar looks like a little world all of its own. In diameter, excluding the outlying *slobody* or suburbs, the town stretches for about three German miles and appears quite beautiful, even entrancing, thanks to its many monasteries and churches. But as you get closer and finally reach the centre you notice that it is in reality just like all Russian towns, that is not much more than a miserable little village, constructed without the slightest notion of architectural order or art.

The streets, for example, are not paved with stone but simply covered over with wooden planks – I would describe them as wooden alleys. And even after a light shower of rain the wood often crumbles away as a result of people constantly walking or riding over it and then such a huge stream of mud shoots up that you can barely pass even on horseback, especially in autumn. And sometimes in really bad weather you can end up head over heels in the mud.

The houses are built just like the ones in other Russian towns, of wood, and in some districts and streets quite badly built. The only exceptions are the houses of some of the boyars, princes, military commanders and courtiers, and also the chief merchants. Their houses are sometimes built of stone and are called 'palaces'. It's true, the last of the late tsars, the brother of the two current rulers, Ivan and Peter, was a most worthy prince. He saw to it that a great quantity of stone was brought to the city. Those who wished to live in the centre were obliged to build new houses of stone and demolish the wooden ones.

Because everything is built of wood, there are lots of fires, especially on their feast days, when they light wax candles. They stick up these candles around their holy pictures to burn all day and all night. Often I observed nocturnal revels, when they rang the alarm bells and shouted and yelled in such a barbaric fashion that I was scared out of my wits and wondered whether a rebellion had broken out. I just couldn't get used to such goings-on. I would leap from my bed and ask the servant, 'Where's the fire?' And back would come the reply, 'Oh, a long way off, it's a mere trifle. Go back to sleep, German, no one is going to come creeping into your bed tonight.' Then he would laugh and say, 'Now when our German goes home he will be able to say that he has seen a little bit of a Muscovite blaze.'

Sophia could not escape the day when Peter, fast maturing, would dispense with her services as regent. This crisis was hastened by the failure of Russia's two campaigns against the Tartars, allies of the Turks, in the Crimea. The commander-in-chief on both occasions was Prince Vasily Vasilievich Golitsyn, Sophia's chief minister, head of the foreign office, and rumoured to be the regent's lover.

A Frenchman using the pseudonym Foy de la Neuville visited Moscow in 1689, acting as agent to King John of Poland. He met Golitsyn and was very impressed by him, as is evidenced by this extract from his account of his visit to Russia, which was published in 1698.

Prince Vasily Golitsyn had an extremely magnificent stone college built, the Slavonic-Greek-Latin Academy. He brought to Moscow from Greece twenty or so doctors and many fine books, exhorted the great to make their children study, allowed them to send them to Latin colleges in Poland and advised them to employ Polish tutors for the remainder; he gave foreigners the right to enter and leave the realm, which had never been done before his time. He also encouraged the Russian nobility to travel and to learn the arts of war in foreign lands, for his plan was to have good soldiers, instead of the legions of peasants whose land remains uncultivated when they are led away to war; to replace this useless service to the state, he meant to impose a reasonable tax on each peasant's head.

The prince also intended to keep ministers in the principal courts of Europe and he planned to have liberty of conscience in his country.

Golitsyn had already received Jesuits in Moscow, with whom he often spoke. These were driven out straight after his disgrace with a declaration from the Tsars Ivan and Peter to the emperor of Austria and the king of Poland, who had sent them, that they would receive no more Jesuits in their country.

If I wished to write down everything which I have learned of this prince I would never be done. Suffice it to say that he wished to people the deserts, enrich beggars, make men of savages, heroes of cowards, and to turn shepherds' huts into palaces of stone. His own palace is one of the most magnificent in Europe. It is roofed with copper, furnished with very rich tapestries and highly curious paintings. He also had one built for foreign ministers, which whetted the appetites of the great and the populace, for during his ministry more than three thousand stone houses were built in Moscow.

Neuville witnessed the overthrow of Sophia and Golitsyn by Peter's supporters in September 1689. He was not sanguine about the capabilities of Russia's new rulers, foremost amongst whom were members of the Naryshkin clan.

Those who most rejoiced at the elder Golitsyn's disgrace are today well aware of their loss, for the Naryshkins who now govern them are ignorant and brutal in equal measure and are starting to destroy everything which that great man did for the glory and advantage of the nation.

They wish to earn renown for themselves by resuming their former guise, a guise which is as foul-smelling as it is black.

These savages have begun by once more forbidding entry to their country to foreigners and by taking away rights of religious expression from Catholics, of whom only the Polish envoy still has a chapel. It is even thought that they will in future restrict Muscovites to learning only how to read and write, as before, making their government tyrannical in that as in other things. This will make everyone miss the great prince.

The Russian Renaissance

For several centuries after the Mongol invasion of 1237–40, Russian culture remained almost untouched by developments in the West. The Russo-Byzantine icon, fresco and church building were the symbols of Holy Russia. Gothic art passed her by and the Renaissance reached her only in fragments and snatches.

It was the second half of the 17th century before the Orthodox Church began to lose its grip on culture, and secularization started to make more and more inroads. These changes resulted from increased contact with the West, especially through Poland, and the influx of foreigners, mostly mercenaries from the Protestant countries of northern Europe, into Moscow, and the schism in the Church, when thousands protested against Patriarch Nikon's reforms of the 1650s. In 1672–6, for example, a court theatre operated in Moscow with the help of German residents, although attendance was restricted to a narrow circle of royalty and courtiers. From the 1650s the first realistic likenesses of rulers were painted; Russian painters made their first experiments in the use of chiaroscuro and perspective, applied mostly to religious painting; a modified classical order system appeared in architecture alongside traditional devices; and the first court poetry was written, based on models imported from Poland. Russian culture was in transition. In the 1680s these semi-westernized trends blossomed in the Moscow baroque style, which has been associated with a delayed Russian Renaissance and which was also distinguished by vivid colours, elaborate decorativeness and high standards of workmanship.

In architecture, Moscow baroque can be seen in churches commissioned in and around Moscow in the 1680s–90s by élite patrons closely associated with court circles. Built by largely anonymous

ABOVE *Tsar Fyodor Ivanovitch (17th century painting on wood showing signs of age).*

Russian master masons – the profession of 'architect' did not yet exist – out of red brick, they were sometimes painted and usually decorated with ornate sculptural details in limestone: pediments, columns, pilasters, decorative scrolls and volutes inspired by western sources, mostly illustrated books and engravings, and capped with golden domes. Commissioned by the regent Tsarevna Sophia in the Novodevichy Convent, three churches, and a bell tower were built in the new style between 1685 and 1689.

Prince Vasily Golitsyn, also a patron of the new fashion, built a mansion decorated with Moscow baroque carving as well as a church. The interior of his house eloquently demonstrated his advanced tastes. He had a gallery of portraits of his family and of Russian and foreign royalty, a new phenomenon in Russia. The ceiling of the

ABOVE The Last Judgement. *17th century Yaroslavl icon.*

reception chamber was painted with the signs of the Zodiac. The rooms were filled with furniture, fittings and objects of foreign origin, and many books on non-religious topics – this at a time when traditional upper-class Russian homes still contained only icons and devotional books. Golitsyn had his own portrait painted and engraved, as did Sophia, the latter in royal regalia surrounded by the seven virtues, probably the first true female likeness in Russian history.

Sophia and Golitsyn's political opponents, the Naryshkin family, were also devotees of the new style; sometimes referred to as Naryshkin baroque, its most remarkable surviving monument is the church of the Intercession of the Virgin at Fili, near Moscow, built in 1690–3 by Peter I's uncle, Lev Naryshkin. The design is the 'octagon on cube', a lavishly ornate tower of receding octagons. Inside, the Naryshkins commissioned an elaborately gilded baroque screen separating the sanctuary from the main body of the church, on which icons were to be placed (the iconostasis), and icons in the new naturalistic style strongly influenced by Catholic art. St Peter and John the Baptist, an allusion to the ruling tsars Peter and Ivan, is an example.

The new trends in painting – light and shade, perspective, realistically depicted landscape, buildings and objects – first appeared in icons, notably in the royal workshops in the Moscow Kremlin headed by the painter Simon Ushakov (1626–86). Ushakov also painted portraits, none of which has survived, but there are examples by his contemporaries. This type of primitive or 'naïve' portrait, known as a *parsuna* (after the Polish word for person), was heavily influenced by icon-painting technique and, in the case of the posthumous portrait of Tsar Fyodor, was for devotional use. Russian painters were still uneasy about attempting to capture a sitter's personality or depicting traits other than piety.

Provincial schools of architecture, painting and applied art flourished, although western influence was less marked outside Moscow. The Volga town of Yaroslavl had a successful school of icon-painting and boasted new churches funded by local merchants, often decorated with coloured tiles and glowing frescos. The craftsmen of Solvychegodsk, the town founded by the Stroganov merchant family, produced coloured enamelware and icons in the miniaturist style. During the 1680s, Metropolitan Jonas constructed an impressive complex of churches in the Kremlin of Rostov-on-Don. All over Muscovy craftsmen produced metalwork, embroidery, enamel and silverware, some of traditional design, some betraying the influence of western art.

Although most of the new trends originated in religious art, they offended orthodox traditionalists, who were ever alert for heretical influences, especially from Catholicism. But their protests came too late. By the 1690s, secular art for state purposes – banners, triumphal arches, engravings, portraits – was being commissioned by the court to supplement or even replace traditional religious imagery.

A landmark in this process is Sir Godfrey Kneller's portrait of Peter I, painted during the tsar's visit to England in 1698. Peter's beardless face, the martial and naval imagery of armour, fortress plans, cannon and anchors, contain not a trace of Holy Russia.

BELOW   *Baroque iconostasis in a Moscow church.*

The arch-conservative head of the Russian Orthodox Church, Patriarch Joachim, welcomed the overthrow of Sophia and Golitsyn as an opportunity to counteract foreign, and especially Catholic, influences. In this extract from his *Testament* written just before his death in March 1690, Joachim warned Tsars Ivan and Peter against foreign 'guile', but to no avail. The hiring of foreign experts was one of the cornerstones of Peter's programme.

May our sovereigns never allow any Orthodox Christians in their realm to entertain any close friendly relations with heretics and dissenters – with the Roman Catholics, Lutherans, Calvinists, and godless Tartars (whom our Lord abominates and the Church of God damns for their God-abhorred guiles); but let them rather be avoided as enemies of God and defamers of the Church. May they command by imperial decree that men of foreign creeds who come here to this pious realm shall under no circumstances preach their religion, disparage our faith in any conversations, or introduce their alien customs derived from their heresies for the temptation of Christians; they should be strictly forbidden to do all this on pain of severe punishment.

I again implore Their Most Serene Majesties, the pious tsars, and call upon them before God, our Saviour, that they prohibit in the whole realm all accursed foreign heretics and dissenters from exercising any kind of command in their regiments: but let them order that these enemies of Christendom be completely removed from such positions. For these dissenters do not agree in faith with us, Christians, who are in possession of true Orthodoxy; they are completely at variance with us in interpreting the tradition of the holy fathers; they are alien to our mother, the Orthodox Church. Of what help could such accursed heretics be to the Orthodox army? They only bring on the wrath of God. The Orthodox pray to God according to the rules and customs of the Church while they, the heretics, sleep, and perform their abominable deeds, despising Christian prayer. The Christians honour the most pure Mother of God, the Virgin Mary, and invoke in every way her aid and that of all the saints; but the heretics – the ungodly military commanders – revile it and blaspheme;

A homesick Scotsman

I now began seriously to consider how I might leave this country, which I not only found disagreeable but which had also fallen far short of my expectations. For example, I saw that strangers were looked on as a company of hirelings. At best they were regarded (as they say of women) as a necessary evil. No honours or advancement were to be expected here, other than military office. Even then the command was limited, and a good patron or patroness, and a bribe, in either money or kind, were required.

The upper classes consider foreigners barely Christian, and the lower classes regard them as outright heathen. No one is accepted as a compatriot unless he first abjures his own religion and accepts theirs. Foreigners cannot marry native Russians. The people themselves are sullen, miserly, avaricious, deceitful, untrustworthy, rude, and cowardly. Despite this they are arrogant and think themselves better than all other nations.

The worst of all is that the rate of pay is low and is, moreover, paid in base copper coin at an exchange rate of four to one with silver. I could thus see that it would be impossible to live from day to day let alone enrich myself, although, before I left Poland, I was led to believe that I would gain profit and wealth. These, and many other reasons I have not mentioned, were all too sufficient for my decision to leave this place.

From General Patrick Gordon, Diary

ABOVE *The domes of the Tsar's Chapel, Moscow (shown in colour on page 86), embodiment of the Russian Church. Patriarch Joachim castigated foreign customs.*

they do not honour the holy icons; they scoff at all Christian piety. Christians observe the fasts; heretics never. No good can come from allowing a heretic – a non-Orthodox man – to hold in bondage, to command, or to judge the Orthodox Christians in the realm of the pious tsars. Are there no Orthodox men fit to fill these positions and to perform in them capably? Indeed, by God's grace, the Russian tsardom abounds in pious men among its subjects, who are well versed in military science and skilled in leading troops.

Let me remind you again not to allow, under any circumstances, the heretic dissenters to bring in any new Roman Catholic and alien customs, nor to introduce the wearing of foreign dress. This is not good but evil in every way. This situation should be dealt with resolutely, both now and later, by pious men and especially by the most autocratic tsars and sovereigns, whom it behoves to provide wise direction to their realm, for its welfare and advantage, but most of all for the glory of God.

Peter I the Great

Peter I (ruled 1682–1725), dubbed 'the Great' in 1721, is arguably the key figure in Russian history. When Sophia and Golitsyn were overthrown in September 1689 it was the latter's military defeats which persuaded Peter to depose him, but the 17-year-old was as yet indifferent to politics, and for a few years his mother's relatives, the Naryshkins, held power at court. Until 1696 Peter ruled jointly with his handicapped brother, Tsar Ivan V, who died in that year.

The autocrat was soon to come into his own, however, as Peter's boyhood passions – boats, warfare, and contacts with foreigners – began to mould his adult policies. Already in 1689 he had assembled the 'play' regiments of Guards which were to provide the backbone of the reformed Russian armies. He had learned to sail, a frustrating pastime in a landlocked country. And he soon began to frequent Moscow's German or Foreign Quarter.

After Peter visited Western Europe itself in 1697–8 he forced his nobles to shave in the western manner and to don western dress. Foreign experts – soldiers and sailors, doctors, shipwrights, architects, painters – were engaged in vast numbers, and institutions on western lines were founded. Between 1700 and 1721 Russia was at war with Sweden. Peter's reforms of the Russian army culminated in victory at Poltava in 1709, although it took another decade to reach a political agreement. Peter founded the navy, using as its base the new port and eventually capital St Petersburg, built on empty marshland near the mouth of the River Neva, won from the Swedes. When Peter adopted the title of emperor in 1721, after final victory over Sweden, a contemporary wrote that he had transformed Russia 'from nothingness into being'.

OPPOSITE *Peter I, the Great (1682–1725)*

Tsar Peter I is very tall, his features are fine, and his figure very noble. He has great vivacity of mind, and a ready and just repartee. But with all the advantages with which nature has endowed him, it could be wished that his manners were a little less rustic. We immediately sat down to table. Herr Koppenstein, who did the duty of marshal, presented the napkin to His Majesty, who was greatly embarrassed, for at Brandenburg, instead of a table napkin, they had given him a basin and ewer after the meal.

He was very gay, very talkative, and we established a great friendship for each other; he exchanged snuff boxes with my daughter. We stayed, in truth, a very long time at table, and we would gladly have remained there longer still without feeling a moment of ennui, for the tsar was in very good humour, and never ceased talking to us. My daughter had her Italians sing. Their song pleased him, though he confessed to us that he did not care much for music.

I asked him if he liked hunting. He replied that his father had been very fond of it, but that he himself, from his earliest youth, had had a real passion for ships and navigation. He showed us his hands, and made us touch the callous places that had been caused by work. His own musicians played Russian dances, which he liked better than Polish ones.

The Russian retinue includes four dwarfs. Two of them are very well proportioned, and perfectly well bred; sometimes Peter kissed, and sometimes he pinched the ear of his favourite dwarf. He took the head of our little princess, Sophia Dorothea, and kissed her twice. The ribbons of her hair suffered in consequence. He also kissed her brother (later George II of England).

He is a prince at once very good and very *méchant*. He has quite the manners of his country. If he had received a better education, he would be an accomplished man, for he has many good qualities, and an infinite amount of natural wit.

In 1695 Russia's war with Turkey was resumed, and with the aim of forming an anti-Turkish league, Peter set off incognito for Europe in March 1697.

The journey, the first ever undertaken by a Russian ruler to the West, took Peter first through the Baltic States and North Germany. In July 1697, at the town of Koppenbrügge, near Hanover, he was invited to a reception by Sophia, the widowed electress of Hanover. The above account is an extract of Sophia's impressions upon meeting her exotic visitors.

From Hanover Peter travelled to Amsterdam, where for most of the next four months he worked in the shipyards of the East India Company and visited factories, museums, and scientific institutions. In Holland Peter met the prince of Orange, King William III of England, who, in January 1698, provided him with a ship and escorts to bring him across the Channel.

Bony ladies

I could embellish the tale of the journey of the illustrious tsar by telling you that he is sensible to the charms of beauty; but, to come to the bare fact, I found in him no disposition to gallantry. If we had not taken so many steps to see him, I believe that he would never have thought of us. In his country it is the custom for all women to paint their faces, and rouge forms an essential part of their marriage presents. That is why Countess Platen singularly pleased the Muscovites; but in dancing, they took the whalebones of our corsets for our bones, and the tsar showed his astonishment by saying that the German ladies had devilish hard bones.

Sophia, electress of Hanover

OVERLEAF *Peter the Great at Deptford dockyard near London. The naval knowledge he gained during his visit to England was put to good use when he returned home.*

ABOVE *Peter the Great's house in Zaandam, Holland.*

Much of Peter's time in London was devoted to shipbuilding in the Deptford dockyards, but the tsar's insatiable curiosity also took him to the Woolwich Arsenal, the Tower, the Royal Observatory, the Houses of Parliament, the Mint, Windsor Castle, Hampton Court and Oxford University. He reviewed the fleet at Spithead. He even showed an interest in ecclesiastical matters. Gilbert Burnet, bishop of Salisbury, was entrusted with briefing the tsar about the Church of England. He met Peter several times, and left an account of his impressions of the 26-year-old ruler.

The tsar came over to England this winter, and stayed some months among us. I was ordered both by the king and the archbishop and bishops to attend upon him, and to offer him such information of our religion and constitution as he was willing to receive.

Peter I is a man of a very hot temper soon inflamed, and very brutal in his passion; he raises his natural heat by drinking much brandy, which he rectifies himself with great application: he is subject to convulsive motions all over his body.

He wants not capacity, and has a larger measure of knowledge than might be expected from his education, which was very indifferent; a want of judgement, with an instability of temper, appear in him too often and too evidently.

But the tsar is mechanically inclined, and seems designed by nature to be a ship's carpenter rather than a great prince. This was his chief study while he stayed here: he wrought much with his own hands, and made all about him work at the models of ships. He told me that he designed a great fleet at Azov to attack the Turkish empire; but he did not seem capable of conducting so great a design, though his conduct in his wars since this has uncovered a greater genius in him than appeared at that time.

Tsar Peter was desirous to understand our doctrine, but he did not seem disposed to mend matters in Muscovy. He was indeed resolved to encourage learning, and to polish his people by sending some of them to travel in other countries, while drawing strangers to come and live among them. He seemed apprehensive still of his sister Sophia's intrigues. There was a mixture both of passion and severity in his temper. He is resolute, but understands little of war, and seemed not at all inquisitive that way.

After I had seen him often, and had conversed much with him, I could not but adore the depth of the providence of God that had raised up such a furious man to so absolute an authority over so great a part of the world.

In 1698 news of another revolt of the *streltsy*, this time in protest at unpopular postings away from their homes in Moscow, ill-treatment by foreign officers

Peter the technician

Westernization, as state policy, began in the reign of Peter the Great (1682–1725), who had a robust enthusiasm for most things western, in particular in the areas of civil and military technology, administration and manners.

He showed an early interest in military and naval matters and in the use of scientific instruments. His friends among the merchants, soldiers and craftsmen in the Foreign Quarter of Moscow encouraged him to look for the best western models, to develop the technologies which Russia needed. Technical books were translated and printed, first in Amsterdam, then, from 1703, in Russia. Throughout his reign young men were sent to Italy, Germany, France, Holland and England, generally to acquire naval skills, and large numbers of foreign technicians were invited to work and teach in Russia. Venetian and Dutch craftsmen built many of the ships in Peter's first fleet, with which he took Azov from the Turks in 1696. Dutch, and later English, builders were prominent in creating his Baltic and White Sea fleets.

In 1697–8, Peter and his suite travelled incognito, first to Holland, where he met Dutch scholars and worked as a ship's carpenter. While there he had a secret meeting with William III, king of England, and stadholder of the States-General. Prompted by the British merchants of the Muscovy Company, and others in the tobacco trade who wished to gain privileges in the Russian market, William induced Peter to come to England by promising him access to English ship design and offering him, as a gift, a small experimental warship, the fastest then afloat.

The tsar was placed in the care of two English admirals and given the use of John Evelyn's house in Deptford, next to a shipyard, where he embarked on a hectic programme of scientific and naval activities. He studied ship construction and navigation with leading experts, visited the Mint and the Royal Observatory, sailed yachts in the Thames and viewed gunnery trials and a mock sea battle.

He also arranged for English craftsmen and technicians to go to Russia, mostly to build and train his navy. Henry Farquharson, a mathematician from Aberdeen, went to Moscow with two young men from the navigation school at Christ's Hospital to staff the new Mathematics and Navigation School – the first secular school in Russia. For the next few decades, the British teachers, with Leonty Magnitsky, trained all Russia's future navigators, draughtsmen, surveyors and astronomers. The school, and the Naval Academy which developed from it and was founded in 1706, produced a new professional class. They also supervised a network of 'cipher schools' that Peter set up in monasteries and episcopal centres, in 1716.

Peter's reforms were also strongly influenced by the German philosophers and mathematicians, Gottfried Leibniz and Christian von Wolff, and scientific links with France – he travelled there in 1717, was elected to the French Academy, met scholars and instrument makers and bought large numbers of scientific instruments.

He was primarily interested in technology and education which could be of use to his modernized state – naval, military, manufacturing, engineering – and in geographical discovery, cartography and canal and port construction. However, he was also interested in astronomy, built up a considerable library in a wide variety of subjects and languages and established a large 'cabinet of curiosities'.

He reorganized the Russian Church, abolishing the office of patriarch and, at the end of his life, Peter the Great founded the Russian Academy of Sciences.

and displeasure at the tsar's sojourn among 'heretics', forced Peter to cut short his tour. He arrived back in Moscow in August 1698, to learn that the former regent Sophia had allegedly sent a letter to the *streltsy* inciting them to rebel in her favour. Peter went to the convent to question Sophia in person, probably the first time they had met since 1689, but she denied everything. Peter did not succeed in convicting Sophia, but hundreds of *streltsy* were cruelly put to death, as the Austrian envoy, Johannes Korb, records in graphic detail in his memoir, here describing events in Moscow in the autumn of 1698. The Russian authorities were later to demand the withdrawal of his book on the grounds that it painted an exaggeratedly barbaric picture of Russian life. Sophia did indeed take the veil, as Korb indicates, probably on Peter's orders.

The tsar invited all the foreign ambassadors to this display of judicial vengeance. His motive was to reassert, on his return, that sovereign prerogative of life and death which the rebels had contested.

There were two rebels whose thighs and other parts of whose bodies were broken while they were in front of the palace of the Kremlin. They were then set, still alive, on the wheel. The corpses of twenty other rebels, who had been executed by blows of the axe, lay near these wheels. Nobody can imagine the desolation conveyed by their howls and screams unless he has truly understood their extreme anguish and the severity of their torture. I saw their mangled thighs tied to the wheel with ropes that were pulled as taut as possible, so that in all that overwhelming and manifold torture which they suffered, I believe none could have been so great as the utter impossibility of any movement, however small.

Their cries of distress even moved the tsar. He went up to the wheels, and at first promised them a speedy death; and then offered them a free pardon in return for a sincere confession. But when he found that they remained obdurate even on the wheel, despite their excruciating torture, and that their only answer was that they would confess nothing, and that they had already all but paid the penalty of their lives, the tsar left them to the agonies of death.

He drove on to the Novodevichy convent. In front of this monastery thirty gallows were erected in a square. From these two hundred and thirty *streltsy* hung. The three chief ringleaders, who had presented a petition concerning the administration of the realm to Sophia, were suspended close to her windows presenting, as it were, the petitions that were placed in their hands. They were so near that the princess could have touched them without difficulty. Perhaps this was done in order to fill Sophia with heavy remorse.

Indeed, I believe that such feelings drove her to take the religious habit, in order to pass to a better life.

Shortly after his return from abroad, Peter set about westernizing his court by forcing the nobles to change their appearance. With images of the West fresh in his mind, Peter was determined to be surrounded by 'decent beardless Europeans', and he himself wielded scissors to cut the beards and hair of his courtiers, impervious to protests that the beard was a God-given ornament, and that to shave it was a mortal sin. A similar assault was made upon the cumbersome Muscovite kaftans and robes. Personal intervention by the tsar was later backed up by a series of decrees specifying the wearing of western dress by men and women (in 1700 and 1701, samples of approved clothing were displayed in public places), and the following edict, dating from 16 January 1705.

Henceforth, in accordance with this, His Majesty's decree, all court attendants, service men from the provinces, government officials of all ranks, military men, all the merchants, members of the wholesale merchants' guild and members of the guilds purveying for our household must shave their beards and moustaches.

If some of them do not wish to shave their beards and moustaches, let a yearly tax be collected from such persons. From court attendants, provincial service men, military men, and government officials of all ranks: sixty roubles per person; from the merchants and members of the wholesale merchants' guild of the first class: one hundred roubles per person; from members of the wholesale merchants' guild of the middle and the lower class and from other merchants and townsfolk: sixty roubles per person; from townsfolk of the lower rank, boyars' servants, stage coachmen, wagoners, church attendants (with the exception of priests and deacons), and from Moscow residents of all ranks: thirty roubles per person.

Special badges shall be issued to them from the Chancery Office which they must wear.

As for the peasants, let a toll of two half-copecks per beard be collected at the town gates each time they enter or leave a town; and do not let the peasants pass the town gates, into or out of town, without paying this toll.

Peter was also determined that his subjects should be better informed and educated. He promoted the translation and publication of books on a wide range of secular topics, including mathematics, fortification, navigation, shipbuilding, warfare, and architecture – and at the end of 1702 he launched Russia's first newspaper, *Vedomosti*.

In 1700 Peter went to war against Sweden, for long Russia's chief rival in Northern Europe. At first things went badly for Russia, but in 1702–3 Russian troops, trained and led by foreigners, won several victories on the Baltic, capturing the Swedish fortress at Nöteborg. Nearby, in May 1703, Peter laid the foundation stone of a new fortress with a church dedicated to SS Peter and Paul on an island in the River Neva.

A new capital city, St Petersburg, was soon to rise from the swamps of the Finnish Gulf. As the following decree shows, Peter wanted a European city, built of stone and regularly planned. Its buildings were designed by foreigneres such as the Swiss Italian Domenico Trezzini, who oversaw much of the construction.

On City Island and Admiralty Island in St Petersburg, as likewise on the banks of the greater Neva and its more important arms, wooden buildings are forbidden and only wattle-and-daub houses are allowed.

Elsewhere, wood may be used for buildings, the plans to be obtained from the architect Trezzini. The roofs are to be covered either with two thicknesses of turf or with tiles. No other roof covering is allowed under penalty of severe fines. The streets should be bordered by the house, not with fences or stables.

The most illustrious and mighty Peter the Great, autocrat of All Russia, has commanded his imperial decree to be proclaimed to people of all ranks. Stone construction in St Petersburg is advancing very slowly, it being difficult to obtain stonemasons and other artisans of this craft, even for good pay. For this reason, all building in stone of any description is forbidden in the whole state for a few years, until construction has sufficiently progressed here, under penalty of confiscation of the offender's property and exile.

This decree is to be announced in all the cities and districts of the St Petersburg province, except the city itself, so that none may plead ignorance as an excuse.

The following is ordered: no building shall be undertaken in St Petersburg on the grounds of houses, between neighbouring back yards, until all the main and side streets are entirely built up.

However, if after this any person needs more buildings, he may build on his grounds, along the neighbour's lot. No stables or barns may be built facing the street, but only inside the grounds.

Along the streets and side streets all the space must be filled by residences as ordered. In the locations where, as ordered by previous decrees, wooden houses may be built, they must be made of squared logs. If the logs are used as they are, the walls must be faced with boards and coated with red, or painted to look like brick.

OPPOSITE *Peter the Great decreed that his subjects must shave or pay a tax on beards.*

The new Peter-Paul fortress was never needed as a defence against the Swedes, who had to relinquish the territories they had lost. In 1709 the Russian armies defeated the Swedes at Poltava in the Ukraine, in one of the crucial battles of European history. Tradition has it that Peter addressed his troops on the eve of the battle, on 27 June, with the following words.

Let the Russian soldiers know that the hour has come in which the very existence of the whole fatherland is placed in their hands: either Russia will perish completely, or she will be reborn for the better. They must think that they have been armed and drawn up in battle array, not for the sake of Peter, but for the sake of the state entrusted to Peter, for the sake of their kin and of the whole of the Russian people which, until now, has been protected by their arms, and which today is awaiting from them the final decision of its fortune. Neither let them be disturbed by the glory of an enemy reputed to be invincible, for they themselves have repeatedly given the lie to this report.

In the action to come let them keep only this before their mind's eye – that God himself and Justice are fighting with us, of which fact, the Lord, who gives strength in battles, has already given them testimony by his aid in many combats: let them rely upon him alone. And as for Peter, let them know for certain that his life is not dear to him, if only Russia and Russian piety, glory, and prosperity survive.

The 1721 Peace of Nystadt marked the end of the war with Sweden. Russia now had its 'window on the West' on the Baltic coast as the former Swedish lands of Estonia and Livonia were annexed. The tsar claimed the title of emperor, conferred upon him by a grateful people.

On 20 October 1721, the following was resolved after deliberation in the Senate and the Holy Synod: to ask His Majesty in the name of all the Russian people, as an indication of their due gratitude for his sublime mercy and the fatherly concern and endeavour it has pleased the tsar to display for the well-being of the state throughout his most glorious reign, and especially during the past Swedish wars; thereby placing the whole Russian state in so strong and advantageous a position, and his subjects in such esteem throughout the world by his leadership alone (as is well enough known to all), that he should be pleased to accept from them, following others' example, the title: Father of the fatherland, Emperor of All Russia, Peter the Great.

Diplomatic and military successes were accompanied by internal reforms aimed at modernizing the state and its personnel, or, as in the following decree of 11 May 1721, improving agricultural methods by imitating the practices of newly acquired subjects on the Baltic. Like much of the legislation of the period, this apparently minor edict was prepared by Peter.

Since it is the custom of peasants in the localities of Courland and Latvia, and among the Prussians, to cut grain with small scythes and rakes rather than sickles; and since this is so much more rapid and efficient compared with our sickles that the average labourer does the work of ten, it is evident that this method would be of great utility in the work, and would thereby increase the supplies of grain.

Therefore, having sought out such people from among the local peasants, we have dispatched them hence in small groups to our grain-producing centres with these scythes and rakes to give instruction, accompanied by special envoys. We have written to the governors and military commanders that they themselves should oversee it, and send them to those areas where the grain grows best, and furnish them with provisions and money. And for better information we enclose herewith a copy of this decree, that you yourselves may have definite confirmation from the ministries that as many as possible are to be taught this summer.

Order also that scythes and rakes be made from the models, to increase their number, and that by next summer all are to use scythes in this manner in the grain-producing areas.

St Petersburg: the making of an imperial city

On 16 May 1703 Tsar Peter I of Russia laid two strips of turf on a bleak island on the Baltic recently captured from the Swedes and, according to popular legend, uttered the words: 'Here there shall be a town.' Just three years later he was referring to this still largely unpopulated and inhospitable spot as 'paradise'. In 1713 'Sanktpetersburgh' replaced Moscow as the capital of Russia. The rapid rise of a new capital and port in a virtually landlocked country which Europeans had, until recently, dismissed as uncivilized, seemed remarkable. In previous centuries foreigners had sneered at wooden Moscow's lack of 'architectural order'. Now they hailed the new capital as a 'brilliant spectacle'.

For Peter, passionate about ships since boyhood, the city was a promise of future naval might as well as a symbol of military prowess. The first building was a wooden fortress, with a church dedicated to SS Peter and Paul. The Admiralty soon followed. Architectural style was determined by Peter's western orientation. His early contacts with foreigners, then visits to Moscow's Foreign Quarter, and finally, in 1697–8, to Western Europe itself, convinced him that in matters architectural, as in most other things, Europeans were more efficient and practical than Muscovites.

There was an additional and vital factor: Peter had a passion for regularity and uniformity which expressed itself not only in architectural proportions but also in edicts, for example, the famous Table of Ranks: new arrivals in the capital were issued with model plans for residences in keeping with their status. Façades were to follow the line of the street. The Swiss-Italian Domenico Trezzini, hired in 1703, acted as Director of Works.

The essential formula during the first decades of St Petersburg, was based on plain northern European style: mainly secular masonry buildings designed by foreigners and laid out according to prescriptions in government edicts. A decree of 1714 banned stone construction in other towns in order to concentrate materials in the new capital.

Unfortunately, little survives from Peter's original city except its layout. There are examples of Trezzini's work, notably the golden-spired cathedral of SS Peter and Paul, the mausoleum of the Romanovs from Peter I onwards; the 12 identical linked façades of the Colleges, or ministries; the Alexander Nevsky monastery; and the Summer Palace on the Neva embankment, with formal gardens which were stocked with statues brought from Italy.

St Petersburg was in some ways an 'artificial' city. Its location and climate made it an inconvenient, even hazardous place in which to live. Supplies had to be transported great distances. But the northern clime provided the charm of winter snowscapes, and the magical white nights in summer when the sun barely sets.

BELOW *Ground plan of St Petersburg; the tsar's passion for uniformity is reflected in its regular grid.*

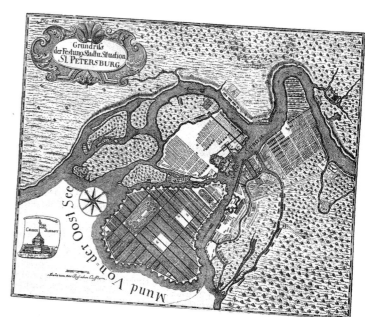

LEFT *View of St Petersburg from the River Neva, showing Elizabeth's Winter Palace and the Academy of Sciences.*

RIGHT *St Nicholas Cathedral; the imperial capital rose from swampy marshland to become the Venice of the North.*

Spacious riverscapes created a spectacular setting for the Venice of the North.

At Peter's death, in 1725, the city still had a temporary feel to it, with many buildings still of wood or wattle and daub, some painted to imitate brick. The tsar's immediate successors lacked the founder's personal commitment to the city, and for a brief period the court even returned to Moscow. Nonetheless, projects started by Peter were completed and extended.

The next major developments are associated with the reign of Peter's daughter Elizabeth (1741–61) and with her leading architect, the Russified Italian Bartolomeo Rastrelli, who came to Russia in 1716 with his sculptor father. During the 1740s and 50s Rastrelli designed a series of sumptuous buildings in the 'Elizabethan baroque' style: the white and gold ballrooms and dining rooms of the Catherine Palace at Tsarskoe Selo (used for only a few months each year) with its 300-metre-long blue and gilded façade; the blues and golds of the baroque-domed cathedral of the Smolny convent, commissioned by Elizabeth in a phase of religious fervour, then abandoned for lack of funds; and palaces for the Stroganovs and other aristocrats.

The most lavish was the Winter Palace (now the Hermitage art museum), said to have been built 'solely for the glory of Russia'. Rastrelli's white-columned, green colour-washed building, with 1945 windows, 1050 rooms and numerous statues, was begun in 1754 and completed in 1762 after Elizabeth's death.

Foreigners were amazed by the lavishness of the court. The Reverend William Coxe wrote in the 1780s: 'The richness and splendour of the

St Petersburg, under the auspices of the Commission for Masonry Construction, a plethora of grand edifices and large-scale ensembles were erected in the classical style favoured by the empress herself. Rastrellian excesses were out.

The new taste is epitomized in the contrast between Rastrelli's baroque Winter Palace and the adjoining small and large Hermitages (de la Mothe, 1764–7, and Velten, 1771–87) and Quarenghi's theatre (1783–7), all of them in the classical style.

Catherine arguably created the grand imperial city which Peter had envisaged but not completed. It was she who ordered the granite-faced embankments for the Neva, and canals, 30 kilometres of them which took 25 years to complete. Public buildings sprang up, monuments to Enlightened absolutism designed in the neo-classical style by the best architects, many of them with foreign names: Giacomo Quarenghi, Antonio Rinaldi, J.-B. Vallin de la Mothe, Charles Cameron.

The last ruler substantially to shape St Petersburg was Catherine's grandson, Alexander I (1801–25). The Empire style of Alexander's city presents a Russian variant of European neo-classicism of the Napoleonic era. Like his predecessors, Alexander was fortunate in his architects and firm in his commitment to a grand city, his vision inspired by Napoleon's retreat from Moscow in 1812 and the entry of the Russian armies into Paris in 1814. Military honours were reflected in such projects as Palace Square, where the Winter Palace faces the superb sweep of Carlo Rossi's general staff headquarters (1819–29), punctuated by its Triumphal Arch, which provides a magnificent setting for the Alexander Column in the centre. Erected in 1834, the 704-ton monolith is inscribed 'To Alexander I from a grateful Russia'.

Russian court surpasses description. It retains many traces of its ancient Asiatic pomp, blended with European refinement.'

Although Elizabeth's reign produced some remarkable individual monuments, the ruler who influenced the shape of the contemporary city more than any other was Catherine II the Great (1762–96). It is no coincidence that the famous 'Bronze Horseman' statue of Peter the Great on Senate Square (by the French sculptor Etienne Falconet, 1782), one of the city's symbols, bears the inscription 'To Peter I from Catherine II'.

Catherine shared Peter's practical bent and devotion to work and considered it self-evident that Russia was a European state. Peter would have approved of her decrees for the remodelling of Russia's provincial towns following a disastrous fire that destroyed the city of Tver in 1763. In

The Baltic conquests of Peter I the Great

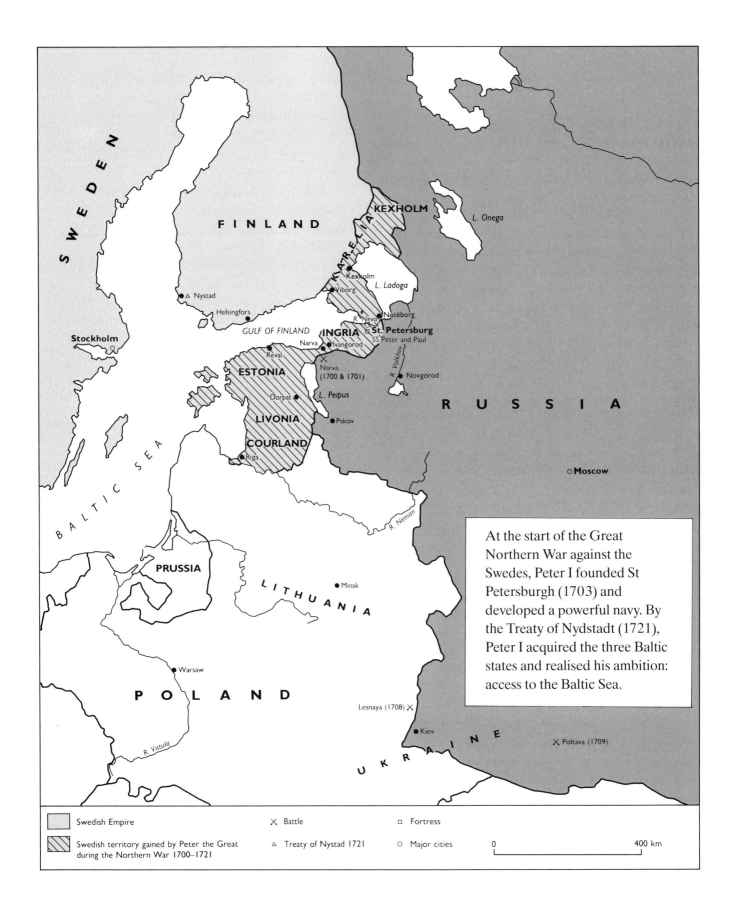

SWEDEN

FINLAND

KEXHOLM

L. Onega

KARELIA

Kexholm

Viborg

L. Ladoga

Helsingfors

△ Nystad

R. Neva

Noteborg

GULF OF FINLAND

INGRIA

St. Petersburg

SS Peter and Paul

Stockholm

Narva

Ivangorod

Reval

R. Volkhov

Novgorod

ESTONIA

Narva
(1700 & 1701)

Dorpat

L. Peipus

RUSSIA

LIVONIA

Pskov

COURLAND

Riga

Moscow

BALTIC SEA

R. Neman

PRUSSIA

LITHUANIA

Minsk

At the start of the Great
Northern War against the
Swedes, Peter I founded St
Petersburgh (1703) and
developed a powerful navy. By
the Treaty of Nydstadt (1721),
Peter I acquired the three Baltic
states and realised his ambition:
access to the Baltic Sea.

Warsaw

POLAND

R. Vistula

Lesnaya (1708) ✕

Kiev

✕ Poltava (1709)

UKRAINE

| | Swedish Empire | ✕ | Battle | □ | Fortress |
| | Swedish territory gained by Peter the Great during the Northern War 1700–1721 | △ | Treaty of Nystad 1721 | ○ | Major cities |

0   400 km

The battle for the Baltic

In the early 17th century, Sweden, under Gustavus II Adolphus (1611–32), gained the eastern Baltic coastline, defeating Poland and Russia, and in 1617 Russia was forced to cede to her the province of Ingria, at the head of the gulf of Finland. However, these gains attracted the ambitious attention of other powers, and in 1656 Tsar Alexis declared war on Sweden and besieged the great Livonian port of Riga, one of the major centres of Baltic trade. Although the siege was unsuccessful, and the Peace of Kardis, signed in 1661, obliged the Russians to accept the Swedish position, they did not abandon the idea of obtaining a Baltic coastline.

In 1697 Charles XII acceded to the Swedish throne at the age of only 15, and in 1699 Frederick IV of Denmark, Augustus II of Poland, and Peter the Great, formed an alliance against Sweden. The intention was that Peter would invade Ingria, Augustus would attack Livonia and Frederick would march into Holstein and then southern Sweden. However, in 1700, before their plan could be put into action, a surprise Swedish landing on Zealand threatened Copenhagen and the king of Denmark, Frederick IV, abandoned the war. And in November of that year, Charles defeated the Russian forces under Peter at Narva on the Baltic.

Rather than follow up this victory, in 1702 Charles invaded Poland, and until 1708 he was embroiled in the complexities of Polish politics. In his absence, Peter took the Baltic provinces in 1703 and, in the same year, founded St Petersburg on the Neva estuary. He also successfully besieged Dorpat and Narva.

In 1708 Charles invaded Russia and turned south into the Ukraine, a move determined by supply problems, the severity of the winter of 1708–9 and the hope that Mazepa, the region's military ruler, would raise the Ukraine against Peter. However, Mazepa was unprepared and this, combined with the swiftness and brutality of Peter's military response and the savage winter, undermined the value of the move south. In early 1709, Charles won the support of the Zaporozhian Cossacks but not of the Don Cossacks, the Tartars or the Turks. On 8 July, hopeful that he would regain the initiative with a major victory, Charles attacked the entrenched Russian forces at Poltava. The army of Peter I repelled the attack and the Swedish king lost about 10,000 men.

The Swedish position around the eastern Baltic collapsed. Viborg and Riga fell in 1710 and in 1713–14 the Russians conquered Finland. In 1716, Peter's army moved into Denmark to prepare for an invasion of Sweden. The invasion did not take place. The Russian move aroused the opposition of George I of Britain, elector of Hanover, who played a major role in mustering the diplomatic support that obliged Peter to withdraw his troops from Germany and Poland.

In 1718 Charles was killed besieging a Norwegian fortress, and the new Swedish government made concessions to George I, Denmark and Prussia in return for an alliance that would oblige Peter to return most of his Baltic conquests. However, Austria and Prussia were unwilling to attack the Russian ruler, while the financial crisis that affected Britain, the South Sea Bubble, sapped British determination. Peter refused to be intimidated by the British navy, and his galleys raided the Swedish coast.

In 1721, as Sweden signed a peace with Russia at Nystad, Peter kept the bulk of his conquests – Livonia, Estonia and Ingria – and, although he returned Finland, retained Kexholm and part of Karelia. He promised to respect their existing privileges and not to intervene in struggles over the Swedish constitution or in the Swedish succession – a commitment that he did not honour.

In 1718 Peter began to replace the haphazardly organized and overlapping Muscovite chancelleries with colleges, or ministries, based on Danish and Swedish models, each run by a committee of officials. The preamble to the *General Regulation* of 1720 listed the colleges and explained their function.

It has pleased his Imperial Highness, our most gracious sovereign, Peter I, for the sake of the correct administration of his affairs of state, the precise definition and calculation of his revenue and the improvement of justice and the police; and also for the fullest possible protection of his loyal subjects; and in order to maintain his naval and land armies, as well as commerce, art, and manufacturing in good condition, to ensure the successful implementation of his marine and land customs duties, and to increase and augment mining works and other state needs, to establish the following state colleges necessary and appropriate to that aim: the Foreign Affairs College, the Revenue College, the College of Justice, the Auditing College, the Military College, the Admiralty College, the College of Commerce, the Estimates Office, the College of Mines, and the College of Manufacture. For each of these, there shall be presidents, vice-presidents, and other appropriate members, clerical and office staff; furthermore these are to be appointed from our own subjects.

Regulations from the tsar affected not only the administration and the economy but also the Church, and even details of everyday life and behaviour. In 1717 the first Russian book on etiquette, entitled *The Honourable Mirror of Youth*, attempted to introduce young Russians to the niceties of polite behaviour.

One of Peter's most important reforms was the Table of Ranks, issued on 24 January 1722. The table was based on the principle of meritocracy; irrespective of their birth, commoners could achieve noble status through service, in the army or in civic office.

How young men should behave

First, clip your nails. Wash your hands and sit down in a refined manner, sit upright and do not be the first to grab the dish.

Do not eat like pigs and do not blow into the bowl so that it splashes everywhere. Do not be the first to drink; hold back and avoid drunkenness; drink and eat only as much as you need; be the last one to finish eating. When you are offered something, take some of it and pass the rest back to the other person, thanking him.

When you drink, do not wipe your lips with your hand but use a napkin, and do not drink until you have swallowed your food. Do not lick your fingers, and do not gnaw at bones, but rather, take the meat off with a knife. Do not pick your teeth with a knife, but use a toothpick and cover your mouth with one hand when picking.

If you want to serve something to somebody else, do not use your fingers as some people have now grown accustomed to doing. Do not munch noisily on the food like a pig, do not scratch your head and do not speak with your mouth full, since that is the way peasants behave. It is bad manners to sneeze, blow one's nose or cough frequently.

When eating an egg, do not smash up the egg shell, and while you are eating the egg do not drink; do not soil the table cloth and do not lick your fingers. Do not accumulate a pile of bones, bread crusts etc. beside your plate. When you have finished eating, give thanks to God, wash your hands and rinse out your mouth.

From *The Honourable Mirror of Youth*, 1717

RIGHT *A table sumptuously set in the Pavlovsk Palace: Peter laid down rules for eating and drinking in the proper manner.*

BELOW *The state room in the palace: young men were instructed in how to behave at court and elsewhere.*

The following points aim to establish the way in which each individual shall conduct himself with respect to ranks:

Princes descended from Our own blood and those who are married to Our princesses, shall on all occasions take precedence and rank over all princes and high servants of the Russian state.

The following ascendancy of command shall exist between naval and land officers: in instances where officers are of equal rank, even if one has greater seniority in that rank, the naval officer shall command the land officer at sea and the land officer shall command the naval officer on land.

Any person who demands honours above his rank, or who takes up a position higher than his designated rank, shall for each offence incur a fine of two months' salary. From the fines levied, a third shall be given to the informant; the remainder will be for the use of the hospital. This observance of rank, however, is not required on such occasions as when several friends or neighbours get together or in public assemblies, but only in church services, court ceremonies such as audiences with ambassadors and formal dinners, in official meetings, weddings, christenings, and other such public ceremonies, and at funerals. The same fine shall be levied on any person who gives up his position to somebody having a lower rank than himself. The financial inspectorate shall carefully monitor this matter in order to provide incentives to service and so that honour is given to those who deserve it and not to idlers and drifters; the above-mentioned fine shall be levied on both men and women guilty of offences.

All married women occupy ranks according to the grades of their husbands, and whenever they behave contrary to that rank, they shall be liable to pay the same fine that their husbands would pay for committing the same offence.

The legitimate children and descendants in perpetuity of all Russian and foreign servants who actually were or are in the first eight ranks, shall be considered equal in all honours and advantages to the highest ancient nobility, even if they are of low birth and have never previously been promoted into the nobility or been given a coat of arms by the crown.

Because civil service grades have not formerly been organized into any order, there is now a pressing need for higher ranks. Therefore whoever is fit for the job must be taken on, even if he does not have a grade. However, because military personnel, who have earned their rank through many years of exacting service, would be offended to find these people appointed their equal or even their superior in rank, any person whose grade is raised must earn his rank by the appropriate number of years' service.

Children of the nobility shall be promoted within the ministries from below. That is, they shall initially be appointed as junior officials, if they are adequately trained, have received a certificate from the ministry, have been presented to the Senate, and have been awarded a patent.

Service in the ranks of corporal and sergeant shall be accredited to all those who have studied and mastered ministerial administration, i.e., everything concerned with justice, foreign and internal trade of the empire and its economy; which matters, they shall be examined in.

Those who study the above-mentioned subjects should be sent abroad to gain practical experience.

Those who perform distinguished service may have their hard work rewarded by being promoted to a higher rank, as is the case of anyone showing zeal in military service, but this may only be done by the Senate and with Our signature.

Military personnel who serve up to commissioned rank but are not of noble birth, on obtaining that rank become nobles, as do their children born while they hold that rank.

But although We and other crowned heads are the only people empowered to grant the honour of nobility with a coat of arms, nevertheless it has many times occurred that certain people have called themselves noble without actually belonging to the nobility. We declare to all that for this reason We have appointed a chief herald, whom everyone having nobility or a coat of arms should approach to submit reports and request decisions in the correct manner, so as to prove by what grant they or their ancestors had them, or that they were raised to that honour by Our ancestors or by Our own munificence.

The greatness of Peter the Great

In October 1721, after peace had been made with Sweden, the Senate and the Holy Synod requested His Majesty to receive the title of Father of the Fatherland, Peter the Great. In a characteristically thoughtful and terse reply, the tsar stated the principles on which he intended to base his future policy: whilst trusting in peace, warlike preparations must not be neglected so that Russia did not share the fate of Byzantium. Also, it was fitting to work within and without for the public welfare, whereby the burden of the people would be lightened.

Four years later Peter died, leaving Russia's territory enlarged but its resources overstrained by his conquests, on the Baltic Sea from Sweden and on the Caspian Sea from Persia. His ultimate aim in waging war had been the enrichment of both state and subject, but the Persian campaign did not yield the expected advantages, and those of the Swedish war were not immediate. Only a minority benefited from the wars – high-ranking military commanders and officials of all kinds were rewarded by the tsar with honours and land, while merchants, manufacturers and richer peasants who supplied the army and navy or had a share in the export trade made fat profits.

Tsar Peter's celebrated reforms did not bring relief to the people because, rather than social, they were political, administrative and fiscal in character. The nature of the Russian service state, to the requirements of which the activities of all social groups were subordinated, remained unchanged. Indeed its power was enhanced in 1721 when the Church was placed under the direction of the Holy Synod, which was no more than a government department analogous to the 11 administrative boards active from 1719 and copied largely from the Swedish model. The workings of the central bureaucratic machine under the direction of the Senate, made up of the tsar's closest advisers, extended into the new administrative regions, 11 'governments' and 45 provinces, and into the larger towns.

One of the failings of the new system of government, intended to be rational and therefore efficacious, was its inability, due among other things to the lack of trained personnel, to collect the poll tax. This was to be levied on the peasant and urban population to cover most of the cost of maintaining the army. In 1722, the task of collection was shifted on to the army itself. Encamped in the countryside, it satisfied its needs in cash or kind at will, causing great misery to the common people. Ultimately the poll tax 'tightened the noose of serfdom', since each landowner was held responsible for the payments due from the peasants on his land.

By contrast, Tsar Peter's last legislative act, the Table of Ranks, was a masterpiece of social engineering. Promulgated in 1722, it determined the composition and grading of the governing class, military and civil, of the new empire and laid down the principles for the promotion of its members. A balance was struck between the claims of merit and lineage: the new men of Peter's making were to enjoy the same status and privileges as the descendants of the ancient families. In theory, merit was to be the sole qualification for entry into the new élite bearing the old name of *dvorianstvo* (the nobility) and for advancement within it. No *dvorianin* (nobleman) was to be promoted to officer rank without having served as a common soldier; conversely a clerk who showed merit was to have the status of *dvorianin*.

Although well suited to the aspirations of a growing class of state servants, the new rules were not strict enough to produce a meritocracy and deepened the divisions between those within the hierarchy and those outside it.

If any person should enquire about an award for outstanding service, enquiries must be made about his services, and if any should prove to be genuinely worthy of reward this should be reported to the Senate and the Senate should make representations to Us. And in the case of men who have served to commissioned rank, whether Russian or foreign, noble or otherwise, these men should be awarded coats of arms according to their services.

Peter's insistence on meritocracy did not exclude himself (the 'first servant of the state' worked his way up through the ranks in the armed services) nor his family. Peter was sorely disappointed in his son and heir Alexis, born in 1690 to his first wife Evdokia. A letter written to Alexis on 11 October 1715 indicates that, in view of Russia's victories over Sweden in the continuing Great Northern War, Peter was most deeply disillusioned by his son's lack of enthusiasm for military affairs. Alexis's reply shows that he was more than willing to relinquish the heavy burdens of government.

Собственноручный указъ сенату, данный Петромъ I.

Declaration to my son:

Everyone knows how, before the beginning of this war, our people were hemmed in by the Swedes, who not only stole the essential ports of our fatherland but cut us off from communication with the whole world. And also later, at the beginning of this war (which enterprise was and is directed by God alone), oh, what great persecution we had to endure from those eternal enemies of ours because of our incompetence in the art of war. But now we have the honour of seeing this enemy trembling before us, trembling, perhaps, even more than we did before him. All this has been accomplished, with the help of God, through my modest labours and through those of other equally zealous and faithful sons of Russia.

However, when, considering our victory – this great blessing given by God to our fatherland – I think of my successor, a grief perhaps as great as my joy gnaws me for I see you, my heir, unfit for the management of state affairs. You have no wish to hear anything about military affairs, which made us honoured who were unknown before. I do not teach you to wage war without a just cause, but to love this art and to endow and learn it by all means, for it is one of the two activities necessary for government: order and defence.

I return again to my original point, thinking of you. I am a man, and subject to death. To whom shall I leave all this sowing, done with God's help, and that harvest which has already grown? To one who, like the idle servant in the gospel, buried his talent in the ground (which means that he threw away everything that God had given him)? I also keep thinking of your wicked and stubborn disposition; for how many times I used to scold you for that, and not only scold but beat you, and also how many years I have now gone without speaking to you, and all without success!

I have pondered this with much grief, and, seeing that I can in no wise dispose you toward good, I have deemed it appropriate to write to you for the last time and admonish you to mend your ways, and that not hypocritically.

If you do not, know that I shall totally disinherit you like a gangrenous member; and do not imagine that, because you are my only son, I write this merely as a threat. I will do it indeed (with God's consent),

because I have never spared my own life for my father-land and people, nor do I now; therefore how can I spare you, unworthy one? Better a good stranger than an unworthy kinsman.

PETER
11 October 1715, St Petersburg

ABOVE *Peter the Great (seated) with his son Alexis, child of his first marriage; the tsar, disappointed in his heir, threatened to disinherit him and later condemned him to death for treason.*

OPPOSITE *Peter the Great's signature.*

Most gracious sovereign and father:

I have read [the letter] that was given me on your behalf on 27 October 1715, after the funeral of my wife. I have nothing to say about it, except that if you wish to disinherit me of the Russian crown because of my worthlessness, let it be as you will. Most humbly I ask you for this very thing, Sire, for I consider myself unqualified and unfit for this task, being most deficient in memory (without which it is impossible to accomplish anything). All my mental and physical capacities are weakened by various illnesses, and I have become unfit to rule such a people, which task requires a man less rotten than I. Therefore, I do not make a claim, nor will I make claim in the future, to the inheritance of the Russian throne after you – God give you health for many years. Let God be my witness; and to show that I testify truthfully I write this with my own hand.

I entrust my children to your will and ask only for maintenance for myself to the end of my life. This is submitted to your decision and merciful will.

Your most humble servant and son,

ALEXIS
31 October 1715, St Petersburg

There was little likelihood of Alexis's securing the quiet life he desired. In August 1716 Peter ordered him to choose between participating fully in the war or becoming a monk, whereupon Alexis fled with his mistress to Vienna. Emperor Charles of Austria was embarrassed by his presence and Alexis was persuaded to move on to Naples, where in 1717 he received this letter from his father.

My son:

The whole world knows how you have disobeyed me and shown contempt for my will; how you have not followed my directions, spurning my words and admonition. Finally, deceiving me, and invoking God as witness at the time of our parting, what did you do? You went away and put yourself under foreign protection like a traitor, a thing unheard of, not only among our children but even among common subjects.

What offence and grief you have thus inflicted on your father and shame on your country! That is why I am sending to you this final message to bring you to conform to my will. Should you fear me, I reassure you and promise you by God and his judgement that no punishment shall be inflicted upon you, but that I will show you my full love if you obey me and return.

However, if you do not, I, as your father, by virtue of the power given me by God, will damn you forever, and, as your sovereign, I will declare you a traitor, and shall leave no means unemployed to punish you as a traitor and abuser of your father; and God will support me in my just cause. Remember, furthermore, that I have not used force with you. If I had wished to do so, why should I have relied on your good will? I would have done as I pleased.

PETER
10 July 1717, Spa

Alexis was reassured by the promise of a pardon. On 4 October 1717 he replied.

Most gracious sovereign and father:

I have received your most gracious letter of 10 July, in which is contained, Sire, your pardon to me, unworthy one, for my self-willed departure, on condition that I return. Thanking you with tears and throwing myself at the feet of your clemency, I beg you to pardon my crimes, though they are worthy of every punishment. Relying upon your gracious promise, I submit myself to your will, and shall presently go from Naples to you, Sire, at St Petersburg. Your most humble and worthless slave, unworthy of the name of son,

ALEXIS
4 October 1717, Naples

Alexis was persuaded by Peter's envoys to return to Russia, arriving back in Moscow in February 1718. Peter's response to his son's repentance was to exclude him from the succession in an edict of 3 February 1718, then to have him interrogated under

torture to name the 'accomplices' in an alleged plot to overthrow his father. Alexis was condemned to death for treason, but died in prison on 7 July 1718, before sentence could be carried out.

We have seen that all our exertions for the upbringing and education of our son Alexis were vain, for he was never forthright in his obedience to us, paid no regard to what is appropriate to a good heir, did not apply himself to study, and did not listen to the teachers we had appointed for him. Later we sent him abroad, in the hope that the sight of well-ordered states would awaken his fervour and induce him to be upright and diligent. But all these efforts of ours were to no avail. The seeds of learning had fallen on stony ground: for not only did he fail to follow good precepts, but he hated them and showed no inclination either for military or for civil affairs; instead, he constantly consorted with worthless and base people whose habits were coarse and disgusting.

In view of his unworthiness and his disreputable behaviour described above, we cannot, in good conscience, leave him as our successor on the Russian

ABOVE *St Peter and St Paul prison where Alexis, held for treason, died.*

throne, knowing that through his disgraceful actions he would forfeit all the glory of our people acquired by God's grace and our tireless toil and squander all the benefits we have gained for the state with so much labour – not only in restoring provinces torn away from our state by the enemy, but also in adding to it many notable cities and lands; it is also well known that we instructed our people in many military and civil sciences to the profit and glory of the state.

Therefore, out of apprehension for our state and faithful subjects – lest they be brought by such a ruler into a worse condition than they had been in before – we, in virtue of our paternal power and as an autocratic sovereign, do, for the good of the state, deprive our son Alexis of the inheritance of our throne of All Russia on account of his faults and crimes, even if there be no person of our family left to rule after us. We proclaim as heir to the said throne our other son, Peter, though he is still a minor, for we have no other heir who is of age.

Peter may have had his detractors, notably those conservatives who had looked to the more traditionally minded Alexis to replace him. But he also enjoyed enthusiastic support. His death on 28 January 1725, precipitated by leaping into the sea to save some soldiers from drowning, fuelled an already flourishing personality cult; Russians and foreigners alike vied to heap praise on a great reformer who was simultaneously lauded as a 'man of the people'. On 8 March Archbishop Feofan Prokopovich delivered a funeral oration in the cathedral of SS Peter and Paul in St Petersburg.

What is this? What has it come to, O Russians? What are we doing? We are burying Peter the Great! Can this be real, or is this a dream or a vision we are see-ing? How heartfelt is our sorrow, how real our misery! The author of our immeasurable blessings and joys, who raised Russia as though from the dead and lifted her to great heights of power and glory; more than this, who gave Russia life and nurtured her, truly the father of his fatherland, and whom, for his great merits, the good sons of Russia wished might live for eternity. Who was this man whom we have lost?

He was your Samson, Russia! He found in you a weak people, but after the meaning of his own name he made you into a mighty Rock. He found an army weak in the field and the object of its enemies' scorn and turned it into an army which is formidable to its enemy and fills the world with its fame and glory.

He was your Moses, Russia! For are not his laws like the strong shield of justice and the unbreakable fetters of crime? Are not his statutes clear, like a light for your path?

He was your Solomon, Russia! receiving from the Lord infinite wisdom and understanding. Is this not sufficiently proved by the diverse philosophical arts displayed both in his own actions and extended to many of his subjects, and the various sciences, skills, and crafts which were introduced by him, about which we had never even heard before? Also, the ranks and grades and the civil laws, the rules of social inter-course and useful customs and codes of behaviour bear witness to this; and he improved our external

Peter I

Peter the Great, a 6 foot 7 inch giant with a preference for rooms with low ceilings, was a man of many contradictions. Most Russians know him best as the 'artisan' tsar, who disguised himself as plain Peter Mikhailov in order to labour in the shipyards of Amsterdam and Greenwich, showing the callouses on his hands to foreign dignitaries. He was a midshipman climbing the rigging, a soldier storming a fortress, a skipper piloting his ship.

He dressed simply and preferred good plain Russian food. But this 'man of the people' never forgot for one moment that he was an autocrat, and did not hesitate to sacrifice thousands of his subjects in the waging of his wars or in the construction of his new capital, St Petersburg.

Every Russian school child knows Peter's motto: 'I am a student and I seek teachers.' But his passion for learning and experiment sometimes made him dangerous to be near. He practised the art of dentistry upon his courtiers (his bag of extracted teeth is still preserved), and exposed them to his even more dangerous experiments in pyrotechnics. He shaved off their beards, forced them into western clothes and into the modern world.

An invitation to the palace could cause panic, for the tsar sometimes had guests detained at gunpoint in order to ensure that they downed the prescribed measures of vodka, supplied by soldiers from buckets. He was an equally unpredictable guest, wrecking John Evelyn's house in Deptford in 1698, tearing off the nose of an Egyptian mummy when the king of Denmark failed to offer it as a gift, and eating and drinking his hosts out of house and home. Yet many foreigners found him charming, including the duke of Saint-Simon, who observed the tsar during his visit to Paris in 1717, and most were impressed

ABOVE *Diamond encrusted imperial orb, part of the regalia of state used by Peter the Great during official ceremonies. He claimed the title of emperor in 1721.*

by the sheer scale of his activity and his desire to learn.

However, there was a dark side to Peter's quest for western enlightenment. His interest in science and technology was tinged with a taste for the curious and the grotesque. He liked to be surrounded by dwarfs and giants, and collected examples of deformed people and animals, along with other freaks of nature, for his first museum, the aptly named St Petersburg Cabinet of Curiosities. He enjoyed watching operations and performing autopsies.

Peter's unpredictable and often cruel nature (epitomized for many by his willingness to condemn his own son to death for alleged treason) has often been attributed to the traumas he experienced in May 1682, when, at the age of nine, he was dragged out of the Kremlin palace in front of the frenzied mob of armed guards (*streltsy*) and saw boyars hacked to pieces; or to another occasion, in August 1689, when he fled for his life in the middle of the night in the belief that his sister Sophia's supporters were out to murder him.

His boyhood also formed his character in more positive ways. Left to his own devices during Sophia's regency, he was free to explore and seek out his own friends, many of whom were foreigners, or of humble origins. Alexander Menshikov, reputedly the son of a pie seller, was one. Peter was also free to devise his own amusements, such as restoring and learning to sail an old boat (the so-called 'grandfather' of the Russian navy), or drilling his boy soldiers, the embryo of the future élite Guards regiments.

The abiding impression of Peter is of sheer energy and the dedication he applied to everything he did, whether it was devising a new law, storming a fortress, designing a fountain or making a pair of shoes. He summed up his frustration at trying to do so many tasks in a letter to his wife Catherine in 1712: 'I'm well, but it's a hard life. I can't use my left hand, so I am obliged to wield the sword and the pen using only my right, and you yourself know how few helpers I have.' In the end, transforming Russia proved too much even for a giant like Peter the Great.

The godfather

Although he was so great a prince, Peter I was not offended when the meanest of his subjects requested him to hold their children at the baptismal font, nor did he refuse people even of the lowest rank. He even condescended to sit at their table, and seemed better satisfied with their meagre food than with the finest entertainment.

He was always a declared enemy of expenses incurred from putting on ceremony or show, and never missed an opportunity of expressing his displeasure on such occasions.

He was godfather to almost every one of the first-born children of all the officers and soldiers of his regiment of Guards, but it was fruitless to expect lavish gifts; he generally contented himself with giving a kiss to the soldier's wife, and putting a rouble under the pillow, according to Russian custom. When the child was an officer's, the present was a ducat.

From Staehlin, *Anecdotes*

appearance, so that our fatherland is now, both externally and internally, incomparably better than before. We are amazed at how greatly it has changed.

He was your David and your Constantine, O Russian church! How zealously he fought against superstition, sycophantic hypocrisy, and the senseless, damaging schism which had taken root among us.

He has gone, but he has not left us poor and destitute; as he has shaped Russia, so she shall remain. He made Russia beloved of good men, and beloved she will continue to be; he made her formidable to her enemies, and she will continue to be formidable; he made her glorious throughout the world, and she will not cease to be glorious. He has left us spiritual, civil and military reforms. Departing from us through the dissolution of his body, he has left us his spirit.

O Russia! In considering how great a man you have lost, consider also how great he has left you. Amen.

Alexander Gordon was a Scottish mercenary resident in Russia. His *History of Peter the Great*, published in 1755, gives a characteristic western view.

Peter the Great conversed with all sorts of people of whom he could learn anything useful; among whom, some of the English and other foreign merchants were frequently his companions. He ate and drank with them, and was often godfather to their children: if his godchild died, Peter often attended the funeral. He was very inquisitive about trade, yet he confessed it was what he least understood. But his establishment of commerce in St Petersburg, and transferring the greatest part of it from the port of Archangel; the premiums he offered to those who should find out new branches of trade; his setting up and encouraging new manufactures of linen and hemp in his own country; the great countenance he gave to foreign

ABOVE *An 18th-century etching of St Petersburg; when Peter died in 1725 many of its buildings were still made of wood.*

merchants, and many other such circumstances, are certain indications that he understood in many instances the means of advancing commerce as well as the great end of it.

This prince made even his pleasures and amusements subservient to the important ends of his government. Peter had more than once received melancholy proof of the impatience his subjects felt under the reforms which he had planned, and was now accomplishing: this rendered him extremely suspicious of them. As men's hearts are generally most open in their cups, he often drank with them liberally; sometimes at court, and more often at their own houses. His manners seemed to be rude, in requiring even the ladies, upon certain occasions, to swallow goblets of wine or other strong liquors; but in this he had his views: drinking is still the vice of Russia, but in a more elegant manner than in past times.

He had frequent convulsive distortions of his head and countenance, contracted by a fright in his youth; it was always the rule of the company he was in to look down, or elsewhere.

To prevent a surprise, or any attempt on his life, Peter would never sleep alone: when he was not with the empress or other companion, he ordered one of his chamberlains to sleep with him; this was an uncomfortable situation for them, since he was very angry if they woke him, and in his sleep he often grasped them very hard.

He proved himself to be a master of exquisite art and acute judgement, in diverting his people from that sordid ignorance which for so many ages had reigned in this country.

Peter I's successors

In 1722, in the aftermath of the struggle with his son and heir Alexis, Peter I had passed a law whereby the sovereign had the right to nominate his or her own successor. On his deathbed, however, Peter is said to have managed to whisper no more than 'Leave all to . . .'

The decision to pass the throne to Peter's second wife, Catherine, whom Peter had crowned as his consort in 1724, was reached by the Senate with a little persuasion from the Guards regiments. For the rest of the century this élite corps was to be instrumental in enthroning or deposing monarchs in a series of palace revolutions.

Catherine I (1725–7) was a kindly, illiterate, and pleasure-loving woman of Lithuanian peasant stock who reigned with the help of Peter's former favourite, Alexander Menshikov. A new governing body, the Supreme Privy Council, was created in 1726. Catherine's nominated successor was Peter's grandson, who reigned briefly as Peter II, dying of smallpox in 1730 at the age of 15. He had been engaged to the daughter of Prince Aleksey Dolgoruky, the leading member of an ancient clan which had hoped to consolidate its power by a marriage link with the crown.

The Supreme Privy Council seized the opportunity of Peter's death to summon Peter I's widowed niece Anna, duchess of Courland. Headed by the Dolgorukys, the Council hoped to control Anna by setting out the conditions of her rule in an official document. Anna accepted these limitations at first, but once in power she dissolved the Council, and reigned freely for the next ten years. Her autocratic regime ended with her death in 1740. With the support of Guards, Elizabeth I, daughter of Peter I, acceded to the throne as empress of Russia. Aged 34, beautiful and charming, Elizabeth imposed an extravagant life style on the Russian court for the next twenty years. It was during her reign that Moscow University was founded, the Winter Palace was built and French influence replaced the German. Upon her death in 1761, her nephew Peter III succeeded her. In 1745, he had married a German princess, Catherine.

OPPOSITE *Elizabeth (1741–61)*

At the beginning of 1730 the unexpected death of the young emperor, Peter I's grandson and successor, Peter II, completely changed the course of events. These were the circumstances.

On the feast of the Epiphany the Orthodox Church holds a solemn ceremony of blessing the waters. At the same time, according to custom, the colours and standards of the troops are blessed. The emperor always takes part in this ceremony, since he is the colonel of the first regiment of the Guards. The river that passes through Moscow had frozen over, and young Peter remained on the ice, at the head of his troops, for at least two hours. The cold was extreme, and he was chilled to the marrow. He complained to Prince Aleksey Dolgoruky that he felt unwell, but the prince, instead of listening, immediately took him hunting. On his return in the evening Peter was forced to retire to bed at once.

Doctors were summoned, and they declared that he already had a fever and was showing symptoms of smallpox. Their opinion was, however, contradicted by the principal physician, who said that the fever was simply that of a chill and treated him in accordance with his own diagnosis.

Some days afterwards the pustules of smallpox appeared, and the infection was so severe that many already despaired of the emperor's life. But everything was kept so secret in the palace that those who were not near his person did not know that he was in danger of his life.

Even on the night of his death, it was commonly rumoured that the emperor was out of danger. The rumours were the more plausible because of the unperturbed behaviour of Prince Ivan Dolgoruky, a favourite of Peter II, who, all the time of the emperor's sickness, took his pleasures in his accustomed manner.

In consequence, most people were surprised when, on 19 January, they heard the news that the emperor had died the night before.

James Keith, a Scots nobleman engaged on state service in St Petersburg, and who later became lieutenant-colonel of Anna's bodyguard, gave the above account of the circumstances of Peter II's death on 18 January 1730. In his *Memoir* of 1730, Keith went on to describe the attempts made by the Dolgoruky clan to cling to power, and the invitation to rule made to Anna, the duchess of Courland, a daughter of Ivan V.

As soon as he had breathed his last, orders were sent to all the ministers, generals, senior officers, and any distinguished people who were in Moscow to assemble immediately in the Senate house. There the chancellor, Count Golovkin, informed everyone that the emperor was dead. Prince Dmitry Mikhaylovich Golitsyn immediately stood up and made a speech, at the end of which he declared that Anna, duchess of Courland, should succeed to the throne. All those present approved. Shortly after, it became known that the Dolgoruky faction had drawn up a scheme of government by which the empress would rule in name only, all power resting in themselves.

Once this meeting had ended, a deputation, headed by Prince Vasily Dolgoruky, was sent to Courland to inform Anna of the election, as they termed it, and to propose certain restrictions on the powers by which she was to govern. She treated the embassy with all possible courtesy, although she was well aware of their plotting and pernicious schemes.

The restrictions which the Supreme Privy Council, headed by the Dolgorukys, hoped to impose upon Anna were set out in a document entitled the Conditions, which took the form of a declaration to be made by the empress.

We hereby give a most binding promise that our main concern and effort shall be not only to maintain but to spread, as far as possible and in every way, our Orthodox faith. Moreover, after accepting the Russian crown, we will not enter into wedlock so long as we live: nor will we designate a successor, either in our lifetime or after. We also promise that, since the safety and welfare of every state depends upon good counsel, we will always maintain the Supreme Privy

Council as it is at present established with its membership of eight persons. Without the consent of this Supreme Privy Council:

○ We will not start a war with anyone.
○ We will not conclude peace.
○ We will not burden our faithful subjects with any new taxes.
○ We will not promote anyone to high rank – above that of a colonel – either in the civil or in the military service, be it on land or on the sea; nor will we assign any important affair to anyone; the Guards and the other regiments are to remain under the control of the Supreme Privy Council.
○ We will not deprive members of the nobility of life, possessions, or honour without due proceedings in a court of law.
○ We will not grant any patrimonies or villages.
○ We will not promote anyone, whether Russian or foreigner, to an office at court without the advice of the Supreme Privy Council.
○ We will not spend any revenues of the state.

And we also promise to maintain an unalterably gracious disposition toward all our faithful subjects. Should we not carry out any part of this promise, we shall be deprived of the Russian crown.

At first Anna accepted these proposals. The Scot James Keith relates the events of February 1730 when she arrived in Moscow and tells how, with the support of the Guards and the vice-chancellor, Count Ostermann, a German, she proceeded to reject the Conditions.

In February 1730 the empress arrived at the village of Vsesvyatskoye, about three miles from Moscow. She decided to stay there for several days, until preparations for her entry into Moscow had been completed. Count Ostermann, who had pleaded sickness ever since the death of Peter II, now found himself well enough to receive her there. Two days later, the empress declared herself to be captain of the Horse Guards and colonel of the Foot Guards, as the Empress Catherine I had been.

ABOVE   *Anna was empress from 1730 to 1740.*

This action fell like a thunderbolt on the Dolgoruky clan, who had resolved that appointments to the great offices of the empire should be made only with the consent of the Supreme Privy Council. But as the decisive action of Empress Anna had met with the general approval of all the officers and of the nobility, they saw that it was equally in her power to override the rest of their schemes.

This prediction indeed proved true, for as soon as the rest of the nobility perceived that the genius of the empress was capable of encompassing everything that her uncle Peter I had formerly undertaken, they presented a formal petition, declaring their dislike of the scheme of government projected in the 'Conditions', and expressing their desire that Her Majesty should rule with the same sovereign powers that her predecessors had enjoyed.

Empress Anna gave her consent, and ordered that the oath of allegiance, worded according to the ancient and accustomed forms, should be taken by all her subjects.

As soon as this was done the whole political balance within the empire changed. Some members of the Dolgoruky family, who had been the chief sowers of discord, were banished to Siberia. Others were prohibited from attendance at court and exiled to their own estates; and the rest, including Field Marshal Prince Vasily Dolgoruky, continued in favour as before. Peace having been restored, Anna was solemnly crowned in Moscow at the end of April. Soon afterwards she went to a country villa at Izmaylovo, where she remained for the rest of the summer.

Empress Anna naturally loved magnificence in her court and household, and luxury and outward display were encouraged until they rivalled that of the court of France. Moreover, because the ancient palace of the tsars in the Moscow Kremlin was not to the empress's taste, for the rooms were too small and many of them dark, she ordered that a palace built of wood should be erected with all speed. This was completed within three weeks, to the surprise of all who saw it. As soon as this palace was ready, Anna left her country retreat at Izmaylovo and journeyed to Moscow. She passed the remainder of the winter there, resolving the matters of state which had not yet been settled.

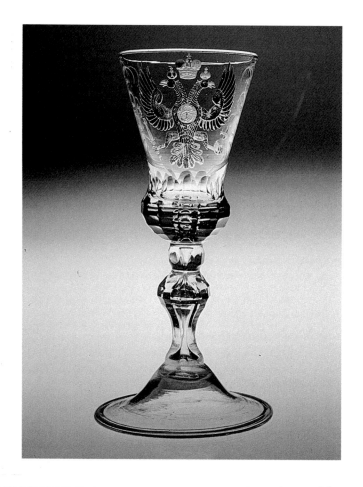

ABOVE *An exquisite goblet, typical of the splendour with which Russia's rulers surrounded themselves.*

ABOVE RIGHT *Peter the Great's Summer Palace was used and enjoyed by his successors.*

LEFT *The kitchen in the Summer Palace. Elizabeth, in particular, was renowned for her lavish receptions.*

Anna's reign was distinguished by the ascendancy of the German party, some members of which had come with her from Courland, and others inherited from the previous regime, for example her vice-chancellor, Heinrich Ostermann. The most notorious of her advisers was Ernst Johann Biron, who was associated with police persecution and a reign of terror. Anna herself took little part in public affairs. The accession in 1740 of her great-nephew Ivan, an infant of five months and son of the duke of Brunswick, looked like extending the rule of Germans. But in 1741, Ivan was deposed by the Guards in favour of Peter I's daughter, 32-year-old Elizabeth.

Her reign is renowned for the lavishness of her court, enhanced by many new buildings designed in baroque style by her favourite architect, Bartolomeo Rastrelli. La Messelière, a member of a French delegation received at the Summer Palace in St Petersburg in July 1757, was suitably impressed. (France was one of Russia's allies against Prussia in the Seven Years War.) His memoir of the delegation's visit, *Journey to St Petersburg*, was published in Paris in 1803.

The moment she was informed of our arrival, the Empress Elizabeth completely broke with etiquette and brought forward the moment to give audience to our ambassador.

During the period for which her residence there is fixed, she never leaves Tsarskoe Selo for any reason whatsoever, but she gave urgent orders for her summer palace to be prepared, and the third day after our arrival, which was on 29 June, she admitted us to her court, amid all the glory of her empire.

All the lords and ladies were resplendent in their robes and jewels. The great crown officers came to the bottom of the steps to receive the Marquis de l'Hôpital. The Russian Chancellor, Count Aleksey Bestuzhev, had a diplomatic illness; Count Vorontsov, the vice-chancellor, stood in for him.

The beauty and richness of the apartments is surprising enough, but they were overshadowed by the agreeable sensation produced by the gathering of over four hundred ladies, most of whom were very beautiful and very finely dressed, who lined the walls of the apartment. A new object of admiration soon succeeded this one: a darkness suddenly created by blinds falling all at once was immediately dispersed by the light of twelve hundred candles which were reflected on all sides in the pier-glasses.

After this ceremony, an orchestra of eighty instruments struck up, and the grand duke and the grand duchess began the ball by taking as partners on his part the countess Shuvalov and on hers the marquis de l'Hôpital. During these first minuets a low, but somehow majestic noise could be heard.

We saw a double door suddenly open to reveal a glittering throne from which the empress arose and, accompanied by her officers, entered the ballroom. The cessation of everyone's movement and a deep silence let the empress's voice be heard. After bowing her head three times to right and left with a majesty mingled with grace and gentleness, she said to the ambassador of France: 'So here you are at last, My Lord Ambassador, and I can learn from you news of your master King Louis XV, and tell you of my feelings for him and my affection for France.'

The ambassador made a most noble speech and presented his credentials, after which he kissed the empress's hand and presented each of us by name to be accorded the same honour. At once the lords and ladies came up to us in the most obliging manner, speaking French as if they were in Paris, and on the spot we were invited to dance, with permission to choose whoever we wished. The room was extremely large and as many as twenty minuets could be danced at once, which made a most singular and very pleasing sight. There were few quadrilles except for some polonaises and anglaises.

The ball went on until eleven o'clock, when the master of ceremonies came and announced to Her Majesty that supper was ready. We passed into a vast

OVERLEAF *Interior of the Catherine Palace, built by Rastrelli, Elizabeth's favourite architect.*

Elizabeth, daughter of Peter the Great

Elizabeth, future empress of Russia, was born on 18 December 1709, the fifth of the 12 children born to Peter I and his wife Catherine, of whom only Elizabeth and her elder sister Anna survived beyond childhood. In 1725 Anna was married to the Duke of Holstein-Gotthorp, but Elizabeth's intended husband, the duke's cousin Karl Augustus, died shortly after their betrothal. She was never officially to marry.

As a woman under the Muscovite system of succession, Elizabeth would not have expected to reign. Even after Peter I's new succession law, which allowed the ruling monarch to choose his or her own successor, she was bypassed several times. Her moment came in 1741: the rule of the 'German party' in St Petersburg, first at the court of her cousin, the Empress Anna (1730–40), then under the regency for the infant Ivan VI (1740–1), caused resentment. She was easily persuaded, at the age of 32, to provide a rallying point for the Guards regiments who deposed the Germans in a bloodless coup.

Although Elizabeth promised that she 'would show herself worthy to be the daughter of Peter the Great', she lacked her father's energy. Elizabeth ruled through favourites rather than institutions. Her most trusted advisers were the Shuvalov brothers: Peter took charge of administration and finances; Alexander ran the security police; and their cousin Ivan pioneered educational reform, submitting a scheme for the foundation in Moscow of Russia's first university, of which he became rector in 1755, and founding the Academy of Arts in St Petersburg in 1757.

In private life, Elizabeth's favourite was Aleksey Razumovsky, a Ukrainian Cossack who, in a 'rags to riches' story, charmed the empress with his beautiful voice and ended up as a prince,

a general and count of the Holy Roman Empire. They may have been morganatically married.

Russia remained a leading power throughout Elizabeth's reign, gaining territory from Sweden after the war of 1741–3, and sending troops as far as Berlin during the Seven Years War (1756–62) against Prussia. She showed firmness in pursuing the Prussian king, Frederick the Great, but all Russia's gains were revoked after her death by her appointed heir Peter III.

The textbook cliché about Elizabeth is that she was good-natured, indolent and extravagant: 15,000 outfits were allegedly discovered after her death, while 4000 were lost in a fire in 1747. Included among these were a number of male garments, which gave Elizabeth the opportunity to display her shapely legs. The court followed her lead, succumbing, in the words of a later commentator, to a 'voluptuousness' which led to 'the ruination of noble houses and the corruption of morals'. The Winter Palace alone cost 1,500,000 roubles at the time of Elizabeth's death, and was unfinished. The Catherine Palace at the royal summer residence of Tsarskoe Selo, also built by her favourite architect Bartolomeo Rastrelli, was almost as lavish.

Elizabeth herself had no intellectual interests. She regarded reading as injurious to health and thought Britain was joined to the continent. But she patronized the opera, ballet and theatre. Her reign also saw increased westernization in thought and art.

German influence gave way to the French influence, which was to reach its height in Catherine II's reign. Elizabeth's father had, after all, once intended to marry her to Louis XV of France.

However, Elizabeth's own upbringing was chiefly Russian. She was drawn to Moscow and its Orthodox monasteries, to church music and pilgrimages. A potent symbol of her reign is the cathedral of the Smolny convent, begun in 1748, which combines Rastrelli's theatrical baroque with the five domes of Orthodox convention. Like the Winter Palace, it was still unfinished when Elizabeth died on Christmas Day 1761.

Elizabeth and her court

The Empress Elizabeth had keen natural intelligence, was of a gay disposition, and indulged in excessive pleasures. I think she was kind at heart; she had great high-mindedness and much vanity; she wanted to shine and was fond of admiration.

Her laziness prevented her from cultivating her mind and her early youth had been very much wasted. Her father, to begin with, had brought up his two daughters like waifs. From their early youth they were looked after only by Finnish maids and after that by peculiar German servants who treated them like playthings.

At her palace at Tsarskoe Selo she assembled around her all the gentlemen- and ladies-in-waiting she favoured most, but they saw Her Majesty but rarely. Sometimes she would not leave her apartments for two or three weeks, and did not summon them into her presence either. At the same time they had no permission to leave the house nor to have anyone to visit them. Their sole entertainment was playing cards and sometimes in the middle of the night, when they were already asleep, they would be ordered to come and assist at Her Majesty's supper. If, half-asleep, they failed to make good conversation, she would throw her napkin on the table and leave them in anger.

In addition, it was not easy to find topics of conversation, as there were many for which she did not care; for instance, one had to avoid mentioning the king of Prussia or Voltaire, illness and death, beautiful women, French manners, and scientific matters. Various superstitions also had to be considered. You will say it was difficult to live at that court. I shall not contradict you, but merely relate things as they were.

From Catherine II, *Memoir*

and very ornate room, lit with nine hundred candles and featuring, outlined, a table laid for four hundred places. In a gallery above the room was a vocal and instrumental ensemble which performed throughout the meal.

There were dishes from all nations, as well as French, Russian, German and Italian waiters who each asked the guests from their country what they wished. With her own hands the empress prepared some milk from her dairy, with strawberries which she sent especially to the marquis de l'Hôpital and the Frenchmen who were with him.

The Grand Duke Peter [later Peter III] drank to our health while naming us, a favour which had never until then been granted to anyone.

While we were partaking of the pleasures of this welcome, the mind of the English ambassador, who was sulking at his home with his followers, was in turmoil.

In the middle of the 18th century, Russia still had no universities, but the omission was to be remedied by the combined efforts of Ivan Shuvalov, a favourite of the Empress Elizabeth, and the scientist and man of letters Mikhail Lomonosov. Lomonosov wrote to Shuvalov in June 1754, welcoming the plans which were then afoot to found a university in Moscow and offering advice.

From the draft report to the Senate which I have received from Your Excellency, I am assured, to my great joy, that the undertaking which I proposed is indeed going to be put into effect, for the advancement of the sciences and, consequently, for the true good and glory of our country.

OPPOSITE *Typical menu from an imperial banquet, written in French, the fashionable court language. The empress entertained favoured courtiers lavishly.*

DINER

DU 24 MAI 1883.

Potage crême de gélinottes

Consommé aux laitues

Bouchées à la Reine et Rissoles

Truites de Gatschina sauce Sicilienne

Noix de jambon aux épinards

Pâté de godiveau à la Périgueux

Chaud-froid Diplomate

Punch à la Romaine

Poulardes et canards sauvages

Salade

Petits pois et choux fleurs, sauce Hollandaise

Gateau Napolitain aux fraises

Parfait au café et glaces

Dessert

In this matter I am well aware how much your natural and matchless talent can be of service; your having read many books can assist it. However, it would be not without value for Your Excellency also to obtain the advice of those persons who have not merely seen universities but have also studied therein for some years, since the institutions, statutes, ceremonies, and customs of these universities will be reflected clearly and vividly in their minds.

My chief and fundamental idea, which I conveyed to Your Excellency, should be kept well in mind, so that the plan for the university may serve throughout all generations to come. To this end, although at present we have not learned men enough, a sufficient number of professors and salaried students should be provided for in the plan. At the beginning, we can manage with however many can be found. As time goes by, the specified number will be made up to strength. Meanwhile, the money corresponding to unfilled appointments would be more usefully employed for assembling the university library; this is preferable to making a meagre and narrow plan now, because of the scarcity of men of learning, then having to apportion the money afresh as their numbers increase, and ask for additional sums.

Lomonosov's project for Moscow University, extracts from which appear below, was implemented when the university opened its doors in the old Pharmacy building on Red Square on 16 April 1755. Its first director was Ivan Shuvalov. The university was remarkable in having no theological faculty, this being deemed the sphere of the Holy Synod. It also admitted a significant proportion of non-noble students, even though instances of former serfs entering it were rare.

For the upkeep of Moscow University and the grammar school attached to it the sum of ten thousand roubles a year will suffice.

It is considered necessary, for the encouragement of learning, that the projected university be placed under the high protection of Her Imperial Majesty

Mikhail Vasilyevich Lomonosov

In 1721, when Mikhail Lomonosov was about ten years old, his father, who made a living on the shores of the River Dvina near Kholmogory, 100 miles from where it ran into the White Sea, built himself 'a new-fashioned hooker', a type of Dutch sailing vessel which Peter the Great had ordered the Russian seamen of the far north to copy. On the *Seagull*, an example of the new western technology introduced by the emperor, the young Mikhail embarked on fishing expeditions to the open seas which linked Russia with Western Europe. But although Mikhail Lomonosov eventually went to the west, he was to take a different route.

Fired by the new opportunities provided by the emperor, Mikhail set off, in 1730, to study at Moscow's Slavonic-Greek-Latin Academy. An exceptionally able student, he was selected in 1735 to transfer to the St Petersburg Academy of Sciences. Within a year he was commanded to study chemistry and mining in Germany where, at Marburg, under the philosopher and mathematician Christian Wolff, he imbibed the moderate, Christian enlightenment of Northern Europe. Lomonosov pursued not only chemistry but other natural sciences, learnt foreign languages and developed a fierce interest in the theory of literature.

In 1739, while at Freiburg in Saxony furthering his practical studies in mining and metallurgy, he heard the stirring news that the Turkish fort at Khotin had fallen to Russian forces. It prompted him to write a patriotic ode which Vissarion Belinsky, the great early 19th-century critic, called the 'beginning of Russian literature'. Along with his *Ode on the Capture of Khotin*, Lomonosov's treatise on a radical new way of verse-making in Russian was sent to the St Petersburg Academy. Out went the flat chant of

existing syllabic Russian verse to be replaced by the muscular, stressed, tonic verse that Lomonosov had heard in German poetry.

By 1741 Lomonosov was back at the St Petersburg Academy of Sciences, where his encyclopaedic enthusiasms and practical bent are reflected in his mosaic of 'The Battle of Poltava': it was the work of Lomonosov, the academy's Professor of Chemistry, the practical technician, the artist, the historian and devoted follower of Peter the Great.

Lomonosov taught Russians how to write poetry, composed an authoritative Russian Grammar (1755), and helped to establish the concept of a literary Russian language which could draw on the riches of Church Slavonic literature as well as the colloquial language.

As he accumulated his modern knowledge, Lomonosov became aware of the dearth of means to bring Enlightenment to the younger generation. Russia needed a modern university

ABOVE *Moscow University; founded by Lomonosov it became Russia's intellectual powerhouse.*

with Russian as its medium of instruction. In 1755, with the support of his patron Ivan I. Shuvalov, Lomonosov opened the doors of Moscow University, which still bears his name. 'He created the first university,' wrote Pushkin, who added, 'He himself, it would be truer to say, was our first university.' Realizing the importance of preparing students for the new venture, Lomonosov pleaded for the establishment of two schools attached to the university, gymnasiums for nobles and non-nobles. Without them, he explained to Shuvalov, the university would be 'ploughed land without seeds'.

Lomonosov died in 1765 and did not live to see his seedcorn thrive and flourish. But in the 18th century Moscow University, with its gymnasiums, produced many of Russia's leading men of letters and thinkers.

Elizabeth, and that, as is customary in other states, one or two of the most exalted persons be appointed as trustees, in order that they may watch over the affairs of the whole institution and report on its needs as these arise.

This institution may not be subject to any authority but the Senate.

To this end it is necessary that a special director be appointed to devote himself to the well-being of the university and look after its revenues; together with the professors, to supervise scholarship in the university and teaching in the grammar school; and to report on all these matters to the trustees, requesting their approval.

Theological studies will properly remain the province of the Holy Synod.

The professors in the university shall be ten in number, in three faculties.

Every professor must, for at least two hours a day, excluding Saturdays, Sundays, and official holidays, deliver a public lecture on his own subject in the university, without requiring any payment from the persons who attend.

All the professors must assemble once a week, on Saturday morning, in the presence of the director of the university, to discuss any regulations and institutions which relate to scholarship and may contribute to its betterment. At these general meetings all matters concerning the students are to be decided, and the fines for rudeness and disorderly conduct determined.

All public lectures must be given either in Latin or in Russian, taking account of the requirements of the subject and of whether the professor is a foreigner or a native Russian.

A list of the new lectures to be provided in each half-year is to be posted up in the university building.

At the end of each month a Saturday is to be set aside when the professors will require the students to defend a thesis in private session.

So that nothing may be left undone that might encourage young persons to apply themselves to learning, once a year, on 26 April, awards are to be made publicly to them; these awards can take the form of small gold or silver medals.

Every student must study for three years at the university, in which time he may be able to graduate in all the subjects offered, or at least in those which may be relevant to his future intentions. Before the termination of this period he is not to be taken away from his studies against his will nor obliged to serve.

Since learning does not tolerate coercion and is rightly included among the noblest institutions of mankind, no serfs are to be admitted either to the university or to the grammar school. If, however, some nobleman perceives exceptional cleverness in the son of one of his serfs and wishes him to acquire learning, he must first emancipate him and renounce all his rights and powers over him.

In so far as in Moscow there are no properly established free schools, where young persons can be suitably prepared for advanced study, Her Imperial Majesty has most graciously decreed that two grammar schools be established in connection with Moscow University and under its administration – one for nobles and the other for persons from the other classes, except serfs.

In order to observe the distinction between nobles and the rest, they are to be taught in different grammar schools, but when the pupils leave the grammar school and become students of higher learning, nobles and the rest are to be mixed together, so as to give the greater incentive to industrious study.

On the European stage, Elizabeth's policy was the maintenance of Russia's alliance with Austria, in order to counteract the growing power of Prussia under Frederick the Great. In 1756 Russia concluded alliances with France and Austria as Frederick invaded Saxony. The Seven Years War that ensued saw many Russian victories, culminating in the taking of Berlin on 28 September 1760.

The gains were short-lived. Immediately after Elizabeth's death in December 1761, her heir Peter III was to renounce all Russia's conquests in Prussia and form an alliance with Frederick.

Elizabeth nominated as her successor her nephew Carl Peter Ulric, known as Peter, born in 1728 to

Elizabeth's sister Anna, duchess of Holstein. In 1742 he was brought to Russia from Germany to be groomed for his future role, and provided with a German bride, Sophia Augusta Frederica. She arrived in Moscow in 1744 at the age of 15, adopted the name Catherine upon her baptism into the Orthodox Church later that year, and in 1745 was married to the heir to the Russian throne. In her *Memoir*, written after she had ascended that throne herself as Catherine II, Catherine recalled her early impressions of Russia and of her husband. Peter was evidently a most unsatisfactory spouse, or so the *Memoir* would have us believe.

In Moscow my mother and I lived quietly. Few people came to visit us and I was prepared for my conversion to the Orthodox faith. I was fifteen. The bishop of Pskov, Simon Todorsky, was asked to introduce me into the dogma of the Orthodox Church. He convinced me of what I already believed, that the celestial crown cannot be separated from the terrestrial one. I had been instructed before by a priest who often told me that before the first communion every Christian could choose the religion that seemed most convincing to him.

My conversion took place without any effort. 28 June 1744 was fixed for the ceremony and the next day, St Peter's Day, for my betrothal to the grand prince. The day before, I went to confession and communion and was confirmed in the public chapel of the court.

The grand prince had shown some interest in me during my illness and continued to do so after I recovered. While he seemed to like me, I cannot say that I either liked or disliked him. I was taught to obey and it was my mother's business to see about my marriage, but to tell the truth I believe that the crown of Russia attracted me more than his person. He was sixteen, quite good-looking before the pox, but small and infantile, talking of nothing but soldiers and toys. I listened politely and often yawned, but did not interrupt him, and as he thought that he had to speak to me, and referred only to the things which amused him, he enjoyed talking to me for long periods of time. Many people took this for affection, especially those who desired our marriage, but in fact we never used the language of tenderness. It was not for me to begin, for modesty and pride would have prevented me from doing so even if I had had any tender feelings for him; as for him, he had never even thought of it, which did not greatly incline me in his favour.

Doubtful paternity

The ceremony of marriage between the Grand Duke Peter and the Grand Duchess Catherine was due to take place in August 1745, when the grand duke came down with smallpox. This illness ravaged him so frightfully that he emerged from his sick room completely unrecognizable. His face had become hideous. The grand duchess did not see him before their wedding; finally, on the wedding day, despite some care to warn the young girl of the grand duke's ugliness, her first glance at his face froze her on the spot. She turned away moaning, and her mother, the princess of Zerbst, threw herself into the arms of the grand duke and held him in her embrace for a long while to give her daughter time to recover from the shock.

Finally they celebrated the marriage, but the grand duke was incapable of having children due to an obstacle which circumcision remedies among eastern peoples. The grand duke, however, thought his case was without remedy. The grand duchess, who had no interest in him and was not yet impressed with the need for children, accepted his malady with some relief.

The Grand Duchess Catherine then met Sergei Saltykov, and became pregnant by him.

From the French Embassy, St Petersburg, 8 September 1758, *Notes*

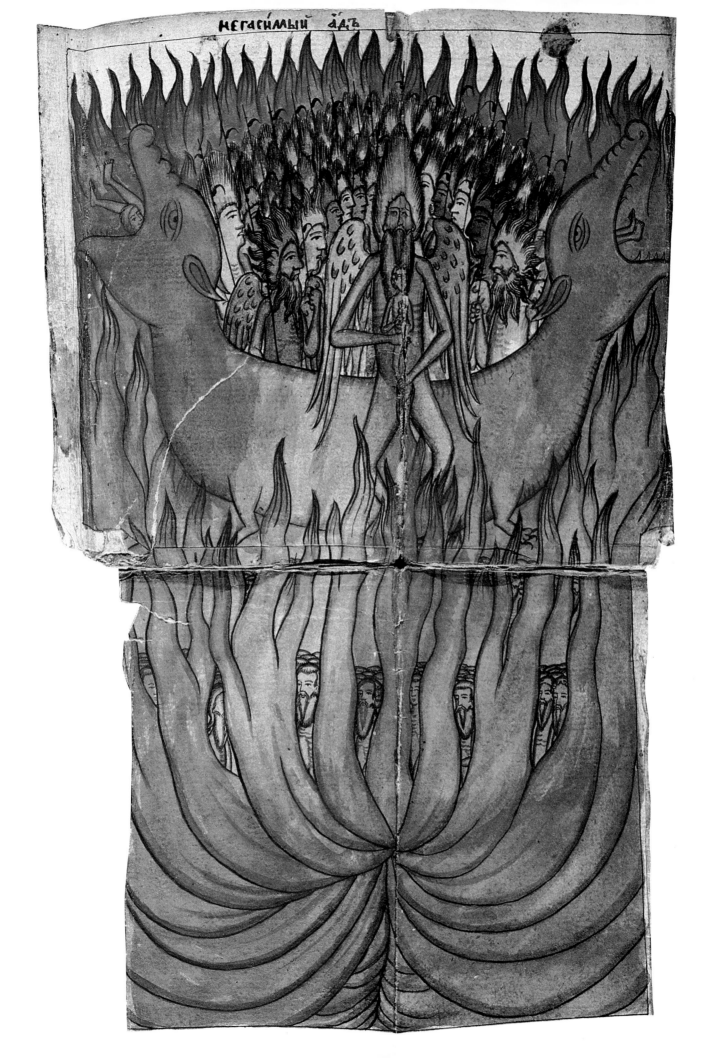

НЕГАСИМЫЙ АДЪ

LEFT *17th-century popular print depicting the torments of Hell. Contemporary belief in eternal punishment did not deter Catherine from sinning through the flesh.*

RIGHT *Celebrating a wedding contract. Catherine's marriage to the future Peter III was unhappy from the start.*

Catherine and Peter's first child, Paul, who, according to Catherine's own *Memoir*, was actually fathered by the courtier Sergei Saltykov, was not born until 1754, and was then immediately removed to the Empress Elizabeth's apartments. But Catherine found ways of keeping herself occupied.

When the required forty days after my confinement had passed, the Empress Elizabeth came a second time to my room for the churching ceremony. I had got out of bed to welcome her but she found me looking so weak and worn that she made me sit down for the prayers read by her confessor. My son had been brought to the room, and this was the first time I had seen him since his birth. I found him beautiful and the sight of him made my heart rejoice, but the moment the prayers were over the empress had him carried away and herself departed.

1 November 1754 was the day fixed by Her Majesty for me to receive the usual congratulations after six weeks of confinement. For this occasion the room next door to mine was richly furnished and there, while I sat on a bedcover of pink velvet embroidered with silver, everybody came to kiss my hand.

The empress came too, and then proceeded to the Winter Palace, where we were to follow her two or three days later. I made the move with the firm resolution that I would not leave my room until I felt enough strength to overcome melancholy.

I was then reading Voltaire's *Histoire de l'Allemagne* and *Histoire Universelle*. After that I read all the Russian books I could get hold of during that winter, among them two immense volumes of Baronius translated into Russian. Then I devoted myself to Montesquieu's *Esprit des Lois*; after that I read the *Annals* of Tacitus which produced a curious revolution in my mind, aided perhaps by the gloomy disposition of my spirit at the time.

I began to see everything in black and searched to find deeper and more intrinsic causes for the various events which presented themselves to my sight.

Catherine's husband came to the throne as Peter III upon Elizabeth's death in December 1761. His reign was to last barely six months, but it contained one notable piece of legislation. In the time of Peter I state service in the army, navy, or civil service had become compulsory for noblemen.

After Peter I's death his successors made a number of concessions, for example reducing the period of

ABOVE *Peter III.*

service. In 1762, with the charter of freedom to the nobility, compulsory service was ended forever.

Noble sentiments have sown in the hearts of true Russian patriots an infinite loyalty to, and love for, us, and great willingness and zeal for our service; therefore we do not see the need for compulsory service, which has been employed up to this time.

Consequently, by the power vested in us from on high, and out of our supreme imperial grace, we bestow freedom and liberty henceforth and forever upon the whole Russian nobility and their descendants, who may continue to serve, in our empire as in other European powers allied to us, on the basis of the following statutes:

All gentlemen in the different sectors of our service may continue as long as they wish and as their circumstances allow; however, those in military service may not seek a discharge or leave during cam-

paigns, nor for three months before they begin, but on their conclusion both inside and outside the country. Those in military service may apply for a discharge from service, or for retirement, to their commanders and await a decision; those in the top eight ranks of all our sectors of service must receive our own imperial confirmation; those in the other ranks must receive a decision from the departments to which they belong.

All serving gentlemen who wish to transfer from the military to the civil service, if there are vacancies, are to be promoted upon appointment after examination, if they have served three years in the same rank, i.e., the rank with which they are transferring to the civil or other service.

Whosoever, having been some time in retirement, or in civil or other service after military service, wishes to re-enter military service, will be accepted if he proves to be worthy of it, retaining the rank he has, converted to a military rank, but with less seniority than all those who had the same rank as he did when he was discharged from military service; if they have all been promoted since, then the person transferring to military service will receive seniority from the day he is appointed; and we ordain this in order that those serving should receive advantage and profit over those not serving.

Whoever wishes to travel to other European states after leaving our service, shall freely receive suitable passports from our ministry of foreign affairs, with the proviso that when necessity demands, gentlemen outside our state present themselves in their fatherland; and that as soon as a proclamation of such a nature is made, everyone in this position is obliged to carry out our orders instantly, on pain of sequestration of his estate.

Russian gentlemen in the service of other European sovereigns may, according to their desires and the available vacancies, enter into our service on returning to their fatherland, those in the service of crowned heads taking the ranks shown on their patents, but those serving others taking a lowering in rank, as established by former legislation.

Since by this our most gracious decree none of the Russian gentlemen shall continue to serve against their will, neither shall they be employed for any kind of local affairs by the administrative bodies established by us, unless special necessity demands it, and even then it shall only be commanded by a decree signed in our own hand.

Though by this our most gracious enactment all the noble Russian gentlemen, apart from the small-holders, will exercise their freedom forever, our fatherly concern for them extends even further to their young children, whom henceforth, for information only, we order them to present at the heralds' office at the age of twelve years, in the provinces or towns, wherever is more practical and convenient, and at the same time their parents, or the relatives in whose charge they are, are to declare what they have learned up to the age of twelve. No one, on pain of our grave anger, should dare to rear their children without instruction in subjects becoming to a Russian gentleman, so we order all gentlemen with one thousand peasants or less to present their children directly to our Cadet Corps, where they will be educated with the most diligent care in all the accomplishments appropriate to a gentleman, and on completion of his studies each will leave with a rank according to his deserts, and may then enter and continue service in the manner set out above.

But since we decree this, our most gracious enactment for all the noble gentlemen, as a fundamental and permanent principle for eternity, we confirm in conclusion in the most solemn terms with our imperial word, that it be held forever to be sacred and inviolable, as enacted and in its privileges. We hope that the whole Russian nobility, aware of how great is our generosity towards it and its descendants, will be inspired by loyalty and zeal for us, not to withdraw from or shun service.

As for all those who have not been in any service anywhere, but spend all their time in idleness and sloth, and do not instruct their children in subjects beneficial to the fatherland, we order all loyal and true sons of the fatherland to scorn and reject them, since they are careless of the common good, nor will they be tolerated at court or at public meetings and celebrations.

Despite this concession, Peter's pro-German sentiments, his neglect of the Orthodox religion and hair-brained military schemes aimed at aiding Frederick the Great of Prussia succeeded in alienating the upper echelons of the nobility. He was deposed in favour of his wife Catherine and soon afterwards, in July 1762, killed in suspicious circumstances. Aleksey Grigoryevich Orlov, brother of Catherine's current lover Grigory and an active participant in the plot to depose Peter III, here describes the events leading to Peter's death in July 1762 in a letter to Catherine:

Your Majesty, I do not know where to begin, fearing Your Majesty's wrath or that you should think that we were the cause of the death of the monster, monster to you and all Russia. Now his valet Maslov has also fallen sick, and the monster himself is so ill that I do not think he will live till night. He has lost consciousness and we, as well as the whole detachment, pray God that He should rid us of him. Maslov can report to Your Majesty in what a state he is, if Your Majesty does not believe me.

Your faithful slave,
[Signature torn off]

Catherine II the Great

Although she was a German by birth, Catherine II, known as Catherine the Great (ruled 1762–96), regarded herself as the spiritual daughter of Peter the Great. This political kinship was symbolized by the equestrian statue of Peter, known later as the *Bronze Horseman*, which she had erected in St Petersburg in 1782. The inscription read 'To Peter the First from Catherine the Second'. Like Peter, Catherine believed firmly that Russia belonged in Europe, but knew that there was still a wide gap to bridge before Russia caught up with its western neighbours. It was said that Peter, whose aims were primarily practical, gave Russians 'bodies' while Catherine gave them 'souls'. It is true that her reign saw the growth of Russian literature and thought, of art and architecture in the classical style, but there were also practical achievements in education, administrative and legal reform, medicine, and town planning.

Most spectacular of all were the triumphs of foreign policy, with the acquisition of the Crimea and a Black Sea coastline as a result of victories over Turkey in the wars of 1768–74 and 1787–92, and parts of what had been Poland and Lithuania to the west after the partitions of Poland in 1773, 1793 and 1795. But maintaining great-power status has its price. Catherine was constantly reminded, most vividly by the Pugachov revolt of 1773–4, that she ruled over a multinational empire in which a large proportion of the population were still serfs or peasants eking out a subsistence living. Dissenters began to appear in the upper classes too, as men like Alexander Radishchev, inspired by the ideals of the French Revolution, denounced autocracy and serfdom. 'Monarchy without despotism' may have been Catherine's own ideal, but, as the future was to prove, there were still too few safeguards against the reappearance of tyranny.

OPPOSITE   *Catherine II, the Great (1762–96)*

Five or six days after Catherine II's accession to the throne in July 1762, she went to the Senate, which she had moved to the Summer Palace in St Petersburg, in order to speed everything up. The first matter presented to her was the country's extreme penury: the army was in Prussia and the nation had been increasingly insolvent for the last eight months. The cost of bread in St Petersburg had doubled. The Empress Elizabeth had, towards the end of her life, hoarded as much as she could and kept her money where she could see it, but she did not use it for the needs of the empire. There was universal want; almost nobody was paid.

Peter III did practically the same. When asked for money to meet the demands of the state, he, like his aunt, grew angry and replied, 'Find it where you like; the money we have here belongs to us.' As Elizabeth had done, he divorced his personal interests from those of the empire.

When Catherine became aware of this situation, she at once declared to the Senate that, as she belonged to the state, she considered that everything she owned belonged to the state, and that there should in future be no difference between her interests and those of the state. This declaration brought tears to the eyes of the whole assembly, which rose and unanimously expressed its gratitude for such reasonable sentiments. Catherine supplied all the money that was needed and for a time stopped the export of corn; these measures within two months restored abundance and reduced all costs.

Although Catherine was raised to the throne by the Guards in a coup masterminded by her current lover Grigory Orlov, she had no intention of being a puppet ruler. In the preceding autobiographical fragments she described (using the third person) the aims of the first years of her reign.

In an undated document, extracts of which follow, Catherine listed her achievements.

In July 1762, Russia had emerged from an onerous war with Prussia, but peace only gave her the advantage of a respite. There was a yearly deficit of seven million roubles, and the state owed about thirteen million in goods to be delivered. Commerce was ruined by monopolies.

The Empress Elizabeth had wanted to borrow two million roubles from Holland during the Seven Years War, but did not succeed, so the crown was greatly discredited. Fortresses crumbled in ruin; the fleet was neglected. At Catherine's coronation, on 22 September 1762, the revenue was counted and the total reached was sixteen million roubles. Two years later the calculation was repeated and the sum arrived at was twenty-eight million.

Nobody knew what the revenue of the state actually was. Corruption reigned everywhere. The Senate remained deaf and lethargic in the affairs of state. Shamefully, there was no headed paper for the Senate before Catherine had it ordered. Prisons were so full that though the Empress Elizabeth, a short time before her death, had liberated about seventeen thousand convicts, there were still at the time of Catherine's coronation no fewer than eight thousand. About two hundred thousand peasants were in revolt, among them members of the clergy and some of the nobility. The seats of legislation had reached a degree of disintegration and corruption which made them scarcely recognizable. Private persons who had laid their hands on money in one way or another considered it unjust if they were asked to account for sums which totalled about four million roubles in cash and seven million in goods. The political situation was such that the Tartars were expected any moment in the Ukraine.

In 1765 there was a credit of five and a half million roubles. The debts of the reigns of Peter the Great, the Empress Anna, and three-quarters of those of the Empress Elizabeth were paid. Commerce was raising its head, monopolies were abolished, the credit of the crown was such that merchants confided their money to the state in one part of the empire to receive it back, on a given date, in another. The value of silver was established once and for all. The civil and army lists were put right, the fleet reorganized, the clergy paid, the rebels pacified: justice ceased to be corrupt, private owners paid their debts without ruin.

A hostel for foundlings was established, a school for the Academy of Fine Arts, a school for noble young girls and another school for daughters of the bourgeoisie; pensions were granted to all those unfit to be employed; a bank was established in Astrakhan; a fund for widows was started, and a pawnbroker's was opened. A great deal of work was put into the reform of the laws, and there was an impressive amount of building.

It is difficult to describe the obstacles Catherine had to encounter among the members of her government. When she first brought her notes on the reform of the laws and declared them to the Senate, they said, '*Ce sont des axiomes à renverser des murailles*' (Axioms such as these could bring walls down). But Catherine persevered.

Catherine's ideas for improving her adopted country were set out in her *Instructions*, or *Nakaz*, of 1767, a document addressed to the delegates or commissioners summoned to Moscow from all classes, except the serfs and the clergy, to discuss the recodification of the laws. Based upon works by Montesquieu, Beccaria, and other European thinkers, the *Nakaz* sought to apply the concepts of the Enlightenment to Russian conditions. It was a statement of ideals rather than a detailed programme for reform. The 526 articles dealt with such issues as crime and punishment, slavery, and definitions of liberty. A few are quoted here.

Russia is a European state.

This is clearly demonstrated by the following observations: the alterations which Peter the Great undertook in Russia succeeded with the greater ease because the manners that prevailed at that time had been introduced among us by a mixture of different nations, and were quite unsuitable to our climate. Peter I, by introducing the manners and customs of Europe among the European people in his dominions, found at that time such means as even he himself was not optimistic enough to expect.

The possessions of the Russian empire extend upon the terrestrial globe to thirty-two degrees of latitude and to a hundred and sixty-five of longitude. Their extent requires absolute power vested in the ruler, to compensate for the delay occasioned by the great distances.

What is the true end of monarchy? Not to deprive people of their natural liberty; but to correct their actions, in order to attain the supreme good.

The intention and the end of monarchy is the glory of the citizens, of the state, and of the sovereign.

The laws ought to be so framed as to secure the safety of every citizen as much as possible.

The equality of the citizens consists in this: that they should all be subject to the same laws.

This equality requires institutions so well adapted as to prevent the rich from oppressing those who are not as wealthy as themselves.

Liberty is the right of doing what the laws allow. The laws ought to be so framed that no one citizen should fear another.

A society of citizens requires a certain fixed order: there should be some to govern, others to obey.

The civil laws ought to guard both against the abuse of slavery and against the dangers which may arise from it. A great number of slaves ought not be enfranchised all at once, nor by a general law.

However, it is still highly necessary to prevent those causes which so frequently incited slaves to rebel; but until these are discovered, it is impossible to prevent the like accidents by laws.

RIGHT *Silver rouble showing Catherine's head; the Imperial eagle is on the reverse (below). Russia's annual deficit was 7 million roubles at the start of the reign.*

The French writer and scholar Diderot, whose library Catherine had purchased and returned to him for life after he fell into debt, visited Russia in 1773–4. As Catherine herself was to observe (here reported by the French ambassador Louis-Philippe de Ségur), many of the philosopher's proposals for Russia were impractical.

I frequently had long conversations with him, but with more curiosity than profit. Had I placed faith in him, every institution in my empire would have been overturned: legislation, administration, politics and finances would all have been changed for the sake of some impracticable theories.

However, as I listened more than I talked, anyone, on being present, would have supposed him to be the commanding pedagogue and myself the humble scholar. Probably he was of that opinion himself, for, after some time, finding that he had not wrought in my government any of those great innovations which he had advised, he exhibited his surprise by a sort of haughty discontent.

Then speaking to him freely, I said, 'Monsieur Diderot, I have listened with the greatest pleasure to all that your brilliant genius has inspired you with; but all your grand principles, which I understand very well, though they will make fine books, would make sad work in actual practice. You forget, in all your plans for reformation, the difference between our two positions. You work only upon paper, which submits to everything. Whereas I, a poor empress, work upon human nature, which is, on the contrary, irritable and easily offended.'

I am satisfied that, from that time, he pitied me, and looked on me as one possessed only of a narrow and ordinary mind. From that moment he spoke to me only on literary subjects, and politics disappeared from our conversations.

Catherine's *Nakaz* had little to say about education. In keeping with Enlightenment ideals, however, Catherine firmly believed that education was one of the main channels for improving society, by creating 'a new type of person'. Experiments in the 1760s included the establishment of foundling homes, reorganization of the élite Cadet Corps (or Military Academy), and the first girls' school, in the Smolny Institute for Noble Girls in St Petersburg.

Catherine wins the heart

A gentleman [identity unknown] who is just returned to London from a long residence at the Court of St Petersburg, has favoured us with the following authentic description and character of the present empress of Russia.

Catherine II is about 41 years of age, of a fine size and shape; her complexion is charming, her eyes bright and expressive; her manner of address is full of dignity, yet easy and engaging, owing chiefly to a most excellent understanding: lively imagination shines in every feature, and excites the admiration of all who behold her. There is a commanding sweetness in her voice expressive of great benevolence, which fixes the attention and wins the heart; and it is a source of wonder that she can sometimes be heard talking with almost every Foreign Minister in his own language.

Her Majesty excels in every accomplishment that adds grace and beauty to one sex, and is acquainted with most of the sciences that are useful and ornamental in the other. She has long been the delight of the people over whom she now reigns; she has studied their genius, and makes their good her principal care.

From *The Reading Mercury, and Oxford Gazette*,
17 September 1770.

In the 1780s, Catherine turned her attention to the creation of a nationwide education system of elementary and secondary schooling, provided free of charge, for both boys and girls from all classes except the serfs, backed up by a training college for teachers and centrally produced textbooks. Corporal punishment was forbidden. Religious instruction was supervised by teachers, not priests. The rules and regulations of the new system were set out in the Education Statute of 1786. The following extracts deal with the four-grade core curriculum.

Institutions are to be established in which young people will be taught in their native language on the basis of general prescriptions. Such institutions must exist in all provinces and districts of the Russian empire under the name of national schools, which are divided into high schools and primary schools.

In every provincial capital there must be one national high school consisting of four grades or classes in which pupils will be taught the following subjects and sciences in their native tongue:

In the first grade they will learn reading, writing, the foundations of Christian law and moral education. Starting with the learning of the alphabet, they will learn to count, then to read the *Primer*, *Rules for pupils*, *Short catechism*, and *Bible history*. In such a manner pupils should by the second half of their first year be able to copy, read out loud and write arabic numbers and Slavonic and Roman numerals, and also be taught the elementary rules of grammar, as contained in the table on the recognition of letters, which is located in the textbook *Handbook for teachers of the first and second grades* [published 1783].

In the second grade they will begin to read the *Full catechism* without the proofs from holy scripture, the book *On the duties of a man and citizen* and *Arithmetic*, part 1, repeat *Bible history*, continue handwriting and learning the rules of grammar from the aforementioned *Handbook*. In this grade pupils will also begin the study of drawing.

In the third grade they will continue drawing lessons, read *Exposition of the gospels*, repeat the *Full catechism*, this time with the proofs from holy scripture, study *Arithmetic*, part 2; the first part of *History of the*

ABOVE *Pupils from the Smolny Institute, Russia's first school for girls. Free education was available to all young people.*

world, *Introduction to European geography* and begin *Geographical description of the Russian empire* and *Russian grammar*, with exercises in spelling.

In the fourth grade [two years] they will repeat *Russian geography*, continue with drawing, *History of the world*, and *Russian grammar*, accompanied by practical writing exercises, such as letters, accounts, lists and so on. *Russian history* and *Mathematical geography* will be taught with exercises using a globe. Also the fundamentals of geometry, mechanics, physics, natural history and civic architecture. In mathematics lessons, geometry and architecture will be studied in the first year and mechanics and physics in the second, together with architecture, which will include technical drawing.

In all the national high schools, in addition to the rules of the Russian language, basic Latin must also be offered for those who wish to continue studying it in higher education, in grammar schools or universities. Also, they should teach whichever foreign language is likely to be most useful for everyday life, with reference to the location of the area where the school is situated.

Catherine was something of a workaholic, drafting much of her own legislation. But the company of friends, and lovers, was important to her. Twelve official favourites have been documented. The most important of her relationships was with Prince Grigory Potemkin. Their love affair lasted for only two years, 1774–5, but he remained her trusted friend and adviser until his death in 1791. The following letters date from the height of their affair. The first is from Catherine to Potemkin.

Now, Sir Hero, may I hope that I will receive absolution for my sins? As you will be pleased to see, there is no question of fifteen lovers but only of one-third of that figure, of which the first occurred unwillingly and the fourth in despair, which cannot be counted as indulgence. As to the other three, God is my witness that it was not through wantonness, for which I have no leanings; had I been destined, as a young woman, to get a husband whom I could have loved, I would never have changed towards him.

The trouble is that my heart is loath to remain even one hour without love. It is said that human vices are often concealed under the cloak of kindness, and it is possible that such a disposition of the heart is more of a vice than a virtue, but I ought not to write this to you, for you might stop loving me or refuse to go to the army fearing I should forget you. But I do not think I could do anything so foolish, and if you wish to keep me for ever, show me as much friendship as affection, and continue to love me and to tell me the truth.

Catherine the woman

Catherine II was 14 years old when she came to Russia in 1744 from her native Germany to marry her second cousin, the 16-year-old Duke Peter of Holstein-Gotthorp; the grandson of Peter the Great, he had been appointed heir to the throne by his aunt, the Empress Elizabeth. It was not a happy marriage, and for many years Catherine failed to produce a child. When she finally gave birth to a son, Paul, in 1754, it was, as she herself records, because she had been urged to choose the father herself.

Having been pushed into unfaithfulness for official reasons, Catherine saw no reason not to continue. She was evidently a highly sexed young woman, and her private life was lampooned in many cartoons and caricatures. She was accused of having over 20 lovers, but the number can be reduced to 12. The first was the father of her son; she made the second, Stanislas Augustus Poniatowski, king of Poland. The third was a handsome Guards officer, Grigory Orlov, who helped to place her on the throne and remained by her side for 12 years.

The great love of her life, the one-eyed giant Grigory Potemkin, came in 1774. He was her lover for only two years, but remained her helpmate, possibly her husband, her closest friend, the commander of her armed forces, and the confidant of her love affairs until his death in 1791. To him she wrote a moving letter in December 1774, explaining that she would have been faithful to Grigory Orlov forever had he not betrayed her. Licentiousness had no charms for her, she wrote, but her heart could not readily survive for a moment without love. Her surviving letters show that she was passionately in love with Potemkin and with Peter Zavadovsky who followed him. She then had seven more lovers. Some deserted her, some she dismissed, one died in her arms, leaving her broken-hearted for months.

Catherine's lovers in later life were much younger than she was – nearly 40 years in the case of the last, Platon Zubov. For there was something maternal in her attitude to them. She believed herself to be educating these young men to take an interest in public affairs, and share in her cultural interests. To some extent they may have replaced her son Paul in her affections; her relations with him had been distorted from the beginning.

Catherine had always been interested in political and historical literature and was a voracious reader, making careful marginal notes and even copying out great chunks from authors who inspired her legislation – the English lawyer Sir William Blackstone was one. She enjoyed English novels, like Smollett's *Humphrey Clinker*, and wrote political tracts, history, children's stories, satires, and many plays, including a Russian version of Shakespeare's *Merry Wives of Windsor*. She also wrote librettos for the opera – a brilliant court needed this form of art – although she herself was not musical. She also loved painting, architecture, and gardens.

Foreigners who were admitted to Catherine's society praised her charm and the ease with which she achieved informality with no loss of majesty. She was vain – yet needed constant reassurance. She showed great courage in the various crises of her reign, as in her actual seizure of power from her husband, Peter III, in 1762, and when she stood up to Prussia and England in 1791, while the guns of the Swedish fleet rattled the windows of her palace in St Petersburg.

Although Catherine was increasingly short-tempered as she grew older, she was normally considerate to those who worked for her. When she died in 1796 her servants and courtiers wept.

ABOVE *Prince Grigory Potemkin*

ABOVE *Catherine the Great*

The second letter, from Potemkin to Catherine, also written about 1774–5, has Catherine's annotations in the right-hand margin.

Allow me, my dearest, to say these last words to end our 'row'. Do not be surprised that I am so anxious about our love. Apart from the innumerable gifts you have bestowed on me, you have given me your heart. I wish to be preferred to all the former ones, to make you understand that no one has ever loved you as much as I, and, as I am the work of your hands, I wish that my repose should also be the work of your hands; that you should find joy in being kind to me, that you should try everything for my consolation and find consolation in me for the great work you have to accomplish, because of your high calling.

I allow.
The sooner the better.
Do not be anxious.
When you wash your hands one hand rubs the other.
You are and will be this for ever.
I can see it and do believe it. My heart is happy. My primary joy.

It will come of its own accord.
Let the mind rest in order that the feelings should be free, they are all love, they themselves will find the best path.
The end of our quarrel. Amen.

Potemkin's greatest influence was in the realm of foreign policy. In 1787 he was awarded the title prince of Tauris, following the annexation of the former Turkish territory of Crimea to Russia in 1783 and the development of the new Crimean or Tauride province.

It was Catherine's acquisitions abroad – from Turkey in 1768–74 and 1787–92, and from Poland as a result of the partitions – that marked her out as one of the most successful rulers in Europe, but the carving up of Poland between Russia, Prussia, and Austria in 1772, 1793, and 1795 was particularly harshly judged by posterity. In the following public pronouncements, Catherine seeks to justify the last two partitions, in the wake of the French Revolution.

Among the disorders and violence stemming from the dissension and discord to which the republic of Poland constantly falls prey, Her Imperial Majesty has always looked with particular sympathy upon the oppression to which the lands and towns adjacent to the Russian empire, which were formerly her property and which were founded on the Orthodox Christian faith, have been subjected.

Now, a number of unworthy Poles, the enemies of their fatherland, imitating the atheistic, frenzied and corrupt rabble of French insurgents, are trying to scatter and spread a pernicious new doctrine throughout Poland and thereby destroy both its own peace and the peace of its neighbours forever.

For these reasons, Her Imperial Majesty is now pleased to take under her power all lands, towns, and regions enclosed within the new frontier line between Russia and Poland, so that henceforth and forever these lands, towns and regions may stand under the sceptre of the Russian empire.

The inhabitants and owners of these lands, whatever their origin or name, shall have citizenship thereof.

The violent force which Her Imperial Majesty was obliged to use to put an end to the revolt which broke out in Poland met with total success, and Poland was brought into complete submission and occupied by the empress's troops. Therefore, Her Majesty hastened to conclude an agreement with her two allies, the Holy Roman Emperor, Leopold II, and the king of Prussia, Frederick William II, with regard to taking the most effective steps to prevent similar disturbances recurring if a stable and strong government is not established.

These two monarchs, convinced by past experience of the absolute inability of the Polish republic, while enjoying any form of independence, to establish such a government in their country recognized that for the good of preserving the peace and happiness of their citizens, it was imperative that they should undertake and execute the complete partitioning of that republic between the three neighbouring powers, Russia, Prussia, and Austria.

BELOW *Mosaic in a Turkish church. Prince Potemkin, the great love of Catherine's life, was created prince of Tauris for his valour against the Turks.*

The empire of Catherine II the Great

SWEDEN

GULF OF FINLAND

R. Neva
○ St Petersburg

INGRIA

ESTONIA

Narva

Novgorod ● NOVGOROD

BALTIC SEA

LIVONIA

Pskov ●

Riga ●

COURLAND

1772

GREAT BRITAIN

DUTCH NETHERLANDS

Vilna ●

P R U S S I A

Minsk ●

1795

P O L A N D

AUSTRIAN NETHERLANDS

HOLY

To Prussia by 1795

Warsaw ○

Pinsk ●

1793

V O L H Y N I A

ROMAN

● Paris

EMPIRE

To Austria by 1795

KIEV

Kiev ●

U K R A I

● Odessa

FRANCE

Vienna ●

A U S T R I A -

H U N G A R Y

E M P I R E

R. Rhine

R. Danube

B L

Russian imperialism in Europe reached a peak during the reign of Catherine II the Great. To the south, Crimea and a Black Sea coastline were acquired, while a tripartite agreement with Austria and Prussia brought about the gradual disintegration of Poland. However, this massive multinational empire was beset with social unrest. The Pugachev rebellion in the south-east was one famous expression of this.

A R C H A N G E L

Archangel

R U S S I A

Ural MOUNTAINS

Perm

KAZAN

R. Volga · Kazan

UFA

Nizhny
Novgorod

NIZHNY
NOVGOROD

ver

MOSCOW

○ Moscow

Orenburg · R. Yaik

R. Oka

Penza

Yaitsk ·

U R A L S K

Orel ·

Uzen

VORONEZH

BELGOROD

R. Don

Guryev ·

ARAL SEA

NE

ZAPOROZHE

Chorny
Yar

ASTRAKHAN

Astrakhan ·

Azov

C A S P I A N

AZOV SEA

S E A

CRIMEA

CAUCASUS

MOUNTAINS

ACK SEA

| | Acquisitions of Catherine the Great |
| | Polish Empire before partitionings |

1795   Date of partition

— — — Russian boundary, 1762

—·—·— Russian boundary, 1795

——▶ Route of Pugachov, 1774

○   Major cities

0   500 km

O T T O M A N E M P I R E

By western standards, 18th-century Russia was a major military and diplomatic power with a backward economy and society. Nowhere was the contrast between East and West more dramatic than in the Russian countryside, where the mass of the population were still serfs, owned by their masters like goods and chattels, and liable to perform labour services or render payment in money and kind to their lords with barely any rights to protect them from abuse. Catherine hoped to improve the lot of the peasantry, but wholesale emancipation was not envisaged, although discussion of the issues was permitted and even encouraged. In 1766, for example, the Free Economic Society in St Petersburg set an essay competition on the subject of peasant rights to land. One of the best entries was written by A. Ya. Polyonov, a translator from the Russian Academy of Sciences, who argued that serfdom was rooted deep in Russian history.

The founders of Russia, after the example of other peoples, were of the opinion that prisoners of war should be turned into slaves.

Wars collected a great number of prisoners, who, by ancient custom, were brought into slavery and included with other plunder. Household management was entrusted to prisoners, who were used as servants in town, and for agriculture outside it.

This harsh and inhuman law of war was preserved in its entirety right up to our times, and we can see clearly the effects of this experience on our peasantry, whose impoverished condition has reached to such extremes that, deprived of almost all human qualities, so to speak, they cannot see the size of their misfortune and seem to be weighed down by a permanent slumber.

Peasants justly deserve all possible care, and neither time nor labour should be spared to bring them into good circumstances. To speak the truth, so many must be obliged to such people who, saving others arduous tasks and worries, feed them abundantly, who, while they have almost nothing, provide others so generously, who, having no joy throughout their whole lives, are exclusively occupied with the increase of the benefit of others. In a word, our life,

our security, all our advantages are in their power and coupled to their condition.

Nothing can bring a man into greater dejection than to deprive him of human rights. Because of this he gradually becomes negligent and lazy. But let a man have human rights, then his strength will return and he will soon become a new man.

The illiterate masses of the peasantry rarely articulated their misery on paper, but examples of popular satire composed by them or on their behalf have come down to us via a vigorous oral tradition of song, fables, and tales, as well as in the form of folk prints and even manuscript collections. The following anonymous works are characteristic examples. The first laments the exploitation of the poor, the slaves, by their masters.

O woe to us slaves living for the masters!
We do not know how to serve their ferocity!
Service is like a sharp scythe;
And kindness is like the morning dew.
And what we make for ourselves – even over that we
    have no power
So in the whole world – there's no such vile existence!
It seems both heaven and earth are angry with us!
Surely we could find ourselves grain without our
    masters!
For what have the woods and fields been created,
When the share of the poor has been taken away?
Why and for what were we born on to this earth?
If we steal from the lord one half-copeck,
The law commands us to be killed like a louse.
And if the master steals ten thousand,
Nobody will judge who should be hanged.
The injustice of the Russian sheriffs has increased:
Whoever brings them a present is right beyond
    argument.
The master can kill the servant like a gelding:
Denunciation by a slave is not believed.
Unjust judges have composed a decree
That we should be tyrannically whipped with a knout
    for that.

Popular arts

The *luboks* were popular prints which appeared at the end of the 17th century, and were the first aspect of Russian popular culture to show western influence, both technically – wood-blocks and later copper-plates were used in their manufacture – and artistically, with the introduction of western motifs, in particular in secular subjects. Mythical figures such as Medusa or the signs of the zodiac, comic narratives and birds, animals, fruit and flowers appear beside figures from Russian legend such as the old witch Baba Yaga, and the Sirin (bird-woman). These motifs also appeared in the applied arts – especially embroidery and ceramics. The techniques of sewing were little altered, but ceramic manufacture was significantly changed by more sophisticated methods of preparing clay (faience, majolica, porcelain) and glazing.

In entertainments, music, and the verbal arts, foreign fashions took hold more slowly. Throughout the period, the Old Russian Shrove and Easter customs of sliding down ice hills and riding on swings remained popular.

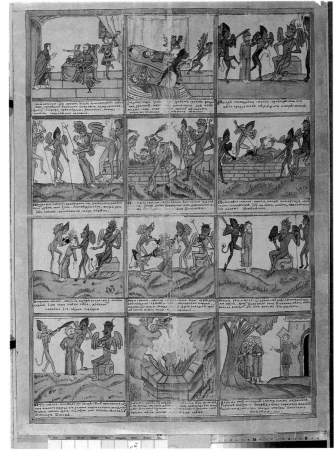

TOP *Fold-out book showing the construction of a church.*
ABOVE *A lubok depicting a sinner's nightmare.*

In music, traditional Russian folk-songs were joined by subjects from abroad: *Marlborough s'en va-t-en guerre* was widely known after 1704. Song and dance melodies were unchanged for many years and traditional ensembles like the 'horn orchestra', a collection of alpenhorn-like instruments each tuned to one note, remained consistently popular.

Drama was also affected by westernization. Peter I, at the beginning of the 18th century, and

ABOVE *An engraving depicting 'The Ox who didn't want to be an Ox', one of the satires that became increasingly popular in the 18th century.*

successive rulers had used plays for propaganda purposes: the 'school plays' – religious and historical dramas modelled on those used for indoctrination by the Jesuits – spawned popular imitations. Short farces ('interludes') and sketches based on those of the Italian *commedia dell'arte* troupes who visited Russia were also popular.

Adaptations of Italian and French romances, such as *Bova the King's Son*, were widely available. *Pesenniks*, collections of popular song texts, ran into dozens of editions, first as manuscripts in the 17th century and then as printed books in the 18th century. Those who could read re-told stories, sang songs and taught theatrical roles to those who could not, so that written texts passed into the oral tradition.

This new popular material began an inexorable erosion of traditional genres, such as oral epics, historical songs and folk tales, which more and more were heard only in remote parts of Russia. Rather than heroic deeds or magic happenings, subjects, by the 18th century, were for the most part down-to-earth. Romance and sexual relations figured widely. New or strange events excited interest: the arrival of an elephant in the 1780s was celebrated in broadsheet verses. Political and social texts ranged from laments on the oppressions of serfdom (*The Serfs' Lament*) to celebrations of the doings of the notorious Stenka Razin, leader of a rebel band of Cossacks in the 17th century. Comic and satirical songs, poems and tales were particularly popular: many works mocked the stupidity of the upper classes and showed servants getting the better of their masters (*The Muzhik and His Master*).

Others illustrated different types of reversal: the 'world upside-down' or characters behaving in a way normally prohibited (*The Ox who didn't want to be an Ox*).

The Russian Empire's great wealth attracted to St Petersburg and Moscow large numbers of foreign entertainers, who presented mechanical theatres, peep-shows, Chinese shades and puppet shows, and performed at *narodnye gulyan'ya*, or seasonal funfairs. Russian entertainers imitated their Italian, French and German counterparts, leading to a fusion of native and western elements which was complete by about 1840.

They try to collect unjust bribes,
And they are not frightened that people die cruelly.
Their power has increased, like the water in the
    Neva;
Wherever you look, everywhere there are lords.
Why do the slaves not get angry with them?
I think that they will soon go crazy with annoyance.
They sell all the good rye to the merchants,
And give us like pigs the bad.
The greedy lords eat meat at fast time,
And even when meat is allowed the slaves must
    cook meatless cabbage soup.
O brothers, it is our misfortune
Always to have rye *kasha*.
The lords drink and make merry,
But do not allow the slaves even to burst out
    laughing.
They go to sleep on a sofa, and order everybody to
    move about quietly,
Not to shout or make a noise.
If anybody carelessly makes a noise,
He receives an unbearable beating.
Only the pipe with tobacco cheers us up
And the green pea in open country.
We'd like to drink from grief a mug of wine,
But there's nowhere to get even sour beer.
The Lord our God!
Give us rest in your heavenly field!
You are our Creator;
Bring us poor people to our end.

There were often dreams of a final reckoning, as in this short piece where the serf 'ox' turns the tables on his 'butcher' master.

The ox did not want to be an ox
And so he became a butcher.
When the butcher went to hit him on the head,
He knocked the blow aside with his horns,
And the butcher fell down.
The ox managed to snatch the axe from him,
Cut off his arms and hung him up by his legs.
And started to pull out the guts and lights.

RIGHT *A stringed musical instrument, traditional to the Tajiks of Central Asia. Its resemblance to a fantastic bird reflects the region's pre-Islamic culture.*

LEFT *Detail from an embroidered woollen skirt. The use of floral motifs is typical of much ornamentation, and is a reflection of the close relationship between peasants and the natural world.*

LEFT *Cotton muslin border for a bed cover. As in the skirt, above, flowers are a recurring theme; here they mingle with birds and animals.*

Occasionally, in the popular imagination, the wily peasant succeeded in getting the better of a member of the gentry.

A certain gentleman was walking ahead along a
	road,
And a peasant was making his way behind,
Taking firewood for sale on a horse.
He shouted to the gentleman, 'Look out, sir,
I'm going along with this load, you see, move to the
	side.'
The gentleman pretended not to hear,
And the peasant caught him in the back with a shaft,
Doing him considerable injury
And tearing his cloak.
Seeing this, the gentleman started to quarrel with
	the peasant,
Seizing him, he said, 'Let's go to court,
Or pay me for the cloak,
And then I won't drag you to the judge.'
The peasant cried, 'Enough, sir, beware,
Let me go, best not to go to court with me,
For you were wickedly haughty with me and too
	much so,
That's why I struck you in the back with the shaft.'
The gentleman said, 'No, you rogue peasant,
I want to get my revenge on you!
Now you've started to quarrel with me,
Let's both go off to court.'
And he went before the judge, and began to explain
The injury the peasant had done him.
The peasant only looked at the judge,
And spoke not a word to him.
The judge at once loudly cried
That the peasant should make some reply.
The judge said, 'I cannot make my decision
When nothing is said to me.'
The gentleman said to the judge, 'To tell the truth,
At the time he was going along quite boldly,
And shouted at me at the top of his voice,
"Get out of the way, sir,
Can't you see that I'm going along with a load, not
	by myself."'
Hearing this, the judge could only burst out
	laughing.

'Why are you complaining?
You only bring shame upon yourself.
When he was polite enough to shout out at you,
Why did you not get out of the way?'
And he ordered the gentleman to be thrown out
With some good bangs on the back on the way.
And so the peasant turned out to be right,
And the gentleman brought upon himself the
	penalty.

In 1773 butchery occurred when a major rebellion erupted in the south, led by Yemelyan Pugachov, a fugitive Don Cossack who claimed to be Tsar Peter III returning to his rightful throne to bring justice to the oppressed.

The edicts which Pugachev issued, always using the titles of Tsar Peter Fyodorovich or Peter III, indicate the wide range of disaffected people who flocked to his banner as he marched through the south. In the Urals, for example, he gathered rebellious tribesmen of Islamic faith.

The great sovereign, tsar of all tsars and worthy Emperor Peter Fyodorovich, upon due deliberation, sends this my personal edict to all my loyal subjects.

Let it be known to every one of you that it is truly I, the great one. And, confident in this belief, know, all of you my subjects, here and everywhere, Muslims and Kalmyks as well as all others, being in all readiness, that you are to come to see me and look upon the radiant image of my face. Nothing must stand in the way of this and, if it pleases you, you should make obeisance to me, breaking your oaths to Catherine.

My order to you is as follows: if any men should rise in opposition, cut off their heads and spill their blood as a warning to their children. And as your forebears, fathers and grandfathers served my grandfather the blessed hero and sovereign Peter Alekseyevich and as he rewarded you, so I will reward you from now on. I have rewarded you with land, water, salt, faith and prayer, pastures, and financial payment; in recognition of this you must serve me to the end of your days.

The Pugachev rebellion

During the first ten years of Catherine's rule, from 1762 to 1772, prolonged war with Turkey exerted mounting pressures in taxation and recruitment on the already burdened serfs (whose protests marked each year of her reign), while the liberation of the gentry from compulsory state service in the 1762 Manifesto raised their hopes of similar relief.

From the year 1762 onwards the serfs lived in expectation of a redivision of all land among the 'black masses' – all those subject to tax – namely, the peasantry.

The Pugachev rebellion, led by a Don Cossack, Yemelyan Pugachev, originated in the southern frontier in 1773 and reverberated throughout the Volga and Ural regions as a series of local uprisings.

Although most of Pugachev's recruits were peasants or had recently been uprooted from the soil (lesser Cossacks, lower clergy, traders and craftsmen from the towns, Volga boatmen, Urals foundry workers) the rebels also included nomads, mountain tribesmen and religious dissenters.

The Pugachev rebellion was concerned more with the encroachment of central government on the freedom of individual groups and the threat to their independence than with peasant issues *per se*. The rising was directed mainly against the nobility – freedom from landlord control being a key demand – and the bureaucracy and the state it administered rather than being directed against the tsar personally.

Religious and social myths played a key part in the spread of the rebellion, and Pugachev was a man who personally appreciated the power of propaganda.

The patent illegality of Catherine's accession and Peter III's abrupt and mysterious death were particularly apposite material, while even the sex of the new sovereign may have undermined her legitimacy in the patriarchal minds of the Russian peasantry.

Sowing seeds of doubt about Catherine's right to rule the empire, Pugachev claimed that he himself was the 'true tsar' (Peter III), who was the 'protector of the people'. As pretender to the throne he was able to air a wide range of political, economic, social and religious grievances and thus to provide a banner of legality for peasant rebellion.

Pugachev's proposals encompassed the grievances of various groups of supporters and offered an alternative form of politics. His seditious letters contained promises to the Yaik Cossacks (in the southern Urals) that traditional liberties, such as fishing and hunting rights, the undermining of which had already led to open revolt, would be restored; promises of freedom for the Bashkirs (in the Urals); promises of redress for the 'Old Believers', religious dissidents who had broken away from the Church in the 17th century in protest against reforms in ritual and service book; and promises of liberation to the peasant workers who were labouring in the Ural factories and mines.

Pugachev's aim was to replace Catherine II's corrupt government with a Cossack-style democracy, which would involve the abolition of serfdom and forced labour in industry: in essence, the people of Russia would become servants of the tsar.

The rebellion failed to undermine the fabric of the tsarist state. Lack of a coherent programme was aggravated by serious rivalries between different groups and the unchallenged superiority of government forces. Yemelyan Pugachev was betrayed to the authorities, captured and executed; and his rebellion was suppressed in 1774 with much bloodshed.

In return, according to this my proclamation, I will be a father and a provider to you and I will not lie to you; I will show great grace. This I have sworn before God. But to anybody who opposes me and is not loyal to me, I will show no grace; his head will be cut off and his pasture seized. To this end we have written this edict with what it establishes.

Saturday, 1 October 1773

Signed by the great sovereign, the Russian tsar, the Emperor Peter III, himself.

As he approached the town of Penza, Pugachev promised the townspeople and the local peasants various rewards and liberties, including religious ones, and incited them to murder their landlords.

By the grace of God, we Peter III, emperor and autocrat, announce for the information of all.

By this personal edict, by our royal and paternal mercy, we grant to all those who were formerly peasants and subject to the landowners to be loyal servants of our own crown. We reward you with the ancient cross and prayers, with heads and beards, liberty and freedom, and you will be Cossacks forever, without being subject to conscription, poll taxes, and other financial demands, with ownership of lands, forests, meadows, fishing rights, and salt lakes without purchase or quitrent.

We release you from all the taxes and financial burdens formerly inflicted on the peasants and all the people by wicked nobility and by bribe-taking town judges.

We order by this our personal edict that those who were formerly noblemen in their estates and who opposed our authority, troubled our empire and ruined the peasants, are to be caught, executed and hanged, and treated in the same way that they, devoid of Christian feeling, treated you the peasants. Upon the elimination of these opponents and dishonest noblemen you will all know everlasting calm and peace in your lives.

Issued 31 July 1774,
signed Peter III

The government, concluding a major war with Turkey, reacted angrily. The strength of the reaction is made clear by Catherine II's manifesto on the revolt in the southern Urals, issued on 23 December 1773.

To our extreme vexation and outrage, we have been informed that not long ago, in Orenburg Province, a Cossack who had run away from the Don and wandered around Poland, collected together a band of vagrants similar to himself and is carrying on terrible brigandage in the region, inhumanly taking the property of the local inhabitants along with their lives. And so that he might henceforth increase his evil band not only with all the miscreants that he meets but also with those unfortunate people whom he hopes to find still oppressed by the darkness of extreme ignorance, this miscreant has had the impertinence to take on himself the name of the late Emperor Peter III.

But the impudence of this miscreant is having harmful consequences for the Orenburg Province. And so, indefatigably concerned for the peace of mind of our loyal subjects, we hereby most graciously announce that we have immediately taken the measures sufficient for the complete annihilation of this miscreant, and with a quantity of troops sufficient for the eradication of that band of brigands, who have already dared to attack small military detachments in that area, and killed in a barbaric fashion those officers who have fallen into their hands, we have sent there our General in Chief, Alexander Bibikov.

However, we confidently hope that all true sons of the fatherland will do their duty and promote the preservation of peace and good order, by guarding themselves against those with evil intentions and through the proper obedience to the authorities.

At last, with great difficulty but without mediators, we managed to conclude the worthy peace with Turkey that we desired, guaranteeing the external security of the empire and affording our loyal subjects the time to take pleasure with thankful hearts in

RIGHT *Pugachev, the rebel leader who claimed to be the 'true tsar'. Defeated by Catherine's forces, he was taken to Moscow in an iron cage and executed.*

praising God for peace and quiet at such a time.

We most fervently pray and ask God to restore everywhere a peaceful life without any revolt, and to strengthen all our true subjects living in it and us ourselves in all the Christian virtues.

Pugachev was captured in September 1774, having been betrayed by some of his own followers. He was taken to Moscow and executed there for treason on 10 January 1775. Andrey Bolotov, a minor nobleman who left a fascinating set of memoirs, describes the scene. Contrary to what he says, it was Catherine herself who ordered, in secret, that Pugachev should not be quartered.

At this time Moscow was preoccupied only with Pugachev. This monster had already been brought there and was kept chained up. All Moscow was talking about him, gathering together to see this miscreant as some kind of freak. By order of Empress Catherine, he was undergoing a formal and most important state trial, like any other state criminal, and nobody doubted that he would be executed.

Pugachev stood in a long, raw sheepskin coat, almost struck dumb and beside himself; he had just crossed himself and prayed. His appearance and manner seemed to me not at all to correspond to the acts for which this monster was responsible. He did not resemble so much a bestial and cruel brigand as some small victualler or shabby cook. His beard was small and his hair dishevelled, his whole appearance completely insignificant.

As soon as judgement had been pronounced the executioners took off the condemned man's coat and all his clothes and started to put him on the block for chopping up as had been decreed: first his arms and legs, then his head.

Then something completely unexpected and strange took place during his execution, for instead of cutting off his arms and legs before quartering him as decreed, the executioner suddenly cut off his head first. God alone knows how this happened: neither had the executioner been bribed to make him suffer less, nor did it occur through the confusion of an inexperienced executioner, but whatever it was, we heard only that some official standing near him suddenly shouted out with emotion, 'Ah, son of a bitch! What have you done?'

Hopes of improving the security and prosperity of the countryside in the wake of the Pugachev rebellion generated the empress's favourite piece of legislation, the Provincial Statute of 1775. It reorganized local administration, aiming among other things to encourage the nobles to devote more time to their estates, and to local and commercial affairs. In 1785 further encouragement was set out in a Charter of Privileges, defining the status and listing the rights of the nobility.

The designation 'noble' is a consequence of the outstanding quality and virtue of men of authority in the past who, having excelled themselves in deeds of service, acquired a noble name which they bequeathed to their posterity.

Not only is it of benefit to the empire and to the throne, but also is it just, that the respected position of the nobility be preserved and confirmed as inviolable; and therefore as of old, so now and forever, the noble state is inalienable and hereditary in those honourable families who possess it.

The nobleman imparts noble status to his wife.

The nobleman imparts noble status to his children, by inheritance.

Since nobility is a fixed state, excluding crime, and since marriage is honourable and founded on divine law, a noblewoman who marries a commoner will not forfeit her noble state; but she will not impart it to her husband and children.

The nobleman cannot be stripped of his noble status without due process of law.

The nobleman cannot forfeit his estate without due process of law.

The nobleman can be judged only by his peers.

A nobleman shall not be subject to corporal punishment.

A touch of class

Imagine a grand and wealthy magnate, the money and costly things showered upon him in plenty by a benevolent fate. Behold him travelling: a gilded carriage on a mass of springs, scarcely affected by the ruts in the street, with its richly moulded windows sealed so that not the smallest breath of wind nor the floating dust-motes can inconvenience him.

This carriage is upholstered in velvet, its cushions stuffed with down or filled with air; in it softness and delicacy combine to create tranquillity. It is drawn by six magnificent horses adorned with gilded harnesses fashioned from Morocco leather; their manes are braided and the reins are of golden silk.

See him step out of the carriage. Gold and precious stones sparkle on his garments. His fur coat is of the finest Siberian sable, his muff of black fox fur; both have the texture of black velvet. In all his apparel no expense has been spared.

Follow him into his house, whose frontage occupies a considerable part of the street. Marble columns support a sumptuous gilded balcony, and bas-reliefs of the same marble grace the tops of the windows. The floor of his entrance hall is of shining marble and porphyry; the steps of the staircase are fashioned from the finest black marble, and pillars of porphyry support the arch. Hand rails of white marble are set upon a gilded bronze baluster. The walls and ceiling are decorated with beautiful paintings.

Go into his apartments and you will see silk, crystal, gold, marble; it appears that all the arts have achieved the impossible in the decoration of this house. Here, the light of a multitude of burning candles is reflected in mirrors of enormous size; there, the facets of the hanging chandeliers sparkle like diamonds. The floors are composed of different woods, sumptuous carpets cover them.

See in the bedroom and the study, deep armchairs, couches, beds to rest upon, and other similar things fashioned to pamper the body.

But the dinner hour has arrived, and the magnate and all his guests repair to the dining-room. Oh heaven, what sumptuous appointments! All the vessels gleam gold and silver; crystal twinkles in the tapestries; a myriad burning candles are reflected in crystal facets.

When at last the food and drink are served, behold at once the finest produce of all the four corners of the earth: great salvers piled high with huge sturgeons; veal, white as snow, in mounds upon the dishes; capons, fatted fowls, quail in winter, pheasant, oysters; early fruits and pineapples for dessert, and others painstakingly preserved, like grapes and melon, excite the eye and delight the vision and the heart. The wines are the finest that France, Italy, and Spain produce, or that the glorious Cape of Good Hope supplies; all are served in plenty.

From Prince M. M. Shcherbatov,
On the Corruption of Morals in Russia

RIGHT *An ornamental vase in the Pavlovsk Palace. The rich enjoyed a standard of living that equalled and even surpassed that of their European counterparts.*

The splendour and opulence of the court increased dramatically in the hundred years after Peter the Great introduced the civilization of Western Europe to Russia.

ABOVE *The 'Golden Drawing Room' in the Winter Palace, St Petersburg.*

RIGHT *The bedroom of Peter the Great, who first westernized Russia.*

FAR RIGHT *The throne room in Peterhof.*

We affirm the freedom and liberty of the Russian nobility for all time, in the families inheriting it.

We confirm the nobleman's privilege of entering the service of other European states allied to us, and of travelling to other countries.

But as the noble designation and status, as of old, now, and henceforward, is acquired by service and by labours beneficial to the empire and to the throne, and as the existing position of the Russian nobility is independent of the security of the fatherland and of the throne; so, at any time of need for the Russian autocracy, when the service of the nobility is a requirement and a necessity for the common good, then, every nobleman is obliged, at the first call of the autocrat, to spare neither his labour, nor his own life in the service of the state.

In his book *On the Corruption of Morals in Russia*, written between 1786 and 1787, but not published until 1858, the conservative Prince Mikhail Shcherbatov, from one of Russia's most eminent families, reserved special condemnation for Catherine.

A woman not born of the blood of our sovereigns and who deposed her husband by an armed insurrection, Catherine, in return for this most virtuous deed, received the crown and sceptre of Russia, together with the title of Pious Sovereign, in the words of the prayer which is recited in our churches on behalf of our monarchs.

It cannot be said that she is unqualified to rule so great an empire, if indeed a woman can bear such a yoke, and if human qualities alone are sufficient for this supreme office. She is endowed with considerable beauty; she is clever, affable, magnanimous, and compassionate on principle. She loves glory and is assiduous in her pursuit of it. She is prudent, enterprising, and quite well read.

Catherine's moral outlook, however, is based on the modern philosophers, that is to say it is not fixed on the firm rock of God's law; being based on arbitrary worldly principles, it is liable to change.

Catherine the reformer

Catherine was a reformer by nature; but reform was also politically wise for a ruler with no right to the throne. In common with her contemporaries, Frederick II of Prussia and Joseph II of Austria, she was deeply influenced by the political literature of the age, notably the French Enlightenment, and the science of good government called 'cameralism'. Developed mainly in Germany in the 17th century, the latter was designed to mobilize human and material resources in the interests of the welfare of the people and the power of the state.

From Montesquieu's *The Spirit of Laws* she derived a vision of a society of 'orders' or 'estates', social groups each with its own function in the state – nobles, townspeople, peasants; this vision of society was particularly influential in her judicial reform in 1775, when separate courts were established for each different social 'estate' on which elected assessors also sat.

From England, she borrowed the concept of *habeas corpus*, whereby any person arrested and not charged for three days could appeal to be released on bail to the Conscience Court, to which each of the three free orders of society could elect assessors. The Charters to the Nobles and to the Towns of 1785, in which she set out the civil and economic rights, and the very limited political rights she was prepared to grant to these two social groups, were also borrowed from abroad.

From the 'cameralists' Catherine borrowed the details of her programme of financial and administrative reform, the organization of a coherent programme of 'law and order', and of social welfare. Institutions such as schools, hospitals and workhouses were placed under the supervision of Boards of Social Welfare, on which the nobles, the townspeople and the peasants who were not serfs, were represented.

The French Enlightenment, embodied in the great *Encyclopédie* edited by Diderot and d'Alembert and, above all, Voltaire, influenced Catherine's attitude towards religious toleration. She never issued a general edict on the subject, but state control of all religions, Protestant, Catholic, Muslim and Jewish, ensured toleration in practice.

Naturally humane herself, Catherine borrowed many ideas on penal law and practice from the Italian jurist Cesare Beccaria, whose *On Crimes and Punishments* (1765) had a tremendous impact on educated public opinion throughout Europe. She was deeply opposed to torture, and although she issued no widely publicized general law abolishing torture, she took steps to eliminate its use in civil and military procedure. She was also opposed to painful forms of execution.

Catherine was aware of Russia's backwardness in relation to the West, in particular, the small size of the middle classes or third estate – that is the merchants, entrepreneurs, industrialists, professional people of all kinds, and craftsmen. She believed it important to increase their number, by following the contemporary practice of inviting 'foreign settlers' to establish themselves in Russia, and by setting up foundling homes to rescue abandoned children.

Education was another means of enlarging the third estate, and for this Catherine borrowed ideas from England (John Locke), France (Fénélon, Diderot, La Chalotais but not Rousseau) and Germany (Johann Basedow). When she became convinced that state initiative was necessary in order to set up an educational system throughout the country, she turned to the method worked out by Abbot Felbiger which was used by Frederick II in Silesia, and subsequently by Joseph II in Austria. In 1782 Joseph sent her an educational expert who was Orthodox by religion, and with his help, over the next 24 years, she set up high schools and junior schools in all the provincial capitals, and junior schools in all the district towns of Russia.

By 1789, in the high school in far-distant Irkutsk in Siberia, Japanese, Chinese, and Manchurian were taught in addition to the main curriculum. The schools were open to all classes of the population, including girls, and serfs, the latter with the permission of their owners.

The total number of children educated in Russian state schools (and in the numerous private establishments) was small in relation to the population as a whole. But there is no doubt that, by the end of Catherine's reign in 1796, increasing demand for literate people, or those with professional qualifications, had led to an increase in the number of educated people.

ABOVE *Voltaire, one of the architects of the French Enlightenment.*

Catherine's bad example

To add to the corruption of women's morals and of all decency, she has set other women the example of the possession of a long and frequent succession of lovers, each equally honoured and enriched. Seeing a shrine erected to this vice in the heart of the empress, women scarcely think it a vice in themselves to copy her; rather, I suppose, each thinks it a virtue in herself that she has not yet had so many lovers!

Although Catherine is in her declining years, although grey hair now covers her head and time has marked her brow with the indelible signs of age, still her licentiousness does not diminish. She now realizes that her lovers cannot find in her the attractions of youth, and that neither rewards, nor power, nor gain can replace for them the effect which youthfulness can produce on a lover.

Trying to conceal the ravages of time, she has abandoned her former simplicity in dress, and although in youth she criticized the Empress Elizabeth Petrovna for leaving a wardrobe large enough for an army, she has started to show a passion of her own for inventing suitable dresses and rich adornments, and has thus given rise to the same luxury, not only in women but also in men.

From Prince M. M. Shcherbatov,
On the Corruption of Morals in Russia

Generally speaking, women are more prone to despotism than men; and as far as Catherine is concerned, it can justly be maintained that she is in this respect a woman among women. Nothing irritates her more than when men, making some report to her, quote the laws in opposition to her will. Immediately the retort flies from her lips: 'Can I then not do this irrespective of the laws?'

The entire reign of this monarch has been marked by events relating to her love of glory. The many institutions she has founded apparently exist for the good of the nation; in fact they are simply symbols of her love of glory. Had she really had the nation's interest at heart, she would, after founding them, have paid attention to their progress. But she has been content simply with their establishment, and with the assurance that she will be eternally revered by posterity as their founder.

LEFT 17th century lubok. *It illustrates a lesson for stupid husbands and clothes-conscious wives. Catherine the Great was a reformer who wished to raise the level of education in Russia: she established free schooling throughout the nation.*

A more radical indictment of fundamental institutions was delivered in 1790 in a book entitled *Journey from St Petersburg to Moscow* by Alexander Radishchev, the son of a wealthy landowner and at that time the director of the St Petersburg customs service. Inspired by the French Revolution, the work denounced a catalogue of the evils of Russian life, among them serfdom.

The story of a certain landowner goes to prove that a man, for the sake of his own personal gain, will forget the humanity of his fellow man.

This landowner had left the capital and acquired a small village of some one or two hundred inhabitants: he was determined to make his living through agriculture. He considered the most reliable way was by using his peasants as tools, having neither will nor motivation of their own. So he took away from them the small plots of ploughed land and hay meadow which are usually given to them by the gentry to provide their necessary sustenance by way of payment for their work. In a word, this nobleman forced all the peasants, their wives, and their children to work for him every day of the year. And so that they did not die of hunger he gave them a certain amount of bread, which was called a monthly ration. Those who did not have any family did not receive a monthly ration, but ate together at the manor, receiving thin cabbage soup on meat days and bread and *kvass* on fast days. If they ever did get any real meat, it was only during Easter week.

Their dress was in keeping with this order of things. They made their own winter footwear; in summer they went barefoot. These prisoners had neither cows, horses, nor sheep. It was not the permission to keep them that the master took away, just the means to do so. If anyone was a little better off or ate sparingly, he would keep a few birds, which the master would sometimes help himself to, paying whatever he saw fit.

Under such conditions it is hardly surprising that agriculture in this man's village was booming. Soon he added to his two hundred serfs a further two hundred martyrs to his greed. And treating them in the same way as he did the first lot, he increased his holdings every year, increasing the number of people suffering in his fields. Now he counts them in their thousands and is renowned as an outstanding farmer.

The fate of Radishchev's book, although it had passed the censor, was sealed by the coincidence of its appearance with the French Revolution, an upheaval which shocked Catherine, as it did most of the crowned heads of Europe. Catherine read it and made copious written comments, some of which are given here. Radishchev was condemned to death for treason, a sentence subsequently commuted to ten years' exile in Siberia.

This book was printed in 1790 without mention of the printing press and without any visible permission at the beginning, although at the end it says: 'With the permission of the Department of Public Morals.' This is probably a lie, or else carelessness. The purpose of

OVERLEAF *A Russian winter landscape, a scene that has hardly changed since Radishchev's journey.*

Radishchev: the first attack on serfdom

In 1766, Alexander Radishchev was one of several young pages from the court of Catherine the Great sent abroad, to the University of Leipzig, to study law. The move was indicative of Catherine's admiration for Western European culture and thought, and of her desire to introduce the fruits of European enlightenment into Russia without compromising the principles of autocratic rule. What Catherine failed to recognize was that the ideological bases of the Age of Reason, with its respect for the rights of man and the concepts of natural and civil law, were essentially incompatible with the traditional pillars of Russian society; autocracy and serfdom.

When Radishchev returned to Russia in 1771 he was struck by the gulf between the Enlightenment ideas he had imbibed in the West and the palpable irrationality, illegality and inhumanity of Russian society.

In 1790, his *Journey from St Petersburg to Moscow* appeared, describing an imaginary journey in the course of which the brutality of serfdom and the fundamental lack of regard for human rights in Russia are disclosed.

It is probable that the work was conceived as an indignant retort to a journey which Catherine had made to the south of Russia in the spring of 1787. The trip was accomplished with all the luxurious trappings of monarchical power. The Governor-General of Novorossia, Catherine's favourite, Grigory Potemkin, lined the royal route with artificial model settlements – the infamous 'Potemkin villages' – designed to conceal the true conditions of peasant life from her eyes.

Radishchev's *Journey* was a harrowingly realistic account of the barbarity of serfdom. It was also clearly a product of the 18th-century Enlightenment, its rejection of both autocracy and serfdom rooted in the belief that a rational society should be based upon a balance of obligations and rights. Drawing upon its concepts of natural law, civil law and the social contract, Radishchev advocates a society where all, including the monarch, are subject to the law and where citizens submit to civil law in exchange for society's undertaking that it will be applied equally to all men. No man shall enjoy rights without accepting social obligations, and none shall endure obligations without enjoying corresponding rights.

In Radishchev's analysis, Russian society was clearly 'unenlightened' in that all the rights belonged on one side, to the monarch and the nobility, while all the obligations belonged on the other, to the serfs. The Journey was conceived as a dire warning that such illegality sanctioned popular revolt in Russia and that Catherine should act before it was too late.

Radishchev printed his book in a small run of about 650 copies on his own private press. Somehow the work had been passed by the St Petersburg Office of Morals and some 30 copies were circulated before Catherine heard of it and the remaining copies were seized.

The *Journey* was the first important example of literature assuming the responsibility of political and moral opposition to the Russian status quo, and its suppression anticipated the regular use of censorship to constrain intellectual dissent in the 19th century. Radishchev committed suicide in 1802, but his career marked the start of a divergence between the government and the intellectual classes that was to have far-reaching consequences for the autocratic state.

BELOW *A Moscow street during Catherine's reign; the relative comfort of urban living was in stark contrast to the misery Radishchev saw when he travelled through the countryside.*

this book is clear on every page: its author, infected and full of the French madness, is trying in every possible way to break down respect for authority, to stir up in the people indignation against their superiors and against the government.

He has learning enough, and has read many books. He has a melancholy temperament and sees everything in a very sombre light; consequently he takes a bilious black and yellow view of things. He has ample imagination, and he is audacious in his writing.

Pages 268–77 are written to bring into contempt those landed proprietors who take the fields away from their peasants. The author lashes out at them, and the government catches it, too.

Pages 278–88 are on the abolition of court ranks. Here monarchs are roughly handled, and it ends with the words: 'how power can be joined with liberty for mutual advantage'. One must assume that he is thinking of the vicious example of France today. This is the more likely because the author seeks occasion everywhere to attack the sovereign and the government. He is doing this now.

Pages 289–305 contain abuse of censorship of books, and here he speaks quite boldly and insultingly about authority and government, which, it is evident, are despised by the author.

Pages 326 and 340 are also about censorship. The strongest passages are marked in pencil. On the last page are these words: 'He was an emperor. Tell me, in whose head can there be more inconsistencies than in an emperor's?' The author does not love monarchs, and wherever he can vilify love and respect for monarchs, he does so with rare audacity and greedy relish.

On page 341 begins the pitiful story of a family sold at auction for their master's debts, and this continues to page 348. Page 349 ends with these words: 'freedom is not to be expected from their counsels (the landed proprietors), but from the heavy burden of slavery itself'. That is, he puts his hopes in a peasant rebellion.

Pages 350–69 contain, in the guise of a discussion of prosody, an ode most clearly, manifestly revolutionary, in which tsars are threatened with the executioner's block. Cromwell's example is cited and

Catherine the ruler

In at least two respects, Catherine as a woman was at a disadvantage compared to a male ruler. First, court opinion in particular did not expect a woman to rule without the advice of a man. Second, a woman could not command armies in the field.

Catherine solved both these problems in a highly personal way. She needed advisers and utterly reliable men in charge of the armed forces, and only present or past lovers provided her with this total trust.

In the first ten years of her reign, therefore, she surrounded herself with a small group of seven high officials. Of these men, her lover Grigory Orlov was placed in command of the artillery; a man who had once been in love with her, Zakhar Chernyshev, was placed in charge of the army, and his brother Ivan in charge of the navy; Count Kyrill Razumovsky, who had also once been in love with her, had a seat on the Council of State. The rise of Grigory Potemkin, from 1774 to 1776, destroyed this harmonious pattern. He took over the armed forces (though not the navy) and saw to it that his own relatives were appointed to crucial posts in the army. By combining love with politics, Catherine succeeded in disarming those who distrusted her capacity to rule, and was seen to be above court factions in a country in which the presence of a woman 'with more hair than wit' on the throne was regarded as unnatural from top to bottom of society.

Fully aware of the importance of public opinion, Catherine was careful to consider important interests throughout her reign, and only acted when she felt she had the public on her side. One of her most interesting experiments in moulding public opinion was the Legislative Commission, convened in 1767. To draft a new legal code from the thousands of laws issued since

the last codification in 1649, Catherine summoned some 540 deputies from government departments, the nobility, townspeople, state peasants, Cossacks, and the numerous settled or nomadic tribes of Russia, including the Tartars, Chuvash, Bashkirs, Votyaks, who startled Muscovites by their picturesque attire when they arrived for the first session. The deputies all brought 'instructions' from their electors, rather like the '*cahiers de doléances*' which deputies to the Estates General brought with them in France in 1789.

In addition, Catherine set out what she considered to be the principles of good government in her 'Great Instruction', a document of over 600 articles, in which she stated her rejection of torture, the principles of the administration of justice she would like to see observed and her idea of a hierarchical society based on 'orders' or 'estates'. Although the Commission never produced a code, Catherine drew on all the materials produced, the instructions to the deputies, the debates, and the drafts of portions of the code in subsequent legislation, so that large areas of public life were codified and officials could act within an established framework of law.

The 'Great Instruction' was on sale in St Petersburg in 1768, and was used as a textbook for the education of Catherine's grandson, the future Alexander I. Though in no sense a code of laws, its humane principles were often used by more merciful judges to mitigate sentences, and it helped to educate a generation of officials in the ideals of the Enlightenment.

A feature of Catherine's reign was the security enjoyed by high officials. No one was disgraced or banished to Siberia when she seized the throne from her husband in 1762, and most of the men she appointed to high office served her for decades, and were well rewarded with titles and grants of estates with serfs. If they were dismissed they suffered no disgrace. Catherine consulted widely, and listened to advice. As she wrote to one of her officials: 'I am very fond of the truth, and you may tell me the truth fearlessly, and argue with me without any danger if it leads to good results . . .'

Shaping foreign policy was one of the principal tasks of a ruler, and from her first day on the throne Catherine made it clear that she was to be consulted. She set herself specific targets: the expansion of Russian influence in Poland, and territorial expansion at the expense of Turkey. Both these aims were achieved, but at the cost of long years of war, destructive of human life and property. In her treatment of Poland she adopted a tone of derision which may have concealed an uneasy conscience at the destruction of a great state. As she grew older, less time was spent on reform and more on warfare, especially after 1789 when Catherine, alarmed by the French revolution, rejected the intellectual heroes of her youth.

OVERLEAF *Louis XVI's execution; Catherine described his rebellious subjects as 'savages'.*

praised. These pages are of criminal intent, completely revolutionary.

Pages 395–400 contain another attack on the wealthy magnates and courtiers.

Pages 410–16 are again about the peasants' miserable existence.

Tell the author that I have read his book from cover to cover, and that in the course of reading it I have come to wonder whether I may in some way have offended him. For I do not want to judge him without hearing him, although he judges sovereigns without hearing their justification.

It seems probable that he has appointed himself the leader, whether by this book or by other means, in snatching the sceptres from the hands of monarchs; he should be questioned on this matter, as well as on his real intentions. And, since he himself writes that he loves the truth, he should be asked to say how the matter stood.

If, however, he does not write the truth, I shall be compelled to seek evidence, and things will be worse for him than before.

Catherine's horror of the 'French madness' increased when news reached Russia in 1793 of the execution of King Louis XVI. She responded by breaking off diplomatic relations with France and restricting the entry into Russia of French publications and personnel, in the edict of 8 February 1793.

The disturbances taking place in France in 1789 could not fail to draw the attention of all well-ordered states. But as long as there was still hope that time and circumstances would serve to bring the misguided rebels to their senses, and that order and the forces of legitimate rule would be reinstated, we tolerated the free presence of French citizens in our empire and all kinds of relations with them.

Now, to everybody's horror, this unfortunate country has been overrun by riotous conduct, when more than seven hundred savages have used the power illegally appropriated by them to such evil ends, that they have raised their hands to the killing of the sovereign anointed by God (carried out in a cruel and agonizing manner on 10 January this year).

We consider it our duty before God and our own conscience not to tolerate any further relations between our empire and France, such as normally exist between well-ordered states, until the justice of the Most High punishes the malefactors, and it pleases His holy will to put an end to the misfortunes of that kingdom, returning to it order and the forces of legitimate rule.

Consequently, we decree as follows: That activities under the trade agreement concluded between us and the late king of France Louis XVI on 31 December 1786 shall cease until such a time as order and legitimate rule is returned to France as described above.

Until such a time, entry into our ports is forbidden to any ships under the French national flag. It is likewise forbidden for our merchants and ship owners to dispatch their goods to French ports.

Former French consuls, vice-consuls, agents and others belonging to them, shall be deported from both of our capitals and other places where they are stationed.

All French people of both sexes, having merchant and bourgeois businesses, artists, craftsmen, and those working for private persons, including teachers, who recognize their country's present government and obey it, shall not be tolerated in our empire and shall be deported from wherever they are.

All our subjects are forbidden to go to France or to have any relations whatsoever with French nationals in their fatherland or in their armies.

The importing into Russia of gazettes, newspapers, and other periodicals published in France is forbidden.

It is strictly prohibited to allow the entry, via land or sea, of French men and women into our empire from abroad, apart from those who want to live in the natural confession of their Christian faith under the protection of our laws. But such people may only be admitted on the basis of a testimonial from French princes.

This does not include all French men and women in Russia who renounce on oath the seditious principles now preached in their country.

ABOVE *Catherine surrounded by her family; the small boy on the left is the future Alexander I.*

Catherine survived Louis XVI by only three years, dying in November 1796. Many grieved her passing, especially those who had worked closely with her. Vasily Popov, former head of Grigory Potemkin's private office, reports her approach to government in a conversation which he had with her grandson, Tsar Alexander I, several years after her death.

Nothing left a greater impression on my mind than the following conversation. The subject was the unlimited power with which the great Catherine not only ruled her own empire but ordered things in other countries. I spoke of the surprise I felt at the blind obedience with which her will was fulfilled everywhere, of the eagerness and zeal with which all tried to please her.

'It is not as easy as you think,' she condescended to reply. 'In the first place my orders would not be carried out unless they were the kind of orders which could be carried out: you know with what prudence and circumspection I act in the promulgation of my laws. I examine the circumstances. I take advice. I consult the enlightened part of the people, and in this way I find out what sort of effect my law will have. And when I am convinced in advance of general approval, then I issue my orders, and have the pleasure of observing what you call blind obedience. And that is the foundation of unlimited power. But believe me, they will not obey blindly when orders are not adapted to the customs, to the opinion of the people, and if I were to follow only my own wishes.'

Catherine II's successors

Despite her frequent threats of bypassing her only son, whom Catherine disliked almost as much as he disliked her, Paul succeeded his mother in 1796. Paul, born in 1754 and sometimes known as the 'Tsar Madman', never won the affection of the court as his mother had done. Probably because he felt that she had spoiled and pampered the nobles, Paul reacted by withdrawing many of their privileges. He held firm and consistent views about duty and morality, yet his behaviour was often violent, petty and unpredictable, especially in his treatment of the nobility and the army; and his foreign policy, which included the expulsion of the Austrian and British ambassadors in 1800, alienated many of Russia's top military men. In 1801 he was strangled in his bedchamber, victim of an assassination plot.

The accession of Paul's son and heir Alexander I, who had approved his father's removal but not his murder, was warmly welcomed by the nobility as a return to normality and perhaps even a promise of reform. The handsome ruler's popularity soared as Napoleon evacuated his troops from Moscow in 1812 and Russians marched into Paris in 1814. But Alexander's reign was to end in reaction, and only a premature death in 1825 saved the tsar from meeting a fate similar to the one suffered by his father.

OPPOSITE *Alexander I (1801–25)*

We, heir to the throne, Tsesarevich and Grand Prince Paul, and we, his consort, Grand Princess Maria.

Having come, after careful consideration and in a tranquil state of mind, to a voluntary and common understanding, we herewith state our joint decree whereby, we appoint as heir, in conformity with natural law, after my death, our eldest son, Alexander, and after him all his male issue. With the surcease of the eldest male issue, the succession rests with the family of my second son, following the order set down for the descendants of my eldest son, and so forth, in the event of my having more sons. This is what is known as primogeniture.

With the surcease of the last male descendants of my sons, the succession will remain in our family but will pass to the female issue of the last reigning sovereign as being the closest to the throne.

Should our family become extinct, the right of succession will pass to the female issue of my eldest son, and the nearest female relative of the last reigning sovereign from the family of my above-mentioned son will succeed to the throne. Failing this, the succession will pass to such male or female person as may stand in her place, always seeing to it that priority is given to a male over a female. This is what is known as substitution.

Having established the rules of succession, I deem it essential to give my reasons. They are as follows: that the state never be without an heir to the throne, that the heir to the throne always be designated by the law itself, that there be not the slightest doubt as to who should succeed to the throne, that the rights and difficulties inherent in the passing of the right of succession from one family to another be avoided.

As the above decree makes clear, Paul was determined to spare his own heirs (four sons and six daughters) the anxiety that Peter I's 1722 Law on Succession had caused him, given that his mother could have disinherited him at any time.

Many of the acts of Paul's short reign represented a protest against his mother's regime; for example, against too much foreign influence (as he viewed it) and laxity in the army. Indeed, the conspirators who assassinated him on the night of 11–12 March 1801 had many causes for grievance. One of their number, General Bennigsen, a Hanoverian in the Russian service, describes the events in the Mikhailovsky Palace in St Petersburg. His companion, Nikolay Zubov, was the brother of Catherine the Great's last lover, Platon. Count Pahlen, military governor of St Petersburg and Foreign Minister, was the mastermind behind the plot. For the next hundred years it was maintained that Paul had died a natural death in his bed.

At about midnight the conspirators set out. Zubov and Bennigsen went straight to the Mikhailovsky Palace, while Pahlen and his detachment made a detour in order to fetch the first battalion of the Semenors regiment. The latter were to intercept the emperor in case he should escape through the apartments of the empress and make an attempt to get away from this side.

Zubov and Bennigsen let the Adjutant Argamakov walk in front. Since he had to submit daily reports to the emperor, Argamakov knew the stairs which led straight to the door of the antechamber where two life hussars and a valet were sleeping.

As Argamakov, Zubov and Bennigsen walked along the passage which led to the room a sentry shouted, 'Halt, who goes there?'

Bennigsen said to him, 'Be silent, you wretched man. You can surely see where we are going.'

The sentry wrinkled his forehead and actually guessed what was going on; but he only shouted, 'Round – passed', and he did so in such a manner that if the emperor heard the noise he would think a round was passing.

Adjutant Argamakov ran on faster and knocked softly at the valet's door, who, without opening it, enquired what he wanted.

'I have come to submit the usual report.'

'Are you crazy? It is just midnight!'

'Really? It is six o'clock in the morning. If you don't open up you will get me into a nice lot of trouble with the emperor.'

Finally the valet opened the door, but as soon as he saw seven or eight people rushing in with bare swords he took refuge in a remote corner.

Bennigsen and Zubov penetrated into the room of the emperor. Not seeing him in bed, Zubov exclaimed, 'He's escaped!' Bennigsen, less excited, searched about with greater attention and discovered the unfortunate monarch behind two wings of a folding screen. He approached him, saluted with his sword, and explained to Paul that by order of the Emperor Alexander he was arrested.

Paul made no reply to Bennigsen's words, and only by the glimmer of a night-light could one see the confusion and terror etched on his face.

Zubov repeated in Russian, 'Sire! In the name of the Emperor Alexander you are under arrest.'

To this Paul replied in a broken voice, 'What does that mean – under arrest?' An instant later he added, 'What have I done to you?'

One of the conspirators shouted, 'You have tortured us for four years!'

The unfortunate Paul was wearing a cotton night-cap; he had only a flannel bed jacket over his shirt and was standing barefoot before the conspirators, who had their hats on their heads and their swords in their hands; those who had decorations wore them on their uniforms.

Bennigsen did not utter a word and remained motionless. In this state of stupor he was found by seven or eight of the conspirators who, intoxicated with wine, had lost their way and were now pushing in with great noise. Prince Yashvil, major-general of the artillery, who had been dismissed from the service some time before, entered at the head of the group, rushed furiously at his sovereign, and threw him down, upsetting the screen and the night-light.

Bennigsen, who during this tumult in the dark had thought that Paul was attempting either to flee or resist, called out to the emperor, 'For heaven's sake, Sire! Don't attempt to escape; you are in mortal danger, and you will be murdered if you put up the slightest resistance!'

Meanwhile Prince Yashvil, Gordanov, Tatarinov, Prince Vyazemsky, and Skaryatin were grappling with the emperor.

At first Paul managed to rise from the floor, but then he crashed down again near a marble table. In falling he hurt his cheek and side. General Bennigsen alone avoided joining in this terrible mêlée; he called out to Paul once more not to defend himself and ran into the antechamber for a light.

On re-entering after scarcely a moment's absence he saw Paul already strangled with a sash. His murderers later maintained that the emperor had put up little resistance; he had only pushed his hand between the sash and his neck, and said in French, 'Messieurs, au nom du ciel, épargnez-moi! Laissez-moi le temps de prier Dieu!'

These were his last words.

ABOVE *Detail from Alexander's throne; he became emperor by conspiring against his father.*

The assassination of Paul was carried out in the name of his eldest son, Alexander, born in 1777. The new tsar always maintained, however, that the intention had been merely to depose his father, for the good of Russia. Be that as it may, the well-educated and handsome Alexander I came to the throne amid general rejoicing. There were those who believed that Russia might at last be on the road to some kind of constitutional reform. The French writer, Mme de Staël, exiled from France for her opposition to Napoleon, visited St Petersburg in 1811 and was struck by the tsar's liberalism. She was, however, well aware that the Russian nobility continued to lack political rights in a most autocratic regime.

As I was conversing with the empress, the door opened and Emperor Alexander I did me the honour to come and talk to me. What first struck me in him was such an expression of goodness and dignity, that the two qualities appear inseparable and, in him, to form only one. I was also very much affected with the noble simplicity with which he entered upon the great interests of Europe, almost among the first words he addressed to me. Sovereigns of Europe are afraid to pronounce a word to which any real meaning can be attached. Alexander, on the contrary, conversed with me as statesmen in England would have done, who place their strength in themselves, and not in the barriers with which they are surrounded.

Alexander I, whom Napoleon has endeavoured to misrepresent, is a man of remarkable understanding and information, and I do not believe that in the whole extent of his empire he could find a minister better versed than himself in all that belongs to the judgement and direction of public affairs. He expressed to me his regret at not being a great captain. I replied that the public feelings of his people, by his example, were achieving the greatest victory, and the first of the kind which had ever been gained. The emperor talked to me with enthusiasm of his nation, and of all that it was capable of becoming. He

expressed to me the desire, which all the world knows him to entertain, of improving the state of the peasants still subject to slavery.

At St Petersburg especially, the great nobility have less liberality in their principles than the emperor himself. Accustomed to be the absolute masters of their peasants, they wish the monarch, in his turn, to be omnipotent, for the purpose of maintaining the hierarchy of despotism. The civil status of citizen does not yet exist in Russia, but it is beginning to emerge: the sons of the clergy, those of the merchants, and some peasants who have obtained from their lords the liberty of becoming artists, may be now considered as a third order in the state.

The Russian nobility bears no resemblance to that of Germany or France; a man becomes noble in Russia as soon as he obtains rank in the army. No doubt the great families, such as the Naryshkins, the Dolgorukys, the Golitsyns, etc., will always hold the first rank in the empire; but it is not less true that the advantages of the aristocracy belong to men whom the monarch's pleasure has made noble in a day. The whole ambition of the citizens is, therefore, to have their sons made officers, in order that they may belong to the privileged class. The result of this is that young men's education is finished at fifteen years of age; they are hurried into the army as soon as possible, and everything else is neglected.

For the earlier part of the reign, however, the focus was on dramatic foreign affairs, as Russia emerged triumphantly from Napoleon's occupation of Moscow in 1812 and, in 1814, marched her troops into Paris. Comte Philippe-Paul de Ségur, whose father Louis-Philippe had been French ambassador to the court of Catherine II, was Napoleon's aide-de-camp in Moscow. His memoir, *The Russian Campaign*, is famous for its description of the great fire of Moscow in 1812.

Napoleon stopped at one of the first houses in the Dorogomilov suburb of Moscow, and it was there that he named Marshal Mortier governor of the capital.

LEFT *The Kremlin in Moscow; after Napoleon's retreat from the city in 1812 Alexander's forces helped to destroy his army.*

'Above all,' he told him, 'there must be no looting. You will answer to me with your life if there is. Defend Moscow against anyone and everything.'

That night was one of sorrow: ominous reports arrived one after another. French residents in that country, and even an officer of the Russian police, came to warn of fire-raising. The latter gave all the details of the preparations which had been made for it. The emperor was, however, still clinging to his disbelief when, at about two o'clock in the morning, he learned that fire had broken out.

It was at the merchants' buildings in the centre of the city and in its richest district. Napoleon immediately issued orders and more orders. At daybreak he went there himself and threatened the Young Guard and Mortier, the governor. The marshal showed him houses with iron bars all over them; they were all locked, all intact and without any signs of penetration. However, black smoke was already issuing from them. Napoleon entered the Kremlin deep in thought. At the sight of the palace of the Romanov and Ryurik dynasties, at once gothic and modern, of their throne which still stood there, of Ivan the Great's cross and of the most beautiful part of the city which was dominated by the Kremlin and which the flames, still confined to the bazaar, seemed bound to respect, his initial hopefulness returned. His ambition was flattered by this conquest; he could be heard crying, 'So I'm finally in Moscow, in the ancient palace of the tsars, in the Kremlin!'

He nevertheless took account of the resources offered by the city, and in this brief moment he optimistically wrote words of peace to Tsar Alexander I. A high-ranking enemy officer had just been found in the main hospital and he was entrusted with the letter. It was in the sinister glow of the flames from the bazaar that Napoleon finished it and the Russian departed. The latter must have brought news of this disaster to his sovereign, from whom the fire was the only reply.

Daylight favoured the efforts of the duc de Trévise: he got the better of the fire. The fire-raisers were in hiding. Their very existence was doubted. Finally,

OVERLEAF *Moscow ablaze; the city burned for five days and Napoleon was aghast at its destruction.*

Napoleon in Russia

On 24 June 1812 Napoleon crossed the river Niemen and entered Russian territory. His *Grande Armée* numbered between 400,000 and 450,000, but it was a multi-national force of which less than half were French. The two main opposing armies under the command of Barclay de Tolly and Prince Bagration were outnumbered and forced to retreat. By 28 June the *Grande Armée* was in Vilna, which only a few days earlier had been the scene of lavish balls hosted by the Russian emperor, Alexander I. Napoleon penetrated further into the Russian empire in the hope that the Russians would be forced to give battle. The two Russian armies joined up before Smolensk, but after resisting the French on 16–17 August, pulled back towards Moscow.

Napoleon had invaded Russia nearly two months earlier with provisions for 24 days; he had clearly hoped to win a decisive battle by this time. When it became obvious that the Russian emperor was not prepared to come to terms, he took the fateful decision to move on towards Moscow, although supplies were already in disarray, and sickness and injuries had taken their toll on his army. Meanwhile Tsar Alexander had appointed Field-Marshal Kutuzov commander of his forces, despite his personal dislike of him.

The *Grande Armée* finally faced the Russians in a pitched battle at the village of Borodino, 72 miles west of Moscow, on 7 September. It was not the decisive engagement Napoleon had hoped for. Losses were horrendous on both sides – the *Grande Armée* lost probably between 30,000 and 40,000 men, including many generals, while the Russians lost over 40,000, possibly a third of their forces. Kutuzov, however, retreated to Moscow in good order and few Russian prisoners were taken. After a conference of war Kutuzov decided to abandon the city, and on 15 September Napoleon entered an almost deserted Moscow.

Moscow burned for five days. Rostopchin, the governor of the city, had deliberately removed fire-fighting equipment and laid explosives before he left; but gales and the indiscipline of the *Grande Armée* contributed to the destruction. Napoleon hoped that Alexander would respond to his peace overtures, but he seemed unable to understand that the tsar could not afford to make peace on any terms while foreign troops were on Russian soil. Napoleon left Moscow on 19 October.

After the battle of Maloiaroslavets the French were forced to retreat along their path of invasion through Smolensk and Vilna. Lack of supplies, harassment by partisan groups and the severe winter weather led to thousands of casualties, and Napoleon abandoned his army on 5 December; its survivors numbered only 25,000. Napoleon had lost over 400,000 men, over 150,000 horses and probably 1000 guns. The way was now clear for his final defeat.

The destruction caused by the campaign was extensive. Three-quarters of the buildings in Moscow were gutted by fire, and towns like Smolensk and Maloiaroslavets were almost destroyed. The countryside was ravaged by both armies; and looting, particularly by the starving troops in the *Grande Armée*, was widespread. The corpses of horses and men that littered the French army's route were a serious health hazard.

Although Napoleon considered making the conflict into one of social revolution by proclaiming the liberation of the serfs, this step would have meant anarchy in the countryside. It would also have made the possibility of bringing Alexander to terms even more remote, and future co-operation with him impossible. Acts of violence by serfs against their masters were not encouraged by the French, who on occasions crushed the rebels.

Napoleon was met with patriotic fervour from

ABOVE *Napoleon on campaign.*

all sectors of Russian society, including the Polish and Lithuanian populations. The nobility volunteered additional recruits, merchants and clergy donated money and goods, groups of peasants attacked stragglers from the *Grande Armée*. Foreigners in Russia were arrested and deported to the interior in an atmosphere of xenophobia, and the war took on the guise of an almost 'Holy War' with Napoleon depicted popularly as the Antichrist. One of his officers commented that the peasants regarded the French as 'a legion of devils commanded by the Antichrist'.

In some sectors of society the rise of patriotism, and the feeling that the Russian people had acted in unison to repel the invader, raised expectations of reform and change which were not to be realized. Ultimately, this affected relations between the tsar and his people more than the economic devastation caused by Napoleon's invasion.

strict orders having been given, suspicion lulled and order restored, everyone went off to requisition a comfortable house or a sumptuous palace, thinking to find there an ease bought with such long and excessive privations.

Two French officers had established themselves in one of the buildings of the Kremlin. From there they could observe the north and west of the city. Towards midnight an extraordinary light woke them. They looked out and saw palaces filled with flames, which at first illuminated but soon demolished their elegant and noble architecture. They noticed that the north wind was driving the flames towards the Kremlin and were concerned for the fortress, where the élite of the army and its leader rested. They also feared for the surrounding houses where our tired and sated soldiers, people and horses were doubtless sunk in deep sleep. Already flames and burning debris were playing about the Kremlin roofs when the north wind, veering to the west, drove them in another direction.

Then, reassured about his army corps, one of the officers went back to sleep, saying, 'Let the others deal with it, it's no longer our business.'

However, a new and lurid glow woke them again; they saw other flames rising in the precise direction from which the wind was now blowing towards the Kremlin, and they cursed French imprudence and indiscipline, to which they attributed this disaster. But three times the wind shifted as it had from north to west, and three times the enemy fires, remorseless avengers seemingly bent on destroying the imperial quarter, proved eager to follow the new direction.

On 19 October 1812, Napoleon's *Grande Armée* withdrew from Moscow at the start of the gruelling retreat through the Russian winter. Alexander I hastened to inform the Russian people of the turn of events, in a manifesto dated 3 November 1812.

We make this declaration to all the people: The entire world knows in what manner the French enemy entered the boundaries of our empire. None of our efforts to observe carefully our peace treaties with him, nor our constant endeavours to avoid a bloody and ruinous war, availed to halt his stubborn

Moscow burning

Could the Muscovites, knowing of the bold and carefree negligence of the French, have conceived the idea of burning Moscow along with our soldiers who were drunk with wine, fatigue and drowsiness? Or did they rather dare to think that Napoleon would be caught up in the catastrophe, and that this man's destruction was well worth that of their capital? That the purpose was great enough for the whole of Moscow to be sacrificed to it?

Everyone had seen men with dreadful faces covered in welts and maddened women wandering amid the flames and putting the finishing touch to a horrible picture of hell. These wretches, drunk with wine and the success of their crimes,

no longer bothered to hide: they went triumphantly through the blazing streets. We surprised them armed with torches, intent on spreading the fire, and had to cut their hands off with blows of the sabre in order to make them let go.

It was said that these bandits had been unleashed by the Russian leaders to burn Moscow and that indeed such a weighty and extreme decision could only have been taken through patriotism and implemented through crime. The order was immediately given to try all the fire-raisers and shoot them there and then.

From Philippe-Paul de Ségur,
La campagne de Russie

ABOVE *A caricaturist's version of Napoleon's ill-fated invasion of Russia.*

intention. With peaceful promises on his lips he never ceased to think of war.

Finally, having prepared a strong army, Napoleon moved with all his forces and great quantities of arms into our land. Murders, fire, and devastation followed in his wake. Looting, burned cities and villages, flaming Moscow, a blasted Kremlin, defiled churches and altars of the Lord, in short, unprecedented atrocities and outrages finally revealed in action what he had hidden so long in his thoughts. The mighty, rich, and prosperous Russian realm has always caused fear and envy in the heart of the enemy. Possession of the entire world could not appease him as long as Russia flourished and remained prosperous. Filled with fear and deep hatred of her, he devised every treacherous means by which he might deal a terrible blow to her forces and wreak boundless ruin upon her wealth.

The whole world turned its eyes to our suffering fatherland and despondently thought to see the last day of its freedom and independence in the flaming skies of Moscow. But the triumph of the enemy did not last long. Soon, hemmed in on all sides by our brave troops and militia, Napoleon realized that he had carried his insolent steps too far and that neither his forces nor his villainies could frighten the valiant and loyal Russians.

After all vain attempts, seeing his huge armies crushed and beaten everywhere, he sought his own personal salvation in speedy flight with the small remnants of his forces. He fled from Moscow with humiliation and fear equal only to the pride and vanity with which he had approached it. Mindful, with fatherly love and a joyous heart, of these great and glorious feats of our beloved subjects, we turn first to bring our warm and fervent thanks to the Source and Giver of all blessings, Almighty God. Then solemnly, in the name of the fatherland, we wish to

RIGHT *Russian troops on the Champs Elysées in Paris; Alexander and his army marched into the city in 1814.*

LEFT *Napoleon's retreat from Russia, defeated by the weather, lack of supplies and partisan troops who harried his demoralized army.*

express our thanks and gratitude to all our loyal subjects, true sons of Russia.

We deem it our duty and obligation by this, our proclamation, before the face of the entire world to express our gratitude and render their just due to the courageous, loyal, and pious people of Russia.

Russian partisan bands, inspired by General Kutuzov, pursued the French armies, picking off stragglers. No more than 50,000 from the total French force of 600,000 managed to leave Russia. And in 1814 Alexander marched into Paris. Previously, on 25 December 1813, as Russian troops were about to enter French territory for the first time in history, the emperor had issued the following order.

Soldiers! Your courage and valour have brought you from the River Oka to the Rhine. They are now taking us further. We are crossing the Rhine, to enter the boundaries of the land with which we are engaged in bloody and cruel war.

May we crown our great accomplishment with the achieving of the much-desired peace.

Entering into the heart of our country our enemies did us much harm, but they have also suffered dire punishment. Let us not be like them: inhumanity and brutality cannot please God, who loves mankind. Let us forget their deeds; let us carry to them, not anger and vengeance, but friendliness and a hand stretched out for reconciliation. It is the glory of the Russian to overthrow the armed enemy and, after wresting the arms from his hand, to be charitable to him and to his peaceful brothers.

This lesson we are taught by the Orthodox faith which we cherish in our hearts; with divine words it speaks to us: love your enemies, and do kindness to those who hate you.

Soldiers! I am fully confident that, through your gentle conduct in the land of the enemy, you will conquer it with your generosity as you have with your arms, and that you will crown your heroic accomplishments by preserving your renown as a courageous and kind people, thus hastening the coming of the goal of our desires – a general peace.

Europe in 1815

The failure of Napoleon's Russian campaign, and his subsequent final defeat in Europe at Waterloo (1815), gave his enemies the chance to retrieve territory lost to the French empire. At the Congress of Vienna in 1815, Russia, Austria and Prussia realigned the national boundaries of Europe. Poland, once again, was incorporated into Russia.

NORWA

NORTH

SEA

DENMA

IRELAND

GREAT

BRITAIN

Edinburgh

Dublin

Hamb

NETHERLANDS

KIN

London

Paris

R. Seine

Strasbourg

Orleans

Nantes

FRANCE

SWITZERLAND

ATLANTIC OCEAN

Geneva

Lyon

Milan

KINGDOM

Turin

LOMBA

Bordeaux

Genoa

PAR

Marseille

OF

Oporto

SPAIN

Barcelona

SARDIN

PORTUGAL

Madrid

R. Tagus

Lisbon

Valencia

Seville

MEDITERRAN

FIN AND

L. Ladoga

Helsingfors

○ **St Petersburg**

SWEDEN

Reval

Novgorod

L. Peipus.

L. Ilmen

Stockholm

Pskov

L. Rubyn • Tver

○ **Moscow**

Vyazma

Riga

Copenhagen

BALTIC SEA

W. Dvina

Vitebsk

Smolensk

Voronezh

Königsberg

Vilnius

Minsk

Danzig

R. Nieman

OM OF PRUSSIA

Bialystock

R U S S I A N   E M P I R E

Berlin

Warsaw

Kiev

R. Don

POLAND

R. Dnepr

Leipzig

Dresden

Cracow

R. Vistula

Azov

Prague

BESSARABIA

R. Bug

AZOV SEA

AUSTRIAN

Munich

Odessa

Vienna

Buda • Pest

E M P I R E

BLACK   SEA

Sebastopol

VENETIA

Venice

Bucharest

Belgrade

A D R I A T I C   S E A

R. Danube

TUSCANY

PAPAL STATES

Sofia

O T T O M A N   E M P I R E

Constantinople ○

KINGDOM

Naples

OF

TWO

--- | Boundary, 1810

--- | Boundary, 1815

☐ | German Confederation, 1815

○ | Major cities

SICILIES

Palermo

0   500 km

SEA

The Russian armies did not participate in the events which saw Napoleon defeated at Waterloo in June 1815. Alexander I was present, however, at the Congress of Vienna (1814–15), which redrew the map of Europe, and in September 1815 at the signing by Austria, Prussia and Russia (and later most European powers) of the Holy Alliance.

In the name of the most Holy and Indivisible Trinity.

Their Majesties the emperor of Austria, the king of Prussia, and the emperor of Russia, in consequence of the great events that have marked the course of the last three years in Europe, having become convinced of the necessity of subjecting the policies to be observed by the powers, in their reciprocal relations, to the sublime truths taught by divine law:

Solemnly declare that the present act has no other object than to publish, in the face of the whole world, their fixed resolution to take for their sole guide in the administration of their respective states, and in their political relations with every other government, the precepts of the holy religion, namely, the precepts of justice, Christian charity, and peace.

Their Majesties have agreed the following:

Consistent with the words of the Holy Scriptures, the three contracting monarchs will remain united by the bonds of a true and indissoluble fraternity and, considering each other as fellow countrymen, they will on all occasions and in all places lend each other aid, assistance, and support.

The sole predominant principle between the said governments and between their subjects shall be to consider themselves all as members of one and the same Christian nation. Their Majesties consequently entreat their subjects to strengthen themselves every day more in the principles which the divine Saviour has taught mankind, as the sole means of enjoying that peace which arises from a good conscience and which alone is durable.

All the powers who shall choose solemnly to avow the sacred principles set out in the present act may be received with ardour and affection into this holy alliance.

Done in triplicate, and signed at Paris, the year of grace 1815, 14/26 September.

The Holy Alliance

On 26 September 1815, while the Great Powers, Austria, Britain, Prussia and Russia, were meeting in Paris to determine the future organization of Europe after Napoleon's defeat at Waterloo, Tsar Alexander I's Holy Alliance was signed by him, Francis I, emperor of Austria, and Frederick William III, king of Prussia. By this alliance, the three rulers bound themselves to each other in brotherly union to 'protect religion, peace and justice', agreed to act according to Christian principles and acknowledged themselves as members of the same Christian nation. After his return to Russia in December 1815, Alexander made the alliance public and instructed that it should be read out in churches throughout his empire. In 1822, the tsar wrote to his friend and adviser Alexander Golitsyn that he had cherished this plan since the Congress of Vienna (1814 and 1815) and that it crowned his work there.

Alexander's contemporaries, however, were less than impressed with this vague and nebulous document. Viscount Castlereagh, the British Foreign Secretary, referred to it as a 'piece of sublime mysticism and nonsense' and doubted whether the emperor's mind was 'completely sound'. Metternich, the Austrian minister for foreign affairs and later the Austrian Chancellor, described it as a 'loud-sounding nothing'.

Alexander I had been brought up in the enlightened atmosphere of Catherine the Great's court. His education had been in the hands of the Swiss republican Frédéric de La Harpe, and religion had formed little part of his instruction. In 1812, however, he underwent a conversion and his religious feelings strengthened in the years leading up to 1815. As he travelled through Germany in 1813 and 1814 with the victorious Russian army, he came into contact with mystics and theologians and read their works. In London, in 1814, he met English Quakers.

His closest confidante in 1815 was Baroness von Krüdener, a religious visionary and widow of a diplomat in Russian service, who contrived a meeting with Alexander at Heilbronn in Germany during which he was overcome with religious emotion. The baroness then set up a *salon* in Paris which the emperor often visited at night in his quest for religious solace. Many contemporaries thought the baroness was the inspiration behind the Holy Alliance, and on occasions she herself claimed this; in more modest moments, she attributed it to the work of God. Although it is on record that Alexander sought her approval before he presented the project to the Austrian and Prussian rulers, and apparently listened to her comments with humility, it is unlikely that she made anything other than minor textual changes. The idea of the alliance was Alexander's own, and the religious sentiments expressed in it reflect his own state of mind in 1815.

Religious enthusiasm was not the only factor to motivate Alexander, who had always had grandiose ideas about the organization of Europe, and the political principles enshrined in the alliance were not new. In 1804, he had proposed to William Pitt, the British Prime Minister, that there should be a league of liberal and constitutional European states and a new code of international law, under the benign protection of Britain and Russia. By 1815, Alexander was at the height of his power and his proposals could no longer be ignored.

The original draft of the Holy Alliance referred to the universal brotherhood of 'subjects' as well as of rulers. Metternich found this unacceptable and removed the offending reference as well as references to a universal European army and to criticisms of previous rulers' policies, although Alexander used the original draft in his

ABOVE *Alexander in Alexander Nevsky church; the tsar's Holy Alliance was described by a critic as a 'loud-sounding nothing'.*

proclamation to his subjects. However, even in this truncated form the Holy Alliance was not a reactionary document. There was no suggestion that the signatories were obliged to intervene in the internal affairs of other powers, nor was it overtly anti-liberal. It was essentially a product of Alexander's optimism about a future in which Europe lived in peace and morality under the wise guidance of Christian rulers who would give their subjects the benefits of just and orderly government.

In the wake of the Holy Alliance, Alexander turned away from thoughts of reform and became more and more introspective. The latter part of his reign was personified by the arch-reactionary Count Alexis Arakcheyev, who virtually ruled Russia during the tsar's absences. Particularly disappointed with the turn of events were those young army officers who had observed the superior standards of the countries in western Europe they were 'liberating'. Discussion groups turned into secret societies some of which were sworn to overthrow autocracy and abolish serfdom. Colonel Pavel Pestel, one of the most extreme members of the revolutionary group later known as the Decembrists, explains the origins of his protest in a testimony given after his arrest in 1825.

I cannot name any person who I could say was directly responsible for inspiring my early free-thinking and liberal ideas, or state the exact time at which they first began to occur to me; for they did not arise suddenly, but gradually and, at the outset, in a way imperceptible even to me. I have the honour, however, of reporting to the investigating commission that I developed a passionate interest in them. I was on fire with enthusiasm and longed for good with all my heart. I saw that the prosperity or hardship of nations lie for the most part in the hands of their governments.

With the sole desire to be some day, in my own time and place, a useful servant of my sovereign and fatherland, I later also began to weigh up whether the laws of political science are observed in the Russian system of government. I did not, at this stage, touch upon the supreme authority, but rather, reflected on ministries, local government, regional authorities, and so forth. In so doing, I then found much that did not tie in with my understanding of the laws of political science, and I began to consider by what enactments they could be replaced, reinforced, or perfected.

I also turned my thoughts and attention to the situation of the people. The servitude of the peasants had always deeply affected me, as had the extensive privileges of the nobility, which I saw, so to speak, as a wall standing between the monarch and his people, hid-

ing the true situation of the people from him, for the sake of personal interests.

Plans to overthrow Alexander I were pre-empted by his death on 19 November 1825. His brother Konstantin had renounced his rights and left Russia. A makeshift plan by army officers to thwart the accession of Alexander's youngest brother as Tsar Nicholas I failed. Many insurgents were killed on Senate (now Decembrist) Square in St Petersburg, and many more were arrested. The Decembrists' Manifesto, discovered among the papers of one of the rebels, Prince Sergey Trubetskoy (who decided at the last minute not to go to the square), outlines a radical scheme of reform.

The manifesto of the Senate declares the following:
The abolition of the existing regime.
Setting up of a provisional government until a permanent one is established, made up of delegates.
Freedom of the press, and therefore abolition of censorship.
Freedom of worship for all faiths.
The abolition of the right to own people as if they were property.
The equality of all estates before the law, and therefore the abolition of military courts and judicial committees of all kinds.
The declaration of the right of all citizens to engage in whatever business they wish. The right to own property of all kinds, namely land, and houses in towns and villages.
The abolition of monopolies; namely, on salt, on the sale of hard liquor, etc.
The abolition of recruitment and the military settlements.
Establishment of local, district, provincial and regional governments and of the procedure for election of members thereto, who shall replace all civil servants hitherto appointed from the civil government.
Public trials.
The introduction of juries in criminal and civil courts.

The establishment of procedure for the selection of delegates to the Chamber of People's Representatives, who shall be responsible in future for sanctioning government procedure and statutes.

The scene on 14 December 1825 on Senate Square itself is described in the memoirs of the Guards officer Baron Andrey Rozen, who was arrested the next day and later sentenced to hard labour in Siberia.

The first shot of a cannon loaded with blank cartridge rang out, and was greeted by a cheer from the crowd; the second and third were loaded with cannon balls, one lodged in the wall of the Senate, the other flew off the corner of the Senate towards the Academy of Arts. The insurgents again replied with a loud, clear 'Hurrah!' Then the Guards loaded up with grapeshot:

Colonel Nesterovsky aimed the cannon and the emperor himself gave the command: 'Fire one!' but the gunner with the slow match began to cross himself. Again, the same voice was heard: 'Fire one!' This time Captain Ilya Bakunin applied the match; in a second the grapeshot from the cannon rained down on the densely packed square.

The guns were moved forward and gave another salvo of grapeshot. From the second, totally gratuitous salvo of grapeshot, the number of those killed, guilty and innocent, soldiers and civilians, was quadrupled, particularly along the narrow gorge of Galernaya Street. Three sides of the Moscow Regiment *carré* fled with Count M. A. Bestuzhev, the third

BELOW *Alexander (left) with the Grand Duke Konstantin Pavlovich on the banks of the river.*

OVERLEAF *The Senate Square, St Petersburg, scene of the Decembrist Revolt.*

towards the embankment, pursued by grapeshot; on the Neva, he wanted to regroup the men, but shot fired from St Isaac's Bridge smashed the ice and many were drowned.

It seems almost incredible that not one of my comrades was killed or wounded; many had their overcoats and hats shot through with bullets. From the salvo fired against the third attack of the cavalry Guards, a bullet took off the left plume of my shako and made a file of soldiers duck their heads to one side. One joker noticed this and asked, 'Why are you bowing your head to one side instead of straight?' In the naval Guards battalion in particular, whole rows of soldiers lay dead; the officers were unharmed. They all fled away from the square.

From ten o'clock in the morning until ten o'clock at night I and my platoon had been parading in nothing but our thin parade tunics. They brought bread for the platoon from the barracks; the merchant Herman Knoop, an acquaintance of mine from Narva, had ordered to give them food and a cup of vodka each and brought me a bottle of the best wine.

During the night they cleaned up Senate Square, Galernaya Street, and the path across the Neva; they took the wounded to hospital. The next day, I saw my wife for two hours, to say goodbye for a long time. I was arrested early on the morning of 15 December by order of the emperor.

The newspapers at that time did not dare to print the truth; they swiftly reached their verdict that all rebel Decembrists were very badly dressed and all looked like animals and had repulsive appearances. The case drawn up showed that the uprising was obviously started openly. On a large square, before the people, some men had dared to express dissatisfaction and had expected general participation in effecting a change for the better.

It is true that when the first cries were heard from the crowd of 'Rather Constitution than Konstantin!' and some people were asked, 'Who is Constitution?', they replied, 'It's Grand Prince Konstantin's wife.' But it is also true that other reasons were declared to grenadiers and reliable non-commissioned officers. For the Decembrists on the square it was easy to foresee a bad ending.

The Decembrist movement

The Decembrist movement derives its name from the military uprising against Nicholas I in St Petersburg on 14 December 1825. Its members were young noblemen, officers of the Guards regiments, who aimed to replace autocracy with a democratic political and social order by means of a *coup d'état*. Anxious to avoid involving the masses in a popular and unpredictable revolution, they tried to keep their revolutionary intentions as secret as possible.

Their ideology was shaped by the writings of the 18th-century European Enlightenment, in particular the French *philosophes*, and by English and German romanticism. A number of Decembrists had direct contact with France, Germany and Poland as Russian army officers during the early 19th-century war of liberation against Napoleon, whose brief occupation of Moscow in 1812 irrevocably altered the political mood of the Russian people, arousing their expectations of far-reaching reforms: 'We were children of 1812' as one Decembrist later put it. Other events in Russia and Europe also had a considerable impact: the regime of Aleksey Arakcheyev, Alexander I's hated chief minister, the mutiny of the Semenovsky regiment in 1820, unrest in the military colonies, the peacetime settlements of the army, and the revolts in Spain, Piedmont, Naples and Greece.

Their main organizations were the Northern Society, based in St Petersburg, and the Southern Society, at the headquarters of the Second Army in Tulchin, Ukraine. Both developed from Guards officers' dining clubs established in 1815. The first Decembrist organization, the Union of Salvation, was formed by members of two of these clubs, nine of them former Freemasons, in February 1816, and aimed to introduce a constitution and to abolish serfdom. In 1818 it was

ABOVE *Five Decembrists were hanged for their part in the rebellion. From left: Pestel, Ryleyev, Kakhovsky, Muraviev-Apostol and Bestuzhev-Riumin.*

replaced by the more cautious Union of Welfare, whose charter was known as the Green Book after the colour of its binding. It grew rapidly in 1819 to around 200 members, pledged to the advance of culture, social justice and philanthropic acts. Disagreements on policy and aims led to its collapse in January 1821 and the Northern and Southern societies emerged from its ruins, joined in 1825 by the Society of United Slavs.

The Decembrists' plans for Russia's future government and society were most fully expressed in the constitutional project of Nikita Muraviev, a member of the Northern Society, and the more radical *Russkaya pravda* (Russian Justice) whose author was Pavel Pestel of the Southern Society. Muraviev's project, greatly influenced by the United States' constitution, proposed a limited monarchy with an emperor whose powers would be similar to those of the US president, a federal system of some 14 states, and the emancipation of the serfs without, however, dispossessing the landed gentry. Pestel, by contrast, formulated the first ever proposal for a Russian republic to be established after the overthrow of the Romanovs. He proposed the abolition of serfdom and of all class-based privilege, a strictly centralized system of government, and the transfer of landownership from the nobility to the state and the peasants. These projects together represent a major landmark in the ideology of the Russian revolutionary movement.

Disagreement over the projects was such that efforts to unite the two societies failed – in particular, Pestel was widely suspected of self-serving ambition – and during the early 1820s both organizations continued to select new members, not only from the army but also from St Petersburg's literary community. A significant group of 'Decembrist poets' emerged around Kondraty Ryleyev and Alexander Bestuzhev-Marlinsky, the editors of a popular, though short-lived journal, *The Polar Star*.

The Decembrists had intended to review the uniting of their secret societies under a common programme in 1826, but Alexander I's death in December 1825 and the succession crisis that followed forced their hand: they were determined to act regardless of the consequences in order 'to awaken Russia'.

Although they knew they had already been betrayed to the authorities, on 14 December members of the Northern Society tried to win support for their cause by persuading troops assembled on Senate Square in St Petersburg that Nicholas was attempting to usurp his elder brother's throne. (Konstantin had, in fact, renounced the throne in favour of Nicholas I for personal reasons some years earlier, but the document had not been published.) From the start their hastily laid plans went wrong. Prince Sergey Trubetskoy, who was to have taken command of the insurrection, lost his nerve and sought refuge in the Spanish Embassy.

The 3000 rebel troops waited in vain for hours in freezing temperatures for further instructions while Nicholas's retinue made desperate efforts to persuade them that Tsarevich Konstantin had abdicated in favour of his younger brother. But darkness was closing in (at around 3 pm), the intentions of the gathering crowd were uncertain

though probably hostile, and the governor-general of St Petersburg was murdered as he tried to placate the troops. Nicholas decided to bring up the artillery, a brutally efficient final resort: two or three salvos were sufficient to disperse the rebels within minutes. At such close range fatalities and casualties were inevitably high.

The Southern Society, led by Pestel and based in the Ukraine, heard of these events two weeks later, and decided to continue the Northern Society's rebellion. However, the authorities already knew about their organization and had arrested Pestel on 12 December. On 3 January 1826, the rebel troops, mostly from the Chernigov regiment, were defeated at Vasilkov near Kiev. The ringleaders were arrested and sent in chains to St Petersburg to share the fate of their Northern confederates.

Three days later, a specially constituted commission started an investigation into the whole uprising in an attempt to establish the conspirators' precise intentions towards the imperial family. Some admitted that they had contemplated regicide, admission that earned them the death sentence, and allowed the conspiracy to be portrayed officially as a desperate attempt to assassinate the emperor. During the six months that it took the Commission to complete its work, in which Nicholas took an absorbing interest, it interrogated 579 men, of whom 289 were found to have been involved, 121 to the extent that they were referred to the Supreme Criminal Court which imposed sentences ranging from forced labour in Siberia to death by hanging. The Decembrists Pestel, Ryleyev, Peter Kakhovsky, Sergey Muraviev-Apostol and Mikhail Bestuzhev-Riumin went to the gallows on 13 July 1826; on the same day the remaining conspirators set off to Siberia to begin sentences which few survived to complete.

In July 1826 five of the ringleaders, including Colonel Pavel Pestel, were executed. One of them was Kondraty Ryleyev, a well-known poet. Just before his execution he penned a last poem in his cell in the Peter-Paul fortress in St Petersburg:

Prison for me is an honour, not a reproach,
I am imprisoned for a just cause.
Why should I be ashamed of these chains
When I wear them for the Fatherland?

ABOVE *Decembrists in exile in Siberia; few survived the forced labour to which they were sentenced.*

PART 6 THE LAST

The 19th century was one of great technological and social achievements in Western Europe. The final vestiges of the 'feudal' order were swept aside. Industrialization, the growth of the railways and the expansion of world trade improved material living standards for a growing proportion of the population. Advances in medicine and improvements in public health extended average life-expectancy. The majority of the population gained the vote, and learned to read and write.

Russia lagged behind in all these fields. Whereas the 1848 revolutions abolished the last remnants of serfdom in Western and Central Europe, it was not until 1861 that the serfs were emancipated in Russia – and even after that (indeed, right up until 1917), the economic position of the individual peasant was, to a large extent, determined by his former status as a serf.

Britain, Belgium, France and Germany were already advanced industrial powers, with burgeoning empires in Africa and Asia, by the time Russia began its first real push towards industrialization in the 1890s. In Britain the annual death rate had been reduced to 18 per 1,000 population by the turn of the century, but in Russia the figure still stood at 35 per 1,000. Cholera, typhus and the long-term effects of poverty killed the tsar's subjects in their thousands. While 83 per cent of the adult population in Britain and France was counted as literate in 1900, in Russia the figure was only 28 per cent. Russia, in short, was the backward country of Europe. Apart from Turkey

and Montenegro, it was the only European country to enter the 20th century without a constitution or a national parliament.

The relationship between autocracy and backwardness stood at the heart of Russian historical development during the 19th century. The reign of Nicholas I (1825–55) was based firmly on the principles of autocracy. The Decembrist revolt was crushed. Censorship was tightened, and the 'western' influence of the Enlightenment, with its calls for individual freedom, was rejected by government and Slavophile philosophers alike. The notion of emancipation was vehemently opposed by most of Russia's noble landowners, despite the growing evidence of its beneficial economic effects in Prussia during the 1820s and 1830s.

Russia's defeat in the Crimean War finally brought home to Alexander II (1855–81) the fact, long argued by leading figures of the intelligentsia, that Russia's military weakness resulted from her political and cultural, as much as her economic, backwardness. If Russia was to compete with the western powers in the scramble for industrial and imperial hegemony, she would have to develop not only a stronger, industrial economy, but also a western-styled 'civil society' based on the rule of law, with universal civil freedoms, stable local self-government and better education. These were the guiding lights of Alexander II's great reforms of the 1860s.

From that point on, the course of Russian history was to be decided by the balance between progress

TSARS (1825-1917)

and order. The gains of industrialization were offset by the problems of poverty and social discontent created by the process of over-rapid urbanization. The transition towards a modern society, with civil freedoms and representative forms of local government, threatened the traditional privileges of the nobility; any government embarking on this course would have to find a means of appeasing them. The new freedoms of expression associated with the great cultural achievements of Tolstoy, Dostoyevsky, Chekhov, Tchaikovsky and Mussorgsky also made possible the growing criticisms of autocracy by the intelligentsia, and the rise of the revolutionary movement itself.

Thus, successive Russian governments were forced to choose between two conflicting policies: on the one hand, encouraging these processes of modernization by relaxing the controls of the autocratic state; and, on the other, maintaining firm political control over society in order to protect the autocracy from the challenges of the liberal intelligentsia, and the revolutionary movement. The first real challenge came in 1905, when workers' strikes and peasant disturbances coincided with the demands for political reform from the liberal gentry and professional classes. Nicholas II agreed to the establishment of a national parliament (the *duma*) in the wake of the 1905 revolution; and his prime minister, Peter Stolypin, embarked on a series of reforms during the following years. But any hope that this would save the tsarist regime was ultimately destroyed by the catastrophic effects of World War I on Russian society.

The most important debates and events of this period are illustrated by a wide variety of documents from government and private sources. Among these are the journals of foreign travellers to Russia, such as the Marquis de Custine from France, and Donald Mackenzie Wallace from Scotland, as well as the written observations of foreign diplomats and correspondents, like William Russell of *The Times*, and Maurice Baring of the *Morning Post*. Their perceptions were often the sharper because they looked at Russia from the outside.

A different perspective may be found in the writings of Russian critics of the tsarist regime, although many of their views were themselves deeply influenced by western humanist values. This part includes the writings of philosophers, such as Piotr Chaadaev (1794–1856) and Alexander Herzen (1812–70); writers such as Ivan Turgenev (1818–83) and Leo Tolstoy (1828–1910); publicists such as Vissarion Belinsky (1811–48) and Semyon Frank (1877–1950); liberal statesmen, such as Pavel Miliukov (1859–1943); and professional revolutionaries such as Sergei Nechayev (1847–82). Here, too, are the voices of tsarist ministers, local officials, and witnesses of events of the period. The feelings of the common man are represented by vivid accounts of the popular demonstrations which shook the Romanov dynasty in February 1917 and then brought it tumbling down.

Nicholas I

The bloody events which inaugurated the reign of Nicholas I (ruled 1825–55) made the new tsar even more firmly attached than previously to the ideals of duty and discipline. Like his father Paul I, Nicholas, born in 1796, was more at home on the parade ground than at court, and the rules and regulations of military discipline, supervised by the Third Section of His Majesty's Own Chancellery, became the norms of civilian life. Education, the press, and publishing were strictly controlled and censored. The slogan of Nicholas's reign was Orthodoxy, Autocracy, Nationalism – in other words, respect for God, King, and Country, which extended to the support of legitimate rulers abroad.

Nicholas acted out his role as gendarme of Europe by helping to crush revolts in Romania in 1848 and Hungary in 1849, as well as putting down the Polish rebellion of 1830. Although this period saw the appearance of the first railways in Russia and some attempts at reform in the countryside, Nicholas's reign was a period of economic and political stagnation culminating in military defeat in the Crimea.

OPPOSITE *Nicholas I (1825–55)*

For all its vastness, this empire is but a prison to which the emperor holds the key. And in this state which can live only by conquest, nothing, if not the sadness of its prince, approaches the sadness of his subjects in time of peace.

Here men know neither the true social pleasures of cultivated minds, nor the absolute and brutal liberty of the savage, nor even the freedom of action of the barbarian. The only compensations I can see for the misfortune of being born under this regime are conceited dreams and hopes of domination. The Russian lives and thinks as a soldier – a conquering soldier.

When Peter the Great established what they call here the Table of Ranks, which is to say, when he applied the military hierarchy to the whole administration of the empire, he changed his nation into a regiment of mutes, of which he declared himself colonel with the right to pass this rank on to his heirs.

Russian government is parade-ground discipline substituted for civil order: it is the state of siege turned into the normal condition of society.

The more I see of Russia, the more I applaud the emperor when he forbids Russians to travel and makes entry to his country difficult for foreigners. The Russian political system would not survive twenty years of free communication with the countries of western Europe.

Do not listen to the Russians' bragging; they take ostentation for elegance, luxury for refinement, the police and fear for the bases of society. To their way of thinking, to be disciplined is to be civilized. They forget that there are savages with very nice manners and very cruel soldiers. Despite all their pretensions to good manners, despite their superficial learning and their profound and premature corruption, and despite their facility for discovering and understanding the positive side of life, the Russians are still not civilized. They are regimented Tartars, nothing more.

The above extracts from the journals of the Marquis de Custine, written after a visit to St Petersburg and Moscow in 1839, offer a damning indictment of the Russia of Nicholas I, from the 'despotic' architecture of St Petersburg to the 'slavishness' of the Russian character. Custine, a monarchist whose father and grandfather had perished during the French

The sad fate of the empress

Alexandra Fyodorovna has given too many idols to Russia, too many children to the emperor. 'What a fate, to exhaust yourself producing grand dukes!' said a great Polish lady who does not hold herself constrained to worship in words what she hates in her heart.

Everyone sees the empress's condition, but no one speaks of it. The emperor loves her. Does she have a fever? Has she taken to her bed? He is caring for her himself. He is watching over her, preparing her drinks, and making her swallow them as a nurse would. But as soon as she is on her feet again, he starts to kill her once more with activity, feasts, journeys, love. To be truthful, as soon as

the danger reveals itself he gives up his plans. He is disgusted by the precautions which would prevent the illness. In Russia, wife, children, servants, relations, and favourites, all are caught up in the imperial maelstrom, going smiling to their deaths.

All must make the effort to obey the sovereign's thought, that single idea which governs the fate of everyone. The closer a person is to this sun of men's minds, the more he is enslaved to the glory that goes with his rank. The empress is dying of it.

From the Marquis de Custine,
La Russie en 1839

RIGHT *Alexandra Fyodorovna, wife of Nicholas I. A contemporary described her as exhausting herself producing grand dukes.*

Revolution, returned to France a partisan of constitutions. Nicholas I, however, regarded parade-ground discipline as the foundations of an orderly state. But the more the tsar fortified his camp, the more vulnerable and isolated he felt. One of his harshest critics, the revolutionary writer and thinker Alexander Herzen, who had fled Russia for Europe in 1847 to escape the censor, sums up the emperor's dilemma in a letter written to the French historian Jules Michelet in September 1851.

The Russian autocracy is now entering upon a new phase. It has created an immense empire, a formid-able army, and a centralized government. But without real roots, without tradition, it is doomed to stagnation. True, it undertook a new task – that of introducing western civilization to Russia, and it was to some extent successful so long as it played the part of enlightened government. That part is now abandoned.

The government, which parted ways with the people in the name of civilization, has lost no time in renouncing Enlightenment in the name of absolutism.

Since then the sole aim of tsarism has been tsarism. It rules in order to rule. But autocracy for autocracy's sake finally becomes impossible: it is too absurd and too sterile.

The government has realized this and has turned to look for some occupation in Europe. The activities of Russian diplomacy are inexhaustible: notes, threats, promises, counsels are showered everywhere; its spies and agents are to be found everywhere.

The Russian emperor regards himself as the natural protector of the German princes; he meddles in all the petty intrigues of the petty German courts; he settles all their disputes, scolding one, rewarding another with the hand of a grand duchess. But this is not a sufficient outlet for his energy. The mainstay of every reaction, every persecution, he undertakes the duty of chief gendarme of the universe. He aspires to represent the monarchical principle in Europe and assumes the airs and graces of a Bourbon.

Surrounded by his generals, his ministers, and his bureaucrats, Nicholas tries to forget his isolation, but grows gloomier, more morose, and more uneasy with every passing hour. He sees that he is not loved; the silence that reigns near him seems all the more deadly because of the distant murmur of the impending tempest. He has openly proclaimed that his aim is the aggrandizement of the imperial power.

There was little scope for regular political activity during Nicholas's reign, but it was this era of stagnation which saw a remarkable flowering of the Russian intelligentsia, who grappled with the 'cursed questions' of Russia's national character. Their debate, which raged on through the 1830s and 1850s, centred upon Russia's relationship with Europe.

The westernizers maintained the 18th-century principle that Russia was a backward part of Europe; the Slavophiles argued, on the contrary, that Russia was fundamentally different from and even superior to the West. Konstantin Aksakov, described as the 'most fanatical of the Slavophiles', expressed his views mainly through analyses of Russian history. In a memorandum written in 1855, he argued that in order to escape from stagnation it was vital to understand the true nature of the Russian people.

The Russian people are not much interested in government: they do not aim to wield power in the state, do not desire political rights for themselves, and do not have within them even the embryo of desire for popular rule. The very first proof of this is provided by the way Russian history begins, with the voluntary invitation to rule by foreigners in the shape of the Varangians, Ryurik and his brothers.

An even stronger proof is given by what happened in the Russia of 1612, when there was no tsar. In that year the people called for political power, elected a tsar, and entrusted their fate to him without restrictions; they then peacefully laid down their arms and dispersed to their homes. Russia's history contains not a single instance of a revolt against authority and in favour of political rights for the people

In view of this, is it not strange that the government of Russia is constantly taking measures against the possibility of revolution, and lives in fear of a political insurrection, a thing most repugnant to the very nature of the Russian people?

Under Peter there began that misfortune which is still with us today. In the West there is this constant enmity and rivalry between state and people, who fail to understand the relationship that exists between them. In Russia we have never had that enmity and rivalry. The Russian people remained true to their outlook and did not encroach upon the state; but the state, in the person of Peter, encroached upon the people, forcibly changing their ways and customs, even their costume. Thus there took place a breach between tsar and people; thus was destroyed the ancient union between the land and the state.

Let us re-establish the ancient union between government and people, state and land, upon the lasting foundation of truly basic Russian principles.

To the government – an unrestricted freedom to govern, exclusive to itself. To the people – full freedom to live, under the government's protection. To the government – the right to act and, consequently, to make laws. To the people – the right to have opinions and, consequently, to voice them.

That is the civil structure of Russia! That is the only genuine civil structure!

KONSTANTIN AKSAKOV

Westernizers and Slavophiles

By the 1830s Russia presented an enigma to intellectuals who sought to define the nature of its culture and to anticipate its historical role. It was poised geographically between Europe and Asia; it had been historically separated from the former, but was thrust into contact with it by the technical and cultural westernization of the 18th century. It possessed two 'capitals' – the native, Byzantine Moscow and the Europeanized St Petersburg, and was divided socially by the gulf which separated the westernized educated classes from the ordinary masses, still steeped in the traditions of the past. This latent cultural ambivalence lay at the root of the Slavophile-westernizer controversy, which was ignited by the appearance in 1836 of Piotr Chaadaev's first *Philosophical Letter*, suggesting that Russia had lost her rightful place in European civilization.

The Westernizers, who included the journalist and critic Vissarion Belinsky and the writer Alexander Herzen, were a loosely knit group whose political differences were disguised by a common antipathy to Slavophilism. Their admiration for European technical, cultural and intellectual achievements led them to argue that Russia's future lay in assimilating the material benefits offered by western civilization and in casting off once and for all the legacy of the period before Peter the Great.

The Slavophiles were a rather more unified group. They argued that Russia was culturally distinct from Europe and that Peter's attempt to turn the country to the West was an eccentric and damaging stage in Russian history. Their view was coloured by the conviction that European civilization was in decline.

This was most clearly articulated by Ivan Kireyevsky in an article of 1852, *On the Nature of European Culture and its Relationship to Russian*

ABOVE *European apparel was a potent symbol of westernization; Peter the Great, who brought the civilization of Europe to Russia, is shown (left) in a skipper's costume.*

Culture. He argued that classical paganism and the Roman influence had led in the West to a disproportionate emphasis on human reason. This had gradually excised man's other cognitive faculties, breaking down the 'integrality' of his personality, fostering intellectual autonomy and leading to progressive social disintegration.

The poet and dramatist Konstantin Aksakov had a vision of an idealized Russia, where the monarch ruled as a benevolent custodian and where people and government obeyed the principle of mutual non-interference. He was hopelessly out of tune with the realities of the time: the backward-looking utopias of Slavophilism had little to offer a Russia poised on the brink of modernization and far-reaching social reform.

Vissarion Belinsky, on the other hand, was a Westernizer, with strong socialist leanings, who believed that Russia must cultivate western values and technology. Of modest background, he was one of Russia's first professional journalists, earning a living from his pen. His *Letter to Gogol*, written in Germany in July 1847, became part of the 'scripture' of the democratic movement in Russia. It was prompted by the writer Nikolay Gogol's book, *Selected Passages from Correspondence with Friends* (1846), which persuaded Belinsky that Gogol, whom he had once idolized as a progressive writer, had deserted to the reactionary camp.

You are only partly right in having detected in my article an 'angry' man: that word is too weak and limp to describe the sort of state into which I was driven on reading your book.

In this beautiful isolation you live as a total stranger, inside yourself, or in a tight little circle fashioned in your image and powerless to resist your influence on it. So it has escaped your attention that Russia sees her salvation not in mysticism, not in asceticism, not in pietism, but in the triumphs of civilization, enlightenment, and humanity. It is not sermons she needs (she has heard enough of them!), nor prayers (she has intoned enough of them!), but for her people to wake up to a sense of human dignity which has for so many centuries been buried in filth and dung; and for rights and laws based not on church doctrine but on reason and justice, and for these to be rigorously enforced.

Instead she presents the horrific spectacle of a country where men deal in men, without even the excuse so cunningly devised by the American planters, who claim that a negro is not a human being; a country where there is not only no guarantee of personal autonomy, honour, and property, but not even an internally ordered society – just vast corporations of various officially appointed thieves and robbers.

In Russia at present the most vital contemporary questions are: the abolition of serfdom, the repeal of corporal punishment, and the introduction of the most rigorous possible enforcement of at least those laws already in existence. And at such a time a great writer, whose artistic genius and profound truthfulness have so masterfully contributed to Russia's self-knowledge, enabling her to gaze on herself as if in a mirror, comes out with a book in which, in the name of Christ and Church, he exhorts the landowner-barbarian to extract more money from the peasants, while cursing them as 'unwashed beasts'! How could this fail to drive me to fury?

You are gravely mistaken if you seriously think your book failed because of the unpalatable truths you supposed you told us all. The public is right: it perceives Russian writers as its sole leaders, defenders, and saviours from the black darkness of orthodoxy, autocracy, and nationalism; and so, while always willing to forgive a writer a bad book, it will never forgive a pernicious one.

If you love Russia, rejoice with me that your book has failed!

The following extract, which is taken from *Selected Passages from Correspondence with Friends*, gives an indication of why the critic was so angry. In these passages Gogol expresses his admiration for the Church and the monarch, those pillars of orthodoxy and autocracy which Belinsky and the Westernizers loathed so much.

Our clergy are not idle. I am pleased that in the depths of the monasteries, in the silence of the cells, irrefutable works are being compiled in defence of our Church. And they are better at their business than we are: they are in no hurry, knowing what the matter calls for, they carry out their work in profound serenity, praying, teaching themselves, and casting out from their souls all unworthy passions and impetuous haste, exalting their souls to the great height of heavenly calm at which one must abide in order to have the authority to speak of such matters.

We must defend our Church with our lives, for it is life itself. We must proclaim its truth through the sweet fragrance of our souls. Let the missionaries of Western Catholicism beat their chests, gesticulate, and by their eloquent oratory wring out fleeting tears-which soon dry up. The preacher of Eastern Catholicism should come before the people in such a way that purely from his humble appearance, his peaceful eyes and quiet, striking voice proceeding from a soul devoid of all worldly desires, all those present are moved, even before he discusses the issue, and proclaim to him unanimously, 'We hear the holy truth of your Church: there is no need to say a word!'

It has not occurred to anybody in Europe to define the significance of the monarch. It is our poets, rather than our legislators, who have seen the sublime significance of the monarchy. They heard with trepidation the will of God to establish it in Russia in its legitimate form. The pages of our history speak all too clearly of the will of Providence. Indeed, this form of power is being established in Russia in its fullest and most perfect form.

Consider also by what marvellous means, even before the full meaning of that power had been explained either to the sovereign himself or to his subjects, the seeds of mutual love had already been sown in their hearts! There is not one imperial house which had such an extraordinary beginning as did the Romanov house. The last and lowest subject in the kingdom sacrificed his life to give us a tsar, and by this pure sacrifice, created an unbreakable bond between the sovereign and his subject. Love entered our blood and a blood relationship began between every one of us and the tsar. Now it would be seen by all of us as a universal disaster if either the tsar should forget and renounce his subjects, or the people should forget and renounce their tsar.

The reign of Nicholas I produced the best works not only of Gogol, but also of Pushkin and Lermontov, and the first efforts of Dostoyevsky, Tolstoy, and Turgenev.

All in their own way raised awkward questions about Russian society and values. Ivan Turgenev's collection of stories about peasant

BELOW *Illustration by the Russian artist, Bakst, of one of Gogol's short stories,* The Nose.

Literature – a social force

In the 19th century the written Russian word became more than an embellishment or entertainment; it began to reflect, and in some cases to determine, the political state of the nation. Given the lack of free institutions, writers of all kinds used their talents to draw attention to the fact that Russian society everywhere was unsuccessful and unhappy. They often went further, calling for and provoking reform. In doing so they ran appalling personal risks. An autocracy which could not prevent subversive ideas slipping past the censor, or circulating illegally, could certainly discourage such practices through harsh reprisals. As a result, many of the great Russian writers of the 19th century were branded by the government as trouble-makers, persecuted and punished.

The poet Kondraty Ryleyev was hanged as a Decembrist revolutionary. Alexander Pushkin was exiled to the Caucasus, confined to his estate, harassed by the police, personally supervised by Tsar Nicholas I and prevented from travelling abroad. Mikhail Lermontov was similarly exiled and debarred from military honours despite his courage in the field. Piotr Chaadaev, though sane, was officially declared to be mad. Ivan Turgenev was arrested for a month and confined to his estate for over a year. Fyodor Dostoyevsky suffered arrest, solitary confinement, mock execution and ten years of Siberian exile. Leo Tolstoy was excommunicated by the Church.

Minor writers like Alexander Herzen, Nikolay Chernyshevsky and Vladimir Korolenko spent more time in exile than at home. What distinguishes Russian writers is the fact that they persisted in their work despite the ever-present threat of censorship and reprisal.

Ivan Turgenev (1818–83) exemplifies their dilemma. His career is marked by a series of compromises between instinctive objectivity and a sense of moral duty, between artistic purity and political involvement. After long experimentation with poetry and drama, he found a truer *métier* in short prose works, ensuring his fame with *A Huntsman's Sketches* (1847–52). This is to Russian society what *Uncle Tom's Cabin* was to America. Consisting of a series of rural portraits and sketches, with little or no narrative interest but a good deal of lyrical expressiveness, these pieces amounted to a devastating indictment of serfdom. Always understated, their message was nevertheless clear. The serfs were shown to be dignified and likeable human beings; their masters were often cruel and ignorant. This slender work, the real quality of which lies in its elegance and sensitivity, is the best example in all Russian literature of a book which helped to change the course of history. Tsar Alexander II certainly took account of it when deciding to emancipate the serfs in 1861.

From then on, the reading public looked to Turgenev for a political statement in everything he wrote. Under such pressure he increased the ideological content of each of his novels, achieving perfection only in *Fathers and Children* (1862), a nicely balanced story which sets universal values against local, historical ones, and succeeds particularly in dramatizing the differences between two generations of Russian reformers, the mild liberals of the 1840s and their radical successors, the Nihilists, in the 1860s. Neither generation, however, thought that it had been fairly depicted, and Turgenev was attacked from both sides.

He was never to repeat this artistic success. Political content, which he felt honour bound to include, detracts from his later novels, *Smoke* (1867) and *Virgin Soil* (1877). Turgenev is a good example of a writer forced by his Russian conscience into political comment.

ABOVE *Alexander Pushkin. Involved in the Decembrist uprising, he was confined to his estate and forbidden to travel abroad.*

RIGHT *Mikhail Lermontov. Guards officer, poet and novelist, he was exiled because of an ode he wrote on Pushkin's death.*

All Russia's historical turning points are reflected in her poems, stories and novels. The Napoleonic invasion and the glories of 1812 are re-created by Lermontov and Tolstoy, the Decembrists are referred to by Pushkin, the Crimean War is described first-hand by Tolstoy, the Act of Emancipation is treated by Nikolay Nekrasov, the Nihilist and Populist movements appear in Turgenev, revolutionary assassins in Dostoyevsky. National institutions are depicted and criticized: the Orthodox Church by Nikolay Leskov, Tolstoy and Chekhov, the prison system and the practice of knouting (flogging) by Dostoyevsky and Tolstoy, the dreaded military conscription by Tolstoy and Nekrasov.

Local government is vividly portrayed by Nikolay Gogol, the merchant and industrial classes by Alexander Ostrovsky and Mamin-Sibiryak, the Civil Service by Gogol and Dostoyevsky.

Not all these literary descriptions of Russian life are critical or satirical. Yet what emerges in the works of these writers is a picture of Russian society which is seldom a happy one, affecting the nation in most aspects of its existence. Dostoyevsky's depiction of urban life, Gogol's pictures of the provincial towns, Ivan Goncharov's representation of the moribund rural aristocracy – all these moved the reading classes and contributed significantly to the growing movement for radical reform.

life, *A Huntsman's Sketches*, published between 1847 and 1851, made a notable contribution to the most vexed question of the day, the abolition of serfdom. The following anecdote comes from the story 'Ermolay and the Miller's Wife', in which the fictional narrator, a young nobleman, recalls an encounter with a serf-owner.

'During my stay in St Petersburg, I happened to get to know Mr Zverkov. He held a fairly influential position and was said to be a knowing and shrewd businessman.

'One day, I somehow ended up travelling out of town in a carriage with him, just the two of us. We got talking and as a practical man of experience, Mr Zverkov set about 'putting me straight' on a few things.

'If you don't mind me saying,' he finally squealed, 'all you youngsters judge and discuss everything without thinking. For instance, you tell me this, that, and the other about the house serfs; but you don't know them, you don't know what kind of people they are.' (Mr Zverkov blew his nose noisily and took some snuff.) 'For example, let me tell you a little story.'

(Mr Zverkov cleared his throat.) 'You know the kind of woman my wife is; you will agree that it would be hard to find a more kind-hearted woman. Well, one day we were driving through our village. At the head-man's, we saw a young girl, his daughter, a very pretty girl indeed. My wife said to me, "Koko (that's her pet name for me, you see), let's take this young girl back to St Petersburg with us. I like her, Koko." "Yes, by all means!" I said.

'The headman, naturally, fell at our feet; he couldn't have hoped for a greater fortune, as you can imagine. Well, the girl, of course, blubbed like an idiot. It was hard for her at first: leaving home, and all that.

'In the maids' workroom, where, naturally, she was trained, the girl made startling progress. My wife took to her in a big way, and finally promoted her above all the rest to be her personal maid, mind! And, we must give credit where credit's due, my wife had never had such a good maid: obliging, discreet, obedient – one simply couldn't ask for more. But then, my wife, I must admit, was very good to her, too good really: she dressed her in the best clothes, gave her tea to drink, and so forth. Well, you can imagine! She served my wife in this way for ten years.

'Then suddenly, one fine morning, imagine, Arina (that was the girl's name) burst into my study unannounced and fell down at my feet; something which I cannot stand. "What do you want?" I asked.

'"Your honour, Alexander Silich, please give me your permission."

'"To do what?"

'"Please allow me to get married."

'I must confess, I was surprised. "But, you stupid girl, your mistress has no other maid but you!"

'"I will wait on my mistress as before."

'"Nonsense! nonsense! your mistress cannot tolerate married maids." I sent Arina away. I thought she would probably come to her senses. I couldn't bear, you know, to believe that any person could be capable of such base ingratitude. Six months later she came again with the same request. This time, I admit, I sent her away angrily. Imagine my surprise, when some time later, my wife came to me in tears, so upset that I was quite alarmed. "What has happened?"

'"It's Arina, you see, I'm ashamed to say it . . ."

'"No! Who was it?"

'"Petrushka, the footman."

'I exploded. That's the sort of man I am, I don't go in for half measures! Petrushka? Well, he could hardly be blamed. He could be punished, but in my opinion, he was not to blame. Arina? Well, need I say more?

'Naturally, I straight away gave orders for her hair to be cut off and that she be dressed in sackcloth and sent back to the village. My wife lost an excellent maid, but there was nothing we could do about it: immorality in a household simply cannot be tolerated.'

Much of Nicholas's foreign policy – especially his attempts to reach an understanding with Britain – had been aimed at avoiding major confrontations. But his refusal to withdraw Russia's right to interfere on behalf of the Orthodox subjects of the sultan of Turkey, and Western fears about Russian influence in the Balkans – following Russian occupation of the

Peasant diet

The peasant's usual fare is extremely simple and monotonous: rye bread, cabbage soup, and gruel make up the meal they eat every day, at lunch and supper alike, with this difference only, that often they do not have supper. Both on fast days and ordinary days the cabbage soup is made from sour cabbage and nothing else, except that, on ordinary days, they sometimes add salt, soured

in northern areas they do not even know it exists. Mushrooms are consumed in great quantity, but berries are gathered only for sale.

On major festival days, and especially before Lent, the amount of food consumed is, one can say, twice as much as usual, but there are times during the year when, on the other hand, even a good farmer goes hungry. The hungriest period

LEFT *17th century popular print depicting peasants planting beets, their daily fare.*

cream, or just milk. Few of them have any notion of seasoning their cabbage soup.

Their gruel is made from buckwheat, wheat, or millet, with milk and vegetable oil, or, during fasts, crushed hemp seeds. To have gruel indicates a certain degree of prosperity. As for meat, that is a great rarity on the peasant's table.

Vegetables are not much eaten, because the peasants lack good kitchen gardens. The potato is not yet in general use. Peas, beetroot, and cucumbers are even scarcer. Cabbage alone is widely eaten, together with onions and radishes on fast days. Their fruit they take to the market, and

for the people is undoubtedly midsummer, before St Peter's Day: the vegetables are not yet ripe and the cabbage in store is nearing its end, so that the usual fare during that fast is *kvas*, with a green onion and cucumbers, if these are ripe. And, to crown it all, at this time the peasant is often without even bread, so he resorts either to borrowing or else, for essential subsistence, he threshes rye that is not yet ripe.

From *Materials for the geography and statistics of Russia collected by officers of the General Staff. Ryazan province, 1860*

Crimean War

The Russians had entertained ideas of Balkan conquests since the reign of Catherine the Great, under whom they had annexed the Crimea in 1783 and Jedisan in 1792. In 1812, under Alexander I, they took Bessarabia and in 1829, under Nicholas I, the Danube delta. They were also advancing in the Caucasus and Central Asia.

Among European powers there was general anxiety about the balance of power, and more specific fears that Russia would become a Mediterranean power and dominate the route to India. Britain, in particular, saw Turkey as a crumbling bulwark against Russian advance. Although the British Prime Minister, Lord Aberdeen, who had made a secret agreement with Nicholas I in 1844, wished to avoid hostilities, Britain's ambassador in Constantinople, Viscount Stratford, played a major role in stiffening Turkish resolve in the face of Russian demands. Russia's ultimatum, demanding suzerainty over the Christian subjects of the sultan, was rejected by the Turks in May 1853, and Nicholas ordered his forces to advance into the Turkish vassal states of Moldavia and Wallachia in July. The Turks declared war two months later, only to see their Black Sea fleet destroyed by Russian ironclads at Sinope in November. On 27 March 1854 Britain and France entered the war. Sardinia also joined to earn their support in her quarrel with Austria.

Naval manoeuvres and engagements ranged from the Baltic to the Far East, but land-fighting was concentrated in the Crimean peninsula where the Russian naval base of Sebastopol was seen as a threat to Constantinople. On 14 June 1854, Lord Palmerston laid a memorandum before the English cabinet in which he argued that driving the Russians out of the Balkan principalities was insufficient, and that it seemed necessary that 'some heavy blow should be struck at the naval power and territorial dimensions of Russia'.

The cabinet accepted his plan for the capture of Sebastopol and the occupation of the Crimea. The Turks drove the Russians from Wallachia and Moldavia and in September 1854 27,000 British, 30,000 French and 7,000 Turks landed on the western coast of the Crimea, 35 miles north of Sebastopol. The Russians sought to block their advance on the southern banks of the River Alma but were forced to retreat. The British infantry stormed the Russian position, but the Russians under Menshikov were allowed to move back to Sebastopol.

Allied incompetence and delays allowed the Russians to consolidate their position in Sebastopol and construct strong fortifications. The allies encamped on the land side, though the Russians were still able to send supplies across the estuary. The position was a wretched one for the besiegers, dry and without water in the summer and freezing in winter. A Russian attempt in October 1854 to cut the Allies off from their supply base at Balaklava was defeated by the British infantry, described by *The Times* correspondent William Howard Russell as a 'thin red streak topped with a line of steel', before being pushed back by the charge of the Heavy Brigade. The Light Brigade were less fortunate, charging, as a result of muddled orders, in the face of Russian artillery, and suffering heavy losses. The following month the Russians attacked the British position, but at the battle of Inkerman on 5 November, they were defeated by the combined British and French forces.

As only a short campaign had been envisaged, preparations for winter operations were negligible. The troops lacked adequate supplies, clothing and shelter, and the nearest hospital was at Scutari 300 miles away. The scandal was exposed by British newspaper correspondents.

The sense that the war was being mismanaged

ABOVE *The ill-fated charge of the Light Brigade.*

played a major role in the fall of the Aberdeen ministry in early 1855. The government was defeated on a motion for a select committee of inquiry into the state of the army in the Crimea, and resigned on 1 February. The more bellicose Palmerston became Prime Minister and the war was waged with new energy. Reinforcements and supplies were sent, the British force rising to 40,000 and the French to 100,000, the hospital service was transformed by the dedication and determination of Florence Nightingale, and a railway replaced the roads between Balaklava and the front.

The war was sapping Russian strength. Large numbers of the men sent to the Crimea died from fatigue and disease during their winter march south. Nicholas I died on 2 March 1855, and his successor Alexander II was less enthusiastic about the conflict. Napoleon III wanted peace but was dissuaded by Palmerston.

A major Allied assault on Sebastopol having failed on 18 June 1855, the Allies battered the town with artillery before another assault on 8 September 1855, in which the French stormed the Malakoff redoubt, a central point of the defences. As a result the Russians set fire to and abandoned the town.

A winter of negotiations followed, exposing differences between Palmerston's marked anti-Russian position and Napoleon III's desire to conciliate the tsar. French and Austrian pressure for peace led to the Treaty of Paris, 30 March 1856.

The integrity and independence of the Turkish empire were guaranteed, the Black Sea was neutralized and the forts of Sebastopol were destroyed.

The war had cost in all about 650,000 lives: 500,000 Russian, 95,000 French, 30,000 Turkish and 25,000 British losses.

ABOVE *The camp of the 4th Dragoon Guards.*

Danubian provinces – prompted Britain and France to invade the Crimea in support of Turkey in September, 1854.

The Crimean War saw bravery and folly on both sides, as recorded by William Howard Russell, *The Times* war correspondent, in his memorable description of the charge of the Light Brigade at Balaklava on 25 October 1854.

The Russians – evidently *corps d'élite* – their light blue jackets embroidered with silver lace, were advancing at an easy gallop towards the brow of the hill. A forest of lances glistened in their rear, and several squadrons of grey-coated dragoons moved up quickly to support them as they reached the summit. The instant they came in sight the trumpets of our cavalry gave out the warning blast which told us that in another moment we should see the shock of battle. Lord Raglan, all his staff and escort, and groups of officers, the zouaves, French generals, officers and bodies of French infantry on the height were spectators of the scene, as though looking on the stage from the boxes of a theatre. Nearly everyone dismounted and sat down, and not a word was said.

And now occurred the melancholy catastrophe which fills us all with sorrow. It appears that the Quartermaster-General, Brigadier Airey, thinking that the light cavalry had not gone far enough in front when the enemy's horse had fled, gave an order in writing to Captain Nolan, 15th Hussars, to take to Lord Lucan, directing his Lordship 'to advance' his cavalry nearer to the enemy. A braver soldier than Captain Nolan the army did not possess. He rode off with his orders to Lord Lucan. God forbid I should cast a shade on the brightness of his honour, but I am bound to state what I am told occurred.

When Lord Lucan received the order from Captain Nolan and had read it, he asked, we are told, 'Where are we to advance to?' and Captain Nolan said, 'There are the enemy, and there are the guns, sir, before them; it is your duty to take them,' or words to that effect, according to the statements made since his death. Lord Lucan, with reluctance, gave the order to Lord Cardigan to advance upon the guns, conceiving that his orders compelled him to do so. The noble earl, though he did not shrink, also saw the fearful odds against him. The only support our light cavalry

OVERLEAF *View from the heights above Balaklava, looking towards Sebastopol.*

The Crimean War

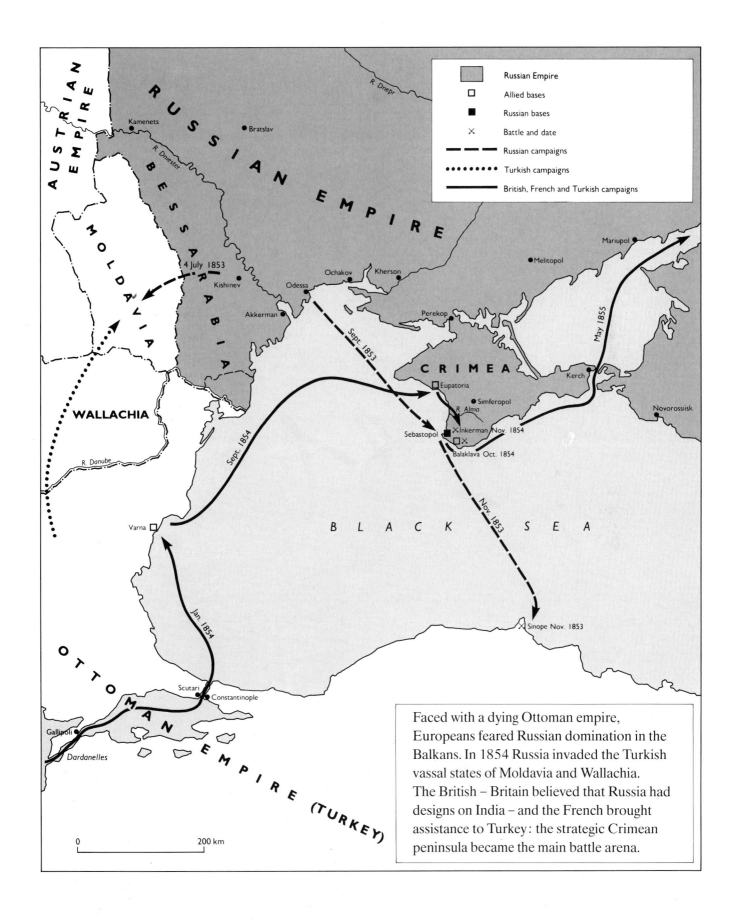

AUSTRIAN EMPIRE

RUSSIAN EMPIRE

Kamenets
• Bratslav

R. Dniester

BESSARABIA

MOLDAVIA

4 July 1853

Kishinev

R. Dnepr

Ochakov   Kherson

Odessa

Akkerman

WALLACHIA

R. Danube

Perekop

Melitopol

Mariupol

May 1855

Sept. 1853

CRIMEA

Eupatoria
• Simferopol

Kerch

Novorossiisk

R. Alma

Sebastopol   ✕ Inkerman Nov. 1854

Balaklava Oct. 1854

Sept. 1854

B L A C K   S E A

Nov. 1853

Varna

Jan. 1854

✕ Sinope Nov. 1853

OTTOMAN

Scutari
Constantinople

Gallipoli

Dardanelles

EMPIRE (TURKEY)

0   200 km

	Russian Empire
☐	Allied bases
■	Russian bases
✕	Battle and date
– – –	Russian campaigns
··········	Turkish campaigns
——	British, French and Turkish campaigns

Faced with a dying Ottoman empire,
Europeans feared Russian domination in the
Balkans. In 1854 Russia invaded the Turkish
vassal states of Moldavia and Wallachia.
The British – Britain believed that Russia had
designs on India – and the French brought
assistance to Turkey: the strategic Crimean
peninsula became the main battle arena.

had was the reserve of heavy cavalry at a great distance behind them, the infantry and guns being far in the rear. There were no squadrons in column at all, and there was a plain to charge over, before the enemy's guns were reached, of a mile and a half in length.

At ten minutes past eleven, our light cavalry brigade advanced. The whole brigade scarcely made one effective regiment, according to the numbers of continental armies; and yet it was more than we could spare. As they rushed towards the front, the Russians opened fire on them from the guns in the redoubt on the right, with volleys of musketry and rifles. They swept proudly past, glittering in the morning sun in all the pride and splendour of war. We could scarcely believe the evidence of our senses! Surely that handful of men are not going to charge an army in position? Alas! it was but too true – their desperate valour knew no bounds, and far indeed was it removed from its so-called better part – discretion. They advanced in two lines, quickening their pace as they closed towards the enemy.

A more fearful spectacle was never witnessed than by those who, without the power to aid, beheld their heroic countrymen rushing into the arms of death. At the distance of twelve hundred yards the whole line of the enemy belched forth, from thirty iron mouths, a flood of smoke and flame, through which hissed the deadly balls. Their flight was marked by instant gaps in our ranks, by dead men and horses, by steeds flying wounded or riderless across the plain.

The first line is broken, it is joined by the second, they never halt or check their speed an instant; with diminished ranks, thinned by those thirty guns, which the Russians had laid with the most deadly accuracy, with a halo of flashing steel above their heads, and with a cheer which was many a noble fellow's death cry, they flew into the smoke of the batteries, but ere they were lost from view the plain was strewed with their bodies and with the carcasses of horses.

Through the clouds of smoke we could see their sabres flashing as they rode up to the guns and dashed between them, cutting down the gunners as they stood. We saw them riding through the guns, as I have said; to our delight we saw them returning, after breaking through a column of Russian infantry, and scattering them like chaff, when the flank fire of the battery on the hill swept them down, scattered and broken as they were. Wounded men and dismounted troopers flying towards us told the sad tale – demigods could not have done what we had failed to do. At the very moment when they were about to retreat an enormous mass of Russian lancers was hurled on their flank. The other regiments turned and engaged in a desperate encounter.

With courage too great almost for credence, they were breaking their way through the columns which enveloped them, when there took place an act of atrocity without parallel in the modern warfare of civilized nations. The Russian gunners, when the storm of cavalry passed, returned to their guns. They saw their own cavalry mingled with the troopers who had just ridden over them, and, to the eternal disgrace of the Russian name, the miscreants poured a murderous volley of grape and canister on the mass of struggling men and horses, mingling friend and foe in one common ruin.

It was as much as our heavy cavalry brigade could do to cover the retreat of the miserable remnants of that band of heroes as they returned to the place they had so lately quitted in all the pride of life. At thirty-five minutes past eleven not a British soldier, except the dead and dying, was left in front of these bloody Muscovite guns.

Captain Nolan was killed by the first shot fired, as he rode in advance of the Hussars, cheering them on. Lord Lucan was slightly wounded. Lord Cardigan received a lance thrust through his clothes.

With the last gleam of day we could see the sheen of the enemy's lances in their old position in the valley; and their infantry gradually crowned the heights on their left, and occupied the road to the village which is beyond Balaklava to the southward. Our Guards were moving back, as I passed them, and the tired troops, French and English, were being replaced by a strong French division, which was marched down to the valley at five o'clock. All our operations in the trenches were lost sight of, as our light brigade was annihilated by their own rashness, and by the brutality of a ferocious enemy.

Russian new year at Sebastopol

Sebastopol, 13 January

Last night the wind changed round to the southward, and the thermometer rose to 34°F. A speedy thaw followed, and the roads and camp will once more suffer from the ravages of our old enemy – the mud. The Russians, who had lighted great watch fires on the north side of the place, illuminated the heights over the River Tchernaya with rows of lights, which shone brilliantly through the darkness of the cold winter's night, and were evidently with all possible pomp celebrating the start of their peculiar new year.

At midnight all the chapel bells of the city of Sebastopol began ringing, and it was evident that a religious ceremony of extraordinary solemnity was about to take place. About a quarter past one o'clock this morning the Russians inside the line of works gave a loud cheer. The French replied by opening fire, and the Russians began one of the fiercest cannonades which we have yet heard.

While the firing was going on, a strong body of Russian men had been pushed out of the town up the face of the hill towards our works in front and on the flank of the left attack. As it was expected that some attempt of the kind would be made, one of the steadiest English sergeants in the service was posted here with twelve men. But somehow or other, the enemy crept up on the little party, surprised them and took them prisoners, and then advanced with such rapidity and suddenness that the parties of the 60th and of the 21st regiments, on duty in the trenches, were obliged to retire almost without firing a shot. They rallied, however, fired, and, supported by the regiments in rear, they advanced, and the Russians were driven back close to the town.

At two o'clock this morning all was silent once more, and the allied armies had opened their new Russian year on Crimean soil.

From *The Times*, 13 January 1855

LEFT *Sebastopol under bombardment, seen from the sea. The city fell to the allies in September 1855.*

Alexander II

When Nicholas I died in 1855 his son and heir Alexander had been made painfully aware, by the defeats in the Crimea, that change was essential if Russia was not to lose her status as a European power and if autocracy was to survive intact. The main obstacle to progress was serfdom. In advocating emancipation Alexander II acted not so much out of liberal or humanitarian convictions as out of a highly developed sense of duty and in the interests of national survival.

The emancipation of 1861 was backed up by reforms in local government, the legal system, finance, education and the army, earning for Alexander's reign the title of the era of great reforms. Alexander probably hoped that the reforms would enable dutiful citizens to fulfil their obligations more efficiently, but many took relaxation for licence, and demanded more. Peasants called for the Golden Charter, which would grant them the land still held by the nobility; non-Russian nationalities rose up in arms; universities became hotbeds of protest; liberals appealed for a constitution; radicals demanded the life of the tsar on behalf of the oppressed masses. In March 1881 they claimed it, when Alexander was blown up by a terrorist group calling itself the People's Will. On that very day he had approved the convocation of an elective body to advise on legislation.

OPPOSITE *Alexander II (1855–81)*

It is rumoured that I wish to emancipate the peasants. This is untrue, and you may tell that to everyone everywhere. But, unfortunately, a feeling of hostility does exist between the peasants and their landlords and, as a result, there have already been some cases of disobedience to the landlords.

I am convinced, therefore, that sooner or later we shall have to grant emancipation. I think that you will, consequently, agree with me that it would be very much better if it were to come from above rather than from below.

Alexander II, who had acceded to the throne in 1855, delivered the above speech to representatives of the nobility assembled in Moscow in March 1856. Fear of revolt from below was one of the arguments used by the tsar to persuade the landowners that emancipation was essential: he could not liberate the serfs without their co-operation.

After five years of deliberations and debates in committees and commissions, the imperial manifesto freeing the peasants from bondage was published on 19 February 1861. The serfs were released from their masters 'in perpetuity', but the new freedom was not without strings.

Serfdom is abolished permanently for peasants settled on landlords' estates and also for house serfs.

The landlords, while retaining ownership of all the lands belonging to them, grant to the peasants, for their use in perpetuity, the farmsteads where they are settled.

In return for the landholdings assigned to them on the basis of the previous article, the peasants are obliged to perform duties for the benefit of the landlords, in the form of labour services or money payments, as defined in the local instructions.

On these bases statutory deeds are to be drawn up to define the relations, in connection with land, between each landlord and the peasants who are settled on his property. The landlords themselves will be responsible for drawing up these deeds.

The peasants released from bondage are to form rural associations to govern their economic activity, and for the purposes of immediate administration and legal proceedings they are to be grouped into rural districts (*volosti*). Supervision of public affairs is to be the responsibility of the commune (*mir*).

The landlord has the power to exercise police authority in a rural association of peasants.

The landlord has the right to oversee the maintenance of public order and public security throughout his property.

In the event of abuse or, in general, improper performance of their duties by the village headman or the landlord's representative, the landlord has the right to demand their replacement.

If a landlord notices that the commune has taken a decision which violates his rights as landlord, he shall, after suspending the implementation of such a decision, report it to the peace mediator, who is obliged immediately to satisfy the legitimate demands of the landlord.

Every rural association is subject, as regards communal land, to joint responsibility in respect of each of its members.

LEFT *Peasant worker; Alexander emancipated serfs in 1861, but his move brought fewer changes than had been expected.*

OVERLEAF *Alexander freeing the serfs.*

RIGHT *Social types; from top left, clockwise: poultry merchant; dairy woman; laundress; tradesman (centre) and his wife; street sweepers; peasant.*

Permanent redemption of lands involved payments spread over 49 years. The requirement to pay went against the traditional peasant belief that those who worked the land should have free access to it.

Acquisition of ownership by the peasants, together with their homesteads, of the land and appendages assigned to them for use in perpetuity, is to be allowed only with the landlord's agreement.

In order that the peasants may take possession, along with their homesteads, of the land allotted to them, assistance from the government is to be made available in the form of a redemption operation. This means that the government will advance a certain sum which is to be repaid by the peasants in instalments over a protracted period. It will itself exact payments from them to cover both the interest on the sum lent and the gradual repayment of the debt.

Peasants and landlords alike protested at the terms of the settlement, the latter sometimes in unselfish tones. In an address of February 1862 the assembly of representatives of the nobility of Tver province appealed to Tsar Alexander on behalf of the peasants. They offered to relinquish some of their privileges and requested the convocation of a nationally elected assembly.

Your Imperial Majesty, Most Gracious Sovereign!

At their first assembly held since the promulgation of the statute of 19 February 1861, the nobility of Tver province hail the Russian tsar who has undertaken to emancipate the peasants and root out all that is wrong in Russia. The nobility of Tver solemnly declare that they sincerely sympathize with the good initiatives taken by Your Imperial Majesty and are ready to follow you along the path that leads to prosperity for Russia's people.

As proof of our readiness and our complete confidence in Your Imperial Majesty we have resolved to submit for Your consideration a frank exposition of our ideas, without any falsehood or concealment.

The manifesto of 19 February proclaiming freedom for the people, while it improved to some extent the material well-being of the peasants, did not liberate them from bondage and did not abolish all the injustices arising from serfdom. The people's good sense cannot reconcile the freedom proclaimed by Your Majesty with their continued relations of obligation towards the landlords and the artificial distinction between estates. The people perceive that, in time, they may be freed only from compulsory labour, but must remain for ever payers of rent, subject to the rule of those landlords nominated by the peace mediators.

Most Gracious Sovereign! We are firmly convinced that You sincerely desire the well-being of Russia, and therefore we regard it as our sacred duty to speak frankly. Between us and the government of Your Imperial Majesty there exists a strange misunderstanding which prevents the fulfilment of your good intentions. Your high officials have devised the condition of temporary obligation, which is unbearable for both peasants and landlords, whereas we our-

The end of serfdom

A number of factors were responsible for Alexander II's Emancipation Manifesto of 19 February 1861, which signalled the end of more than two centuries of Russian serfdom. The possibility that the agrarian economy faced a growing crisis, official fear of peasant disorder, the discrediting of serfdom in the eyes of many officials and influential commentators, defeat in the Crimean War, and Alexander II's personal inclinations and the apparently close connection between serfdom and Russia's economic backwardness, were all important. The actual terms of the Emancipation Manifesto were the result of a compromise between the government's desire for reform, hedged about by a fear of acting incautiously, and the interests of the landowners, whose co-operation it needed.

The terms were disappointing to many peasants, one reason being that former private serfs were denied immediate freedom. For the first two years after the Edict, they were obliged to serve their lords as formerly, while the land was surveyed and valued. After this, they were 'temporarily obligated': they paid rent to their lord and were subjected to his jurisdiction until they could redeem the land.

Because the government feared that the emancipation of the serfs might lead to unrest or mass migrations, the peasants were also made subject to the authority of a communal organization which might or might not correspond to their traditional commune. It was responsible for their financial obligations and they were forbidden to leave their localities without its permission.

In general, the new administrative arrangements which were introduced on emancipation reinforced the peasant's separate and inferior status within Russian society.

LEFT *Peasant housing: in spite of emancipation, money owed to landlords and a rapid increase in the population often caused hardship.*

Former household serfs were freed without land, while provisions for serfs who worked on the land varied throughout Russia, according to the local situation. In each region the state laid down maximum and minimum sizes of the allotments awarded to peasants. The actual area depended on negotiations between the landowner and his former serfs. The state compensated the former for most of the land that was allocated in this way; anything above this had to be paid for in cash or in kind by the peasants, who were also obliged to recompense the state over a 49-year period.

Similar but more generous arrangements were made for state peasants, who were freed five years later, in 1866.

Because of its cautious and inflexible provisions, the manifesto brought fewer immediate social changes than might be expected.

Most peasants continued to live in their villages and cultivated their strips in time-honoured fashion. Only gradually did the development of a market economy and of industry, arguably encouraged by emancipation, help some to grow wealthier than others and it induced the adventurous and enterprising or the needy and poverty-stricken to migrate to the towns, often temporarily at first.

However, in the long run, difficulties such as the heavy redemption payments which were owed by the peasants and the loss of valuable land to their former lords were a grave defect in the emancipation measures.

Exacerbated by rapid population growth, these difficulties caused social distress in many areas and gradually undermined tsarist authority in the countryside.

selves, who are more than anyone else interested in this matter, desire that these privileges be abolished. This general discord provides the best of proofs that the transformation which is now a question of extreme necessity cannot be carried out by bureaucratic methods.

We are sure that all the changes will remain unsuccessful because they are being introduced without the people's permission and consent. An assembly of elected representatives of the whole country is the only way to achieve a satisfactory resolution of the problems arising from but not solved by the manifesto of 19 February.

In presenting for Your Imperial Majesty's consideration our humble request for the convening of an Assembly of the Land, we hope that the sincere desire for the common good which has animated the nobility of Tver will not be misinterpreted.

Peasant reaction took more elemental forms.
In the village of Bezdna, in the Kazan province, a peasant named Anton Petrov succeeded in persuading villagers, angry at the obligations they still had to perform, that the tsar really had intended to grant them complete freedom without ties, and that this was clear if one interpreted the manifesto correctly. The official record of the investigating commission gives this account of the consequent rumours in the Bezdna area.

Nearly all the temporarily obligated peasants were convinced that the promulgation of the manifesto meant that they were to be given complete freedom. In some settlements the peasants were voicing this expectation long before they heard of Anton Petrov. For instance, the peasants of Akhmetevo village, on Mr Bakunin's land, having had the manifesto read to them and hearing that for two years they would have to perform labour service just as before, refused to believe this and, neglecting the work due to their master, spent three days looking for someone else to read the text to them. Though the peasants did not say so outright, it was clear that throughout these

three days they were trying to find a person who would read the manifesto to them in such a way that it would seem to bear out their beliefs.

The position was the same in Kuznechikha village, among the peasants settled on Prince Dadiani's land; they, while not refusing to work for their landlord, also doubted the words of the person who read them the manifesto. They made him read the whole manifesto, from the first page to the last, and when he left out the formulas and tables, explaining that there was no need to read these, the peasants said, 'Read everything, because it may be that freedom is in there somewhere.'

The peasants explain their conviction like this: 'They did not send books to our fathers and grandfathers, and they knew well that they were serfs and had to work for the landlord, but people had been saying for a long time that we were to be freed, and then, after that talk, they sent us books and had them read to us.

'We are sorry, but we thought, why would they send us these books if freedom is not in them . . .'

All this shows that the peasant understands freedom as meaning nothing less than his complete deliverance from work for the landlord. Having to work in payment for use of the land was beyond his comprehension.

Given this state of mind among the peasants, it is easy to see why the news that some peasant in Bezdna village had read 'freedom' in the manifesto was all over the district within a couple of days. The peasants lost no time in passing on this rumour to their neighbours and talked in the markets about freedom. On the third day, when Anton proclaimed freedom, several thousand peasants assembled in Bezdna.

There was no need for any incitement in order to gather the crowd: everyone made their way to Bezdna, attracted by the rumours about freedom.

The revolt that ensued, in April 1861, had to be put down by government troops, as described here in the eye-witness account of N. A. Krylov, the manager of one of the local landed estates.

ЕРЕМА   ПАРАМОШКА   ФОМА

ABOVE Lubok *portraying Toma and Yeryoma, the Russian version of 'Tom and Jerry'. Like their western counterparts, they depict resistance to oppression.*

I went to Volostnikovka, to the house of the landlord Gorlov, to spend the night.

As dusk fell I arrived at Kokryaty. 'Sidor isn't in.' 'Where is he?' 'At the office,' the woman told me, 'he's gone to be registered as a free man. The peasants have succeeded in getting true freedom, so now they have all gathered at the office. It is said there are orders to slaughter the landlords.'

I went to the office. There was a crowd – noise, uproar, people crushed together, and a sort of bestial boldness in their faces. They were assembled to decide how to share out their master's rye and how to thresh their master's corn, or how to divide the sheaves among themselves. They decided to thresh the master's corn for the commune.

I listened to their talk, about knifing, hanging, or chopping up the gentry, about fixing axe heads on long poles. Altogether it was like Pugachev's rebellion. They had driven away the village headman.

Somebody who could write was writing down the names of the peasants who were to have true freedom, and the crowd was distinguishing between them. 'Don't put his name down,' they cried. 'He's always hobnobbing with the masters, don't give him any land.' From conversation with a number of persons there I learnt what was behind all this.

I sought out Sidor at the gathering. While he was getting horses ready for me I expressed admiration for the 'Pugachov revolt' and delight with the representatives of authority. Some peasants told me openly how they had driven the police chief and the marshal out of Bezdna, said that they were going to burn the marshal, and claimed that the tsar had ordered that no mercy be shown to the gentry, that they must be beheaded.

By order of the authorities thirteen companies of soldiers and two guns were sent into the district. On 12 April a company arrived at Bezdna, along with the tsar's aide-de-camp Count Apraksin, Molostvov, the local marshal of nobility, Shishkin, the police chief, and several adjutants. They all stationed themselves opposite Anton's house, at a distance of about a hun-

dred and fifty paces. Anton's house, his yard, his roof, and the street for fifty paces in front of the house were full of people.

The soldiers first appealed to the people, asking them to disperse or to hand over Anton. They got nothing from the crowd except shouts and coarse remarks.

A priest also tried to address the crowd. They answered him with curses.

'Give the command, captain!' There was a volley from several rifles and in the midst of the crowd three men fell to the ground. 'Cease fire!' The appeals began afresh, and they went on talking to the peasants for as long as before. Nothing but abuse from the crowd.

'Command!' Another volley, five men killed. 'Cease fire!' Appeals once again, as unsuccessful as before. The number of rifles brought to bear was increased, and after further volleys fifteen more men had fallen, without any noticeable effect on the crowd.

After each volley, the peasants were called upon either to disperse or to hand over the guilty Anton, but apart from rude shouts and threats, nothing was

St Anne's cross for 10%

In Bezdna village, a certain Old Believer named Anton Petrov had discovered, in the manifesto, the announcement of true freedom, which nobody had been able to make out until he found it.

Where a 'model statutory deed' is given in the manifesto, what is written is: 'house serfs 00, peasants 00, land 00', and so on. Anton was not puzzled by these zeros, but explained that what was meant was true freedom, sealed with St Anne's cross. As for St Anne's cross – turn back a page, and there, right in front of 'house serfs 00' stands 10%. This sign, he said, was St Anne's cross, by which means true freedom was sealed in secret fashion.

Anton was sitting in a hut in Bezdna, looking at these zeros, and reading without hesitation: 'the landlords' lands – hills and dales, ravines and roads, sand and reeds, not a twig from the forest for him. If he sets foot off his land, send him away with kind words, and if he won't listen, cut off his head; the tsar will reward you for that.'

The people liked this freedom so much that crowds flocked in from all directions to hear about the true freedom, bringing with them the manifesto, for Anton to point out the place where true freedom was to be found. Anton preached this for five days in succession.

From *Khrestomatiia* . *1861–1917*

ABOVE *Village house. Although there was unrest in villages and settlements throughout the country, the rebellion in Bezdna was the most serious.*

heard from the crowd. The entire company was now ordered to shoot: forty men fell but the crowd remained recalcitrant. Another volley from the company and this time they all began rushing about, running away; those who could not get out owing to the crush cried, 'We will give him up!' The firing stopped.

Anton was brought out of the house, and a crowd of people followed him out of the yard. He had put the manifesto on his head. As soon as Anton had separated himself from the crowd, the Cossack troops advanced and seized him.

Anton is thirty-five years old, thin, and short of stature. His face white as a sheet, he was terribly frightened: he thought they were going to shoot him there and then. The crowd dispersed, the corpses were brought together, the wounded taken to hospital. Altogether, a hundred and fifty persons had been killed or wounded.

In the summer of 1861 the revolutionary writer and thinker Alexander Herzen, who had been living in exile since 1847, responded from London through the pages of his political journal *The Bell* with a rhetorical address to the Russian people.

You hate the landlord, you hate the government official, you fear them – and you are quite right. But you still have faith in the tsar and the higher clergy. Don't have faith in them. The tsar is with them and they are his men. You can see him now, you, the father of a youngster killed at Bezdna, you, the son of a father killed at Penza.

With this pretence of liberation, Tsar Alexander has taken upon himself to open the people's eyes, and, to make this happen sooner, he has sent to all four corners of Russia aides-de-camp, bullets, and birches.

The Scotsman Sir Donald Mackenzie Wallace, an inveterate traveller and writer on Russia at the end of the last century, describes a meeting of one of the newly instituted *zemstvo*, or local assembly of deputies, which he attended in Novgorod. He remarks on the range of classes represented there.

Not long after my arrival in Novgorod I had the opportunity of being present at a district assembly. I found thirty or forty men seated round a long table covered with a cloth. Before each member lay sheets of paper for the purpose of taking notes, and before the president – the marshal of nobility for the district – stood a small handbell, which he rang vigorously at the commencement of the proceedings and on all the occasions when he wished to obtain silence. To the right and left of the president sat the members of the executive bureau, armed with piles of written and printed documents, from which they read long and tedious extracts, till the majority of the audience took to yawning and one or two of the members slept.

At the close of each of these reports the president rang his bell – presumably for the purpose of awakening the sleepers – and enquired whether anyone had remarks to make on what had just been read. Generally someone had remarks to make, and not infrequently a discussion ensued. When any decided difference of opinion appeared, a vote was taken by handing round a sheet of paper, or by the simpler method of requesting the ayes to stand up and the noes to sit still.

What surprised me most in this assembly was that it was composed partly of nobles and partly of peasants – the latter being decidedly in the majority – and that no trace of antagonism seemed to exist between the two classes. Landed proprietors and their *ci-devant* serfs, emancipated only ten years before, evidently met for the moment on a footing of equality. The discussions were carried on chiefly by the nobles, but on more than one occasion peasant members rose to speak, and their remarks, always clear, practical, and to the point, were invariably listened to with respectful attention. Instead of that violent antagonism which might have been expected considering the constitution of the assembly, there was too much unanimity – a fact indicating plainly that the majority of the members did not take a very deep interest in the matters presented to them.

One of the *zemstvos'* main tasks was the provision of medical services to the local population. Mackenzie Wallace approved of their work.

The old conceptions of disease, as something that may be most successfully cured by charms and similar means, are rapidly disappearing. The *zemstvo* – that is to say, the new local self-government – has done much towards this end by enabling the people to procure better medical attendance.

In the towns there are public hospitals, which generally are – or at least seem to an unprofessional eye – in a very satisfactory condition. The resident doctors are daily besieged by a crowd of peasants, who come from far and near to ask advice and receive medicines.

Besides this, in some provinces, medical assistants are placed in the principal villages, and the doctor makes frequent tours of inspection. The doctors are generally well-educated men, and do a large amount of work for a very small remuneration.

The reform of the judiciary was one of Alexander II's most important achievements. Trial by jury and a proper system of appeal courts were introduced, on the Western European model. All citizens were, nominally at least, deemed equal before the law. As Mackenzie Wallace found out, this proved unpopular in the new justice of peace courts in the provinces, where the nobles were accustomed to a privileged status.

The extreme popularity of the justice of peace courts did not last very long. The discontent appeared first among the so-called privileged classes. To people who had all their lives enjoyed great social consideration, it seemed monstrous that they should be treated in the same way as the peasant. When a general, who was accustomed to be addressed as 'Your Excellency', was accused of using abusive language to his cook, and found himself seated on the same bench with the menial, he naturally supposed that the end of all things was at hand; or perhaps a great

OPPOSITE *The church of St Blaise (1365) in Novgorod. In this city – famous for its history of independence – was held one of the first, newly instituted, democratic* zemstvo.

civil official, who was accustomed to regard the police as created merely for the lower classes, found himself, to his inexpressible astonishment, fined for a contravention of police regulations!

Naturally the justices were accused of dangerous revolutionary tendencies, and when they happened to bring to light some injustices on the part of the *chinovniki* they were severely condemned for undermining the prestige of the imperial authority.

Another major reform was the extension of public education. But the government feared that an educated populace would prove a rebellious one. In 1866 Count Dmitry Tolstoy, who was regarded as a pillar of conservatism, was appointed Minister of Public Instruction. In the countryside, the Church was encouraged to play a dominant role. In higher schools it meant an emphasis on classical discipline, as Mackenzie Wallace observed.

Count Dmitry Tolstoy received the mission of protecting the young generation against pernicious ideas, and eradicating from the schools, colleges, and universities all revolutionary tendencies. He determined to introduce more discipline into all the educational establishments, and to supplant to a certain extent the superficial study of natural science by the thorough study of Latin and Greek.

This scheme, which became known before it was actually put into execution, produced a storm of discontent in the young generation. Discipline at that time was regarded as an antiquated and useless remnant of patriarchal tyranny, and young men who were impatient to take part in social reorganization resented being treated as naughty schoolboys.

To them it seemed that the Latin grammar was an ingenious instrument for stultifying youthful intelligence, destroying intellectual development, and checking political progress. Ingenious speculations about the possible organization of the working classes and grandiose views of the future of humanity are so much more interesting and agreeable than Latin syntax and Greek irregular verbs!

Peasantry and serfdom

In 1858–9, the population of Russia totalled about 60 million, 12 million of whom were 'free men'. The other 48 million (about 80% of the population) were divided equally into state peasants (bound to land owned by the state) and proprietary peasants, serfs in the proper sense of the word who lived on private estates and were the property of individual landowners. These constituted 37.7% of the empire's population and were divided into peasants who fulfilled their obligations exclusively or primarily by paying rent, and who lived mainly in the forest zone to the north, and those who performed labour services in the fertile 'black-earth belt' in the south and south-east.

There were two basic types of obligation: *obrok*, where serf dues and obligations were payable in kind or in cash, increased, in the 18th century, especially in the less fertile non-black-earth regions; *barshchina*, or labour dues, which were particularly prevalent on the black-earth soils, where landlords were determined to extract as much work as possible from their peasants. Although a law restricting *barshchina* to three days was passed at the end of the 18th century, it was not always implemented.

The burdens of the state peasants, who were not serfs, were less onerous. From the 1830s, when Nicholas I instituted the Ministry of State Domains for the administration of the state peasants, and gave them title to their land and permitted them to form organs of serf government, they were effectively free men. In 1838, they comprised 30–40% of the male population. As with proprietary serfs, all males were subject to poll tax and paid rent. However, they did not have to provide labour and were generally better treated than serfs proper. In law, they were regarded as free men although they

ABOVE *Cossack. Soldiers served in the army for a term of 25 years.*

needed passports to travel, and if a young woman wished to marry outside her village, her family had to pay a fee.

The paternalist relationship of landlord to serf was a microcosm of that between the tsar and his people. A landlord exercised virtually total control over his serfs. Although he was supposed to provide for them in times of famine and help them when harvests were poor, he also policed his estate, acted as judge, enforced capital punishment with the *knout* (whip) or sent peasants into exile in Siberia. In practice, landowners were tsars on their estates. Serfs could

be given as presents, and could be bought and sold in the market place as chattels, their value varying according to their attributes. Landlords periodically submitted lists of males on their estates to the State Domains, for tax purposes.

Peasant farming was generally fairly primitive with, in most areas, communes where open-field farming with multi-strip cultivation was the norm. Techniques were backward and the extended family and the household formed the core institution together with the village community and the *volost*, the parish or group of closely knit villages. In an attempt to ensure that the tax burden was equitably distributed according to work capability, and the age and sex composition of a household, land was regularly redivided within the community. As the population increased in the 19th century, there was pressure to redivide the limited amount of land.

Serfdom was concentrated in two main areas: in the central provinces, where the system had originated, and in the western provinces, acquired in the partitions of Poland, where more than half the population were serfs. It was never established in the northern and eastern regions and in Siberia.

The army was recruited from the tax-paying population (both peasants and the lower middle class); five or six men in every thousand served for 25 years. The few serfs who survived became free men. It was possible for a peasant to avoid military service by paying another serf to take his place, but this was a costly exercise. Men were called up annually for the army and trained for a year in the reserve; when the next annual levy was mobilized, trainees became regular troops. Reducing the term of service would have greatly increased the number of recruits and freed serfs at a rapid rate, releasing landless peasants, trained in the use of firearms and military tactics, onto a society that was not ready to absorb them.

Despite their noble intentions, the reforms of
Alexander II had little effect on the lives of the
peasants. They continued to be governed by
customary law, while the *zemstvos* were not
established at the village level until 1917. The
peasants were left to administer – and provide welfare
services – for themselves through the traditional
village assembly. Mackenzie Wallace describes it
vividly.

The simple procedure or rather the absence of all formal procedure at the assemblies, illustrates admir-
ably the essentially practical character of the
institution. The meetings are held in the open air,
because in the village there is no building – except
the church, which can be used only for religious purposes – large enough to contain all the members; and
they almost always take place on Sundays or holidays, when the peasants have plenty of leisure.

Any open space may serve as a forum. The discussions are occasionally very animated, but there is
rarely any attempt at speech-making. If any young
member should show an inclination to indulge in
oratory, he is sure to be unceremoniously interrupted
by some of the older members, who have never any
sympathy with fine talking. The assemblage has the
appearance of a crowd of people who have accidentally come together, and are discussing in little
groups subjects of local interest. Gradually some one
group, containing two or three peasants who have
more moral influence than their fellows, attracts the
others, and the discussion becomes general.

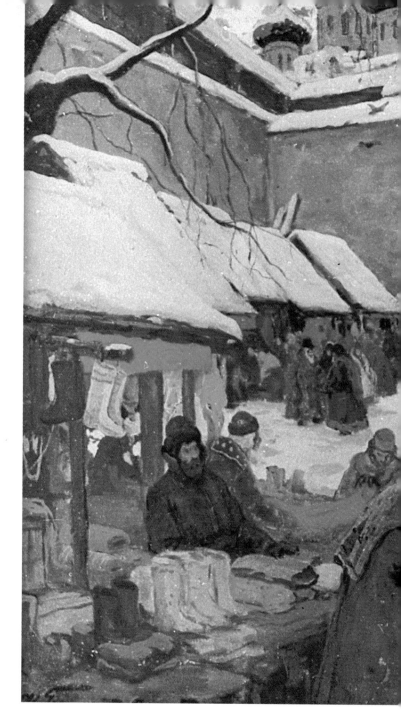

The friendly Russians

No class of men in the world are more good-
natured and pacific than the Russian peasantry.
When sober they never fight, and even when
under the influence of alcohol they are more
likely to be violently affectionate than disagree-
ably quarrelsome.

If two of them take to drinking together, the
probability is that in a few minutes, though they
may never have seen each other before, they will
be expressing in very strong terms their mutual
regard and affection, confirming their words with
an occasional friendly embrace.

From Sir Donald Mackenzie Wallace, *Russia*

LEFT *Market day in an old city. A contemporary described Russian peasants as being among the most good-natured men in the world; even animated political discussions normally ended in embraces rather than blows.*

, Two or more peasants may speak at a time, and interrupt each other freely, using plain, unvarnished language, not at all parliamentary, and the discussion may become a confused, unintelligible din; but at the moment when the spectator imagines that the consultation is about to be transformed into a free fight, the tumult spontaneously subsides, or perhaps a general roar of laughter announces that someone has been successfully hit by a strong *argumentum ad hominem* or by a biting, personal remark.

In any case, however forceful the arguments, however sharp the remarks, there is no danger of the disputants coming to blows with one another.

The democratic customs of the peasantry were romantically idealized by young radicals and intellectuals from the new universities, Russia's emergent intelligentsia. Those who called themselves 'populists' believed that the peasant village assembly could form the basis for a revolutionary renewal of Russia. About 3000 of them followed a dedicated revolutionist, Sergei Nechayev's appeal to 'go to the people' as doctors, teachers, and agitators in what came to be known as the 'mad summer' of 1874.

Pursued by the police, and mistrusted by the peasantry, these populists began to despair at the difficulties involved in stirring the inert population to revolution. The temptation to resort to more violent methods soon became too great, as one of the populist newspapers later explained.

The revolutionary movement in Russia began with the so-called 'going in among the people'. The first Russian revolutionaries thought that the freedom of the people could be obtained only by the people itself, and they imagined that the only thing necessary was that the people should absorb socialistic ideas. It was supposed that the peasantry were naturally inclined to this, because they already possess, in the rural commune, institutions which contain the seeds of socialism, and which might serve as a basis for the reconstruction of society according to socialist principles. The propagandists hoped, therefore, that the people would joyfully accept the new teaching.

But the people did not understand its friends, and showed itself hostile to them. With pain in their hearts the revolutionists had to confess that they were deceived in their hopes of the people. Around them were no social revolutionary forces on which they could lean for support. Terrorism was the only means that remained, and it had the advantage of giving a natural vent to pent-up feelings, and of appearing to be a reaction against government persecution.

A party called *Narodnaya Volya* (People's Will) was accordingly formed, and during several years the world witnessed a spectacle that had never been seen before in history. The *Narodnaya Volya*, insignificant in numbers but strong in spirit, engaged in single combat with the powerful Russian government. Neither executions, nor imprisonment with hard labour, nor ordinary imprisonment and exile, destroyed the energy of the revolutionists. Under their shots fell, one after the other, the most zealous and typical representatives of arbitrary action and violence.

The aim of *Narodnaya Volya* was to disorganize the government apparatus by assassinating officials, and finally Tsar Alexander II himself on 13 March 1881. The same day his assassins issued the following statement.

Workers of Russia!
Today, 13 March, Alexander the tyrant has been killed by us, socialists. He was killed because he did not care for his people. He burdened them with taxes. He deprived the peasant of his land; he handed over the workers to plunderers and exploiters. He did not give the people freedom.

He cared only for the rich. He himself lived in luxury. The police maltreated the people and he rewarded them instead of punishing them. He hanged or exiled any who stood up on behalf of the people or on behalf of justice. That is why he was killed.

A tsar should be a good shepherd, ready to devote his life to his sheep. Alexander II was a ravening wolf and a terrible death overtook him.

Ten days later, the leaders of *Narodnaya Volya* published an open letter which was addressed to the dead man's son, the new tsar, Alexander III. This letter warned the new tsar of the dangers ahead.

Your Majesty:
While fully comprehending your deep sorrow, the executive committee would not be justified in postponing this explanation out of a feeling of natural delicacy.

There is something higher than the most legitimate of personal feelings: it is the duty to our country, to which all individual sentiments must be sacrificed. The issue remains unchanged. It is the circumstances of the age that create revolutionaries, the whole nation's discontent, the urge of all Russia towards a new social order.

There are but two ways – either revolution, inevitable, unavertible by any executions, or the voluntary transfer of supreme power into the hands of the people.

We turn to you, disregarding that suspicion which the misdeeds of the administration have aroused; we turn to you as a citizen of our country and as a man of honour.

We trust that no sense of personal bitterness will

cause Your Majesty to forget your duty or to cease to wish to know the truth.

We too have cause for bitterness. You have lost a father. We have lost fathers, brothers, wives, children, and our dearest friends.

We are prepared to suppress our own personal feelings if the good of our country Russia demands it; and we expect the same of you.

We do not impose conditions, as these have been imposed by history; we merely state them. The conditions are:

A general amnesty for all political crimes, as those were not crimes, but rather the fulfilment of social duty.

The summoning of representatives of the whole

nation to consider the existing social and economic order and its modification in accordance with the nation's desire.

And so, Your Majesty, decide.

There are two ways before you. The choice to be made is yours.

We can only beg of fate that your judgement and your conscience will lead you to choose the only path consistent with the good of Russia, with your honour, and with your duty.

Alexander III

The assassination of Alexander II brought to an end the period of liberal reform under his reign. The new tsar, Alexander III, who reigned from 1881 to 1894, oversaw a clamp-down on the revolutionary movement, and tighter censorship laws. Plans for constitutional limitations on the powers of the government, initiated under Alexander II, were now rejected, and the principles of autocracy upheld.

This failed, however, to stem the revolutionary movement, which now found a new basis of support among the exploited workers of Russia's expanding industries, as well as the non-Russian nationalities, who had reason to protest against Alexander's programmes of Russian colonization. It was no surprise that Jews played such a prominent part in the socialist parties, given the anti-Semitism of the Russian government, and its failure to control the violent pogroms against Jews.

Several aspects of Alexander's reign explain and illuminate the growing strength of the revolutionary movement, among them the heart-rending protest of Marya Tsebrikova, a revolutionary publicist, against the injustices of the regime – a protest which earned her several years exile in the bitter cold of the far north. Many of the problems encountered by the government as it sought to build up Russia's fledgling economy stemmed from the shortage of indigenous capital to finance the new industries. This meant that the government had to squeeze revenues from the already impoverished peasant farmers. The outcome was widespread poverty in the countryside, culminating in the terrible famine of 1893.

This particular concentration on the growing revolutionary movement leaves little room to describe the cultural achievement of Russia's great writers and composers, illustrated on pages 352–67. In many ways, cultural achievement reached its heights under Alexander III, despite his tightening of censorship. Perhaps this was not surprising, for writers such as Tolstoy, Dostoyevsky and Chekhov increasingly saw it as their duty to focus on the great social problems of their time. And each of them, in his own way, foresaw the impending crisis.

OPPOSITE *Alexander III (1881–94)*

We by the grace of God, Alexander III, Emperor and Autocrat of All Russia, Tsar of Poland, Grand Duke of Finland, etc., hereby make known the following to all our faithful subjects: that it has pleased the Almighty, in His inscrutable will to visit Russia with heavy blows of fate, and to call her benefactor, the Emperor Alexander II, to Himself.

The emperor fell by the hands of impious murderers who had repeatedly sought his gracious life, and made their attempts because they saw in him the protector of Russia, the foundation of her greatness, and the promoter of the welfare of the Russian people. Let us bow to the unfathomable will of Divine Providence, and offer up to the Almighty our prayers for the repose of the pure soul of our beloved father.

We ascend the throne, which we inherit from our forefathers, the throne of the Russian empire, the tsardom of Poland, and the grand dukedom of Finland, inseparably connected with it. We assume the heavy burden which God has imposed upon us with firm reliance upon His almighty help. May He bless our work for the welfare of our beloved fatherland, and may He guide our strength for the happiness of all our faithful subjects.

Given at St Petersburg in the year of Our Lord 1881, and the first year of our reign.

The above proclamation was made by the new tsar, Alexander III, on ascending the throne. It was prepared by the new tsar's old tutor, Konstantin Pobedonostsev, Procurator of the Most Holy Synod, a jurist and former professor of law, and an arch-reactionary and critic of Alexander II's liberal reforms.

Pobedonostsev argued that Russia's untrustworthy people could only be governed by strict hierarchy and firm authority. On 6 March he wrote to the new tsar, warning him not to accept the constitution which was being prepared by Alexander II's Minister of the Interior, Count Mikhail Tariyelovich Loris-Melikov.

If they begin to sing the old siren's song, that it is necessary to be calm and to continue in the liberal direction, that it is necessary to yield to so-called public opinion, for God's sake, Your Majesty, do not believe and do not listen! It will be the ruin of Russia and of you: this is as clear as day to me. It is necessary to end at once, now, all the talk about freedom of the press, about popular meetings, about a representative assembly.

These are all lies spoken by superficial and weak people; it is absolutely essential to reject them for the good of the true people.

Following Pobedonostsev's advice, Alexander issued an imperial manifesto rejecting the modest limitations on government envisaged by Loris-Melikov and proclaiming his divine right to uphold autocracy. This foreshadowed a regime of repression, forcing the revolutionary movement into retreat, but equally alienating the rest of educated society.

A revolutionary writer exiled in Paris, Maria Tsebrikova, in an open letter to the tsar published in all the leading newspapers of Europe, accused him of tyranny, injustice and misrule.

Your Majesty,

The laws of my country forbid free speech. All that is honest in Russia is forced to look on at the arbitrary despotism of the officials, the persecution of thought, the moral and physical ruin of the rising generation, the slavery of the oppressed and plundered people – and to be silent.

The Russian emperors see and hear only what they are allowed to see and hear by the officials who stand between them and the masses. The fearful death of Alexander II cast an ominous gloom over your succession to the throne, and your advisers have persuaded you that his death resulted from the free ideas fostered by the best part of his reign.

Our terrorists were created, not by the reforms of the last reign, but by the insufficiency of those reforms.

Your advisers scare you from a progressive policy simply because it is dangerous to the absolute power of ministers and officials who find secrecy and despotism to their advantage.

RIGHT *Tsarist soldiers discover a clandestine printing press in Kiev. Alexander III's accession to the imperial throne brought in an era of repression that drove dissenters underground and turned them to revolution.*

The whole system is driving even those to whom blood and violence are hateful into the ranks of malcontents, into revolutionary propaganda. For one incautious word – for a few pages of underground literature (often taken up out of mere curiosity), a youth – a child – is a political offender. There have been political prisoners, children of fifteen – even fourteen – years old in solitary confinement. The government that rules over one hundred million is afraid even of children.

The broken-down, embittered young generation turns to revolution. Blood is horrible to me on whichever side it is shed, but when bloodshed on one side is rewarded with a decoration, and on the other side with the gallows, it is easy to understand which bloodshed will have for the young the charm of heroism.

Political prisoners are the defenceless victims of arbitrary despotism that extends to downright brutality. But measures of coercion and terror, from 'administrative' exile to the gallows, never attain their end.

Freedom of speech, personal security, freedom of meetings, full publicity of justice, education accessible to all talents, suppression of administrative despotism, the convoking of a national assembly for which all classes can choose their delegates – in these alone our salvation lies.

You, Your Majesty, are one of the most powerful monarchs in the world; I am a working unit in the hundred million whose fate you hold in your hands; but nonetheless, I, in my conscience, fully recognize my moral right and duty as a Russian woman to say what I have said.

Maria Tsebrikova

Alexander, having read through the letter, was said to have exclaimed, 'That is all very well; but what on earth does all this matter to *her*?' On her return to Russia, Maria Tsebrikova, then in her 54th year, was arrested and sent into internal exile in Yarensk, a small town in the far north.

One aspect of Alexander's reactionary rule was his

policy of Russification – colonizing the non-Russian territories of the empire and imposing on them the customs and language of Russia. As Mackenzie Wallace pointed out, such policies were bound to create a revolutionary movement among the subject nationalities.

The policy of Russifying subject nationalities, inaugurated by Alexander III, has increased the use of the Russian language in official procedure, modified the system of instruction in the schools and universities, and brought a few schismatic and heretical sheep into the Eastern Orthodox fold; but it has entirely failed to inspire the subject populations with Russian feeling and national patriotism; on the contrary, it has aroused in them bitter hostility to Russian nationality, and to the central government.

In such of them as have retained their old aspirations of political independence – notably the Poles – the latent disaffection has been stimulated; and in those of them which, like the Finns and the Armenians, desire merely to preserve the limited autonomy they formerly enjoyed, a sentiment of disaffection has been created.

All of them know very well that in an armed struggle with the dominant Russian nationality they would be crushed. They hail, however, with delight the liberal and revolutionary movements, in the hope that the Russians themselves may undermine and possibly overthrow the tyrannical autocratic power. Towards this end they would gladly co-operate.

While sympathizing with every form of opposition to the government, the men of the subject nationalities reserve their special affection for the socialists, because these proclaim, like the liberals, the principles of extensive local self-government and universal equality before the law. This explains why so many Poles, Armenians, and Georgians are to be found in the ranks of the Social Democrats and the Socialist Revolutionaries.

Of the recruits from oppressed nationalities the great majority come from the Jews, who, though they have never dreamed of political independence, or even of local autonomy, have most reason to complain of the existing order of things.

Nationality groups in Russia around 1900

In 1897, Russia's population of 125 million consisted of about 170 ethnic groups. Russians, or East Slavs, made up slightly less than half the total, but, together with 28 million Ukrainians and Belorussians, were a clear majority. Historically, the regime tended to favour them over non-Russians, as it favoured Orthodoxy over other religions, nobles over non-nobles, and officials over everybody else.

The seven million West Slavic Poles were another matter. Roman Catholicism, a tradition of conflict with Russians, memories of national independence, and industrial development resulted in a national consciousness that ensured that a crisis of Russo-Polish relations would be a by-product of any other crisis in the empire.

Almost two million Germans were concentrated in the South and along the Volga, where they had been enticed in the 18th century, and in the Baltic provinces of Latvia, Lithuania and Estonia, where they had held sway for centuries, filling a disproportionate share of élite positions in the bureaucracy and the military. In the later 19th century they faced new Russifying pressures in the Baltic region that had long been their preserve.

The four million Latvians, Lithuanians and Estonians responded to their double subjugation by Russia and Germany with furious cultural activity – the Baltic provinces had the highest literacy rates in the empire – and, in the revolutions of 1905 and 1917, surpassed other areas in revolutionary turmoil.

In Transcaucasia lived 2.5 million Georgians and Armenians. Both had ancient Christian traditions and distinctive, non-Slavic languages; remarkably they adapted to Russian ways without sacrifice of their own culture. Transcaucasia held

A settlement in Georgia; the region's inhabitants retained their distinctive culture while adapting to Russian ways.

the potential for many-sided conflict: between Armenians and Georgians, between either or both and the Russians, between all of these and foreigners who owned most of its mineral wealth and between any or all of these and the Azerbaijanis, the region's third major nationality.

The Azerbaijanis were among the empire's 12 million Turkic people whose conquest by Russia had started in the 16th century. In the latter 19th century, Russia expanded into Central Asia, which was inhabited by Kazakhs, Bashkirs, Turkomens, Uzbeks, Kalmuks and Kirghiz.

The range of lifestyles among the Turkic peoples was wide. Volga Tartars had coexisted peacefully for centuries with their Slavic neighbours and were, like them, settled agriculturalists. Most of the peoples of Central Asia were pastoral nomads, and all, including the Kirghiz, spoke a Turkic language. All were Muslims. Although some Turkic intellectuals were drawn to secularism, nationalism or both, national consciousness for most began and ended with Islam.

The *inorodtsy*, peoples of other stock, lived mainly in the far North or Eastern Siberia. Few in number, they were economically and culturally primitive. Yakuts, Samoeds, Aleuts and Eskimos were classified as *inorodtsy*.

Jews and anti-Semitism

With only a few exceptions, Russia's Jewish population was forced to live within a Pale of Settlement in the empire's western provinces. This encouraged the traditional *shtetl* or Jewish village, isolated (except economically) from the surrounding world, and dominated by teachers, the rabbis, who guided every aspect of daily life with religious and customary sanctions. Learning and piety were prized; women bore toil and privation so that their menfolk could spend their time studying Hebrew and religious books.

As such a visible minority, Jews were the focus of prejudice and persecution. This came partly from Russian Orthodox stories of the struggle between Christians and Jews which found their way into the traditional literature of the Orthodox Church and were familiar to the faithful. From these, Russians acquired a disposition against the Jewish name, such as other Christians might have against 'Philistines'.

Also important were the hostility and suspicion which peasants (and not just in Russia) held for outsiders. Jews were quintessential outsiders, and one rationale for confining them within the pale was the government's plea that otherwise it could not protect them from peasant violence.

Peasants did not, however, make the laws which enshrined anti-Semitism in endless prohibitions; ethnic Russian officials copied colleagues who came from areas with a Jewish population and a tradition of anti-Semitism, pervasive from the Black Sea to the Baltic.

The élite believed in an idealized Russia, where rural Eastern Europe was a harmonious world of sturdy, deferential peasants and chivalrous, benevolent squires. All would have liked to close their eyes to money, the squire because it was beneath him, the peasant because almost every transaction except barter was a misfortune. Because they were barred by the laws from many occupations, Jews took whatever work was left, such as peddling, horsedealing, money-lending.

LEFT *The military stand by while the mob assaults a Jew. The pogroms that started in 1881 resulted in the great waves of emigration that took Jews as far afield as the United States.*

A dead horse meant buying a new one from a Jewish horsedealer, borrowing money to pay for it from a Jewish money-lender, and borrowing again to pay the rent for which the squire's steward, possibly another Jew, was dunning him.

In truth, each and every one of the Jews was as poor as his peasant neighbour, but as scapegoats nearest to hand, alien in language and religion, they were an easy target. Local and central officials were not loath to divert to the Jews antagonisms that might otherwise have been directed against themselves, the social system, and the regime.

Between Alexander III's accession to the imperial throne in 1881 and the 1905 revolution, popular anti-Semitism found ghastly expression in a series of pogroms; these were mob attacks on Jewish houses, property and people, incited in many cases by low-level police officials.

Although the government in St Petersburg could not openly encourage such violations of public order, it preferred the mobs to attack the Jews rather than officials' own homes or government offices.

Official ambivalence towards anti-Semitism was shown in the notation which Tsar Alexander III made on a police report: 'I am glad in my heart when they beat the Jews, but it cannot be permitted.'

With the obvious official connivance at the hatred and violence, Jews began slowly to tear themselves from the country they considered their only known homeland, and began the great wave of emigration which was to take them westwards to settle in the countries of Central Europe, England, and especially across the Atlantic to the United States, then the melting-pot of the poor and homeless from all over the world.

Anti-Semitism was a pervasive influence in the corridors of power in St Petersburg, and the first two years of Alexander's reign were marked by terrible anti-Jewish riots (pogroms) in the Pale of Jewish Settlement. Arnold White, an English publicist, writing in the *Contemporary Review* for May 1892, after spending eight months in Russia, explained the anti-Semitism of Russian nationals. The tsar himself was one of the worst offenders.

The main object pursued by the governing classes in repressing the Jew in Russia is sheer self-defence. Russians hold that the bright Jewish intellect, if allowed free play, would contaminate the whole empire within a short space of time. It has been calculated that if the repressive laws of Russia were repealed, and the Jews allowed access to any and every post in

Scientific anti-Semitism

In St Petersburg there exists a powerful group of Poles and Yids which has direct control of banks, the stock exchange, the bar, a great part of the press, and other areas of public life. Through many legal and illegal ways it exerts an enormous influence over the bureaucracy and the general course of affairs. Parts of this group are implicated in the growing plunder of the exchequer and in seditious activity. Preaching the blind imitation of Europe, these people recommend the granting of the most extensive rights to Poles and Jews, and representative institutions after the Western model. Every honest voice is silenced by the shouts of Jews and Poles who insist that one must listen only to the 'intelligent' class and that Russian demands must be rejected as backward and unenlightened.

From N. P. Ignatyev, Minister of the Interior, *Memorandum to Alexander III*

the service of the empire, eight years would not pass before every post worth having outside the army and navy would be filled by an official of the Hebrew faith. I believe the statement to be little if at all exaggerated. The average Jew towers above the average Russian. Intellectual jealousy and fear of supersession supply the effective force to anti-Semitic prejudices in Russia. In point of fact, religious antipathy has little part in the measures directed against Russians of the Hebrew faith.

Alexander III's reign witnessed the first real wave of industrial expansion shaped by Alexander's two great ministers of finance. Ivan Vyshnegradsky, appointed in 1886, pursued a policy of squeezing extra revenues from the peasantry by increased indirect taxes. But this left the peasants without reserves of food or money. Hundreds of thousands died from starvation when the harvest failed in 1891. Vyshnegradsky was forced to resign. He was replaced by Sergei Witte, a young star from the railway department. His policies were based upon a stable rouble and increased grain exports to attract foreign capital for Russia's industries, especially her railways. Rapid expansion created a new class of blue-collar workers, poorly paid, living in terrible conditions. To limit the worst excesses of factory-labour exploitation, a law was passed in 1886 stipulating that workers had to be employed according to contracts overseen by factory boards. Details of factory conditions were given in the state council.

Unrest among factory workers of Moscow and Vladimir provinces, and the consequent disorders in some factories, clearly revealed many unattractive aspects of factory life. Furthermore, the causes of these disorders were not accidental, but were conditioned by improper relations between management and labour.

The owners of several factories, taking advantage of their superior position, do not hesitate to violate the conditions agreed upon with their employees and to resort to various means for extracting increased

LEFT *Repairing a rail line. Sergey Witte, Minister of Finance from 1892, understood the vital importance of an efficient rail system.*

BELOW LEFT *The Trans-Siberian railway, instigated by Witte, still traverses Russia's great plains.*

BELOW *Factory. Under Alexander III, workers were unprotected by labour legislation.*

profits. In violation of the labour contract, wages are reduced either openly or by understating the number of hours and days worked per week. Also, deductions and fines exacted from the workers for the benefit of management attain huge proportions, in several instances totalling about forty per cent of wages paid.

Finally, the workers' obligation to purchase all their necessities at company stores, and the sale of these products at high prices, were found to be a common occurrence. The situation of the workers becomes more and more deplorable. Oppressed to extremes by their hopeless indebtedness to the owner, they are frequently unable not only to pay their taxes and maintain their families, but even to earn enough to feed themselves.

The resultant animosities against the manufacturers, given the difficulty that is encountered in seeking legal redress for the defence of their rights, constantly prompt the workers to seek the reinstatement of these rights by creating disturbances and crude manifestations of lawlessness and violence.

The costs of this ceaseless exploitation of factory labour in terms of human suffering were most obvious among the cheapest sources of labour, women and children.

A female doctor working for the *zemstvo* in Kostroma, L. Katenina, made the following observations in a report of 1913.

One cannot help but note the premature decrepitude of the factory woman. A woman worker of fifty who has worked' at the factory thirty or more years frequently looks ancient; she sees and hears poorly, her head trembles, her shoulders are sharply hunched over. She looks about seventy years old.

It is obvious that only dire need keeps her at the factory, forcing her to work beyond her strength.

While in the West, elderly workers have pensions, our women workers, having given decades to the factory so that they are prematurely enfeebled, can expect nothing better than to live out their last days as latrine attendants.

The institution of land captains in 1889 was another aspect of Alexander III's repressive rule. They were appointed by the ministry of the interior to oversee virtually every aspect of law enforcement and government in the countryside. Accordingly, they were given wide powers of intervention in village affairs and rights to execute summary justice. V. I. Gurko, an assistant Minister of the Interior, thought that the main problem with the land captains was that they were left too much to their own devices, and this made them both lazy and corrupt.

Not until 1904, fifteen years after the institution was established, was there an inspection of the land captains; and this first one was to embrace twenty-four districts in three provinces. From the outset it was evident that there was a multitude of problems in need of immediate solution.

It soon became apparent that there was virtually no supervision over the activities of the land captains other than that some of their administrative decisions were revised as a result of complaints lodged against them.

ABOVE   *Alexander III's study. In contrast to his father, he presided over an era of oppression and terror.*

One reason for this lack of supervision was that the legal supervisors, the district marshals of nobility, very seldom carried out their duties, and even avoided them lest they offend their subordinate land captains who played an influential part in electing the marshals. It also became clear that the chief sin of the land captains was not arbitrariness but laziness and indifference.

Nicholas II

The reign of Nicholas II (1894–1917) marks the final struggle of the Romanov autocracy to keep itself in power, despite the mounting pressures for reform from the liberal intelligentsia, the new urban middle classes, blue-collar workers, and peasants. The basic dilemma of the regime stemmed from the fact that its two main goals were incompatible: the creation of a modern, industrial society while retaining the autocracy. Nicholas believed he could engineer an industrial revolution without conceding political rights to its bourgeois vanguard, the merchants and employers, but without concessions to the blue-collar workers themselves. The result was that both rose against him in 1905.

Conditions in Russia's industrial centres, and the nation-wide feeling of political injustice, brought to a head the wave of strikes and demonstrations that started the revolution of 1905. A wave of optimism followed the manifesto of 17 October, in which Nicholas granted Russia's first constitution, and called for a national parliament, the *duma*, elected on a popular franchise. But bitter disappointment ensued at the bloody repression of the revolutionary movement in 1906–7, the closure of the first two *dumas*, and their replacement by a more conservative body.

During the following years, Prime Minister Stolypin attempted to stabilize the regime by carrying through a series of agrarian and administrative reforms. But this initiative proved highly unpopular. From that point on, the sense of imminent catastrophe pervaded the whole of Russian educated society, as reflected in the growing conservatism of intellectuals and artists, as well as the scandals at court connected with the 'holy man', Rasputin. This sense of foreboding was proved correct by the events of February 1917.

OPPOSITE *Nicholas II (1894–1917)*

I rejoice to see gathered here representatives of all estates of the realm, who have come to express their sentiments of loyal allegiance. I believe in the sincerity of these feelings, which have been those of every Russian from time immemorial. But it has come to my knowledge that latterly, at some meetings of the zemstva (local assemblies), voices have been heard from people who have allowed themselves to be carried away by senseless dreams about the participation of representatives of the zemstva in the general administration of the internal affairs of the state.

Let it be known to all that I devote all my strength to the good of my people, but that I shall uphold the principle of autocracy as firmly and unflinchingly as did my ever-lamented father.

The accession speech of Nicholas II in 1894, quoted above, was written by the reactionary Pobedonostsev, as Alexander III's had been. This, alone, was enough to make it clear from the start of his reign that the last Russian tsar would stick firmly to the principles of autocracy and a policy of political repression, until forced into reform by the revolution of 1905.

Under Nicholas II, the apparatus of the police state, with its infamous security wing, the Third Section, grew to resemble a 20th-century totalitarian state. Prince V. P. Meshchersky, the talented and cynical publisher of *Grazhdanin*, a liberal-minded periodical, described its activities.

The police knew who subscribed to and read foreign publications which had been prohibited; they knew who criticized the government and how severe the criticisms were; they knew what was being written about the Minister of the Interior in letters between friends: the police knew many things which it was not absolutely necessary for them to know.

One thing only the police did not know, and that was the most important: they did not know what was going on in the terrorist circles. This state of affairs had come about under the Third Section, formed in 1826, whose function it had been to direct and control Russian thought. To this function was now added the surveillance of purely personal affairs.

The regular routine work of secret police – that is, the safeguarding against and prevention of unlawful actions – was but a drop in the ocean compared with the tireless and meticulous efforts of the Third Section to ferret out information about people's private lives. Nonetheless, the Third Section proved to be unable to thwart various recent plans of the terrorists, who carried out their plots unhindered. Inquests invariably showed that the success of a terroristic act was directly due to the unpreparedness of the police. At the same time numbers of people were being put under arrest for the opinions they held. The police department had inherited the logic of the Third Section and now its main concern was to discover what the people were thinking.

The Third Section was kept increasingly busy watching the movement of workers, activated by the industrial recession at the turn of the century. The movement was influenced by the Russian Social Democratic Workers' Party, a Marxist group led by Martov, Plekhanov and Lenin, and the Socialist Revolutionary Party, founded in 1901 by neo-populist groups. The crisis was especially severe in the Polish city of Lódź, as reported by the local paper, *Syn Otechestva* (Son of the Fatherland) in 1900.

The crisis, like a raging hurricane, has swept through Lódź. It spared nothing and no one, affecting everything and everyone. Some it touched only slightly and caused them no particular harm, whereas others were severely maimed, and many were crushed and buried beneath its ruins. One needs only to walk down Petrokovskaia Street, to look at the intensely gloomy faces gazing all about them, to see how many victims there are. Yes, all these gentlemen bustling about, sombre creatures with downcast heads, are people who have closed down or are closing down factories and small workshops; they float like shadows, unable to come to their senses from the blow.

ABOVE *Coronation proclamation of Nicholas II, the last tsar,*
and the empress, Alexandra.

Death by starvation

A few days ago a young woman, not over twenty-one, was seen in the streets. She walked swaying like a drunkard, provoking the mockery of passers-by. She scarcely had the strength to say that she was not drunk but had not eaten for seven days. The same day a man, who turned out to be an unemployed weaver, collapsed in the street. He had not eaten for several days, and had no place to live. At the same time, a twelve-year-old boy, a girl of twenty-one, and an elderly man of fifty-five were picked up on the street completely exhausted from hunger. In one day five persons were picked off the streets! And how many such remained unnoticed, lacking the courage, or perhaps the strength, to go outside?

Lódź, like many other industrial centres, had to endure the full force of the crisis that curtailed work in factories and mills, and threw out into the streets masses of people deprived of wages and bread.

From *Rozwój Lódzki* (*Lódź's Development*)

Over the next few years conditions failed to improve, partly because of a series of poor harvests and partly because of the costly war against Japan in 1904–5. Strikes and demonstrations became commonplace, not all of them inspired by political extremists. Father Gapon, a St Petersburg priest and prison chaplain, established his Assembly of Russian Factory Workers in 1904 with the approval of Vyacheslav Konstantinovich Pleve, Minister of the Interior, to provide tea-rooms and lectures for its members. On Sunday, 9 January 1905, Gapon led a march of 120,000 workers, some of them bearing religious banners and icons, to the Winter Palace, where they planned to present the following petition directly to the tsar.

O Sire! we working men of St Petersburg, our wives and children, and our parents, helpless and aged men and women, have come to you, our ruler, in quest of justice and protection. We are beggars, we are oppressed and overburdened with work; we are insulted, we are not regarded as human beings but are treated as slaves who must suffer in silence.

Our first wish was to discuss our needs with our employers, but this was refused us: we were told that we have no legal right to discuss our conditions. We asked that wages of casual labourers and women should be raised to one rouble a day, that overtime should be abolished, and that more adequate medical attention should be provided for us with care and without humiliation. We asked that the factories should be rebuilt so that we could work in them without suffering from draughts, rain, and snow.

Your Majesty! We are here, many thousands of us. We have the appearance of human beings, but in fact we have no human rights at all, not even the right to speak or to think. We are turned into slaves by your officials. Any one of us who dares to raise his voice in defence of the working class is thrown into prison, sent into exile.

The bureaucracy of the government has ruined the country, involved it in a shameful war, and is leading Russia nearer and nearer to utter ruin. We, the Russian workers and people, have no voice at all in the expenditure of the huge sums collected in taxes from the impoverished population. We do not even know how our money is spent. The people are deprived of any right to discuss taxes and their expenditure. The workers have no right to organize their own labour unions to defend their own interests.

Is this, O Sovereign, in accordance with the laws of God, by whose grace you reign? How can we live under such laws? Break down the wall between yourself and your people. Let all be equal and free. And to this end let the election of members to the Constituent Assembly take place in conditions of universal, secret, and equal suffrage.

This is our chief request; all else depends upon it; this is the only balm for our sore wounds; without it our wounds will never heal, and we shall be borne swiftly on to our death.

A new proletariat

Russian industrialization gathered pace during the 1880s and 1890s, adding new and large factories to the already impressive numbers of smaller workshops in St Petersburg and Moscow. Some factory workers, of whom there were around two million in 1900, were the children of people who had themselves worked in factory industry. Others were newly arrived from the countryside, 'snatched from the plough and hurled into the factory furnace', in Trotsky's memorable phrase. Some workers settled only temporarily in the towns, before returning to their villages: with the high urban cost of living and no prospect of government support when redundancy or old age came upon them, many had good reason to return. Others remained, their numbers regularly swelled by fresh waves of migrant workers. By 1913, the industrial working class, including workers in mining, construction and transport, had grown to six million.

The average working day during the 1880s was at least 12 hours. By 1913, it had fallen to ten hours. Meal breaks and other rest periods, as well as the time taken for the journey to and from home, added two or three hours to these figures. The reduction in hours of work is attributable only in part to government legislation, which, in 1897, stipulated a maximum of $11\frac{1}{2}$ hours. Of much greater consequence was the revolution of 1905–6, which forced employers to concede reductions.

Most workers were paid by the hour and received a daily or weekly wage. There were significant differentials between skilled and unskilled workers and between those in different occupations. Women made up one-quarter of the total industrial labour force and were overwhelmingly concentrated in low-paid jobs, including sweated trades such as clothing, where

ABOVE *Detail from a traditional cloth hanging. The feminine skills which produced superb embroidery like this were used in the textile and clothing industries; but end products and surroundings were both very different.*

the rate of pay never exceeded one-half the average industrial wage.

The main target for workers' anger was the foreman, who wielded virtually absolute power on the shop floor. He employed them, ensured that they completed the tasks he assigned and could fine or even dismiss them for sub-standard work or breaches of factory discipline, such as lateness or absenteeism. Some foremen abused their position, by demanding bribes or sexual favours.

Most spare time was spent at home or in factory barracks, the latter a characteristic means of accommodating (and monitoring) workers in newly industrializing regions. A survey of printers in Saratov in 1900 revealed that food and rent represented three-quarters of the household budget. Clothes, laundry and baths accounted for most of the remainder.

The 1905 revolution

On Sunday, 9 January 1905, a crowd of St Petersburg working men and women assembled in front of the Winter Palace to present the tsar with a petition. Its tone was submissive, monarchist and naive, but the substantive demands – representative government, amnesty for political prisoners, separation of church and state – were drawn from the standard repertoire of European liberalism and radicalism.

The guards opened fire and hundreds of demonstrators were killed. The shooting provoked a wave of strikes that would, with ebb and flow, continue through the year.

After Bloody Sunday – as this day of slaughter became known – the workers dropped the rhetoric of naive monarchism, and educated Russians stopped believing that the common people loved the monarchy.

The government attempted to repair the damage by convening a commission to investigate the 'real needs' of St Petersburg's workers. The workers boycotted the commission, but the election of the worker delegates to it mobilized the working class and so facilitated the formation of the St Petersburg soviet in the autumn. On 18 February, the government announced its plans for the election of a purely consultative assembly. Prior to Bloody Sunday, the announcement would have swung a portion of educated public opinion behind the government; now it seemed like a sign of weakness – and its value was undercut by the publication of a manifesto calling for prayers for the institution of autocracy.

The most important element of the revolution in 1905 was strikes by industrial workers. The railroad system, constructed with government funds, carried revolutionary contagion as the strike movement advanced in waves along it.

The government had routinely used the military to repress civil disorders; now, unsure how soldiers would respond when ordered out against workers, peasants, or their own fellows, it lacked confidence to issue the orders.

The revolution moved at a slower pace in the countryside, but by the autumn, peasants were resorting increasingly to the plunder and destruction of manor houses (*razgrom*).

The liberal Union of Liberation, which had been clandestine, came into the open and undertook to recruit professional men and women into organizations to support their agenda.

Liberals achieved their most remarkable successes in the *zemstvos*. These agencies of local administration were dominated by the landed nobility. Yet in 1905, almost every provincial *zemstvo* assembly passed a resolution calling for an end to autocracy and for measures that would do away with all the privileges, and many of the advantages, of the nobles who voted for them.

It seemed that the general strike in St Petersburg in October would provide the appropriate denouement for the government to grant a constitution, the liberals to make peace with the regime, and the workers and peasants to settle down under a new order. Every kind of enterprise was shut down. The government, paralysed by the general strike, issued the October Manifesto, which provided for civil liberties and a parliament, but this did not wind down the revolution as left, centre and right expected.

A party that called itself 'Octobrist' emerged to greet the manifesto, saying it was exactly what was wanted; but the constitutionalist activists, who would coalesce into the Cadet party, were not propitiated by the manifesto. They kept up their campaign for a constituent assembly and a government responsible to a legislature elected by universal, equal, secret and direct suffrage.

Ardent monarchists greeted the October

Manifesto with lamentations. They vented their feelings in widespread acts of violence against those who, they believed, had forced the tsar to issue the manifesto: students, Jews, workers, and intellectuals. This rightest response coalesced into the 'Black Hundred' organizations, which attempted to mobilize the masses on behalf of monarchist and patriotic goals. The government patronized these organizations, despite their scurrilous propaganda and intermittent violence, but it did not direct or fund them.

Unmollified by the October Manifesto, the workers of St Petersburg kept up their general strike, suspending it only on 30 October 1905. The St Petersburg soviet, their council, continued to meet; only in December could the government arrest the executive committee of what amounted to a rival government in the capital.

In response to the arrest of the St Petersburg soviet, a general strike was called in Moscow; the strikers took up arms, but they neither launched a vigorous assault – nor made a determined effort to win over the garrison troops of Moscow. Prime Minister Witte staked everything on a desperate gamble, an attempt to send the Semenovsky Guards regiment by rail from St Petersburg to suppress the insurrection in Moscow. The regiment retook the city by assault and put the working-class district of Presnia, the heart of the insurrection, under artillery siege.

By 1 January 1906, it was clear that the urban revolution was over. Counter-revolutionary violence had succeeded where political concessions had not. Peasants perpetrated more agrarian outrages in 1906, but the most restive areas were subdued by rail-borne army units. In the countryside as in the city, it was effective repression that brought the revolution to an end.

The crowd was dispersed by live rifle-fire: about 150 were killed and several hundred wounded. The day was to become known as Bloody Sunday, the first in the revolution of 1905–6.

After Bloody Sunday the people of Russia heard a new refrain, launched in a New Year's article by the conservative newspaper *Novoe Vremya* (New Times): 'It is no longer possible to live this way.' Doctors, teachers, students, lawyers, merchants, and manufacturers joined in a popular movement against the autocracy. Strikes and demonstrations took place in all the major industrial centres.

The French consul in Kharkov, the industrial centre of the Ukraine, wrote to Paris at the height of the strike movement in October 1905.

Work stopped everywhere: on the railways, in all factories, workshops, in shops of all types, in the university, in all schools, in all administrative offices, even the telegraph offices; the whole population was on the streets, either as sightseers or as demonstrators. From the evening, people began to ransack arms stores and to smash the windows of the large stores and conservative journals.

Students, directed by lawyers, doctors, and teachers and helped by workmen and Jews, seized the district neighbouring the university and set up ten barricades made of heavy oak planks, poles, and large paving stones. The rioters seized the law courts where the archives were and threw those into the streets.

All the police could do was to organize a poor demonstration (paying the demonstrators one rouble a head), with a portrait of the emperor and the national flag. This was a pitiful failure. The students tore the tsar's portrait and the flag to shreds.

With the state weakened, the peasantry resumed its long-standing war with the landowners by confiscating property and burning manor houses.

Under pressure from his ministers, Nicholas II issued the following manifesto on 17 October 1905, in the hope of appeasing the revolutionary movement. It was Russia's first real political constitution.

Unrest and disturbances in the capitals and in many parts of Our empire fill Our heart with great and heavy grief. The welfare of the Russian sovereign is inseparable from the welfare of the people, and the people's sorrow is His sorrow. The unrest, which now has made its appearance, may give rise to profound disaffection among the people and become a menace to the integrity and unity of Our state.

The great vow of tsarist service enjoins Us to strive with all the force of Our reason and authority for the quickest cessation of unrest so perilous to the state.

We therefore impose upon the government the obligation to carry out Our inflexible will:
(1) To grant the population the unshakeable foundations of civic freedom based on the principles of real personal inviolability, freedom of conscience, speech, assembly, and union.
(2) Without halting the scheduled elections to the state *duma* (parliament), to admit to participation in the *duma*, as far as is possible in the short time remaining before its call, those classes of the population which at present are altogether deprived of the franchise.
(3) To establish it as an unbreakable rule that no law can become effective without the approval of the state *duma* and that the elected representatives of the people should be guaranteed the supervision of the legality of the actions of authorities appointed by Us.

We call upon all the faithful sons of Russia to remember their duty to their fatherland and together with us to make every effort to restore peace and quiet in our native land.

Issued at Peterhof on the seventeenth day of October in the year of Our Lord, nineteen hundred and five, and the eleventh year of Our reign. The original text signed in His Imperial Majesty's own hand.

NICHOLAS

Yet it was not clear whether political reforms would satisfy the socio-economic grievances of the working masses, or the revolutionary demands of the Menshevik (minority) and Bolshevik (majority) wings of the Russian Social Democratic Workers' Party.

RIGHT *The battleship Potemkin; its crew's mutiny in 1905 was immortalized in Eisenstein's film, made 20 years later.*

The latter greeted the tsar's manifesto with the following proclamation in the *Bulletin* of the newly established Soviet (council) of Workers' Deputies on 20 October.

Now we have been granted a constitution.

We have been granted freedom of meetings, yet meetings are being surrounded by soldiers.

We have been granted freedom of speech, yet the censorship remains unshaken.

We have been granted freedom of knowledge, yet the universities are occupied by military force.

We have been granted personal inviolability, yet the gaols are full of prisoners.

We have been granted a constitution, yet autocracy remains.

We have been granted everything, and we have been granted nothing.

After a national – and by European standards fairly democratic – election campaign in the winter of 1905–6, the first state *duma* (parliament), the '*Duma* of National Hopes', assembled in the Tauride Palace in St Petersburg on 14 May 1906. The correspondent of the *Morning Post*, Maurice Baring, attended one of its first sessions.

I had the good fortune to gain admission to the *duma* yesterday afternoon. I think it is the most interesting sight I have ever seen.

When you arrive at the Tauride Palace, which outside has an appearance of dignified stateliness, you walk through a spacious front hall into what looks like a gigantic white ballroom built in the late Louis XIV style. This is the lobby; beyond it is the Hall of the *duma*. In this long gallery members and visitors were already flocking, walking up and down, talking and smoking cigarettes, and throwing the ashes and the ends on the polished floor.

One saw peasants in their long black coats, some of them wearing military medals and crosses; popes [priests], Tartars, Poles, men in every kind of dress except uniform.

When the sitting began I went up into the gallery. The Hall of the *duma* itself is likewise white, delicate in

LEFT *Nicholas with members of the Senate; a true autocrat, he closed down the First* Duma *six weeks after it had been established.*

decoration, an essentially gentlemanlike room. The sitting began about three o'clock. The members go to their appointed places, on which their cards are fixed and the impression of diversity of dress and type becomes still stronger and more picturesque.

You see dignified old men in frock coats; aggressively democratic-looking intellectuals with long hair and pince-nez; a Polish bishop dressed in purple; men without collars; members of the proletariat; men in loose Russian shirts with belts, and men dressed in the costume of two centuries ago.

The president walked in to his seat under the portrait of the emperor, which is a rather shiny study in blue and white. One thanked heaven the *duma* had not been redecorated in the art nouveau style, for almost all the modern buildings in Russia, from Moscow to Harbin, are built in the mixture of Munich, Maple, and Japan which is called art nouveau (modern style), and in Russia 'decadent'.

Nicholas II, however, was reluctant to let go of his autocratic powers. Four days before the *duma* met, on 23 April 1906, he passed a series of 'fundamental laws': the tsar retained the title of autocrat, and extensive authority in all legislative matters; the *duma* was reduced to a consultative body. Nonetheless, finding its deputies too radical, Nicholas closed down the First *Duma* after only six weeks, in July 1906.

The Second *Duma*, assembled in February 1907 after fresh elections, proved no more amenable to the government, the largest parties being the socialist Trudoviks (Labour Group), and the oppositionist Constitutional Democrats (Cadets).

On 3 June this *duma* was dissolved and a new electoral law passed, to produce a third *duma* assembly dominated by gentry delegates. Meanwhile, field courts martial were set up in the provinces to deal with any revolutionary disturbances: death sentences were carried out within 24 hours without right of appeal. By the end of 1907 over 2000 people had been executed. Leo Tolstoy wrote this in reaction to the news of one such execution in 1907.

I cannot stay silent. Today in Kherson on the Strelbitsky field, twelve peasants were hanged for a so-called 'attack with intent to rob' on a landed proprietor's estate in the Elisavetgrad district. These were twelve men by whose labour we live, the very men whom we have deprived by every means in our power – from the poison of vodka to the terrible falsehood of a faith we impose on them with all our might, but do not ourselves believe in – twelve men strangled by cords by those whom they feed and clothe and house.

Twelve husbands, fathers and sons from among those upon whose kindness, industry, and simplicity alone rest the whole of Russian life, are seized, imprisoned, and shackled. Their hands are tied behind their backs, lest they could seize the ropes by which they are to be hanged, and they are led to the gallows. Several peasants similar to those about to be hanged, dressed in clean soldiers' uniforms with good boots on their feet and with guns in their hands accompany the condemned men.

This is dreadful, but most dreadful of all is the fact that it is not done impulsively under the sway of feeling that silences reason, as occurs in fights, war, and even burglary, but on the contrary it is done at the demand of reason and calculation.

Everything now being done in Russia is done in the name of general welfare, in the name of the protection and tranquillity of the people of Russia.

And if this is so, then it is also done for me who lives in Russia. For me, therefore, exists the destitution of the people deprived of the first and most natural right of man – the right to use the land on which he is born; for me, these hundreds of thousands of unfortunates dying of typhus and scurvy in fortresses and prisons which are insufficient for such a multitude; for me, the mothers, wives, and fathers of the exiled, the prisoners and those who are hanged and suffering; for me, the spies and the bribery; for me, the interment of these dozens and hundreds of men who have been shot; for me, the horrible work of the hangman goes on.

It is impossible to live so! I at any rate cannot and will not live so. That is why I write this and will circulate it by all means in my power, both in Russia and abroad.

During the period of the Third *Duma* (1907–12) some political progress was made towards democracy, despite the fact that the constitution of October 1905 had been blatantly overturned. One factor for progress was the new Prime Minister, Peter Stolypin, who although a landowner and patriotic monarchist, did not share the political views of the tsar and the reactionary nobles. Stolypin set out to re-establish the country's administration on a modern and legal basis. His land programme, for instance, consisted of breaking up the ancient land commune into private plots, for the richest peasant farmers. This was supposed to create a law-abiding stratum of peasant landowners producing for the market. Stolypin explained his policy to the state *duma* in May 1907.

The government wants above all to promote and enhance peasant landownership. It wants to see the peasant earning well and eating well, since where there is prosperity there is enlightenment and also true freedom. But for this it is necessary to give opportunity to the capable, industrious peasant, who is the salt of the Russian earth. He must be freed from the vice of his present situation. He must be given the chance to consolidate the fruits of his labour and consider them his inalienable property.

Let property be general where the commune is operative still; let it be household ownership where the commune no longer exists; but let it be hereditary, with firm legal guarantees. The government should then assist such peasant smallholders with advice and credit facilities.

The government has already taken steps in this direction. The interest rates charged by the Peasant

RIGHT *Postcard depicting Nicholas as a tyrant; in reality he was shy and retiring.*

Bank have been temporarily reduced. Now if, together with this, there were a programme of planned re-settlement; if land loans were easily available, and if expanded agricultural credit facilities were created, hope would be seen, even if the full programme of land reforms which the government has proposed is not enacted.

Stolypin found support for his policies of conservative reform among the Octobrists, a liberal-capitalist party dominant in the *duma*. But he increasingly alienated the conservative nobles, who were worried about the loss of their traditional privileges in local government and suspicious of Stolypin's growing personal power. V. I. Gurko follows Stolypin's fortunes.

Stolypin was successful in establishing good working relations with the majority of the Third *Duma*; harmonious relations developed between the ministry of the interior and the *zemstva* (local administrations). In a word, under Stolypin's direction and to a great extent owing to his clever policy, calm and peace spread over the country. After the tumult of recent years, Russia once again trod the road of enrichment and progress. Prosperity increased rapidly. It is enough to say that while in 1900 the average income of a citizen was ninety-eight roubles yearly, in 1912 it was a hundred and thirty roubles, an increase of over thirty per cent.

As the country calmed down, and as his personal position became more secure, Stolypin himself underwent a marked change. Authority went to his head, and the flatterers surrounding him did the rest. He became intolerant of adverse criticism and difference of opinion.

Finally Stolypin parted company with the Octobrist party because he considered it not meek enough. Now the great merit and entire significance of the Octobrist party was precisely this, that while it recognized the necessity of supporting the Russian government in order to strengthen the position of the lawful authority, it judged all matters upon the basis of their usefulness to the country and did not hesitate to

oppose the government when its party opinion differed from the official one.

To the Stolypin of 1910 this situation was unacceptable. He needed men who would be subordinates in word and deed, so he transferred his sympathies to the Nationalist party, and began to look to it for support.

Stolypin also engaged in open conflict with the party of the Right. For all its shortcomings, this party was not a governmental one; it considered itself the party of the state, and everything that tended to lessen the imperial authority was to be sharply opposed. It goes without saying that all personal enemies of Stolypin who had conservative opinions had joined this party. They flaunted their devotion to the throne and, playing upon the weakness of Nicholas II, used every pretext to blacken Stolypin's reputation in the eyes of the monarch.

In many cases there was evidence of an intrigue against Stolypin on the part of a group of State Council members, among whom were Durnovo and V. F. Trepov. This was illustrated, for instance, by opposition in the State Council to the legislative project dealing with the establishment of the *zemstvo* institutions in the nine western provinces. This project had been initiated by the government and had already passed the *duma*, but under Durnovo's leadership the right wing of the State Council used every means in its power to have the project rejected. This positively enraged Stolypin. He announced to the tsar that with the systematic opposition to his programme which he found in the State Council he saw no possibility of continuing any fruitful work. He tendered his resignation.

For several days the situation was uncertain. The right wing of the State Council, especially Durnovo, was already celebrating a victory; but Stolypin's prestige in the eyes of the thinking public was still great, and the tsar appreciated him so much that he did not desire to let him go. Stolypin, too, stood his ground firmly. He agreed to remain chairman of the council of ministers on three conditions: (1) an enforced leave of absence of an indefinite period for Durnovo and V. F. Trepov; (2) the appointment of new members for the State Council by the crown but with his,

Stolypin's, knowledge and approval; and (3) the prorogation of the Third D*uma* for a period of several days, so that the statute on the western *zemstva* might be confirmed by sovereign power.

The tsar agreed to Stolypin's conditions, but never forgave him for having forced his hand.

On 14 September 1911 Stolypin was assassinated by a terrorist named Dmitry Bogrov in the Kiev opera house. Tsar Nicholas II describes the scene in a letter to his mother.

My daughters Olga and Tatiana were with me at the time. During the second interval we had just left the box, as it was so hot, when we heard two sounds as if something had been dropped. I thought that an opera glass might have fallen on somebody's head, and ran back into the box to look. To the right I saw a group of officers and other people. They seemed to be dragging someone along.

Women were shrieking, and, directly in front of me in the stalls, Stolypin was standing; he slowly turned his face towards us and with his left hand made the sign of the cross in the air. Only then did I notice that he was very pale and that his right hand and uniform were bloodstained. He slowly sank into his chair and began to unbutton his tunic.

People were trying to lynch the assassin. I am sorry to say the police rescued him from the crowd and took him to a room for his first examination. Then the theatre filled up again, the national anthem was sung, and I left with the girls at eleven.

BELOW *Pre-revolutionary bank notes. Interest rates charged by the Peasant Bank were reduced temporarily to encourage peasant smallholders.*

With the death of Stolypin, tsarism lost its last chance of reform before 1917. The years leading up to the outbreak of war witnessed a growing mood of conservatism among the educated classes, and a growing divide, marked by increasingly hostile relations, between the latter and the working classes. The increasing divide which existed between bourgeois and non-propertied elements was highlighted by the violent wave of strikes across Russia in the summer and autumn of 1913. A government report notes how strikes flared up.

They happen sometimes for the most trivial causes, and with extraordinary rapidity embrace wide areas with tens of thousands of workers. But apart from that, the strike movement we are now experiencing has a more threatening social significance in that it arouses hostility and bitterness between employer and worker, unites the workers on the basis of an irreconcilable relationship to the existing state and social structure, and in this way creates among the workers ready cadres to reinforce the revolutionary parties.

Under the influence of agitators and the Social Democratic press, there has recently developed among the workers a harmony of action such as indicates their close solidarity and organized nature. The places where strikes take place are put under a boycott; those workers who approach are exposed to bitter persecution and are excluded from work. Orders at strike-bound factories and plants are also placed under a boycott, and any factory that might accept them risks a strike among its own workers.

In this context, a war with Germany was almost bound to prove fatal. Durnovo warned Nicholas II of this in a prophetic memorandum of February 1914.

A struggle between Germany and Russia undoubtedly involves the weakening of the conservative principle in the world, of which our two great powers are the only reliable bulwarks. Moreover, a general European war is mortally dangerous both for Russia and Germany, no matter who wins.

It is our firm conviction, therefore, that there must inevitably break out in the defeated country a social revolution which, by the very nature of things, will spread to the country of the victor.

Death of a statesman

If the persons who headed the secret service did not actually organize the attempt on Stolypin's life, they at least did not try to prevent it. It looked very suspicious that Stolypin's assassin, Bogrov, was the agent of the secret service section, and was hanged in a hurry before the arrival in Kiev of Senator Trusevich, who had come with special instructions to investigate the murder. On his return to St Petersburg, Trusevich told me of his impressions, which only confirmed my earlier suspicions.

I am still inclined to think that the assassination of Stolypin was at least tolerated by those in high positions. They did not know how to get rid of Stolypin and did not dare remove him without a serious reason. At one time it was intended to create for him the high post of viceroy of Siberia, but for some reason this was given up. Stolypin had many enemies among the bureaucrats and the people at the court. To add to this, he ordered an inspection of the secret funds of the department of police. So, as the revolutionists at that time were organizing an attempt on his life, it was decided not to interfere with their plot.

From A. I. Guchkov

An especially favourable soil for social upheavals is found in Russia, where the masses undoubtedly profess, unconsciously, the principles of socialism. The peasant dreams of obtaining a gratuitous share of somebody else's land; the worker, of getting hold of the entire capital and profits of the manufacturer. Beyond this, they have no aspirations. If the government permits agitation along these lines, Russia will be flung into anarchy, such as she suffered in 1905–6.

War with Germany would create exceptionally favourable conditions for such agitation. Both military disasters – partial ones, let us hope – and all kinds of shortcomings in our supply are inevitable. In the excessive nervousness and spirit of opposition of our society, it will be well if the government does not yield, but declares that in time of war no criticism of the governmental authority is to be tolerated and resolutely suppresses all opposition.

Durnovo was right. The Russian economy was unable to cope with the strains of war. By Christmas 1914, the war, only just beginning, had already created a serious crisis of munitions production. General Belayev, army chief of staff at the Ministry of War, explained the situation to Maurice Paléologue, the French ambassador.

Our losses in men have been colossal, though if it were merely a matter of replacing wastage we could soon do so as we have more than eight hundred thousand men in our depots. But we're short of rifles to arm and train these men. Our original reserve was five million six hundred thousand rifles; at least we thought so. The Grand Duke Nicholas thought so; I thought so myself. We have been criminally deceived;

TO ALL MILITARY AND NAVAL FORCES

Today I have assumed command of all the military and naval forces operating in the theatre of war.

With firm trust in divine mercy and unshakeable confidence in ultimate victory, we shall fulfil our sacred duty of defending our country to the death, and we will never allow Russian soil to be dishonoured.

Given at General Headquarters, 5 September 1915.

signed NICHOLAS

RIGHT *Empress Alexandra; pious and neurotic, she ruled arbitrarily when Nicholas was at the front in 1915.*

our magazines are nearly empty. Forgive me for giving no further explanation of a very painful matter.

To make good the deficit, we are about to purchase a million rifles in Japan and America and we hope to arrive at an output of one hundred thousand a month in our own factories. Perhaps France and England could also let us have a few hundred thousand.

The position is hardly less difficult as regards gun ammunition. Our entire reserve is exhausted. The armies need forty-five thousand rounds per day. Our maximum daily output is thirteen thousand: we hope it will reach twenty thousand by about 15 February. Until that date, the situation of our armies will not only be difficult but dangerous.

As the army suffered defeats in Galicia, Nicholas II assumed command of all military and naval forces. But at home the growing shortage of shells, the mounting losses, and the wave of revolutionary strikes from the autumn of 1915 gave rise to calls for a 'government of public confidence'. Maurice Paléologue, recorded the event in his diary.

Today, Monday, 27 September 1915, the Union of *zemstvos* and the Union of Towns, which have been in session in Moscow the last few days, passed the following joint motion.

'In the tragic difficulties which Russia is experiencing, we deem it our first duty to send a warm greeting to our stoical, glorious, and dearly loved army. The Russian people are more determined than ever to continue the war to victory, in loyal association with their faithful allies. But on the path of victory there lies a fatal obstacle, an obstacle created by all the old vices of our political system: we mean irresponsible power, the absence of any link between the government and the country, etc.

'A drastic change is required. In place of our present governors, we must have men who enjoy the confidence of the nation. The work of the *duma* should be resumed without delay.

'The two unions have appointed three delegates each, and commissioned them to lay the country's wishes before the tsar in a personal audience.'

A major cause of public concern about the government was the dominant influence of Rasputin, the 'holy man' whose spurious spiritualism was accepted as gospel by Tsaritsa Alexandra. Many believed the tsaritsa's court was under the influence of German agents.

Rasputin's well-publicized orgies and other misdeeds created such an uproar that by March 1916, M. V. Rodzianko, president of the Fourth *Duma*, thought it his duty to confront Tsar Nicholas II on the issue.

Following the tsar's arrival at Tsarskoe Selo, I asked for an audience and was received by him on 8 March. The audience lasted an hour and a half. I told him everything – of the intrigues of the ministers who worked against each other through Rasputin, of the lack of a definite policy, of the abuses everywhere, of the failure to take public opinion into consideration, and of the limit of public endurance.

I reminded him of the adventures of 'heroes' of the home front and of their contacts with Rasputin; also of Rasputin's dissipations and orgies, and that his relation to the tsar and his family, and his influence on state matters in these times of war, deeply aroused honest people. There was no doubt that Rasputin was a German agent and spy.

'I must tell Your Majesty that this cannot continue much longer. No one opens your eyes to the true role which this man is playing. His presence in Your Majesty's court undermines confidence in the supreme power; it may have an evil effect on the fate of the dynasty and turn the hearts of the people from their emperor.'

While I was enumerating these sad truths, the tsar was either silent or showed astonishment, but was at all times affable and courteous. When I had finished, he asked, 'How do you think the war will end – in our favour or against us?'

Nicholas was far too weak-willed to cross his headstrong wife, Alexandra. In a last effort to save the reputation of the monarchy, the Grand Duke Dmitry Pavlovich, Prince Yusupov (a nephew by marriage of the tsar), and the reactionary Purishkevich, who had denounced Rasputin in the *duma* as a 'filthy, vicious, and venal peasant', invited the supposed monk on 17 December 1916 to late evening tea at the Yusupov Palace, where they murdered him. Piecing together all the contemporary accounts, the French ambassador, Maurice Paléologue, offered the following version of this gruesome event.

Yusupov walked casually to the far end of the room, stopped at a table on which various *objets d'art* were laid out, and said, 'As you're on your legs, come and have a look at this fine Italian Renaissance crucifix I bought recently.'

'Show it me; you can't look too often at the image of Our Lord crucified.'

Rasputin walked up to the table.

'Here you are,' said Yusupov. 'Isn't it beautiful!'

Rasputin: saint or sinner?

Rasputin, born Grigory Yefimovich Novykh in 1872, spent a profligate and wanton youth; the name by which he is known translates as 'Debauchee'. In 1904, he left his family and devoted himself to religion, learning to read and write, and making a pilgrimage to the Holy Land. He abandoned his job as a Siberian carter and began to organize prayer meetings in competition with the local Orthodox Church.

His striking presence, hypnotic powers and insight into human character gave him a powerful hold on the local peasants, and it was probably the Orthodox Church which started rumours that his meetings often degenerated into mass orgies. Certainly, he had a powerful sexual appetite, and women who came to him for spiritual guidance were sometimes persuaded that such guidance would be more effective if they removed their clothes first. When Rasputin moved into St Petersburg society in 1905, a minority of female admirers believed his bed was the closest any mortal could get to God.

His most significant admirer, Empress Alexandra, was spiritually but not physically possessed by Rasputin. A German princess who had converted to the Orthodox faith when she married Nicholas II in 1894, she was neither happy nor popular in the Russian court. Her miseries were intensified by the knowledge that her only son, Alexis, was a haemophiliac who could die as a result of even a minor injury.

the royal family. Close to the people, he had insights that the emperor's advisers lacked.

With the outbreak of World War I, both Alexandra and Rasputin became even more unpopular. Although politicans, clergymen, and police chiefs portrayed Rasputin, on copious evidence, as a lecherous charlatan, the royal couple chose not to listen. As defeat followed defeat, Alexandra was regarded resentfully as 'that German woman', under the influence of Rasputin, her evil genius. He, in common with

FAR LEFT *Rasputin; he became the Romanov family's evil genius.*

LEFT *Rasputin surrounded by members of the Russian court.*

Introduced to the royal family as a potential healer, Rasputin had an uncanny ability to handle Alexis, and after 1907, when he pulled the young boy out of what seemed to be a fatal decline, the empress became unshakeably convinced of his holy powers.

Nicholas, less impressed than his wife, nevertheless valued his healing ability. In fact, Rasputin offered the tsar good advice, which was usually not taken. He emphasized, for example, that war would be disastrous for Russia and for

other unpopular people at this time, was said to be a German spy, and it was widely believed that Nicholas was under the thumb of his wife. An appropriate Russian saying reinforced this anxiety: 'It's a sad home where the cow instructs the bull.' Although Alexandra under Rasputin's influence sent countless letters of advice to Nicholas, the emperor was not unduly influenced by them. Rasputin's murder in 1916, by a group of noblemen led by Prince Felix Yusupov, made not the slightest difference to the course of the war.

ABOVE *Yusupov Palace, home of Rasputin's chief assassin. The 'Debauchee' died in its garden.*

As Rasputin was bending over the sacred figure, Yusupov stood on his left and fired twice into his ribs, almost point-blank.

Rasputin cried out, 'Oh!' and he fell in a heap on the floor.

Yusupov stooped down to the body, felt the pulse, examined the eye by raising the lid, and could see no sign of life.

At the sound of the shots, the accomplices upstairs rushed down at once. The Grand Duke Dmitry said, 'Now we must throw him in the water quick. I'll go and find my car.'

His companions went back to the first floor to arrange how to move the body.

Twelve minutes later Yusupov returned to the room downstairs to have a look at his victim. He shrank back in horror. Rasputin had half risen, supporting himself on his hands. With a supreme effort he staggered to his feet, brought his heavy fist down

with the other conspirators to the room on the ground floor.

Rasputin had gone. He had strength enough to open the door leading to the garden and was dragging himself over the snow. Purishkevich fired one bullet into his neck and another into his body, while Yusupov, now a yelling maniac, fetched a bronze candlestick and battered in his victim's skull.

It was a quarter past two in the morning.

Rasputin's murder had little impact on the course of events. Changes of personnel in the upper reaches of power could not satisfy hungry workers and war-weary soldiers. The following events in the capital – renamed Petrograd instead of the German-sounding St Petersburg during the war – were reported in a memorandum of 24 February by the Third Section. It was International Women's Day, and the first day of the 1917 revolution.

On 23 February at 9.00 a.m. the workers of the plants and factories of the Vyborg district went on strike in protest against the shortage of black bread in bakeries and groceries. The strike spread to some plants located in the Petrograd, Rozhdestvensky, and Liteiny districts, and in the course of the day fifty industrial enterprises ceased work; eighty-seven thousand five hundred and thirty-four men on strike.

At about 1.00 p.m., the workmen of the Vyborg district, walking out in crowds into the streets and shouting, 'Give us bread', started to become disorderly in various places at the same time, taking with them on the way their comrades who were at work, and stopping tramcars. The demonstrators took away the keys to the electric motors from the tram drivers, which forced fifteen tramcars to quit the lines and retire to the Petrograd tram yard.

The strikers, who were resolutely chased by police and troops summoned for this purpose, were dispersed in one place but quickly gathered in other places, showing themselves to be exceptionally stubborn. In the Vyborg district order was restored only towards 7.00 p.m.

on Yusupov's shoulder and tore off his epaulette, saying in a last whisper, 'You wretch! You'll be hanged tomorrow! I'm going to tell the empress everything!'

Yusupov shook him off with great difficulty, ran out of the room, and went upstairs again. White to the lips and covered with blood, he called to his accomplices in a choking voice, 'He's still alive! He spoke to me!'

Then he collapsed on a sofa in a dead faint. Purishkevich seized him in his rough hands, shook him, lifted him, took away his revolver, and dragged him

Revolution in Culture

Up to the early 19th century, the western attitude to Russian art was one of comfortable ignorance. There had always been one or two exceptions – for those who loved the art of decorative and seductive living, Carl Fabergé, caviar and sable furs might be said to have shone like stars in an otherwise darkened sky. The rest was ignorance.

Slowly these few symbols gave way to the growing international recognition of a very national Russian style. First, writers like Dostoyevsky and Tolstoy created powerful works of fiction, complex stories peopled with unforgettable characters. Then the now familiar melodies began to be heard in concert halls outside the Russian cities. The national addiction to haunting sounds full of melancholy seems to have a particular appeal to the European and American sensibility.

If Bach and Beethoven are the touchstones of the classics, then Tchaikovsky and Rachmaninov are the romantics of all time. There are few people who were not taken as children to a performance of *The Nutcracker Suite*, while a whole modern generation has succumbed to the oriental strings of Borodin without realizing that his music is the source of *Kismet*'s 'Stranger in Paradise'.

ABOVE   *The 'Pine Cone' egg by Fabergé. Guilloché enamel.*

OPPOSITE   *Moscow, 1880. Chekhov loved the city where he spent 20 years.*

And with the new century came two new revolutions. First, an irresistible explosion of unique quality; Serge Diaghilev's Ballets Russes, so full of brazen colour that costumes and sets by the most revolutionary of modern artists in Paris and New York could only reflect glory on the greatest male dancer of all time, Nijinsky.

The other couldn't have been more different; a quiet revolution, quiet plays, spoken with quiet intensity, from the pen of Anton Chekhov, still played in the theatres of the world, almost certainly second only to Shakespeare in the number of performances.

And his friend and collaborator Konstantin Stanislavsky, an actor and producer at the Moscow Art Theatre, in trying to help his fellow actors feel at home in their parts, to become the people they portrayed on the stage, created almost unintentionally a method of achieving this that became The Method, continued by performers such as Marlon Brando and Elia Kazan: the essence of our contemporary theatre.

If the 18th century belongs to the cool calm dignity of Georgian England, the 19th century to the experimental mastery of French painters, then

surely the early 20th century belongs to the
emotional charge generated by Russia's
emergence into the artistic limelight of the world.

ABOVE *A. Ivanov.* The Appearance of Christ to the
People *which took him 20 years to complete.*

Art and architecture

In the early years of the 18th century, as artists
gradually liberated themselves from the primarily
religious artistic language of medieval Russian
icon-painting, they came into closer contact with
the European baroque and with realistic
tendencies in portrait-painting. Russian society
began to take an interest in the human
personality; the predominant genre of the age was
the portrait, painted by such artists as Ivan Nikitin
(*c.* 1680–*c.* 1742), Andrey Matveyev (1701/4–39),
Aleksey Antropov, Ivan Vishnyakov and Ivan
Argunov.

At the beginning of the 18th century, the so-
called Painters' Brigade was set up in the St

Petersburg Chancellery of Building. They painted
murals and worked on the interior decoration of
the new buildings of St Petersburg and other
towns. At the same time, the brigade served as a
school for the training of artists. In 1757, the St
Petersburg Academy of Arts was created on the
initiative of Mikhail Lomonosov. It trained
professional painters, sculptors, engravers and
architects. Other types of painting made their
apppearance, such as historical, landscape and
genre, and developed alongside the art of the
portrait which blossomed in the late 18th century,
with Fyodor Rokotov (1730s–1808), Dmitry
Levitsky (1735–1822) and Vladimir Borovikovsky
(1757–1825). All continued to move towards a
more informal, realistic depiction of the sitter, and
attempted to convey the subject's spiritual state.

The first quarter of the 19th century was a time of growing national self-awareness and an upsurge in patriotism inspired by the war of 1812. The spread of libertarian ideas in turn brought fresh subject matter to painting. Subjects taken from classical antiquity gave way to themes from

Russian history, although painting continued to develop stylistically within the bounds of classicism. The work of 18th-century Russian portrait painters was developed by early 19th-century masters of the genre, in particular Orest Kiprensky (1782–1836); Vasily Tropinin (1780–1857), who was interested in genre painting; Aleksey Venetsianov (1780–1847), probably the first Russian artist to paint in a

BELOW   *The green dining room of the Catherine Palace, Tsarskoe Selo, in Rastrelli's baroque style.*

markedly national style; Silvester Shchedrin (1791–1830), whose reproduction of nature was both realistic and poetic; Karl Bryullov (1799–1852), a successful and prolific portrait painter; Alexander Ivanov (1806–58), who bridges classicism and realism; and Pavel Fedotov (1815–52), who heralded the advent of a new generation of Russian realist painters.

Theatre

At home in Russia, Anton Chekhov (1860–1904) is honoured first and foremost for short stories which capture mood or atmosphere: sadness, boredom, frustration and unfulfilled dreams. Their settings are Russian but their applicability is universal.

Abroad, however, Chekhov is regarded as Russia's greatest playwright. His reputation rests on the four mature plays written in the last eight years of his life: *The Seagull* (1896), *Uncle Vanya* (1897), *The Three Sisters* (1901) and *The Cherry Orchard* (1904). They are plays of atmosphere and psychological insight rather than incident and sensation, set apart by a sense of melancholy.

In his lifetime, Chekhov's plays were meticulously directed at the Moscow Art Theatre by Konstantin Stanislavsky (1865–1938).

Stanislavsky created a naturalistic style in which actors used their own psychological reaction to 'live' their roles. Instead of capturing the audience's eyes and ears with bold gestures, brilliant lighting and music, Stanislavsky wanted to capture their hearts with a shock of recognition.

'Constructivist theatre', developed later by the director Vsevolod Meyerhold (1874–1940), in

RIGHT *Bathers from Iasnaya Poliana, home of Leo Tolstoy. He is sitting in the foreground.*

reaction to naturalism, used his 'bio-mechanics' system of acting, based on mime and acrobatics, in strikingly modern, 'machine'-style sets.

Literature

By the age of 20 Alexander Pushkin (1799–1837) was known to the public as a major new poetic voice, and to the tsarist autocracy as a troublemaker with revolutionary sympathies.

Pushkin read classical and European literature avidly from boyhood onwards. His reputation as a poet extends over 800 lyrics and a dozen narrative poems. He came to fame with a long mock epic, *Ruslan and Ludmilla* (1820); brought the narrative genre to perfection in *The Bronze Horseman* (1833); composed a novel in verse, *Eugene Onegin* (1823–31); and made excursions into drama with the Shakespearean tragedy *Boris Godunov* (1825) and four *Little Tragedies* (1830). For the last six years of his life Pushkin turned increasingly to prose, which he wrote with inimitable precision: *The Tales of Belkin* (1830), *The Queen of Spades* (1833), and *The Captain's Daughter* (1833–5).

The creator of modern Russian and the greatest single progenitor of Russian literature, he is best remembered as a man who, in his own words, 'exalted freedom in an age of cruelty'.

Born into an ancient aristocratic family in 1828, Leo Tolstoy (1828–1910) married in 1862 and settled down to family life and serious literature. The next two decades produced the two great novels *War and Peace* (1865–9) and *Anna Karenina* (1875–7) but at 50, Tolstoy was permanently haunted by a sense of the futility of human existence. The insoluble problems of self-awareness, mortality, sexuality, brutal and immoral behaviour were unbearable.

For the last three decades of his life he attempted to live a morally pure existence and to perfect his ideas on love, God, non-violent resistance to evil and the use of art solely to infect others with a spirit of noble sensitivity. The great sage preached charity and brotherly love while withholding these very qualities from those near and dear to him.

From the totality of Tolstoy's writing there emerges such a sense of the mystery and complexity of human life that, despite the anguish of the author himself, his finest stories and novels are more than enjoyable and relevant – they have a unique quality that is both fascinating and inspirational. Whether viewed as reformer, philosopher, or creative artist, Leo Tolstoy will continue to be ranked among the most prolific and significant writers of western civilization.

Fyodor Dostoyevsky (1821–81) won critical praise for his first novel, *Poor Folk* (1846), with its compassionate and psychologically penetrating portrait of a downtrodden hero lost in the bureaucratic hierarchy. Praise turned the head of this sickly, withdrawn and touchy young man. But *The Double* (also 1846) and *The Landlady* (1847) were criticized.

In April 1849, Dostoyevsky was arrested for participation in a clandestine discussion group, charged with subversion, and sentenced to death; his sentence was commuted to four years' hard labour followed by a further four years of exile as a common soldier. In January 1850, he arrived at the Omsk penal settlement in Siberia.

Dostoyevsky found himself among the dregs of humanity. This first-hand experience of the criminal mind disclosed to him the profound irrationality of human nature, and disabused him of the belief that political solutions could ever redeem a corrupt soul. From his New Testament he learned that salvation was to be found not in political or institutional change but in the complete religious transformation of human nature. He was to return from Siberia in 1859 a writer with a religious mission. The period also revealed to him the profound spiritual resources of the ordinary people; from then on religious populism and deep faith in the superiority of native Russian cultural and moral values dominated his thought.

Dostoyevsky's two great novels of the mid-1860s, *Notes from Underground* and *Crime and Punishment*, transcended polemics to become works of profound philosophical and artistic importance. *The Idiot* (1868) advocated the Christian virtues of meekness and humility as embodied in 'the positively good man' and *The Devils* (1872) mounted a pugnacious attack on the revolutionary movement and the spiritual bankruptcy of the contemporary age.

Respected by the left for his 'radical' past and admired by the right for his nationalism and religious values, he achieved his masterpiece in *The Brothers Karamazov* (1879–80).

Ballet

One of the strongest Russian artistic influences on the West started in St Petersburg during the last decade of the 19th century. Alexandre Benois (1870–1960), art historian and painter, gathered round him a number of other young artists, poets and critics who shared his ideas. They met to discuss artistic ideals, although with no definite objectives except to explore the world of art. In

1890 they were joined by the painters Leon Bakst (1866–1924) and Nicolas Roerich (1874–1947), and by Serge Diaghilev (1872–1929) from the distant provincial town of Perm.

Diaghilev, considered to be the 'country bumpkin', uncouth but dashing with a silver quiff, displayed more energy than the others and soon had the vision to develop and exploit their talents.

RIGHT *Costume for Igor Stravinsky's* The Firebird, *designed by Leon Bakst.*

ABOVE *Serge Diaghilev, director of the Ballets Russes.*

OPPOSITE *Submarine monster, a Bakst costume for Rimsky-Korsakov's opera Sadko.*

He was the catalyst. He formed the group into a team with the prime objective of publicizing Russian art. He became the editor of a magazine called *Mir Iskusstvo* ('The World of Art') which was published from 1898 to 1904 and to which all the members of the group contributed. They also now called themselves *The World of Art* and arranged exhibitions. But Diaghilev was

determined to promote Russian art in the West. The first 'season' in Paris was an exhibition of Russian paintings at the Grand Palais in 1906 in a winter-garden setting designed by Bakst, followed by concerts of Russian music in 1907 and the first productions of opera and ballet in 1908 and 1909 when Fyodor Chaliapin (1873–1938), Anna Pavlova (1881–1931), Tamara Karsavina

ABOVE *Anna Pavlova, most famous ballerina of the time.*

(1885–1978), Vaslav Nijinsky (1889–1950) and other Russian artists first performed in the West. *The World of Art* became Diaghilev's Ballets Russes.

Diaghilev's troupe with Michel Fokine (1880–1942), an innovative choreographer of genius, reinvented the art of ballet. Diaghilev believed that ballet, where the composer, choreographer and designer worked together, could achieve a synthesis of all the arts and be the supreme art form. Short, dramatic, startling ballets burst on Paris in 1909 and in particular the revolutionary oriental setting and costumes designed by Bakst for *Cléopâtre* shattered all notions of the art of the theatre.

After the first season Chaliapin, the great dramatic bass, began a lucrative career touring the opera houses of the world, and Pavlova, jealous of Nijinsky, also preferred to form her own company. Later, Nijinsky, Diaghilev's lover, left him and married. Diaghilev never forgave him. Nijinsky, who danced for the last time in 1917, finally went mad.

In 1910 Diaghilev presented his first complete programme of ballets; Paris discovered the exoticism of *Shéhérazade* and was overwhelmed. For the early seasons the team was Russian. Music was by Rimsky-Korsakov, Mussorgsky, Glazunov, Tcherepnine and the great new discovery Igor Stravinsky (1882–1972) with *The Firebird* (1910) followed by *Petrushka* (1911) and *The Rite of Spring* (1913): settings and costumes by Benois (*Le Pavillon d'Armide*, *Petrushka*), Bakst (*Shéhérazade*, all four new productions in 1912), Roerich (*The Rite of Spring*), Natalia Gontcharova (*The Golden Cockerel*). Stranded in the West during World War I and finally exiled after the Revolution, Diaghilev commissioned French, Spanish and English composers and artists, including Ravel, Debussy, Poulenc, Richard Strauss, Constant Lambert, Erik Satie, Matisse, Picasso, Derain, de Chirico and Marie Laurençin: a comprehensive catalogue would include all the major composers and painters of the first quarter of the 20th century, for Diaghilev, the impresario, always searched for the best and the truly original. And found it.

The irony is that the Ballets Russes never performed in Russia. Diaghilev died in Venice in 1929 and his legacy is the art of ballet. Paradoxically while ballet as an art form ossified in Soviet Russia, it flowered in the West. It was developed by Serge Lifar in Paris, George Balanchine in New York and Ninette de Valois and Marie Rambert in London; all had begun their careers with the Ballets Russes, which had astonished the world for twenty years.

Music

Peter Ilich Tchaikovsky (1840–93) never attached himself to any artistic grouping and did not share in the radicalism of the new Russian school of music, which established itself in the late 1850s and early 1860s. Unlike the members of the new school, he was primarily interested in humanity's spiritual and emotional struggles.

Tchaikovsky wrote 11 operas, among them *Eugene Onegin* (1879) and *Queen of Spades* (1890). They concentrated on the personal and dramatize one person's emotional experiences through showing individual psychology.

Tchaikovsky's exploration of the problems of human existence found its fullest expression in his symphonies, notably the fourth (1877), the fifth (1888) and the sixth, known as the *Pathétique* (1893). His work owes much to the French and German models, but the tone of his musical language and the form of his musical thought remained profoundly Russian. It strongly influenced his friend, the composer Sergey Rachmaninov (1873–1943), who became one of the greatest pianists of his generation.

Tchaikovsky's operas and symphonies, his ballets – especially *Swan Lake* (1876), *The Sleeping Beauty* (1889) and *The Nutcracker Suite* (1891–2) – and his chamber music are a high point of European culture, the major achievement of Russian music in the late 19th century.

Russian national opera, and in 1842, *Ruslan and Ludmilla*, based on a poem by Pushkin. Glinka's work reflects the development of original music with national characteristics.

In the late 1850s and early 1860s, following Glinka's death in 1857, music moved away from the private salon into the public hall. Merchants, tradesmen and clergymen joined the audiences. In 1859 the composer, pianist and teacher Anton Rubinstein founded the Russian Musical Society, which held regular concerts for a broad-based audience in St Petersburg. Branches sprang up in other towns. In 1862 the Free School of Music opened in St Petersburg to attract office workers, tradesmen and students to musical training.

Opera remained the leading musical genre in Russia throughout the 19th century. In the late 1850s and early 1860s, a group of young Russian

Tchaikovsky (1840–93)

Mussorgsky (1839–81)

Rachmaninov (1873–1943)

Glinka (1804–57)

Opera

Opera was popular in early 19th-century Russia, but most performances were put on at home by amateur musicians from the upper classes. Mikhail Glinka (1804–57), the father of Russian classical music, who shaped the course of Russian music for the rest of the 19th century, was an amateur, interested in folk-music and in the history and everyday life of the common people as source materials. When he came to write opera, he turned for inspiration to his own native traditions. In 1836 he wrote *Ivan Susanin*, later renamed *A Life for the Tsar*, which was the first

musicians established itself. It was led by the composer Mikhail Balakirev (1836–1910) and the other members, all composers, were Alexander Borodin (1833–87), Modest Mussorgsky (1839–81), Tsesar Cui (1835–1918) and Nikolay Rimsky-Korsakov (1844–1910). The group has gone down in the history of Russian music as the Mighty Handful. All were talented musicians and they shared the desire to serve their fellow Russians through their art. They had a strong sense of national pride and a feeling for popular culture. They romanticized Russia's past to reveal its ideals to their contemporaries and they used the images of folk-music to carry their message to the people.

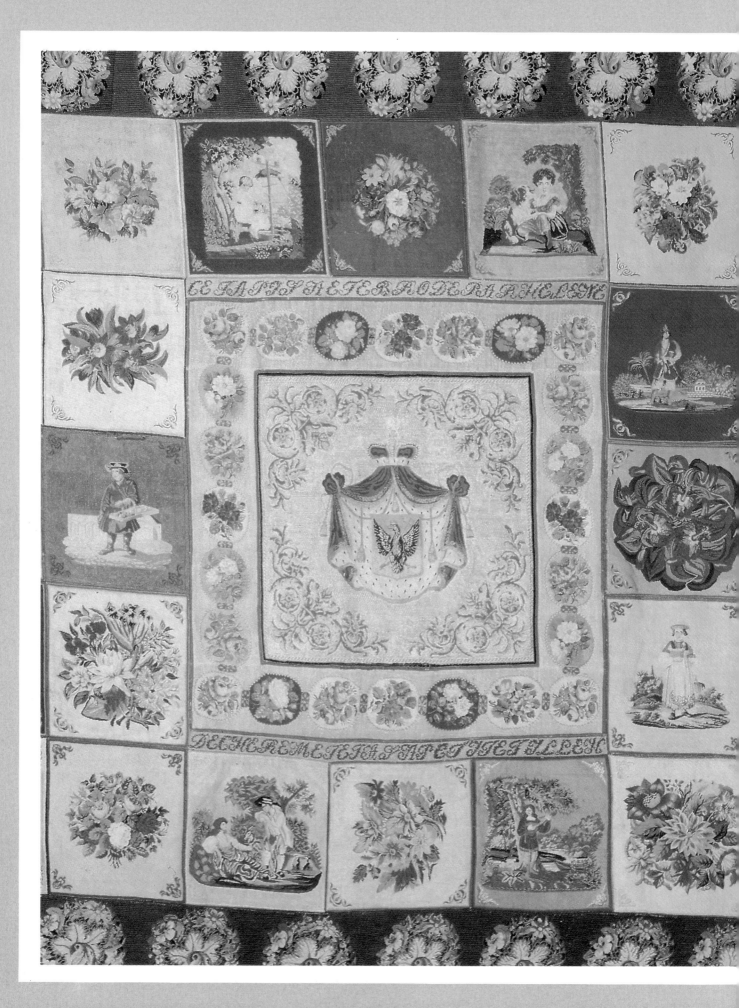

Decorative arts

At the beginning of the 18th century, Peter the Great's absolutist government destroyed the traditional features of everyday Russian existence, determined to transform Russia into part of Europe. Only the peasants retained the outward appearance and life-style of the past. Medieval artistic traditions were denounced as indications of bad taste and obscurantism. Peter's 1718 Decree on Assemblies (social gatherings of the nobility in imitation of European salons), had a dramatic effect on the way Russians behaved and how they dressed and decorated their homes. The government banned traditional clothing at the assemblies and ordered all who attended to appear in Western dress.

Administrative buildings and the homes of eminent citizens were furnished after the European model, and large quantities of furniture, mirrors, chandeliers, and fabrics in the baroque style were imported from Holland, England and France. Traditional furniture – benches with folding backs, chests for keeping money and documents, trunks for clothing – which had been used by all classes of society, survived mainly in the provinces. Wall hangings were used to decorate palaces, their production organized by Peter I in a new factory in St Petersburg. By the middle of the century, Russian

RIGHT *Simple glass bowl in primitive style; geometric enamelling. Probably provincial, c. 1900.*

LEFT *A rare needlework carpet; the central coat-of-arms is of the Gorchakov family. Mid-19th century.*

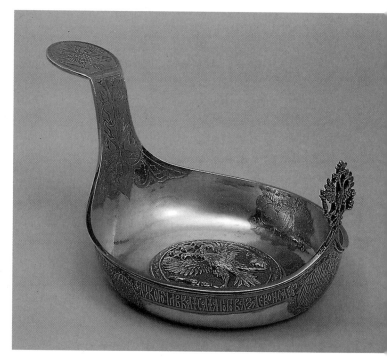

weavers, trained by specially invited French specialists, began to work independently.

By the time the baroque style reached its height, in the 1750s, furniture was being manufactured in Russia. In palaces, it shows the influence of the architect Bartolomeo Rastrelli, creator of the 'Elizabethan baroque' style, in its lavish gilded carving. Baroque stylistic features in interior decoration later gave way to the neo-classical, with its simplicity and clarity of composition, symmetry, and motifs derived from classical antiquity. Carved decoration became flatter and craftsmen used the natural properties of the wood.

Developments towards the end of the 18th century were closely linked with the work of the leading architects Andrey Voronikhin, Vasily Stasov and Karl Rossii, with architectural details – columns, capitals, cornices – on furniture. This was the era of the 'Russian Empire' style, which reached its height in applied art after the Franco-Russian war of 1812, and remained popular throughout the reign of Alexander I (1801–25). The monumental forms of Doric and Tuscan architectural orders borrowed from French Empire style, stylized Roman and ancient Egyptian motifs, military trophies and winged sphinxes all appear regularly in applied art.

Two types of glass were produced in Russia in the first half of the 18th century: colourless panes embellished with monograms, military emblems and inscriptions for palaces; and painted glass decorated with pictures. The baroque influenced the designs and ornamentation of both. By the 1750s, Russian glassware rivalled that of the rest of Europe. The State Glass Works produced tableware made of fine coloured glass decorated with gold or silver. Crystal was also widely used.

At the beginning of the 1750s, after many years of experimentation, the chemist Dmitry Vinogradov succeeded in obtaining porcelain clay from local deposits and in producing it locally – porcelain had previously been imported from China and Western Europe. The Imperial Porcelain Factory, established in 1744, produced a wide variety of items, including dinner and tea services, of which the most famous are 'Arabesque' made for Catherine the Great, and the 'Royal' tableware for the Empress Elizabeth.

Although porcelain figures first appeared in the 1760s, reflecting realistic tendencies in Russian art, the most famous series, the 'Peoples of Russia', dates from the 1780s. Of the private porcelain factories opened in the late 18th century, one of the biggest was Franz Gardner's works, best known for its figurines depicting various classes of townspeople. From the 1820s come those of Aleksey Popov, Sergey Batenin and Prince Nikolay Yusupov.

New designs in precious metalware included women's European-style jewellery, and small decorative items such as snuff boxes, *nécessaires*, fans, beauty spots, and perfume bottles. At the beginning of the 18th century tea became a popular drink, creating a demand for samovars, silver tea pots and sugar bowls. As in Paris, it also became fashionable to make everyday utensils – cups, salt-cellars, glasses and snuff boxes – from precious metals. Snuff-taking, a habit imported from the West, became popular, and, with it, the fashion for snuff boxes made by Russian and foreign craftsmen. In the middle of the 18th century baroque and rococo decoration on gold- and silverware was replaced by motifs inspired by the neo-classical style. Everyday utensils, as well as objects for special occasions, were adorned with representations based on the ideals and images of classical antiquity, episodes from the campaigns and victories of the Russian army and military regalia. Motifs borrowed from the empire style in architecture appeared at the beginning of the 19th century.

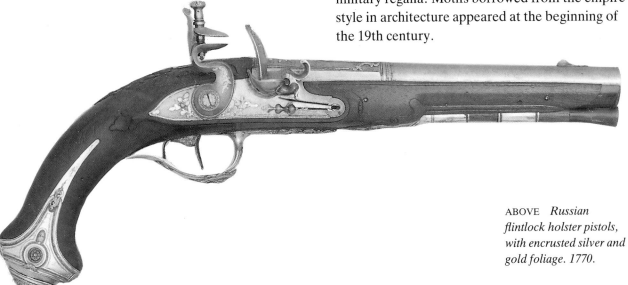

ABOVE *Russian flintlock holster pistols, with encrusted silver and gold foliage. 1770.*

In Moscow, where the Kremlin gold and silver workshops (later transferred to St Petersburg) had been leading centres in the 17th century, craftsmen were generally more conservative than their counterparts in the new capital; they often used traditional decorative devices and disregarded the baroque and rococo styles. However, the Moscow enamellers Grigory Musikilsky and Andrey Ovsov introduced the miniature portrait into the jeweller's craft.

The best known of a number of provincial centres were in the northern Russian cities of Vologda and Solvychegodsk and in Veliky Ustyug, a major trade and industrial centre whose craftsmen were renowned for niello or black enamel technique applied to silverware. Vologda masters were famous for engraving, Solvychegodsk for painted enamel and yarned ornament work.

ABOVE *Russian gold, enamel and citrine necklace, made by the Moscow jeweller Ivan Chichelev in 1873.*
OPPOSITE *Enamelled plaque with the imperial eagle.*

The city of Tula, 150 miles to the south of Moscow, was the country's first centre for the manufacture of steelware. The Tula Armaments Factory was established in 1710 and, in addition to armaments, the city's masters made steel domestic wares – elegant mirrors, candelabra, chandeliers, writing sets – richly decorated with carving, engraving and the technique known as 'diamond faceting'. All are sought after today.

Artistic techniques developed throughout the 19th century and Russian decorative art culminated in the exquisite designs and masterly workmanship of Peter Carl Fabergé (1846–1920), the Russian goldsmith and jeweller.

PART 7 THE RUSSIAN

The Russian Revolution was probably the most important political event of the 20th century. The division of the world into two hostile camps, communist and capitalist, which dominated much of the history of the century, had its origins in the events of 1917 and their aftermath in Russia.

It was the attempt to prosecute the First World War that finally overtaxed the Russian system and most clearly demonstrated the inadequacies and inequalities of the Romanov autocracy. The Russian forces in World War I were ill-equipped and, when coupled with poor leadership, suffered terrible casualties. Loss of prestige alone might not have been sufficient to bring about revolution, but rampant inflation and scarcity of food set the scene.

By 1917, after three years of war, the bond between the Tsar and the majority of his people had been shattered. In February, food rioters in the capital, Petrograd, were joined by most of the military garrison and Nicholas was forced to abdicate. When his brother, Grand Duke Michael, decided to refuse the throne, over three centuries of Romanov rule came to an abrupt end and the Imperial government was overthrown. The Provisional Government, appointed by a committee of the *duma*, attempted to maintain Russia's participation in the war and thereby faced a growing swell of popular discontent. Although it was

reorganized four times between March and October, the government was unable to cope with the critical problems affecting the country, which included peasant land seizures, nationalist independence movements in non-Russian areas and, in particular, the collapse of army morale at the front. There was also the ever-present threat of insurrection.

In April, Lenin issued an open call for 'All Power to the Soviets' and the overthrow of the Provisional Government. Subsequently, during the 'July Days' in Petrograd, there were violent mass demonstrations which led to the outlawing of the Bolshevik Party, the arrest of Trotsky and the escape of Lenin to Finland. But, from his temporary refuge, Lenin was still able to inspire the Bolsheviks in their propaganda campaign. By the autumn of 1917, the slogan of 'peace, land and bread' had won a considerable number of converts among the hungry urban masses, and with the soldiers and sailors who were beginning to desert in droves.

Russia was in military, economic and political turmoil. Despite opposition from the Bolshevik Central Committee, Lenin advocated armed insurrection to overthrow the existing regime. Fearing a government crackdown, when soldiers were sent to close their newspapers, the Bolsheviks responded by calling out sympathetic troops and workers' Red Guards as a defensive measure to protect the Petrograd

REVOLUTION (1917)

Soviet. However, these improvised forces encountered little effective opposition and the way, therefore, was now clear for Bolshevik and Left Socialist Revolutionaries to topple the existing government in an almost bloodless coup on 7 November 1917. In the event, resistance was limited and power lay there for the taking. Public buildings and utilities fell easily, and the storming of the Winter Palace which followed was something of an anticlimax. More by accident than deliberate strategy, therefore, the Bolsheviks and their political allies now found themselves holding the reins of power.

The Bolshevik Revolution was the first real attempt to put Marxist theory into practice. But instead of liberating the people of Russia, it returned them to bondage. The communist state which grew up under Lenin bore a remarkable resemblance to the tsarist autocracy which it replaced. The parliamentary aspirations of the people were once again crushed when the Constituent Assembly, the great liberal hope of the February Revolution in 1917, was forcibly closed down by the Bolsheviks in January 1918. The institutions of local self-government – which the people had developed during 1917 through the *zemstvos*, the soviets, and various local committees – were forced out of existence or subordinated to the Bolshevik state dictatorship during the ensuing years

of civil war (1918-20). The press freedoms and civil rights, which in April 1917 had given Lenin cause to declare Russia the 'freest country in the world', were soon abolished once the Bolsheviks took control. With the outbreak of civil war, a secret police terror was launched against 'counter-revolutionaries', the bourgeoisie, nobles and intellectuals. Indeed, it was to be applied against the whole Soviet population during the campaigns of forcible collectivization and industrialization in the 1930s.

In the following section may be found eye-witness accounts describing, for example, the 'February Days' and the unrest among the peasantry. Here are recounted the words of Nicholas II; also, those of the arch-revolutionary, Lenin, and the views of those who opposed him; while the exciting atmosphere of October is captured in the writings of journalist John Reed.

Ironically, nearly all of the Bolsheviks who had carried out and defended the October Revolution were later destroyed by Joseph Stalin during the terrible purges which he instigated in 1937-8. The ruthless pursuit and use of power, which had helped to achieve the revolution, developed into a prime instrument of the Soviet state. Force became the order of the day, where once ideology and idealism had sufficed. The roots of this tragedy, however, can only be understood by reference to the road to power in 1917.

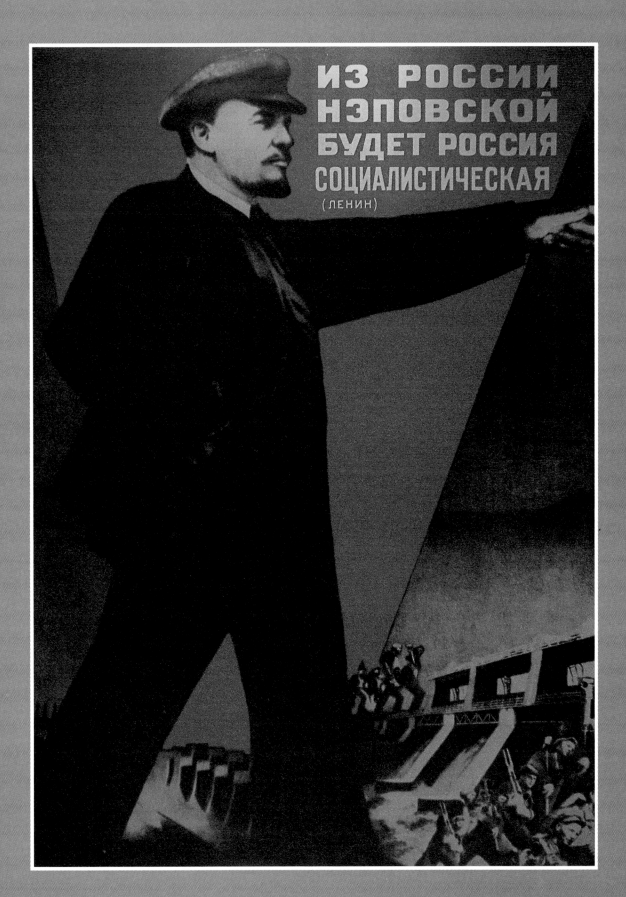

Lenin

The collapse of the tsarist regime in February 1917 resulted from a series of workers' demonstrations and strikes in Petrograd, followed by the decisive mutiny of the garrison there. But it led on to a series of local revolutions right across the country – in the factories, the towns, the trenches, the villages, and the non-Russian parts of the empire – each of which displayed a growing dissatisfaction with the provisional government.

The Bolsheviks succeeded in overthrowing the government and consolidating their own state dictatorship. In 1917-18, they encouraged the revolutionary initiatives of the people to complete the destruction of the old political and social order. But in the following years of civil war, they used their campaign against the Whites to legitimize the construction of a centralized Bolshevik state, with political control over all social institutions. Indeed, by 1921 the Bolsheviks had won the civil war, but killed the revolution.

The giant figure of Lenin straddles this period as head of the new Soviet state. In particular, it is his role as inspirer and leader of the October Revolution that immediately seizes the imagination. As a theoretician, he formulated the ideology of Marxism-Leninism; as a man of action he demanded that the Bolshevik Central Committee adopt a policy of armed insurrection and lent his considerable powers of oratory to the cause of Communism. From 1922, however, he was incapacitated with serious health problems and died in January 1924.

The experience of the revolutionary period is reconstructed through the memoirs and written accounts of those who lived through it. All shades of opinion are represented, from out-and-out monarchists to the most radical Bolsheviks. Documents have also been selected to represent a wide range of perspectives.

OPPOSITE *Lenin (first head of the Soviet state, 1917-24).*

In Petrograd, the Suvorov Prospect is black with people; a political meeting is being conducted in the Zaiats Alley, diagonally opposite the academy. A dray cart has been unhitched, and orator follows orator on to this shaky platform, which towers above the crowd. Visored caps follow fur hats, which follow bowlers. About three dozen women shuffle by; they are wearing prison gowns and their slippers scuff through the snow. On Suvorovsky they say their goodbyes and scatter. Still hatless and without their overcoats, the Preobrazhensky soldiers whom we had hidden are stealthily leaving our gates and mingling with the crowd on the Prospect.

My wife returns from the centre of town: she says it is the same thing there. Everywhere, there are automobiles and crowds. The arsenal has been taken. They say that about twenty thousand automatic pistols alone have been handed out.

There is a lot of firing in the streets, but it all seems to be for show; mostly it is the adolescents who are doing the shooting, almost all of them have revolvers. 'Did you see the women? The criminals from the Litovsky prison? The jails have been opened.'

The area continues to be a bubbling cauldron of activity. A boy hidden behind a cornice whistles sharply, with all his might. All at once, everyone turns towards Tauride Street. The crowd surges towards the pavement – a mad crush follows. Pushing their way forward through the retreating crowd, the safety catches of their rifles clicking, come armed students and workers. They fan out in a chain across Tauride Street.

An artilleryman, on a magnificent, deep-chested Caucasian stallion, rides up to the human chain and salutes it with his officer's sabre. 'Hurrah!' Everyone crowds around horse and rider. Street urchins escort him through the crowd, holding on to his stirrups. Caps are thrown into the air. The youths on the pavement madly fire their pistols into the air. Slowly, with a dancing step, the officer rides by, showing off, making the horse arch its neck by sawing on the iron bit. The Guards Artillery must have mutinied.

This was how Sergey Mstislavsky, a Socialist Revolutionary leader in Petrograd, described the

capital during the 'February days' of 1917.

The power of the people on the street was enough to bring down the Romanov dynasty. On 2 March Nicholas II issued his abdication order.

It has been God's will to visit upon Russia a new and grievous trial. The internal disturbances which have begun among the people threaten to have a calamitous effect on the future conduct of a hard-fought war.

The whole future of our beloved fatherland demands that the war be carried to victory.

In these decisive days in the life of Russia, we have deemed it our duty in conscience to help our people to draw closer together, and to unite all the forces of the nation for a speedier attainment of victory.

Consequently, in agreement with the state *duma*, we have judged it right to abdicate the throne of the Russian state and to lay down the supreme power.

Not wishing to be parted from our beloved son, we hand over our succession to our brother, the Grand Duke Mikhail Aleksandrovich, and bless him on his accession to the throne of the Russian state. We enjoin our brother to conduct the affairs of the state in complete and inviolable union with the representatives of the people in the legislative bodies on the

principles to be established by them, and to take an inviolable oath to this effect.

We call upon all true sons of the fatherland to fulfil their sacred duty to it by their obedience to the tsar at this time of national trial, and to help him, together with the people's representatives, to lead the Russian state on to the path of victory, prosperity, and glory. May the Lord God help Russia!
Pskov, 2 March 1917, 3.00 p.m.

NICHOLAS

Given the popular mood, the Grand Duke Mikhail Aleksandrovich was well advised to refuse the throne, pending the convocation of a new sovereign parliament, the Constituent Assembly. On 3 March he issued the following proclamation.

A heavy burden has been laid upon me by the will of my brother, who has given over to me the imperial throne of All Russia at a time of unprecedented warfare and popular disturbances.

Inspired by the thought, which is shared by all the people, that the good of our native land is above everything else, I have taken a firm decision to assume the supreme power only in the event that

such is the will of our great people, upon whom it devolves by a general vote through their representatives in the Constituent Assembly, to determine the form of government and the new fundamental laws of the Russian state.

Therefore, invoking God's blessing, I ask all citizens of the Russian state to pay allegiance to the Provisional Government which is to be endowed with full power until such time as the Constituent Assembly, to be convened in as short a period as possible on the basis of a universal, direct, equal, and secret vote, by its decision on the form of government, expresses the will of the people.

During the next few days, a fire-engine went round the public buildings of Petrograd with ladders and iron hooks to remove the tsarist emblems. Meanwhile, the Petrograd Soviet (council) and the *duma*'s temporary committee negotiated the formation of the Provisional Government. The Soviet declined to participate; however they set conditions for its support – some of which are quoted below – which were unanimously accepted by the *duma* committee.

Complete and immediate amnesty for all charged with political, religious, terroristic crimes, military uprisings, etc.

Political freedom in all its forms: freedom of speech, press, unions, meetings, and strikes: this freedom to apply equally to the army.

The organization of the army on the basis of self-government.

The organization of a citizen militia to enforce order; this militia to be subject to the local authorities, elected on the basis of universal, equal, direct, and secret suffrage.

The abolition of all class, nationality, and religious restrictions.

The garrison of Petrograd not to be removed from the city and not to be disarmed.

During the first few weeks of its existence, the Provisional Government introduced democratic political reforms and high-sounding moral declarations on the desirability of ending the imperialist war.

The Bolsheviks, led at this stage by Stalin and Kamenev, joined the other socialist parties in giving the government conditional support. But on 4 April 1917 Lenin returned to Petrograd from Western Europe and began to preach a much more revolutionary policy. The following brief extract includes what were considered to be the major points from his April Theses.

The specific feature of the present situation in Russia is that the country is passing from the first stage of the revolution – which placed power in the hands of the bourgeoisie – to its second stage, which must place power in the hands of the proletariat and the poorest sections of the peasants.

No support should be given to the Provisional Government. The utter falsity of all its promises should be made clear. The masses must be made to see that the Soviets of Workers' Deputies are the only possible form of revolutionary government.

Lenin gradually won over the majority of Bolsheviks to his policy of agitating among the masses for a second revolution, transferring power from the Provisional Government to the soviets. In the countryside, the land-hungry peasants began to confiscate the property of the landowners. A report from the Saratov province in the autumn of 1917 gave this vivid impression of the condition in which the estates had been left by the peasants.

As far as the manor buildings are concerned, they have been senselessly destroyed, with only the walls left standing. The windows and the doors were the worst to suffer; in the majority of the estates no trace is left of them. All forms of transport have been destroyed or taken; cumbersome machines like steam-threshers, locomotives, and binders were taken out for no known reason and discarded along the roads and in the fields; agricultural tools were also taken; anything that could be used in the peasant households simply disappeared from the estates. On the estates that used to have collars and harnesses for a hundred or two hundred horses, such as those belonging to the Ikonnikovs and the Gagarins, it is now difficult to find enough harness for a single horse and cart.

The peasants were equally violent in their resistance to the government's policy of compulsorily purchasing their foodstuffs at fixed prices. A report by the provincial commissar in Simbirsk in August 1917 makes this clear enough.

On 20 August, in the village of Chirikov, in the Sengileyev district, the population assaulted Lobanov, a member of the Chertanov food supply board, while he was on duty. An investigation is now being conducted.

In the village of Maliachkin, in the Syzran district, the population refused to submit to the registration of grain and threatened members of the food supply committee.

The district commissar has been requested to take urgent and drastic measures to deal with this.

ABOVE   *Painting depicting the death of a policeman at the hands of Petrograd revolutionaries. In that time popular anger was directed against any person or object reminiscent of tsarist rule. In the country, peasants turned on landowners, confiscating and destroying property and possessions. But they also protested violently against the fixed purchase price imposed by the government.*

The Timoshkin village food supply committee of the Sengileyev district telegraphed about the agitation of local townsmen Abdriaznikov, Baimashev, and Absaliamov against the village food supply committee. This agitation had a detrimental effect upon the population and interfered with work. According to information from the Syzrań district food supply board, the population refuses to surrender grain at fixed prices, which it considers too low. The situation in the city and the whole district is critical. The commissar has been requested to take most energetic measures to introduce the law on the grain monopoly, resorting, in case of need, to armed force.

Popular discontent in the capital, Petrograd, grew during 3 and 4 July into a mass armed

demonstration, which had to be dispersed by gunfire. The Bolsheviks had tried to prevent it, realizing they lacked enough strength in the country as a whole to seize and retain power. Yet the following report by the public prosecutor found the Bolsheviks guilty of plotting the uprising, in league with the German command, a verdict in tune with the right-wing backlash that followed the 'July days'.

On the basis of the data outlined, as well as of data that cannot as yet be made public, Vladimir Ulyanov (Lenin), Ovsei-Gersh Arenov Apfelbaum (Zinoviev), Alexandra Mikhailovna Kollontai, Mecheslav Ulyevich Kozlovsky, Evgenia Mavrikievna Sumenson, Helfand (Parvus), Iakov

---

Lenin the billiard ball

Lenin is a typical outcome – I would even say a victim – of those abnormal political conditions that have existed in Russia up to this time. By his endowments he is an outstanding figure, distorted by the abnormal conditions that prevail.

Lenin possesses an imposing wholeness. He seems to be made of one single piece of granite. He is all round and polished like a billiard ball. You cannot get hold of him. He rolls with irrepressible speed. But he could repeat to himself the well-known phrase, 'Je ne sais pas ou je vais, mais j'y vais résolument' (I don't know where I am going, but I am going there resolutely).

Lenin is devoted to the revolutionary cause. But to him revolution is embodied in his person.

Lenin was never distinguished by excessive moral sensitivity or by inordinate tact. He substituted inflexibility for them. He has a great militant temperament and a tremendous reserve of energy. But deprived of an arena to pour out his energy in great political actions, he pours it out in great polemic words.

His settling of accounts with opponents screeches crunchingly like iron over glass. His socialism is uncouth, for Lenin employs a clumsy axe where a sharp and fine scalpel is called for.

There is almost always, in Lenin, some grain of unquestionably vital and political truth. But, good God, what does he not contrive to do with this poor little truth that falls into his hands! He supports it strongly and firmly as a rope supports a hanged man.

From Viktor Chernov, *Delo Naroda*, 16 April 1917

The Russian peasantry

More than 15 million men were conscripted between the outbreak in August 1914 of World War I and 1917. However, although landowners lost many of their labourers, the primitive and backward methods of farming could not ensure full employment. By late 1916, rapid inflation had rendered the rouble virtually valueless, while industry's transfer to war production resulted in a dearth of manufactured goods. Peasants cut back on crops for sale in the market and relied more on local exchanges, converting grain into homebrew (*samogon*). Government food supply officials, desperate to resolve the growing food crisis, resorted to coercion, but defeated their own objectives by forcing a further withdrawal from the market while simultaneously provoking peasant hostility.

By early 1917, Russia was ripe for revolution. After the fall of the tsarist regime and the emergence of the provisional government, peasant disturbances spread throughout the countryside. Using their traditional institutions, the village commune and parish (*volost*), as vehicles for this revolutionary transformation of rural Russia, peasants arrested local officials, village policemen and guards, and replaced them with peasant representatives. The new village and parish committees (later called soviets in some places) were generally established when the post of parish elder was abolished. At village level, the number of those eligible to participate expanded considerably, while equal electoral rights to all were given at parish level.

The pinnacle of success was to gain control of landed estates. Village communities, and even whole parishes on occasion, with their carts and horses, would demand grain, equipment and livestock from their neighbouring landowner or steward and share out the spoils. Anyone who refused to participate was immediately (and often brutally) punished.

As 1917 wore on, peasant demands for land merely increased. As a consequence of the Russian Revolution, the holding of private property was abolished. In the autumn, the Bolsheviks issued the Land Decree of October, which sanctioned the confiscation of estates and the redistribution of their property, and forged an alliance with one wing of the Socialist Revolutionary Party, which was traditionally associated with the peasantry. However, their hopes of encouraging direct exchange of products between town and countryside were short lived. The lack of raw materials and fuel for industry, and the return of many workers to villages, meant that there was a shortage of manufactured goods. With inflation still rampant and local organizations strengthened, peasants became increasingly self-sufficient. Bolshevik policies of forcefully requisitioning grain and other agricultural products, supported in 1918 by a class attack on alleged *kulaks* or wealthy peasants, failed to remedy the crisis and, by mid-1920, had provoked widespread peasant unrest. In some regions, famine ensued. Thereafter, the propensity to emphasize industrial growth over agricultural development continued to afflict the Soviet state.

ABOVE Kulaks *being deported from their village.*

Furstenberg (Kuba Ganetsky), Midshipman Ilin (Raskolnikov), and ensigns Semashko, Sakharov, and Roshal are accused of having entered – in 1917, while Russian citizens – into an agreement with the enemy to assist in the disorganization of the Russian army, in order to weaken the fighting strength of the army. For this purpose, and with the money received from the enemy, they organized propaganda among the civilian population and in the army, appealing to them to refuse immediately to continue military actions against the enemy; also, toward the same end, to organize in Petrograd, from 3 July to 5 July 1917, an armed insurrection against the existing supreme state authority. This resulted in murders and violence and attempts to arrest some members of the government.

As a consequence of this, some military units refused to carry out orders of their commanding personnel and arbitrarily abandoned their positions, thus aiding in the success of the enemy's armies.

Lenin was forced into hiding in Finland; but as the date for a new Congress of the Soviets approached, he bombarded the central committee of the Bolshevik party with demands to stage an insurrection and seize hold of state power. But the central committee was more cautious: at first, they even burned Lenin's letters, lest they should fall into the hands of local Bolshevik hotheads. Finally, Lenin wrote to the central committee on 29 September, offering his resignation from the party, unless it adopted his plans for an immediate uprising.

If we were to attack at once, suddenly, from three points, Petrograd, Moscow, and the Baltic fleet, the chances are a hundred to one that we would succeed with smaller sacrifices than in the July days, because the troops will not advance against a government of peace. Even though Kerensky has loyal cavalry, etc., in Petrograd, he would be compelled to surrender since we enjoy the sympathy of the army. If, with such good

RIGHT *Demonstration in front of the Winter Palace, former home of the tsars and an enduring focus for popular discontent.*

LEFT *Women soldiers. Members of the women's battalion were sent to the front in World War I and also guarded the Winter Palace.*

chances, we do not take power, then all talk of transferring the power to the soviets becomes a lie.

In view of the fact that the central committee has left unanswered the persistent demands I have made for such a policy ever since the beginning of the democratic conference, and in view of the fact that the central organ is deleting from my articles all reference to glaring errors on the part of the Bolsheviks, I am compelled to regard this as a subtle hint at the unwillingness of the central committee even to consider this question, a subtle hint that I should keep my mouth shut, and as a proposal for me to retire. Therefore I see no alternative but to tender my resignation from the central committee, which I hereby do, reserving for myself freedom to campaign among the rank and file of the party and at the party congress.

For it is my profound conviction that if we wait for the Congress of Soviets and let the present moment pass, we shall ruin the revolution.

The central committee, however, continued to wait for the Soviet Congress, convened for 25 October, on the grounds that they could gain a majority there among all the socialist parties for a Soviet government without the need to resort to a violent seizure of power. John Reed, a young American journalist, described the scenes at the Smolny Institute, where the congress was to meet, on 24 October.

The Smolny Institute, headquarters of the Central Committee and of the Petrograd Soviet, lies beside the wide River Neva. I went there on a streetcar, moving snail-like with a groaning noise through the cobbled, muddy streets, and jammed with people. At the end of the line rose the graceful smoke-blue cupolas of Smolny Convent outlined in dull gold, beautiful; and beside it the great barracks-like façade of the Smolny Institute, two hundred yards long and three lofty storeys high, the imperial arms carved hugely in stone still insolent over the entrance.

A famous convent school, under the old regime, for the daughters of the Russian nobility, patronized by the tsaritsa herself, the Institute had been taken over by the revolutionary organizations of workers and soldiers. Within were more than a hundred huge rooms, white and bare, on their doors enamelled plaques still informing the passer-by that within was 'Ladies' classroom number 4' or 'Teachers' Bureau'; but over these hung crudely lettered signs, evidence of the vitality of the new order: 'Central Committee of the Petrograd Soviet' and 'Central Executive Committee' and 'Bureau of Foreign Affairs'; 'Union of Socialist Soldiers', 'Central Committee of the All-Russian Trade Unions', 'Factory Shop Committees', 'Central Army Committee', and the central offices and caucus rooms of the political parties.

The long, vaulted corridors, lit by rare electric lights, were thronged with hurrying shapes of soldiers and workmen, some bent under the weight of huge bundles of newspapers, proclamations, printed propaganda of all sorts. The sound of their heavy boots made a deep and incessant thunder on the wooden floor. Signs were posted up everywhere: 'Comrades! For the sake of your health, preserve cleanliness!'

On the evening of 24 October, Lenin, no longer able to restrain himself, came out of hiding, and made his way in disguise to the Smolny Institute. Calling a meeting of the central committee, he won over his comrades to implement his plans for the immediate seizure of power, culminating in the storming of the Winter Palace on 25 October, where the last session of the Provisional Government was in session. S. L. Maslov, the Minister of Agriculture, recalls the events.

On Wednesday morning, at 11.30, I was summoned by telephone to a special meeting of the Provisional Government. It was reported to us that the Bolsheviks had seized the Petrograd news agency, the State Bank, the post and telegraph. It was agreed that Polkovnikov, the man in charge of the defence, had not acted with decision, and N. M. Kishkin was appointed in his place with two assistants, Palchinsky and Rutenberg. It was decided that the Provisional Government should remain in continuous session.

At 7.00 p.m. Kishkin, who was at the general staff, was handed a note signed by Antonov demanding the surrender of the Provisional Government and the disarming of the guard. Kishkin was given twenty minutes in which to decide. When the ministers learned of this demand they decided that only the Constituent Assembly could take over their powers.

The guard of the Winter Palace was made up of some cadets, part of the Engineering School, two companies of Cossacks, and a small number of the Women's Battalion. At 10.00 p.m. a shot was fired in the palace, followed by cries and shots from the cadets. About fifty hostile sailors and soldiers were arrested and disarmed. In the meantime more and more sailors and soldiers arrived, until the guard seemed helpless. Outside the palace, rifles, machine guns, and even cannon were being fired.

About 2.00 a.m. on 8 November, there was a loud noise at the entrance to the palace. The insurrectionists were trying to break in and thirty of the cadets were trying to hold them back. Members of the Provisional Government took a hand and stopped further trouble. The armed mob of soldiers, sailors, and civilians, led by Antonov, broke in. They shouted threats and made jokes. Antonov arrested everybody in the name of the Revolutionary Committee and proceeded to take the names of all present.

We were placed under arrest, and told that we would be taken to Peter-Paul fortress. We picked up our coats, but Kishkin's was gone. Someone had stolen it. He was given a soldier's coat. A discussion started between Antonov, the soldiers, and the sailors as to whether the ministers should be taken to their destination in

Lenin: the first successful revolutionary

Vladimir Ilyich Ulyanov (or Lenin as he called himself from 1901 onwards) was born on 22 April 1870 at Simbirsk. His father was a school inspector, a loyal and conservative official. The eldest son, Alexander – four years Lenin's senior – studied in St Petersburg University but was arrested and hanged for participation in a plot to assassinate the tsar. Shortly afterwards, Lenin was expelled from his university, Kazan, after student demonstrations. In 1891, he enrolled as an external student in law at St Petersburg while living under restrictions a thousand miles away in Samara. Two years later, Lenin moved to St Petersburg where he began his political apprenticeship.

Lenin first made his mark in revolutionary circles as a theorist. After travelling abroad, where he met the founding fathers of Russian Marxism (Georgy Plekhanov and Pavel Akselrod) he returned to Russia. Helped by periods of prison detention, he continued to study and to write. His major work, the *Development of Capitalism in Russia* (1899) was the first systematically to apply the western doctrine of Marxism to Russian conditions. He dedicated the rest of his life to bringing about the revolution in Russia.

Lenin subordinated private life to public activities. Maksim Gorky once recalled him listening to Beethoven with astonished delight, but then rejecting the 'escapism' it provided from 'hellish reality'. His remedy for reality was political dictatorship imposed on the working class by its alleged vanguard.

The rise in October 1917 took him by surprise, as did the enormity of the problems the revolution inherited. It soon became clear that his political vanguard, so suitable for seizing power, was unable to rule Russia other than by force. Yet any relaxation would make reiteration of the old order likely.

Lenin worried over these problems and about the future of the Communist Party under the leadership of such forceful personalities as Trotsky and Stalin. But a series of strokes from 1922 broke his health and reduced his influence. He died on 21 January 1924 at Gorky, near Moscow.

BELOW *Lenin, the founder of Bolshevism and the major force behind the 1917 revolution.*

OVERLEAF *The storming of the Winter Palace, the culmination of the Bolshevik seizure of power.*

automobiles or on foot. It was decided to make them walk.

Each of us was guarded by two men. As we walked through the palace it seemed as if it were filled with the insurrectionists, some of whom were drunk. When we came out on the street we were surrounded by a mob, shouting and threatening.

At the Troitsky Bridge the mob recovered its voice and shouted, 'Throw them into the river!' The calls were becoming louder and louder. Just then a machine gun opened fire from the other side of us. We threw ourselves down, while some of the mob ran, and with them one of the arrested officers.

During the following weeks, the Bolsheviks consolidated their dictatorship. The Constituent Assembly was forcibly closed down during its first and only session on 6 January 1918.

The Bolsheviks had come to power offering peace, bread, and land. But how was peace to be obtained? What should the Bolsheviks do if the Central Powers refused to sign a peace? They started by sending a delegation to negotiate with the German high command at Brest-Litovsk; it included a representative from the soldiers, the sailors, the workers, and the peasants. The peasant delegate was in fact a last-minute addition, as Lieutenant-Colonel I. K. Fokke recalls.

Lastly there was the peasant delegate, old Roman Stashkov, a good-natured, simple old fellow with yellowish-grey hair and beard, and deep wrinkles in his brick-tanned face. He was utterly and completely bewildered by the whole proceeding, and still – despite the times – addressed his revolutionary colleagues as *bariny* (master). He had been a last-minute addition to the party. Not until they were on their way to the station did the leaders of the delegation realize that the peasant class was unrepresented among

them, and, as their motor sped through the dark and deserted streets of Petrograd, there was consternation among them at this omission.

Suddenly they turned a corner and came upon an old man in a peasant's coat plodding along in the snow and carrying a bag. The car stopped.

'Where are you going, *tovarishch* (comrade)?'

'To the station, *barin* – I mean *tovarishch*,' replied the old man.

'Get in; we'll give you a lift' – and they sped on.

The old man was mildly pleased at the unusual attention he received from his new friends, but as they neared the Warsaw station he showed signs of worry.

'This is not the station I need, comrades; I want the Nikolayevsky station. I've got to go beyond Moscow.'

This would never do, thought Joffe and Kamenev, and they began to question the old peasant about his politics.

'What party do you belong to?'

'I'm a Socialist Revolutionary, comrades,' was the slightly disconcerting reply. 'Everybody in our village is a Socialist Revolutionary.'

'A left or a right one?'

Something warned the old man, perhaps it was the tone of his questioner, that he had better not say 'right'.

'Left, comrades, of course, the very leftest.'

No other requirements were needed for a 'mandatory representative of the Russian peasantry', and it was getting near train time.

'There's no need for you to go to your village,' the old man was told. 'Come with us to Brest-Litovsk and make peace with the Germans.' A little more persuasion, a little money promised, and thus, incredibly, the lacuna in the delegation was filled.

As the negotiations wore on, the prospects of a revolution in Germany seemed to diminish, while the German high command began preparations for a renewed attack on the weakened Russian state.

RIGHT *Red Guards, here in front of the Smolny Institute, were in the forefront of the Revolution.*

The left wing of the Bolshevik party favoured fighting a guerrilla-type war against the Germans, in the belief that this would present a model of anti-imperialism to the proletariat of Western Europe. But Lenin rejected this argument on pragmatic grounds, and put his own views to a meeting of the Bolshevik Central Committee in January 1918.

It is now only a question of how to defend the homeland – the socialist republic. The army is utterly exhausted by war; our supply of horses is such that in an attack we will not be able to withdraw the artillery; the German position on the Baltic islands is so good that if they attacked they could take Reval (Tallinn in Estonia) and Petrograd with their bare hands. If we continue the war in conditions like this, we will strengthen German imperialism, and we will have to make peace all the same.

Of course, this peace we are going to conclude will be a shameful peace; but we need a respite to put social reforms into practice (take only transport); we need to gain strength and for that we need time. The bourgeoisie has to be throttled, and for that we need both hands free.

The peace of Brest-Litovsk, finally signed on 3 March 1918, gave the Bolsheviks the breathing spell they needed to reconstruct the failing economy and consolidate their revolution. But there was still one more important act in the Russian tragedy. After the abdication, the imperial family was imprisoned for five months near Petrograd. As tension mounted, the family was moved to Tobolsk in Siberia. In spring 1918, the Bolshevik leaders ordered their return to Moscow because the government was afraid that the family might be rescued by monarchist forces. Instead, apparently on the initiative of the local Soviet organizations, they were moved to Ekaterinburg in western Siberia. Then, to prevent them falling into the hands of the advancing Czechoslovak Legion, Tsar Nicholas II and his family were executed on the orders of the Urals Soviet in Ekaterinburg on 16 July 1918.

Glossary

Altyn A coin (three copecks).

Appanage The territory ruled by a prince under the suzerainty of the grand prince or tsar.

Archimandrite A senior churchman, usually the abbot of a large monastery.

Assembly of the Land An assembly of representatives from all over Muscovy convened to discuss matters of state. Prominent in the reign of Mikhail Romanov, it declined in importance with the consolidation of a central autocracy.

Barshchina Corvée, the work that a serf was obliged to perform on his master's land.

Boyar A nobleman, one of the entourage of a prince, grand prince or tsar. The title was not hereditary and was conferred by the ruler upon individuals. It was abolished by Peter the Great.

Brodniki A section of the East Slavonic population living on the steppes outside the jurisdiction of the princes.

Cheka The Bolshevik secret police, forerunner of the KGB.

Chiliarch Originally, the commander of a thousand in the armed muster of a Russian town; later, an important official, especially in Novgorod and towns with a similar constitution.

Copeck A copper coin (one hundredth of a rouble).

Decembrists Participants in the abortive insurrection of December 1825.

Derevlyanins An East Slavonic tribe.

Desyatina A measure of land.

Duma The parliament that Russia acquired after the reforms of 1905.

Dvoryanstvo Originally, the personnel of the grand prince's court (dvor), the servitor class; from the time of Peter the Great, the gentry, to whom all holding a rank in the civil or armed services belonged, hereditary status being acquired above a certain rank.

Golden Horde Name given by medieval Russians to the western division of the Tartar (Mongol) empire.

Grivna A monetary unit which altered in value at various times and in different parts of the country; in the later period, equivalent to ten copecks.

Häme A Finnic tribe, later absorbed by the Finns.

Kagan The ruler of various oriental peoples; occasionally used as a title of the princes of Rus.

Kasogy The Circassians, a Caucasian people.

Kremlin The citadel of a Russian town.

Krivichi An East Slavonic tribe that formed a significant element in the population of Novgorod.

Kulak Literally 'fist': an opprobrious term applied by the Bolsheviks to the more prosperous peasants whom they dispossessed.

Kvass A drink made from fermented rye bread.

Latinism Medieval Russian term for Roman Catholicism.

Liturgy The usual name for the Eucharist in the East.

Marshal of Nobility A dignitary, elected by the dvoryanstvo of a given area, who played a prominent part in local government.

Merya A Finnic tribe, now extinct (unless they are to be identified with the present-day Mari).

Mir The peasant commune.

Obrok Quit rent, paid annually by a serf to his master to discharge his obligations to him.

Oprichnina Originally, the personal possessions of a prince or the dower of his widow; under Ivan the Terrible, those persons (oprichniki) and sections of the country under the tsar's personal command, and outside the normal administrative structure of the state.

Pech A stove.

Pechenegs A nomadic people, predominantly Turkic, who occupied the steppe region from the ninth to the mid-11th centuries.

Pessenik A songbook.

Poltina A coin (half a rouble).

Polovtsy A nomadic Turkic people, also known as Kipchaks or Cumans, who displaced the Pechenegs in the steppes in the mid-11th century. After their power was destroyed by the Tartars, they were assimilated by the surrounding peoples.

Polychronion A prayer for the long life of a person or persons, sung mostly on festive occasions.

Posadnik The highest administrative official in Novgorod and other oligarchic cities, elected by the town assembly. In the later period the number of posadniki was increased, and their terms of office limited.

Rezana A coin (fraction of a copeck).

Rouble Russian monetary unit; in early times, equivalent to about one English mark.

Servitor A person engaged in state service; a forerunner of the dvoryanstvo.

Slavophiles A 19th-century group who believed that Western European models were not applicable to Russia, and that it should seek a basis for its future development in its native traditions.

Sloboda A suburb, typically inhabited by members of a single professional group: in Moscow there was also a 'German sloboda' where Western Europeans lived.

Slovenins An East Slavonic tribe occupying the north of the East Slavonic territory.

Spiritual father/mother An individual's confessor and spiritual adviser.

Streltsy The Musketeers, the professional armed forces of Muscovy, replaced by a regular army by Peter the Great.

Synod The governing body of the Russian Orthodox Church after the suspension of the patriarchate under Peter the Great, effectively controlled by the tsar through his representative.

Torki A Turkic people, originally nomadic, who later adopted a sedentary way of life on the borders of the Kievan principality and were often allied with Rus against the Polovtsy.

Tsarevitch A tsar's son.

Tsarevna A tsar's daughter.

Tsaritsa The wife or widow of a tsar; also a reigning empress.

Udmurts A Finnic people now inhabiting a territory west of the Urals.

Versta A measure of distance (⅔ mile).

Volost A region.

Vyatichi One of the East Slavonic tribes.

Westernizers A section of the 19th-century intelligentsia, radical and rationalistic in outlook, who believed in the development of Russia along Western European patterns.

Yasy A Caucasian people related to the present-day Ossets.

Zemstvo The major organ of local government after Alexander II's reforms.

Bibliography

This is not intended as a comprehensive bibliography of all relevant works, but is a selection of books relating to the topics discussed in the essays and the chronicles. Articles have not been included because they are more difficult for the general reader to obtain. Most of the works cited here contain bibliographies which are a good starting point for more detailed reading on individual subjects.

Acton, E. *Rethinking the Russian Revolution*. Harlow, Essex, 1990.

Acton, E. *Russia*. Longman, 1986.

Aksakov, S. T. *A Russian Gentleman*. Oxford, 1984.

Aksakov, S. T. *A Russian Schoolboy*. Oxford, 1983.

Aksakov, S. T. *Years of Childhood*. Oxford, 1982.

Alexander, J. T. *Catherine the Great: Life and Legend*. Oxford, 1989.

Anderson, M. S. *Britain's Discovery of Russia, 1553-1815*. London, 1958.

Anderson, M. S. *Peter the Great*. London, 1976.

Anisimov, E. V. *Podotnava Reforma Petra I*. Leningrad, 1982.

Ascher A. *The Revolution of 1905*.

Avrich, P. *Russian Rebels 1600-1800*. New York, 1972.

Barratt, G. *Voices in Exile: The Decembrist Memoirs*. Montreal and London, 1974.

Bartlett, R. P., Cross, A. G. and Rasmussen, K., eds. *Russia and the World in the Eighteenth Century*. Columbus, 1988.

Bartlett, R. and Hartley, J. M., eds. *Russia in the Age of the Enlightenment: Essays for Isabel de Madariaga*, 1990.

Berlin, I. *Russian Thinkers*. New York, 1978.

Bird, A. *A History of Russian Painting*. Oxford, 1987.

Black, J. M. *Eighteenth Century Europe*.

Black, J. M., ed. *The Origins of War in Early Modern Europe*. Edinburgh, 1987.

Black, J. M. *The Rise of the European Powers 1679-1793*.

Blum, J. *Lord and Peasant in Russia*. Princeton, 1961.

Bonnell, V. E., ed. *The Russian Worker: Life and Labor under the Tsarist Regime*. Berkeley, 1983.

Boss, V. *Newton and Russia: the Early Influence, 1698-1796*. Cambridge, Mass., 1972.

Bowlt, J. E., ed. *Russian Art of the Avant-Garde, Theory and Criticism 1902-1934*. New York, 1976.

Bruce Lincoln, W. *Nicholas I, Emperor and Autocrat of All the Russias*. Illinois, 1989.

Bruce Lincoln, W. *The Romanovs*. London, 1983.

Bushnell, J. *Mutiny Amid Repression: Russian Soldiers in the Revolution of 1905-1906*. Indiana, 1986.

Catherine II. *Memoirs*. London, 1955.

Chamberlin, W. N. *The Russian Revolution, 1917-1921, Vol. I*. 2 vols. New York, 1935.

Cherniavsky, M. *Tsar and People*. New Haven, 1981.

Christoff, P. K. *An Introduction to Nineteenth-Century Russian Slavophilism, Vol. I*. The Hague, 1961.

Ibid. Vol. II. The Hague, 1972.

Ibid. Vol. III. Princeton, 1982.

Clardy, J. V. *The Philosophical Ideas of Alexander Radishchev*. London, 1963.

Cohen, S. *Bukharin and the Bolshevik Revolution*. Oxford, 1980.

Coughlan, R. *Elizabeth and Catherine*. 1974.

Cracraft, J. *The Petrine Reform in Russian Architecture*. Chicago and London, 1988.

Cross, A. G., ed. *An English Lady at the Court of Catherine the Great: The Journal of Baroness Dimsdale, 1781*. Cambridge, 1989.

Cross, A. G., ed. *Britain and Russia: Contacts and Comparisons, 1700-1800*. 1979.

Dashkova, Princess E. *Memoirs*. London, 1958.

Dawidowicz, L. S., ed. *The Golden Tradition*. Northvale, N. J., 1989.

Dubnow, S. *History of the Jews in Russia and Poland*. 3 vols. Philadelphia, 1916.

Duffy, C. *Russia's Military Way to the West: Origins and Nature of Russian Military Power, 1700-1800*. London and Boston, 1981.

Dukes, P., ed. *Russia in Europe*. 1990.

Dukes, P., ed. *Russia Under Catherine the Great, Vol. II*. Newtonville, 1977.

Dukes, P. *The Making of Russian Absolutism, 1613-1801*. London, 1982.

Edie, J. M., Scanlan, J. P. and Zeldin, M. B. *Russian Philosophy*. 3 vols. Chicago, 1965.

Eidelman, N. *Conspiracy Against the Tsar: A Portrait of the Decembrists*. Moscow, 1985.

Falkus, M. E. *The Industrialization of Russia, 1700-1914*. London, 1972.

Farnsworth, B. *Aleksandra Kollontai: Socialism, Feminism and the Bolshevik Revolution*. Stanford, 1980.

Fennell, J. *The Emergence of Moscow 1304-1359*. London, 1968.

Fisher, A. W. *The Russian Annexation of the Crimea, 1772-1783*. Cambridge, 1970.

Frank, J. *Dostoevsky, Vol. I: The Seeds of Revolt, 1821-1849*. London, 1977.

Ibid. Vol. II: The Years of Ordeal, 1850-1859. London, 1984.

Ibid. Vol. III: The Star of Liberation, 1860-1865. London, 1986.

Garrard, J., ed. *The Eighteenth Century in Russia*. Oxford, 1973.

Gatrell, P. W. *The Tsarist Economy, 1850-1917*. London, 1986.

Geyer, D. *The Russian Revolution*. Oxford, 1987.

Gleason, A. *European and Muscovite: Ivan Kireyevsky and the Origins of Slavophilism*. Cambridge, Mass., 1972.

Hamilton, G. H. *The Art and Architecture of Russia.* London, 1976.

Hellie, R., ed. *Ivan the Terrible: A Quarcentenary Celebration of his Death.* Irvine, 1967.

Hughes, L. *Sophia Regent of Russia, Ambitious and Daring Above her Sex.* New Haven, 1990.

Johnson, R. E. *Peasant and Proletarian: The Working Class of Moscow in the Late Nineteenth Century.* Leicester, 1979.

Jones, W. G. *Nikolay Novikov: Enlightener of Russia.* Cambridge, 1984.

Josselson, M. and Josselson, D. *The Commander: A Life of Barclay de Tolly.* Oxford, 1980.

Kahan, A. *Russian Economic History: The Nineteenth Century.* Chicago, 1989.

Kaiser, D. H., ed. *The Workers' Revolution in Russia 1919: The View from Below.* Cambridge, 1988.

Kaplan, H. H. *Russia and the Outbreak of the Seven Years' War.*

Keep, J. L. H. *Soldiers of the Tsar: Russian Army and Society, 1462-1874.* Oxford, 1985.

Kennett, A. and Kennett, V. *The Palaces of Leningrad.* London, 1984.

Kimerling Wirtschafter, E. *From Serf to Russian Soldier.* Princeton, 1990.

Kjetsaa, G. *Fyodor Dostoyevsky: A Writer's Life.* London, 1988.

Kochan, L. *Russia in Revolution, 1890-1918.* London, 1970.

Kochan, L. *The Making of Modern Russia.* London, 1973.

Kopelev, L. *The Education of a True Believer.* New York, 1980.

Lang, D. M. *The First Russian Radical: Alexander Radishchev.* London, 1959.

Leatherbarrow, W. J. and Offord, D. C. *A Documentary History of Russian Thought.* Michigan, 1987.

Longworth, P. *Alexis, Tsar of All the Russias.* London, 1984.

McConnell, A. *A Russian Philosopher: Alexander Radishchev.* The Hague, 1964.

McKay, J. P. *Pioneers for Profit: Foreign Entrepreneurship and Russian Industrialization, 1885-1913.* Chicago, 1970.

Madariaga, I. de. *Catherine the Great of Russia: A Short History.* New Haven, 1990.

Madariaga, I. de. *Russia in the Age of Catherine the Great.* London, 1981.

Mamonova, T. *Women and Russia.* London, 1984.

Mandelstam, O. *Selected Essays.* Texas, 1977.

Marchioness of Londonderry and Hyde, H. M., eds. *The Russian Journals of Martha and Catherine Wilmot.* London, 1934.

Markov, V. *Russian Futurism: A History.* Berkeley, 1968.

Marsden, C. *Palmyra of the North: First Days of St Petersburg.* London, 1942.

Massie, R. K. *Peter the Great: His Life and World.* London, 1981.

Mazour, A. *The First Russian Revolution 1825: The Decembrist Movement.* Stanford, 1964.

Mochulsky, K. *Dostoyevsky: His Life and Work.* Princeton, 1967.

Nicolson, H. *The Congress of Vienna: A Study in Allied Unity: 1812-1822.* London, 1989.

O'Meara, P. *J. K. F. Ryleev: A Political Biography of the Decembrist Poet.* Princeton, 1984.

The Oxford Companion to Gardens. Oxford, 1986.

Palmer, A. *Alexander I: Tsar of War and Peace.* 1974.

Palmer, A. *Russia in War and Peace*. 1972.

Papmehl, K. *Freedom of Expression in Eighteenth Century Russia*. The Hague, 1971.

Parkinson, J. *A Tour of Russia, Siberia and the Crimea, 1792-1794*. London, 1974.

Peace, R. *Dostoyevsky: An Examination of the Major Novels*. Cambridge, 1971.

Peterson, R., trans. *The Russian Symbolists: An Anthology of Plays and Critical Texts*. Ann Arbor, Michigan, 1986.

Pushkin, A. *The Captain's Daughter*. London, 1969.

Rabinowitch, A. *The Bolsheviks Come to Power: The Revolution of 1917 in Petrograd*. New York, 1976.

Raeff, M. *Origins of the Russian Intelligentsia*. New York and London, 1966.

Raeff, M., ed. *The Decembrist Movement*. Englewood Cliffs, 1966.

Raeff, M. *The Well-Ordered Police State: Social and Institutional Change Through Law in the Germanies and Russia, 1760-1800*. New Haven, 1983.

Ragsdale, H., ed. *Paul I: A Reassessment of his Life and Reign*. Pittsburg, 1979.

Riasanovsky, N. V. *A History of Russia*. Oxford and New York, 1984.

Riasanovsky, N. V. *A Parting of Ways: Government and the Educated Public in Russia, 1801-1855*. Oxford, 1977.

Richardson, W. *Zolotoe Runo and Russian Modernism: 1905-1910*. Ann Arbor, Michigan, 1986.

Rogger, H. *Jewish Policies and Right-Wing Politics in Imperial Russia*. London, 1986.

Schapiro, L. *1917: The Russian Revolution and the Origins of Present-Day Communism*. 1984.

Schapiro, L. *Russian Studies*. London, 1986.

Scott, J. *Behind the Urals*. Indiana, 1989.

Segel, H. B., ed. *The Literature of Eighteenth Century Russia*. New York, 1967.

Shcherbatov, M. M. *On the Corruption of Morals in Russia*. Cambridge, 1969.

Shukman, H., ed. *The Blackwell Encyclopedia of the Russian Revolution*. Oxford and New York, 1988.

Sked, A., ed. *Europe's Balance of Power, 1815-1848*. 1979.

Smith, S. A. *Red Petrograd: Revolution in the Factories, 1917-1918*. Cambridge, 1983.

Stites, R. *The Women's Liberation Movement in Russia, 1860-1930*. Princeton, 1978.

Sutherland, C. *The Princess of Siberia*. London, 1984.

Tikhomirov, M. *The Towns of Ancient Rus*. Moscow, 1959.

Trotsky, L. *1905*. New York, 1971.

Walicki, A. *A History of Russian Thought from the Enlightenment to Marxism*. Oxford, 1980.

Walicki, A. *The Slavophile Controversy*. Oxford, 1975.

Webster, C. *The Congress of Vienna*. London, 1934.

Westwood, J. N. *Endurance and Endeavour: Russian History 1812-1986*. Oxford, 1987.

Williams, R. C. *Artists in Revolution: Portraits of the Russian Avantgarde, 1905-1925*. Bloomington, 1977.

Wolfe, B. *Three Who Made a Revolution*. New York, 1948.

Sources

Part 1

Primary Chronicle, (anon.), eds. V. P. Adrianova-Peretts and D. S. Likhachev in *Povest'vremenykh letopis*, Akademia Nauk Soiuza Sovetskikh Sotsialisticheskikh Respublik, Moscow, 1950. Extracts

Emperor Maurice, *Strategicon*, ed. G. Vernadsky in *A Source Book for Russian History from Early Times to 1917*, Yale University Press, New Haven and London, 1972. Extracts.

Ibn Rusta, *On the Russians, c. 903–913*, Ibid. Extracts.

Constantine Porphyrogenitus, *De Administrando Imperio*, Ibid. Extracts.

Part 2

Primary Chronicle, op. cit. Extracts.

Patericon, (anon.), Kiev, 13th century. Extracts.

The Legend of the Princes of Vladimir, (anon.), 16th century. Extracts.

Vladimir II Monomakh, *Testament* (or *Instruction*), 12th century. Extracts.

Sadko, (anon.), in *Pesni, sobrannye P. N. Rybnikovym*, Moscow, 1861. Extracts.

The First Novgorod Chronicle, (anon.), in

Novgorodskaia pervaia letopis, AN SSSR, Moscow, 1950. Extracts.

Typography Chronicle, (anon.), Vol. 24, Petrograd, 1921. Extracts.

The Lay of Igor's Campaign (anon.), trans. Dimitri Obolensky, in *The Penguin Book of Russian Verse*, Penguin. Extracts.

The Life of Prince Alexander Nevsky in *Pamyatniki drevney pismennoisti i iskusstya*, Vol. CLXXX, Moscow. Extracts.

Part 3

Sofony of Ryazan, *Zadonshchina*, 14th century. Extracts.

Yepifany (Epiphanius) the Wise, *The Life of St Sergius of Radonezh, c. 1392–1417*. Extracts.

The First Novgorod Chronicle, op. cit. Extracts.

Yepifany (Epiphanius) the Wise, *The Life of St Stephen of Perm*, ed. V. Druzhinin in *Zhitie sv. Stefana, yepiskopa Permskogo*, St Petersburg, 1897. Extracts.

The Third Will of the Grand Prince Vasily Dmitryevich, c. 1423. Extracts.

Nikon Chronicle, (anon.), Vols. 9–14, St Petersburg, 1862–1910. Extracts.

Moscow Compilation, (anon.), Vol. 25, Moscow and Leningrad, 1949. Extracts.

Sophia Chronicle, (anon.), Vols. 5–6, St Petersburg, 1853. Extracts.

Filofey, *Epistle to Vasily III*, c. 1520. Extracts.

Nikon Chronicle, op. cit. Extracts.

Ivan IV, *Law Code*, 1550. Extracts.

Prince A. M. Kurbsky and Tsar Ivan IV of Russia, *Correspondence*, 1564–1579. Extracts.

Richard Chancellor, *On Muscovy, 1553* in *A Source Book for Russian History from Early Times to 1917*, op. cit. Extracts.

Giles Fletcher, *Of the Russe Commonwealth*, Ibid. Extracts.

Yermak the Cossack, Conqueror of Siberia, (anon.), in V. Miller, *Istoricheskie pesni russkogo naroda, XVI–XVII vv*, Petrograd, 1915. Extracts.

Part 4

Nikon Chronicle, op. cit. Extracts.

Richard James, *Notebook*, ms. in Bodleian Library, 1619. Extracts.

Avraamy Palitsyn, *Skazanie Avraamiia Palitsyna*, AW SSSR, Moscow, 1955. Extracts.

"J.F.", *A Brief Historical Relation of the Empire of Russia*, early 17th century. Extracts.

Tsar Mikhail, *Decree on runaway peasants, 1634–5*. Extracts.

Paul of Aleppo, *Travels of Macarius*. Extracts.

Archpriest Avvakum, *Life*, 1660s. Extracts.

Life of the Boyarina Morozova, Princess Urosova and Marya Danilova, ed. N. Subbotin in *Materialy diya istorii raskola*, Moscow, 1886. Extracts.

Moscow Chronicle, op. cit. Extracts.

Ludwig Fabricius, *Account of the Razin Rebellion, 1667–71*. Extracts.

Part 5

Dvorsovye Razriady (Court Records), Vol. 4, *(1676–1701)*, St Petersburg, 1885. Extracts.

Andrey Matveyev, *Zapiski* in *Russian Memoir Series, No. 27: St Petersburg, 1941*, Oriental Research Partners. Extracts.

Heinrich Butenant, *Warhaftiger Relation*, ed. N. G. Ustrialov in *Istoriia tsarstvovovaniia Petra Velikogo*, Vol. I, St Petersburg, 1858. Extracts.

Credential of the Russian Ambassador Vasily Postnikov. Extracts.

Georg Adam Schleissing, *Description of Moscow*, c. 1687. Extracts.

Foy de la Neuville, *Recit de mon Voyage*, ms. in Bibliothèque Nationale, 1690. Extracts.

Patrick Gordon, *Diary*, Aberdeen, 1858. Extracts.

Patriarch Joachim, *Testament* in *Istoriia tsarstvovovaniia Petra Velikogo*, op. cit., Vol. II. Extracts.

Bishop Burnet, *History of His Own Time*, Clarendon Press, 1823. Extracts.

Johannes Georg Korb, *Diary of an Austrian Secretary of Legation*, trans. and ed. Count Macdonnell, London, 1863. Extracts.

Peter I, *Decrees on Western dress and shaving*, 1701 and 1705, in *Polnoe Sobranie Zakanov Imperii. 1649–1913*, 1st series. Extracts.

Peter I, *Three decrees on the building of St Petersburg*, 1714. Extracts.

Peter I, *Order on the eve of the battle of Poltava*, 27 June, 1709. Extracts.

Peter I, *Edict on Agricultural Methods*, 11 May, 1721. Extracts.

Peter I, *Preamble to the General Regulation*, 1720. Extracts.

Peter I, *Table of Ranks*, 1722. Extracts.

The Letters of Peter and Alexis, in N. Ustrialov, *Istoriia tsarstroviianiia Petra Velikogo*, Vol. 6, St Petersburg, 1858–63. Extracts.

Manifesto depriving Alexis of succession, 3 February, 1718, Ibid. Extracts.

Feofan Prokopovich, *Funeral Oration to Peter I*, 1725. Extracts.

Staehlin-Storcksburg, Jacob von, *Original Anecdotes of Peter the Great*, London, 1788. Extracts.

Alexander Gordon, *History of Peter the Great, Emperor of Russia*, Aberdeen, 1755. Extracts.

James Keith, *A Fragment of a Memoir of James Keith written by Himself, 1714–1734*, Edinburgh, 1843. Extracts.

The conditions of Anne's accession to the throne, 1730, ed. L. Vesdrovnyi in *Khrestomatiia po istorii SSSR*, VVII, vek, 1963. Extracts.

La Messelière, *Journey to St Petersburg*, Paris, 1803. Extracts.

Catherine II, *Memoir*. Extracts.

Catherine II, *Manifesto on the freedom of the nobility*, 18 February, 1762. Extracts.

Aleksey Grigorovich Orlov, *Letter to Catherine II*, 1762. Extracts.

Catherine II, *Nakaz*, 1767. Extracts.

Louis-Philippe, Comte de Ségur, *Memoirs and Recollections*. Extracts.

Catherine II, *National School Statute*, 1986. Extracts.

The Reading Mercury, 17 September, 1770. Extracts.

Oxford Gazette, 17 September, 1770. Extracts.

Correspondence between Catherine and Potemkin, 1774–5.

Catherine II, *Public pronouncements on the partition of Poland*, 1773, 1793, 1783. Extracts.

A. Ya. Poyonev, *On the Serf Condition of the Peasants*, c. 1768. Extracts.

Folk song, (anon.), 18th century. Extracts.

Pugachev, *Edict to the Urals, 1 October, 1773*, eds. L. G. Brestrovyni and B. B. Kafengauz in

Khrestomatiia po istorii SSSR, XVII, Moscow, 1963. Extracts.

Pugachev, *Edict to the Peasants, 31 July, 1774*, Ibid. Extracts.

Catherine II, *Manifesto on the revolt of the Cossack Pugachev and on the measures taken for the elimination of this miscreant*, 23 December, 1773. Extracts.

Andrey Bolotov, *Memoirs* in *Khrestomatiia po istorii SSSR*, op. cit., XVIII. Extracts.

Catherine II, *Charter of the Rights, Freedoms and Privileges of the Noble Russian Dvoryanstvo*, 1785. Extracts.

Prince M. M. Shcherbatov, *On the Corruption of Morals in Russia*, 1858. Extracts.

Alexander Radishchev, *Journey from St Petersburg to Moscow*, 1790. Extracts.

Catherine II, *Notes on Radishchev's Journey*, ed. Osip Maksimovich Bodyansky in *Chetniya*, LIV, 1865. Extracts.

Catherine II, *Decree on the breaking off of relations with revolutionary France*, 8 February, 1793. Extracts.

Vasily Popov, *Conversation with Alexander II*. Extracts.

Paul I, *Decree on the succession to the imperial throne, 5 April, 1797* in *Polnoe Sobranie Zakanov Rossiiskoi Imperii. 1649–1913*, op. cit. Extracts.

General Benningsen, *Memoirs*, comp. L. Kelly in *St. Petersburg, a Traveller's Companion*, London, 1981. Extracts.

Madame de Stael, *Ten Years' Exile*, London, 1821. Extracts.

Philippe-Paul, Comte de Ségur, *La Campagne de Russie*. Extracts.

Alexander I, *Order to the Russian troops about to enter French Territory*, 25 December, 1813. Extracts.

Alexander I, *Holy Alliance*, 1815, Extracts.

Pavel Pestel, *Pravda Russkaia*, 1825. Extracts.

Prince Sergei Trubetskoy, *Decembrists' Manifesto*, c. 1825. Extracts.

Baron Andrey Rozen, *Memoirs of December 14 Revolt*. Extracts.

Kondraty Ryleyev, *Last Poem*, 6 June, 1826. Extracts.

Part 6

Marquis de Custine, *La Russie en 1839*. Extracts.

Alexander Herzen, *Letter to Jules Michelet*, September 1851. Extracts.

Konstantin Sergeyevich Askakov, *Memorandum to Alexander II*, 1855. Extracts.

Vissarion Belinsky, *Letter to N. V. Gogol, July 1847* in *Polnoe sobranie sochinenii*, Vol. X, Moscow, 1956. Extracts.

N. V. Gogol, *Selected Passages from Correspondence with Friends*. Extracts.

Ivan Turgenev, *Huntsman's Sketches*, 1847–51. Extracts.

Materials for the geography and statistics of Russia collected by Officers of the General Staff. Ryazan Province, 1860. Extracts.

William Howard Russell, in *The Times*, 13 January, 1855. Extracts.

Alexander II, *Address to Moscow representatives of the nobility, 30 March, 1856*, comp. S. S. Dmitriev in *Khrestomatiia po istorii SSSR 1861–1917*. Extracts.

Alexander II, *Manifesto on the release of the peasants from bondage*, 19 February, 1861, Ibid. Extracts.

Acquisition of ownership by the peasants and payments made by them. Ibid. Extracts.

Petition from the landowners of Tver, 1862, Ibid. Extracts.

Official record of the peasant riots in Bezdna, 1861, Ibid. Extracts.

N. A. Kyrlov, *Eye-witness account of revolt, April 1861*, Ibid. Extracts.

Alexander Herzen, *The Bell*, Ibid. Extracts.

Donald Mackenzie Wallace, *Russia*, Cassell & Co, London, 1905. Extracts.

Narodnaya Volya, Manifesto to the Workers of Russia, 13 March, 1881. Extracts.

Narodnaya Volya, Open letter to Alexander III, 23 March, 1881. Extracts.

Alexander III, *Proclamation*, 11 May, 1881. Extracts.

Kontantin Probedonostev, *Letter to Alexander III*, 6 March, 1881. Extracts.

Maria Tsebrikova, *Letter to Alexander III*, March, 1881. Extracts.

Arnold White, in *Contemporary Review*, May, 1892. Extracts.

N. P. Ignatyev, *Memorandum to Alexander III*. Extracts.

Minutes of the State Council debate on the factory-labour law, Litvinov-Falinskii, 61, 1886. Extracts.

L. Katerina, *Report on the health of women factory workers to the zemstvo*, Kostroma, 1913. Extracts.

V. I. Gurko, *Features and Figures of the Past, Government and Opinion in the Reign of Nicholas II*, Stanford University Press, 1939. Extracts.

Nicholas II, *Accession speech*, 1894. Extracts.

Report on the industrial crisis in *Syn Otechestva (Son of the Fatherland)*, 1900. Extracts.

Assembly of Russian Factory Workers, *Petition to the Tsar*, 9 January, 1905. Extracts.

Rabut, *Report on the strike movement*, October 1905. Extracts.

Nicholas II, *Manifesto of 17 October, 1905*, in *Polnoe sobranie zakonov*, Vol. XXV, Part II. Extracts.

Bulletin of the Soviet Workers' Deputies, 20 October 1905. Extracts.

Maurice Baring, in *Morning Post*, May 1906. Extracts.

Peter Stolypin, *Speech to the duma Stenograficheskie Otchety*, St Petersburg, 10 May 1907. Extracts.

V. I. Gurko, in Maria Petrovna von Bock, *Vospominaniia o moem ottse, P. A. Stolypine*, Chekov Publishing House of the East European Fund, New York. Extracts.

Nicholas II, *Letter to his mother*, 1911. Extracts.

Government report on strikes, October 1913. Extracts.

P. N. Durnovo, *Memorandum to Nicholas II*, 14 February, 1914. Extracts.

Maurice Paléologue, *An Ambassador's Memoirs, 1914-1917*. Extracts.

M. V. Rodzianko, *Audience with Nicholas II*, March, 1916. Extracts.

Okhrana Section, *Memorandum to precinct superintendents*, 24 February, 1917. Extracts.

Part 7

Sergei Msistlavsky, *Five Days Which Transformed Russia*, 1923. Extracts.

N. de Basily, *Diplomat of Imperial Russia, 1903-1917: Memoirs*. Extracts.

Mikhail Aleksandrovich, *Proclamation*. 3 March, 1917. Extracts.

N. N. Sukhanov, *The Russian Revolution 1917*, London and New York, 1955. Extracts.

Leon Trotsky, *The History of the Russian Revolution*. New York, 1932-57. Extracts.

V. I. Lenin, *April Theses*, 1917. Extracts.

Viktor Chernov, *Description of Lenin* in *Delo Naroda*, *No. 26*, 16 April, 1917. Extracts.

Saratov Province Report in TsGANKh, f. 478, op. 1, d. 202, II.7-8. Extracts.

M. Martynov, *Agrarnoe dvizhenie v 1917 godu po dokumentam Glavnogo Zemel'nogo Komiteta* in KA, XIV, 1926, 218. Extracts.

V. I. Lenin, *Letter to Central Committee*, 29 September, 1917. Extracts.

John Reed, *Scenes at the Smolny Institute, 24 October, 1917*, ed. R. Pethybridge in *Witnesses to the Russian Revolution*, George Allen and Unwin, 1964. Extracts.

S. L. Maslov, *Statement on the taking of the Winter Palace* in *Delo Naroda*, No. 193, 11 November, 1917. Extracts.

Leon Trotsky, *Address on the seizing of power by the Bolsheviks*, ed. N. N. Sukhanov in *The Russian Revolution, 1917*, op. cit. Extracts.

Ivan Grigoreyevich Fokke, *Na stsene i sa kulisami brestskoi tragikomedii*, ed. I. V. Hessen in *Arkhiv Russkoi Revolutsii*, XX, Berlin, 1925-34. Extracts.

Index

Page numbers in italic refer to illustrations and/or captions

A

Aberdeen, Lord 278, 279
Academy of Arts 184, 346
Academy of Sciences 190, 191
Agrippina, Grand Princess 83
Airey, Brigadier 280
Akhmetevo 294
Aksakov, Konstantin 270, 271
Akselrod, Pavel 373
Alexander, Emperor 32
Alexander, Prince of Novgorod 84,
    85
Alexander I, Emperor *237, 238, 255,*
    257
  accession 243
  and his father's assassination 243
  and St Petersburg 163
  death 256, 262
  education 254
  education of 237
  manifesto (1812) 248-50
  religious beliefs 255, 256
Alexander II, Emperor *286,* 287-305,
    290-1, 306
  and Crimean War 279, 287
  and emancipation of serfs 274,
    287, 288, 282-3
  and reforms 264, 265, 287, 298,
    300, 302
  assassination 287, 304
Alexander III, Emperor 304, *306,*

307, 317
Alexander Column 163
Alexander Nevsky 76, 79, 84
Alexander Nevsky Monastery 161
Alexandra, Empress 338
Alexandra Fyodorovna, Empress 268,
    269
Alexis Mikhailovich, Tsar 105, 127,
    130, 134, 135, 139
Alexis, Romanov 341
Alexis, St 87
Alexis, Tsarevich 151, 170-84
All Saints Bridge (Moscow) *125*
Alma river 278
Amsterdam 152, 156, 174
Anastasius of Cherson 56
Andrew, St 24
Andrey, Prince 98
Andrey Bogoliubsky, Prince 71
Andrey the Younger 98
Andronyev Monastery 132
Anna, Princess of Byzantium 52
Anna, Empress 179, 180-4, *181*
Antian tribes 19
anti-semitism 312-16
Antony, St 64
Antropov, Aleksey 346
appanage 97
Apraksin, Count 296
Arabs 19, 20, 28
Arakcheyev, Count Alexis 256, 260
Archangel 176

architecture 145, 159, 161, 163
Argunov, Ivan 346
Arkady, Bishop 72
Armenians 310, 311
Askold, Prince 24, 28, 32
Assembly of Russian Factory
    Workers 322
Astrakhan 107, 116
Augustus II, King 165
Austria 165, 192, 206, 254
Avvakum, Archpriest 105, 127, 132-4
Azerbaijanis 311
Azov 156

B

Babel, Tower of 19, *19*
Bagration, Prince 244
Bakst, Leon 350, 351, *351,* 352
Bakunin, Captain Ilya 257
Balaclava 278
Balakirev, Mikhail 353
Balanchine, George 352
Balkans 278, 281
Ballets Russes 345, 351, 352
Baltic Sea *164,* 169
Baltic States 152, 160, 165, 310
bank notes *335*
Baring, Maurice 265, 329
baroque style 355, 356
barshchina (labour dues) 300

Basil, Emperor 50
Batenin, Sergey 357
Batu Khan 80, 82, 83, 84, 85
Beccaria, Cesare 225
Belayev, General 237-8
Belgorod 48, 56
Belinsky, Vissarion 190, 265, 271, 272
Bell, The 297
Belorussians 310
Bennigsen, General 240, 241
Benois, Alexandre 352
Berestovo 48, 56, 64
Berlin 185, 192
Bessarabia 278
Bestuzhev, Count Aleksey 183
Bestuzhev, Count M. A. 257
Bestuzhev-Marlinsky, Alexander 262
Bestuzhev-Riumin, Mikhail 262
Bezdna 312-17
birchbark scrolls 29
Birgir, Earl 84
Biron, Ernst Juhann 183
Bityagovsky, Danilko 120
Bityagovsky, Mikhail 120
'Black Hundred' organization 330
Black Sea 199
Blackstone, Sir William 205
Bloody Sunday 324-5, 326-7
Boards of Social Welfare 224
Bogoliubsky, Prince Andrey 72, 79
Bogrov, Dmitry 335, 336
Bolotov, Andrey 220
Bolsheviks
    and Lenin 371
    and Provisional Government 366
    dictatorship consolidated 363
    Land Decree 369
    Petrograd uprisings 370
    revolutionary demands 328
    seize news agency 372
Boris, Prince, son of Vladimir I 48, 56, 59, *59*, 60
Boris and Gleb, Church of (Smyadino) 72
Boris Godunov (Mussorgsky) 120
Borodin, Alexander 74, 353-5, 358
Borodino 244
Borovitorsky, Vladimir 346

Brest-Litovsk 376, 377
Bryullov, Karl 347
Bulgaria 20
Bulgars 20, 41, 48
Burnet, Gilbert 153
Butenant, Heinrich 139
byliny 69
Byzantium 28, 31, 34, 48, 56

C

Cadet Party 324, 331
Calvinist 148
Cameron, Charles 163
Cardigan, Lord 280, 284
Caspian Sea 169
Castlereagh, Viscount 254
Catherine I, Empress 179
Catherine II, Empress *198*, 199-237, *226*, *237*
    achievements 200-1
    and boundaries *208-9*
    and education 202-4, 225
    and local administration 220
    and Pugachev 218-20
    and the Enlightenment 201
    and St Petersburg 163
    and torture 225, 233
    arrival in Russia 193
    as reformer 224-5
    as ruler 232-3
    criticisms of 224
    death 237
    description 202, 204
    foreign policy successes 199, 208-9
    French influence 185
    German birth 199
    Great Instruction 233
    husband deposed 195, 205
    Instructions 201, 202
    interest in literature 205
    letter to Potyomkin 204
    lovers 204-5
    marriage 193, 195
    reaction to French Revolution 236
    reading 195
    spiritual kinship with Peter I 199
Catherine, Princess 179

Catherine Palace 162, 185, *186*
Catholics 144, 147, 148, 149
Chaadayev, Pyotr 265, 274
Chaliapin, Fyodor 351, 352
Chancellor, Richard 112-14
Charles XII, King 165
Charles of Austria, Emperor 172
Chekhov, Anton 265, 275, 307, 345, *347*, 348
Chelyadin, Ivan Andreyevich 100
Chernigov 20
Chernyshev, Ivan 232
Chernyshev, Zakhar 232
Chernyshevksy, Nikolay 274
Cherson 48, 50, 52
Cherven 61
Chester, Sir William 112
Chichelev, Ivan *358*
children, attitude to 110
'cipher schools' 156
civil war 361
collectivization 361
Congress of Vienna 254
Constantine Monomachus, Emperor 67
Constantine Pavlovich, Grand Duke *257*
Constantinople 20, 24, 28, 32, 33, 35, 40, 44, 67, 77, 87, 95, 278
Constituent Assembly 376
Copenhagen 165
corruption 200
Cossacks 117, 165
Courland 160, 183
Coxe, Reverend William 162-3
Crimea 139, 144, 199, 206
Crimean War 264, 267, 275, 278-85
Cui, Tsesar 353-5
currency 93
Custine, Marquis de 265, 268-9
Cyrillic script *57*

D

Dadiani, Prince 294
Daniil, Prince of Volynia 84
Daniil, Archpriest 132
Danilo Dmitrievich, Prince 98

Danube River 20, 36
death rate 264
Decembrists 256, 260-3, 264
Deisis of Zvenigorod *102*
Denmark 113, 165
Deptford 153, *154-5*, 156, 174
Derevlyanins 31, 36, 38
Diaghilev, Sergei 345, 350-2, *351*
Diderot, Denis 202
Dimitri Donskoy, Prince 77, 87
Dimitri False 104, 119, 121, 122, 123, 124
Dimitri Ivanovich, Grand Prince 88, 89, *89*, 90, *90*
Dimitri Ivanovich, Tsarevich 116, 120, 122
Dimitri Mikhailovich Pozharsky, Prince 119
diplomacy 134, 142
Dir, Prince 24, 28, 32
Dmitry Pavlovich, Grand Duke 340
Dnepr River 19, 20, 24, 52, 60, 89
Dolgoruky, Prince Aleksey 179, 180
Dolgoruky, Prince Vasily 182
Dolmatov, Tretyak 100
Don River 89
Dormition Cathedral (Moscow) 109, 140, *146*
Dorpat 165
Dostoyevsky, Fyodor 265, 273, 274, 275, 345, 350
duma 265, 319, 329, 331, 332, 334, 363, 365
Durnovo, I. N. 334, 336-7

E

East India Company 152
education 156, 300
Education Statute (1706) 203-4
Edward III, King 114
Ekaterinburg 377
Elizabeth I, Empress 178
    accession 179, 183
    death 192
    description 184-5, 188
    German influence 185
    lavishness 183, 185

Elizabeth I, Queen 111, 113
embroidery 131
Encyclopédie 225
Enlightenment, the 191, 224, 260
Estonia 24, 60, 84, 160, 165, 310
etiquette 166
Evdokia Lopukhina 170
Evelyn, John 156, 174
Evpraksia, Princess 82

F

Fabergé, Peter Carl 345, *345*, *356*, 358
Fabricius, Ludwig 135
Falconet, Etienne 163
family 320
famine 80, 121, 307, 369
Farquharson, Henry 156
Fathers and Sons (Turgenev) 274
Fedotov, Pavel 347
Felbiger, Abbot 225
Feodosy, St 64
Feofil, Archbishop elect 98
Filaret, Metropolitan 127, 128
Filipp, Metropolitan 96
Filofey, Monk 95, 100
finance 93
Finland 165
Finnish Gulf 158, 165
First Novgorod Chronicle, The 70, 80, 84
Fletcher, Giles 114
Fokine, Michel 352
Fokke, Lieutenant-Colonel I. K. 376
foremen 323
France 182, 183, 192, 278
Francis I, Emperor 254
Frank, Semyon 265
Frederick II, King (Frederick the Great) 185, 192, 197, 224, 225
Frederick IV, King 165
Frederick William II, King 207
Frederick William III, King 254
Free Economic Society 210
Freitburg 190
French Revolution 228, 236
furniture 355, 356

Fyodor, Prince of Ryazan 82
Fyodor I, Tsar 116, 119, 120
Fyodor III, Tsar *138*, 139, *139*, 140, 146
Fyodor Davydovich, Prince 98
Fyodor Ivanovich *145*
Fyodor Nikitich 122, 128

G

Galicia 28, 338
Gapon, Father 322
Gardner, Franz 357
George I, King 165
George II, King 152
Georgians 310, 311
Gerasim, Bishop 90
German residents 145
Germany 79
Germogen, Patriarch 125
glass *355*, 357
Glazunov, Alexander 352
Gleb, Prince, son of Vladimir I 48, 59, *59*, 60
Glinka, Mikhail 353, *353*
Godunov, Tsar Boris 104, *118*, 119, 120, 121, *121*, 122
Gogol, Nikolai 273, 275
Golden Charter 287
Golden Horde 76, 79, *81*, 85, 90, 92
Golitsyn, Alexander 254
Golitsyn, Prince Dmitry Mikhaylovich 180
Golitsyn, Prince Vasily 139, 144, 145, 146, 148, 151, 180
Golovkin, Count 180
Goncharov, Ivan 275
Gontcharova, Natalia 352
Gordon, General Patrick 148
Gorky, Maxim 373
Grazhdanin 320
Great Britain 254, 278
Great Schism 105
'Greek fire' 34, *36*
Greeks 19, 32, 34, 36, 40, 44
Green Book 261
Greenwich 174

Guchkov, A. I. 336
Gurko, V. I. 334
Gustavus II Adolphus 165
Gyurgy, Prince 72

H

habeas corpus 224
Harpe, Frédéric de La 254
Hart, Sir William 112
Hastings, Lady Mary 113
Herzen, Alexander 265, 269, 271,
    274, 297
Hilarion, Metropolitan 29, 64
Holland 152, 156, 200
Holstein 165
Holstein, Duchess of 193
Holstein-Gotthorp, Duke of 184
Holstein-Gotthorp, Duke Peter of 204
Holy Alliance 254-5
Honourable Mirror of Youth 166
Hungary 267

I

Iasnaya Poliana *349*
Ice, Battle of the 84
icons 101, 145, 146, 149
Ignatyev, N. P. 313
Igor, Prince 24, *31*, 32, 34, 36, *37*
Igor, Prince 65, 72
Igor of Novgorod-Seversk 72, 74, 75,
    75
Ilmen, Lake 98
Image of Christ Not Made by Hands,
    Church of the 140
Imperial Porcelain Factory 357
India *281*
industrialization 264, 361
inflation 369
Ingria 165
Inkerman, Battle of 278
International Women's Day 343
Intercession of the Virgin, Church of
    146
Irkutsk 225
Iskorosten 36, 38

Ivan, Prince of Ryazan 82
Ivan III, Grand Prince (Ivan the
    Great) 77, *94*, 95-103
Ivan IV, Tsar (Ivan the Terrible) *106*,
    107-17
    adopts title 'tsar' 104, 107, 109,
        113
    coronation 109
    crown of *111*
    cruelty of 104
    writings of 104
Ivan V, Tsar 139, 141, 142, 151
Ivan VI, Emperor 183
Ivan Neronov, Archpriest 132
Ivan Obolensky, Prince 98
Ivanov, Alexander 346, *346*
Ivanovich, Tsaritsa Irena Fyodorovna
    120
Ivan Vasilyevich, Prince 96, 98
Izmaylovo 182
Izyaslav, Prince, son of Vladimir I 48
Izyaslav, Prince, son of Yaroslav the
    Wise 59, 65

J

James II, King 142
Japan 322
Jedisan 278
Jesuits 144, 212
Jewish people 307, 310, 312-16
Joachim, Archimandrate 134
Joachim, Patriarch 140, 148, *149*
Job, Patriarch 120
John of Poland, King 144
Jonas, Metropolitan 147
Joseph II, Emperor 224, 225

K

Kachalov, Mititka 120
Kakhovsky, Peter 262
Kalka, Battle of the 79
Kalka River 78
Kamenev, Lev 366, 376
Kanev 64
Kardis, Peace of 165

Karelia 165
Karsavina, Tamara 351
Kayala River 74, 75
Kazan 107, 109
Keith, James 180, 181
Kerensky, Alexander 370
Kexholm 165
Khabar, Ivan Vasilyevich 100
Kharkov 328
Khazar 20, 24, 40
Khotin 190
Kiev 20, 22, 23, 28-9, 31, 47, 61, 65,
    72, 73, 74, 79, *81*, 84, 139
Kipernsky, Orest 346
Kireyevsky, Ivan 271
Kirghiz 311
Kirill of Rostov 89
Kishkin, N. M. 372
Kneller, Sir Godfrey 147
Knoop, Herman 260
Koppenbrugge 152
Koppenstein, Herr 152
Krob, Johannes 157
Korolenko, Vladimir 274
Kostyantin, Mayor 71
Kremlin *53*, 87, *121*, 140, 141, *141*,
    147, *149*, 182, *242*
Krivichi 24, 32
Krüdener, Baroness von 255
Krylov, N. A. 294
Kuchum Khan 116
Kulaks 369
Kuliko Polo 87
Kulikovo 77, 88, 90
Kurbsky, Prince Andrey 104, 109-10,
    112, 113
Kurya, Prince 45
Kutuzov, Field-Marshal 244, 250
Kuznechikha 294

L

Ladoga 24, 71
Ladoga, Lake 70
land captains 317
language 57
Latvia 160, 310
Lavrentyevich, Astaska 116

Lay of Igor's Campaign 77
Lazar, Priest 134
Legislative Commission 232-3
Lenin (Vladimir Ilich Ulyanov) *362*,
        363-77, *373*
    and Brest-Litovsk 376-7
    and Social Democratic Workers'
        Party 320
    April Theses 366
    death 363
    emerges 372
    history 373
    inflexibility 368
    in hiding in Finland 370
Leo, Emperor 32, 33
Leopold II, Emperor 207
Lermontov, Mikhail 273, 274, *275*
Leskov, Nikolay 275
Letter to Gogol (Belinsky) 272
Levitsky, Dmitry 346
Lifar, Serge 352
Light Brigade 278
Lipensky, St Nikolai *103*
literacy 264
literature 274-5
Lithuania 77, 79, 87, 96, 104, 109,
        113, 128, 199, 310
Livonia 160, 165
local government 334
Łódź 320, 322
Lomonosov, Mikhail 188, 190-1, 346
London 142
Lopatin, G. Ya 353
Loris-Melikov, Count Mikhail
        Tariyelovich 308
Louis XV, King 185
Louis XVI, King 184, *234-5*
luboks 211
Lucan, Lord 280, 284
Lutherans 148
Lyubech 32

M

Macarius, Patriarch 134
Magnitsky, Leonty 156
Mal, Prince 36, 38
Maloiaroslavets 245

Mamay, Prince 88, 90
Marburg 190
Maria, Grand Princess 96
Martha, Tsaritsa 141
Martier, Marshal 243, 244
Martov, L. 320
Maslov, S. L. 372
Matveyev, Andrey 140, 141, 346
Maurice, Emperor 19
Mazepa, Ivan 165
Meletius, Patriarch 134
Mensheviks 328
Menshikov, Alexander 175, 179
Merya 32
Meshchersky, Prince V. P. 320
Messeliere, La 183
metalware 131, 357, 358
Method, the 345
Meternich, Prince 254, 255
Meyerhold, Usevolod 348
Michael III, Byzantine Emperor 20,
        24, 32
Michelet, Jules 269
Mighty Handful 353-5
Mikhail Aleksandrovic, Grand Duke
        364, 365
Mikhail Fyodorovich, Tsar *127*, 128,
        128, 129, 130
Mikhail of Chernigov, Prince 85
Mikhailovsky Palace 240
Miliukov, Pavel 265
Miloslavskaia, Maria 139, 140, 141
Minin, Kuzma 119
mir 129, 288
Miracle, Monastery of the 133, 134
Moldavia 278, *281*
Molostvov, Marshal 296
Monastery of the Caves (Kiev) 19,
        28, 64-5, 72
Mongols 79, 145 *see also* Golden
        Horde
Morning Post 329
Morozova (St Feodora) 134
Moscow 87, 90, 119, 124, 143, *143*,
        144, 145, 156, 161, *229*, 243-8,
        246-7, 323, 325, 345
Moscow Chronicle 134
Moscow University 179, 184, 188,
        191, 191-2, *191*

Mothe, J.-B. Vallin de la 163
Mount Elbras *43*
Mstislav, Prince, son of Vladimir I
        48, 59, 60, 61
Mstislav, Prince, son of Vladimir II
        Monomakh 68
Mstislav Andreyevich 72
Mstislav Izyaslavich, Prince 72
Mstislavsky, Sergei 364
Muraviev, Nikita 261
Muscovy Company 107, 113, 156
Musikilsky, Grigory 358
Mussorgsky, Modest 120, 121, 265,
        352, 353-5, *353*

N

Naples 172
Napoleon Bonaparte, Emperor 163,
        243, 244-5, *245*, 248, 249, *250*,
        254, 260
Napoleon III, Emperor 279
Narodnaya Volya 304, 305
Narva 165
Naryshkin, Ivan 141-2
Naryshkin, Lev 146
Naryshkina, Natalia, Tsaritsa 141,
        144
Naryshkins 140-2, 144, 146
Nationalist Party 334
nationality groups in Russia 16, 310-
        11
    German 310
    Lithuanian 245
    Polish 245, 310
Naval Academy 156
Nechayer, Sergei 265, 303
Nekrasov, Nikolai 275
Neophyte, Metropolitan 68
Nepryadva River 68
Nesterovsky, Colonel 257
Nestor, Monk 28-9
Neuville, Foy de la 144
Neva River 84, 151
new proletariat 323
Nicholas I, Emperor *266*, 267-85
    attempt to thwart accession
        thwarted 256

crushes revolt 267
death 279
description 267, 269, 270
foreign policy 276
Nicholas II, Emperor *318*, 319-43, *330-1, 333*
  abdication 364-5
  accession speech 320
  and police state 320
  coronation proclamation *321*
  description of Stolypin's assassination 335
  Fundamental Laws 331
  October Manifesto 328
  pressures for reform 319
  weakness 334
Nifont, Archbishop 72
Nightingale, Florence 279
Nijinsky, Vaslav 345, 351, 352
Nikitin, Ivan 346
Nikon, Abbot 64
Nikon Patriarch 127, 132, 133, *133*, 134, 135, 145
Nikon Chronicle 96, 109, 116, 120, 122, 123, 125
Nizhny Novgorod 84, 119
nobility, liberation of 217
Nolan, Captain 280, 284
Nöteborg 158
Novgorod 19, 20, 24, 32, 59, *70*, 72, 76, 77, 79, 95, 96, *108*, 119
Novodevichy Convent 155
Nystadt, Peace of (1721) 160, *164*, 165

O

Ob River 113
obrok 129, 300
obshchina 129
October Manifesto 324, 325
Octobrists 324, 334
'Old Believers' 105, 117, 127, 132, 134, 135
Oleg, Grand Prince 24, 28, *31*, 32, 33
Oleg, Prince, son of Svyatoslav 41, 47
Olga Romanova 335

Olga, Saint 31, 36, 38, 40, *41*, 44
opera 353
oprichniki 113, 114, 116
Orlov, Aleksey Grigoryevich 195
Orlov, Grigory 200, 204, 232
Ostermann, Count Heinrich 181, 183
Ostrovsky, Alexander 275
Otrepyev, Grishka 122
Ovsov, Andrey 358

P

Pahlen, Count 241
Painters' Brigade 346
painting 346
Paisius, Patriarch 134
Palace Square (St Petersburg) 163
Paléologue, Maurice 337, 338
Palitsyn, Avraamy 122
Palmerston, Lord 278, 279
Panshin 135
Parfany, Bishop 92
Paris 163, 250, 251
Paris, Treaty of (1856) 279
parsuna 146, 346
Patericon 64
Paul I, Emperor 239-43
  accession 239
  assassination 240-3
  paternity 193, 195, 204
  reaction against mother 240
  relations with mother 205
Paul of Aleppo, Deacon 132
Pavlova, Anna 351, 352, *352*
Pavlovsk Palace 167
Peasant Bank 332-4, *335*
peasants 300-1
  conscription and 369
  decree on runaways 129
  diet 277
Pechengs 36, 40, 41, 44, 47, 56, 60, 61, 80
Peipus, Lake 84, 85
People's Will 287
Pereyaslavets 41, 44, 45, 47
Permian 90, 92
Pesenniks 213
Pestel, Colonel Pavel 256, 261, 262,

263
Peter I, Emperor (Peter the Great) *150*, 151-77, *154-5, 171, 175*
  and agriculture 160
  and Alexis 170-4
  and education 156, 157
  becomes Emperor 151, 160
  condemns son to death 151, 171
  Decree of Assemblies 355
  dentistry 174
  descriptions 152, 174-5, 176, 177
  interest in ships 152, 156, 190
  named joint tsar 142
  parentage 139
  regiment of guards 176
  reorganization of ministries 166
  signature *170*
  taste for curious and grotesque 175
  western influences on 151, 156, 157, 161, 271, 355
  western visits 152, 153, 156
Peter II, Emperor 179, 180
Peter III, Emperor 179, 185, 188, 192-3, 195, 197
Peter and Paul, church of (St Petersburg) 158, 161
Peter-Paul fortress 160
Petrich 44
Petrograd 343, 363, 364, 365, *365*, 370, 372, 377 see also St Petersburg
Petrograd Soviet 365
Petrov 294, 296
Philip, Metropolitan 255
Platen, Countess 152
Plekhanov, Georgy 320, 373
Pleve, Vyacheslav Konstantinovich 322
Pobedonostsev, Konstantin 308, 320
pogroms 307, *312*, 313
Poland 60, 77, 113, 119, 124, 145, 165, 199, 206-7, 233, 252-3, 267, 301
Poland, Treaty of Eternal Peace with (1685) 139
Polar Star, The 262
Polotsk 48, 65
Poltava 151, 160, 165
Polyanins 24

Polyonov, A. Ya 210
Poniatowski, Stanislas Augustus 204
Popov, Aleksey 357
Popov, Vasily 237
popular arts 211-13
porcelain 357
Postnikov, Vasily 142
Potemkin, the battleship 329
Potemkin, Prince Grigory 204, *205*, 206, 232
Primary Chronicle 19, 20, 24, 28, 31, 32, 33, 40, 48, 52, 60, 61, 64, 65, 67, 68, 72
Privileges, Charter of 220-4
Proclamations, Place of 140
Prokopovich, Archbishop Feofan 174
Provincial Statute (1775) 220
Provisional Government 366, 372, 373
Prussia 160, 165, 185, 192, 200, 206, 254
Pskov 71, 76, 77, 95, 100
Pugachev, Emelyan Ivanovich 117, 199, *208-9*, 216-20, *219*
Purishkevich *340*, 343
Pushkin, Alexander 120, 191, 273, 284, 285, *348*, 349
Putivl 75
Pyotr Veliky, Prince 100

Q

Quarenghi, Giacomo 163

R

Rachmaninov, Sergey 345, 353, *353*
Radishchev, Alexander 199, 228, 227-36
Raglan, Lord 280, 284
rakes 160
Rambert, Marie 352
Rasputin, Grigori 319, 338, *340*, 340-1, 343
Rastrelli, Bartolomeo 163, 183, 185, 356

Razin, Stenka 135, *135*, 213
Razin, Stepan 117
Razumovsky, Aleksey 184
Razumovsky, Count Kyrill 232
Red Guard *377*
Red Square 140, 190
Reed, John 371-2
religion 49, 52-3, 132
Renaissance 145-7
repression 309
Revolution, of 1905 319, 323-5
    Bloody Sunday 324-5, 326-7
Revolution, of 1917 360-1, 364-77
Riga 165
Rimsky-Korsakov, Nikolay 69, 352, 353-5
Rinaldi, Antonio 163
Rodzianko, M. V. 338-40
Roerich, Nicolas 350, 352
Rogned, wife of Vladimir I 48
Rogvolod, ruler of Polotsk 48
Rokotov, Fyodor 346
romances 213
Romania 267
Romanov, Anastasius 113
Romanov family 122 *see also under names of members*
Romanus, Emperor 34, 36
Rosii, Karl 356
Rossi, Carlo 163
'Rossiya' 16
Rostislav, Prince 72
Rozen, Baron Andrey 257
Rubinstein, Anton 353
Rublyov, Andrey 87, *102*
Rus, land of 16-17, *21*, 22-3
    neighbours of 42-3
Russell, William Howard 265, 278, 280
Russia, boundaries of 16-17
    capitals of 271
    national character of 270
    origins of 18-19, 24
    population of 293, 300, 301
'Russian Empire' style 356
Russkaya pravda 261
Ryazan 77, 80, 82, 83
Ryleyev, Kondraty 262, 263, 274
Ryurik, Prince 24, *24*, *25*

S

Sadko 29, 69-70
St Basil's Cathedral (Moscow) 140
St Blaise, Church of (Novgorod) *299*
St George Monastery *62*
St Nicholas Cathedral 163
St Peter and St Paul prison 173
St Petersburg 151, 158-9, *158-9*, 161-3, *161*, *162*, *177*, *185*, 323, 324, 325, 328 *see also* Petrograd
Saint-Simon, Duke of 174
St Sophia (Kiev) *54-5*, 59, *63*
St Sophia (Novgorod) 64, 72, *99*
St Vladimir's Cathedral *47*
salt bag *131*
Saltykov, Sergei 193, 195
Samara 373
samovars 357
Santa Sophia (Constantinople) *39*
Saratov 323
saunas 122
Schleissing, Georg Adam 143
Scutari 278
scythes 160
Seagull 190
Sebastopol 278, 279, 285
Ségur, Louis-Philippe de 202
Ségur, Comte Philippe-Paul de 243, 248
Selected Passages from Correspondence with Friends 272-3
Senate Square (St Petersburg) *258-9*
serfdom 109, 113, 127, 129, 169, 227-8
    abolition of 260, 261, 276, 287, 288, 292-7 *see also following entry*
serfs 151, 199
    emancipation 210, 264
Serfs' Lament 213
Sergius, St 77, 87, 89, 90
Shchedrin, Silvester 347
Shcherbatov, Prince M. M. 221, 224, 227
Shuvalov, Countess of 184
Shuvalov, Alexander 184
Shuvalov, Ivan 184, 188, 190, 191

Shuvalov, Peter 184
Shuysky, Vasily 119, 123
Siberia 107, 116, *117*, 182
Sibir, Khan of 117
silversmiths 130-1
Sineus 24
Sinope 278
Slavonic-Greek-Latin Academy 144
Slavonic tribes 19
Slovenins 19, 24, 32
Smolensk 20, 32, 245
Smollett, Tobias 205
Smolny convent 162
Smolny Institute 202, 371-2, *377*
snuff-taking 357
Socialist Democratic Workers' Party
        320, 328
Social Revolutionary Party 320, 369
Solvychegodsk 146, 358
Sophia, Electress of Hanover 152
Sophia Alekseyevna (Regent) 139,
        140, 142, 144, 146, 151, 153,
        157, 175
Sophia Augusta Frederica *see*
        Catherine II
Sophia Chronicle 98
Sophia Dorothea, Princess 152
Sophia Palaologina 95, 107
Soviets, Congress of 371, 372
Soviets of Workers' Deputies 366
Spiridon, Archbishop 80, 84
Staël, Mme de 243
Stalin, Joseph
        and Provisional Government 366
        purges 361
Stanislawski (Konstantin Sergeivitch
        Alexeyev) 345, *348*
Stashkov, Roman 376
Stasov, Vasily 356
State Domains, Ministry of 300
steelware 358
Stefan, brother of St Sergius 89, 90
Stephen of Perm, St 77, 92
Stolypin, Peter 265, 319, 332, 334-5,
        336
Stratford, Viscount 278
Stravinsky, Igor *351*, 352
streltsy 113, 139, 140, 141, 142, 157,
        175

strikes 324, 325, 328
Stroganov family 117, 146, 162, 358
Strus, Pan 128
Sudislav 59
Summer Palace 161, 182, *183*
Svyatopolk, Prince 48, 59, 60
Svyatopolk II, Prince 67
Svyatoslav, Prince, son of Vladimir I
        36, 40, 44, 45, 48
Svyatoslav, Prince, son of Yaroslav
        the Wise 59, 61, 65
Svyatoslav Olgovich 71
Sweden 79, 84, 113, 151, 158, 160,
        165, 170, 185
Syn Otechestva 320

T

Table of Ranks 161, 166, 168, 169
*Tale of Bygone Years see Primary
        Chronicle*
Tartars 28, 76, 79, 80, *81*, 82, 84, 85,
        87, 88, 95, 104, 113, 139, 144,
        148, 165, 200, 311
Tatiana, Princess 335
Tauride Palace 329
Tauris Palace 207
taxation 157-8, 169, 316
Tchaikovsky, Peter 265, 345, 352-3,
        353
Tcherepnine, Alexander 352
Tchernaya river 285
tea 357
terrorism 320
Teutonic Knights 84
Theophanes 87
Third Section 320
Times, The 278, 280, 285
Tmitorokan 59
Todorsky, Bishop Simon 193
Toktamysk Khan 90
Tolly, Barclay de 254
Tolstoy, Count Dmitry 300
Tolstoy, Leo 265, 273, 274, 275, 307,
        345, 349, *349*
trade and tribute 26-7
Trans-Siberian Railway *315*
Trepov, V. E. 334

Trévise, duc de 244
Trinity Monastery 77
Tripole 65
Triumphal Arch 163
Tropinin, Vasily 346
Trotsky, Leon 323
Troubles, Time of 105, 119, 124
Trubetskoy, Prince Sergey 256, 262
Trudoviks 331
Trusevich, Senator 336
Truvor 24
tsar, title 104, 109
Tsarskoe Selo 162, 185, *187*, 188,
        189, 195, *347*
Tsebrikova, Marya 307, 308-9
Tula 358
Turgenev, Ivan 265, 273-6
Turkey 113, 139, 152, 190, 199, 217,
        276, 278
Tushino, Brigand of 125
Tver 76, 77, 87, 95, 163, 292
Typography Chronicle 84

U

Uglich 116, 120
Ukraine 165, 200
Ukrainians 310
Union of Liberation 324
Union of Salvation 260
Union of Towns 338
Union of Welfare 261
Union of *zemstva* 338
United Slavs, Society of 261
Ushakov, Simon 146
Ust-Vymm 92

V

Valois, Ninette de 352
Varangians (Vikings) 20, *21*, *22*, 24,
        31, 42
Vasilkov 262
Vasily, Grand Prince Vasilyevich 92,
        96
Vasily III, Grand Prince 77, 95, 98,
        100, *108*

Vasily IV, Tsar 123-5
Vedomosti 158
Veliky Ustyug 358
Velten 163
Venetsianov, Aleksey 346-7
Vepsa 24
Viborg 165
Vienna 172
Vikings *see* Varangians
Vinogradov, Dmitry 357
Vishnyakov, Ivan 346
Vitichev 20
Vladimir 79, *83*
Vladimir, Prince 71
Vladimir I, Prince (Vladimir the
    Great) *46*, 47-57, *49*
  and Cherson 50, 52
  and Pechenegs 56
  arrival in Novgorod 48
  baptism 50, 52
  becomes sole ruler 31
  death 56
  eye disease 52
  in Kiev 41
  raiding Byzantium 47
  religion 29, 47, 48, 52-3, 56
  sexual habits 48
  stability of rule 59
Vladimir II Monomakh, Grand Prince
    67, *69*, 72
Vladimir Andreyevich, Prince 89, 90
Vladimir-Suzdal 28
Volga River 113
Vologda 358
Volokhov, Danilko 120
Volokhova, Marya 120
volost 301
volosti 288
Voltaire, François *225*
Voronezh River 82
Voronikhin, Andrey 356
Vorontsov, Count 183
Vorotynsky, Prince Ivan 125
Vsesvyatskoye 181
Vsevolod, Prince, son of Vladimir I 48
Vsevolod, Prince, son of Yaroslav the
    Wise 65, 67
Vsevolod, Prince of Novgorod 71
Vyacheslav, Prince, son of Yaroslav

the Wise 61, 65
Vyatichi 41
Vyatka 77
Vyazemsky, Prince 241
Vym River 92
Vyshegorod 48, 60
Vysheslav, Prince, son of Vladimir I
    48
Vyshnegradsky, Ivan 316

W

Wallace, Sir Donald McKenzie 265,
    297, 298, 300, 302, 310
Wallachia 278, *281*
Waterloo *252-3*, 254
westernization 151, 156, 157, 201, 271
White, Arnold 313
William III, King 152, 156
Winter Palace 162, 163, 179, 185,
    195, *222*, 322, 324, *371*, 372,
    374-5
Witte, Count Sergei 315, 325
Wladislaw, Prince 119, 124
Wolff, Christian 190
World War I 265, 337, 364, 369

Y

Yaropolk I 41, 47, 48
Yaroslav 146
Yaroslav I, Prince (Yaroslav the
    Wise) 48, 59, 60, 61, 65
Yashvil, Prince 241
Yapifany the Wise 77, 89, 90
Yermak Timofeyevich 116
Yury Ingvarevich, Grand Prince 82
Yury Vsevolodovich, Grand Prince 82
Yusupov, Prince *340*, 341, 343
Yusupov, Prince Nikolay 357

Z

Zaandam *153*
Zadonshchina 77
Zavadovsky, Peter 204

Zealand 170
zemshchina 113
zemskie 116
Zemskii sobor 121
zemstvos 297-8, 302, 320, 324, 334,
    361
Zerbst, Princess of 193
Zhidyata, Bishop 61
Zinoviev 368
Zoltiewski, Pan 124
Zubov, Nicolay 240, 241
Zubov, Platon 205, 240
Zyapunov, Prokofy 125

Notes on illustrations

Details are given, where available, for paintings, prints, engravings and other non-photographic illustrations.

(b. = bottom; t. = top; r. = right; l. = left)

6 *Sts Vladimir, Boris and Gleb*, icon (anon.), 16th century, Tretyakov Gallery, Moscow.

15 *Catherine II, 'The Great'*, painting by D Levitsky, Tretyakov Gallery, Moscow.

Part 1

18-19 *Tower of Babel*, painting by Pieter Breughel the Elder (c. 1515-69), Kunsthistorisches Museum, Vienna.

Part 2

37t. *Igor I*, illustration from A. Howard and E. Newman, *Pictorial History of Russia*, Hutchinson & Co, London, New York and Melbourne, 1943.
37b. *Greek Fire*, from a Byzantine manuscript, Prado Museum, Madrid.
41b. *The Baptism of Olga*, illustration from *Pictorial History of Russia, op. cit.*
43 *The Mountain of Elbrus*, painting by N. A. Jaroshenko (1846-94), Russian Museum, Leningrad.
49 *Vladimir, grand duke of Kiev*, from an ancient banner.
69 *Vladimir Monomakh in Council with his Advisers*, wood carving, anon., 1551, on the imperial seat of Ivan IV, Church of the Assumption, Moscow.
75 *Fighting the Tartars*, illustration from *The Tale of Igor and his Sword.*

Part 3

78 *Genghis Khan in his tent*, from a Persian manuscript by Rachid ad-Din, Bibliothèque Nationale, Paris.
91 *Dimitry Donskoy reviewing his troops*, miniature from *The Tale of the Bloody Encounter with Mamai*, 14th century, British Library, London.
101 *The Annunciation of Ust jug*, icon, 12th century.
102t.l. *The Old Testament Trinity*, icon by Andrey Rublyov, 1410s or 1420s.
102t.r. *The Dormition of the Virgin*, icon by Andrey Rublyov, early 15th century.
102b.l. *Archangel Michael*, icon by Andrey Rublyov, early 15th century, Dormition Cathedral, Zvenigorod.
103 *St Nikolai Lipensky*, icon attributed to Andrey Rublyov, early 15th century.

Part 4

106 *Tsar Ivan Vasilyevich the Terrible*, painting by V. Vasnetsov, 1897, Tretyakov Gallery, Moscow.
115t. *Russian costumes*, lithograph, c. 1890-1900, Germany.
115b. *Russian merchants and boyars at the court of Maximilian II*, woodcut print by Michael Peterle, 1576, Victoria and Albert Museum, London.
117 *The Conquest of Siberia by Yermark*, painting by V. I. Surikov, 1895, Russian Museum, Leningrad.
118 *Boris Godunov*, miniature from the *Titulyarnik*, 1672, Historical Museum, Moscow.
125 *The Flourishing of the Kremlin*, painting, anon., late 17th century.
132 *The Patriarch Nikon and his Clergy*, painting, anon., mid-17th century.

Part 5

143 *Cathedral Square, Moscow Kremlin*, painting by F. Ya. Alekseyev (1753-1824).
144 *Tsar Fyodor Ivanovich*, painting by I. M. Sheginev, from *Pamyatniki Moscovski*.
146 *The Last Judgment*, icon, 17th century, Yaroslavl.
150 *Peter the Great*, painting, anon., collection of Countess Bobrinskoy.
154-5 *Peter the Great at Deptford*, painting by Daniel Maclise (1806-70), University of London, Royal Holloway and Bedford New College, Egham.
161 *Plan von St Petersburg*, illustration from *Das Veränderte Russland*, Frankfurt and Leipzig, 1738.
162 *View of St Petersburg from the River Neva*, print, 18th century, British Library, London.
171 *Peter I with his Son*, painting by N. Nikolai (1831-94), Tretyakov Gallery, Moscow.
177 *Nevsky Prospect, Leningrad*, etching, 18th century.
178 *Empress Elizabeth Petrovna*, portrait from N. N. Bozherdnov, *Trista Let Tsarstovivaniya Doma Ronanovykh*, St Petersburg, 1912.
194 *Wizards, apostates, enchanters, idolaters and devil-worshippers*, lubok, anon., 17th century.
195 *Celebration of a Wedding Contract*, painting by M. Shibanov, 1777, Tretyakov Gallery, Moscow.
196 *Peter III*, mosaic painting, British Museum, London.
198 *Catherine the Great*, portrait from *Trista Let Tsarstovivaniya Doma Ronanovykh*, op. cit.
203 *Smolny Schoolgirls*, painting by D. Levitsky, 1770s.
212 *The Ox who did not want to be an ox and so became a butcher*, print, anon., from D. A. Rovinsky, *Popular Prints*, 1881.
219 *Yermelyan Pugachev*, painting by N. D. Vakurov (1879-1952).
226 *A Lesson for stupid husbands and clothes-conscious wives*, lubok, anon., 17th century.
233 *Catherine II*, engraving by R. Woodman, print by Caroline Watson, after a portrait by Rofselin.
235-6 *The execution of Louis XVI*, lithograph, c. 1793, Bibliothèque Nationale, Paris.
237 *Catherine II surrounded by her family and courtiers*, engraving by Sido, 1913, Hermitage Gallery, Leningrad.
238 *Portrait d'Alexandre Ier*, painting by F. Gérard (1770-1837), Château de la Malmaison, France.
242 *Moscow Kremlin*, lithograph, 19th century.
245 *Napoleon on a campaign*, painting by Ernest Meissonier (1851-91), Musée d'Orsay, Paris.
246-7 *View of the Kremlin during the Moscow Fire*, painting by Schmidt (after d'Oldendorf), Bibliothèque Nationale, Paris.
249 *Napoleon*, caricature, Russian Museum, Leningrad.
250 *Napoleon's retreat from Russia 1815*, Musée de l'Armée, Paris.
251 *Bivouac des Troupes Russes aux Champs-Elysées 1814*, painting by Sauerweid, Musée Carnavalet, Paris.
255 *Alexander I in the Alexander-Nevsky Lavra, September, 1825*, engraving by Chesky, from a painting by Chernetsov.

Part 6

266 *Tsar Nicholas I*, painting, anon., private collection.
269 *Alexandra Fyodorovna with Alexander Nikolayevich and Alexandra Nikolayevna*, Roman Gallery, Winter Palace, Leningrad.
275l. *Alexander Pushkin*, portrait by Frankenberg, 1835, collection of Countess Bobrinskoy.
277 *Peasants growing vegetables*, lubok, anon., 17th century.
279 *The Charge of the Light Brigade, Balaclava*, print, 1854, private collection.
282-3 *View from the heights above Balaclava*, print, c. 1855, National Maritime Museum, London.
285 *Sevastopol in December*, illustration by Pyotr Pavlinov from Leo Tolstoy, *Tales of Sevastopol*, Foreign Languages Publishing House, Moscow, 1950.
289 *Types populaires russes*, illustration from *L'Univers Illustré*, France, 1881.
290-1 *Alexander II freeing the serfs*, painting by K. Lebedev.
300-1 *Types populaires russes*, illustration from *L'Univers Illustré*, op. cit.
303 *On a market day in an old city*, painting by I. Goryushkin, Penza Art Gallery.
305 *Assassinat de Sa Majesté l'empereur de Russie le 13 mars à Saint-Petersbourg*, illustration from *L'Univers Illustré*, op. cit.
306 *Alexander III*, portrait from C. A. Toluzakov, *Podvig 300-Lednyago Suzhenya Rossii Gosudarei Doma Romanovykh*, St Petersburg, 1913.
309 *Découverte d'une imprimerie clandestine à Kiev*, illustration from *L'Univers Illustré*, op. cit.
312 *Assault on a Jew in the presence of the military*, print by Schombeer, 1881.
315 *Repair work on the railway*, painting by K. A. Savitsky (1844-1905), Tretyakov Gallery, Moscow.
333 *Tyrans payez vos dettes*, from postcard series *Les Armoiries de Nicholas II*.

Revolution in culture

346 *The Appearance of Christ*, painting by A. Ivanov (1806-58), Tretyakov Gallery, Moscow.
350l. *Submarine monster*, costume design by Leon Baskst, for Rimsky-Korsakov's opera, *Sadko*, 1898.
350r. Costume design by Leon Baskt, for Stravinsky's ballet, *The Firebird*, Paris, 1910.

Acknowledgements

Our grateful thanks to the many museums, libraries and individuals, including those listed below, who provided us with illustrations.

(b. = bottom; t. = top; r. = right; l. = left)

Barnaby's Picture Library 34-5, 288
Bibliothèque Nationale, Paris 78
G. Bertin 66
Bodleian Library 212
Bridgeman Art Library 18-19, 43, 154-5, 171, 201, 234-5, 245, 246-7, 266, 279, 282-3, 316-17, 326, 355r.
British Library 37
British Museum Publications 26, 27, 34
Christie's Colour Library 345, 355l., 356t. and b., 357, 358, 359
Cinzano 182t.
E. T. Archive 250
Martine Franck/Viva 311
Giruadon, Paris 238, 251
Robert Harding Picture Library 39, 62, 85, 97, 149, 182b., 191, 206-7, 222t. and b., 223, 347
Michael Holford 75, 115b., 150, 159, 162, 275
Lindsey Hughes 97, 146, 147, 203, 346
Hulton-Deutsch Collection 159, 229, 340, 341l., 371
Image Bank 2
Index, Florence 41
Oxana Ivanchenko 101, 102t.l. and b.l.

Jourdes/Edimages, Paris 45, 115t., 289, 301, 305, 309, 349
Victor Kennett 196, 221, 249
Mansell Collection 25, 94, 161, 176, 205l. and r., 225, 233, 261, 280, 312, 332r., 351b., 352, 353(4)
John Massey Stewart 49, 53, 63, 69, 83, 86, 117, 121, 123, 126, 128, 133, 135, 138, 141, 143, 145, 153, 163, 167t., 170, 173, 178, 181, 183, 185, 186-7, 198, 237, 241, 255, 257, 263, 269, 271, 273, 286, 290-1, 306, 314-15t., 318, 321, 325, 329, 300-1, 333, 335, 339, 342-3, 350, 351t., 362, 367, 374-5
Fred Mayer/Magnum 230-1
Mingei International Museum, San Diego 89, 130, 131l. and r., 214t. and b., 215, 323
Newsweek Book Division, New York 6
David Nicolle 97
Novosti London 15
Novosti Press Agency 55, 93, 118, 175
Pyotr Pavlinov/Foreign Languages Publishing House, Moscow 285
Popperfoto 337, 364, 365, 369, 370
Russimage-Bank 195, 211t. and b., 226, 277, 295
SCR Library 23, 46, 51, 58, 71, 75, 99, 102t.r., 103, 111, 167b., 177, 219, 222, 275r., 293, 297, 299, 302-3, 314-15b., 315, 344, 348t. and b., 373
USSR Photo Library/Ilya Glazunov 30
Viking Ships Museum, Oslo 22